Praise for *Vocation: The Astrology of Career, Creativity and Calling*

"What am I here for?" This question – of career or calling, direction or destiny – will arise in everyone's life at some point. The astrological insights in this book are thorough, considered and imaginative; this creates a very engaging 'exploration space' which is sure to invite intuitive clarity in the reader.

      Melanie Reinhart, author of *Chiron and the Healing Journey*

Brian Clark synthesizes the best of the astrological, psychological, and mythopoetic ways of knowing. At a time when technique is ascendant in astrological circles, his work returns us to the rich imaginal realm which nourishes and feeds all good interpretive work. I can think of no one better suited to guide astrologers in our efforts to make the 'vocatus' of the Soul discernible to those we would help.

      Jason Holley, Astrologer and Psychotherapist

For some what we do as a career to earn a living is the same thing as what we do as our vocational calling and contribution as a member of society; but for others it is different. Using an astrological perspective, learn how to clarify our creative impulse towards a purposeful role in the world within the context of our career.

      Demetra George, author of *Asteroid Goddesses*
      and *Astrology and the Authentic Self*

ISBN: 978-0-9944880-1-5

First edition published 2016 by Astro*Synthesis
PO Box 111
Stanley, Tasmania 7331
Australia
www.astrosynthesis.com.au

The author can be reached at: brian@astrosynthesis.com.au

Charts calculated using Solar Fire software
Cover Designer: Cat Keane
Proof-reader: Jane Struthers
Project Manager and layout: Frank C. Clifford

Front Cover: I often imagine the vocation as if it were a meandering path
through the woods. Walking its trail we keep coming across forks and diversions.
But as Robert Frost so delightfully wrote, taking the course 'less travelled by'
makes 'all the difference'.[1]

VOCATION

The Astrology of Career, Creativity and Calling

BRIAN CLARK

Astro*Synthesis

Acknowledgements

First, my thanks to all the students who have participated in our classes on Vocational Astrology and who willingly shared with me their anecdotes and experiences. I have been enormously privileged to witness the stories of many clients who have searched for and participated in their vocation, and it is these clients and students who have contributed so valuably to my understanding.

A heartfelt thank you to Stephanie Johnson who asked me write the Vocation Solar Writer Report for Esoteric Technologies which focused my ideas and how I might present them. I have been well supported by friends and colleagues who have read, proofread and assisted me to present the manuscript. My thanks to all those who have lent a hand; in particular Mary Symes and Barb Thorp for helping with edits and suggestions, and Frank Clifford for his motivation and direction. Thomas Moore has been instrumental in this book, as his writing on vocation and the soul has been inspiring. I thank him for allowing me to use his case study.

I would also like to express enormous appreciation to my Asian colleagues who have been supportive of my work perhaps in ways they do not fully appreciate. So a sincere thank you to Jupiter Lai in Hong Kong, Rod Chang and Yvetta Chang in Taiwan and Mayumi Sakuya in Japan, all of whose dedication to astrology is admirable.

I feel blessed to have been able to follow my vocation and be encouraged each step of the way by my family. Thank you to Glennys for sharing the continuing journey with me.

TABLE OF CONTENTS

– PREFACE –
A QUESTION OF VOCATION

All work is a vocation, a calling from a place that is the source of meaning and identity, the roots of which lie beyond human intention and interpretation.[2]

A vocation is a calling. The English word originates from the Latin *vocare*, to call, and in early English this was understood to be a spiritual calling, an intimate invitation to follow the course of one's passion. The root *voca* means 'voice' and the original implication of having a vocation was that one followed one's inner calling.

In contemporary terms, vocation is often thought as a 'spiritual calling'. Equally, it epitomizes the quest to find our authentic voice in the world. Vocation is an internal tone; a poignant moving feeling that there is a place for us to be in the world. Since the language of the inner world is articulated through images and feelings, this inner voice is not logical, but experienced intuitively and imaginatively. It arises through images, symbols, felt senses, fantasies and dreams; therefore, it is often ambiguous and unclear. Nonetheless, it is deeply felt and lives through our imagination.

And because vocation is deeply felt, it prompts us to give it meaning, form and life. It demands something of us, but that something eludes being identified or articulated. It is a yearning, a hope, a drive that even our creativity, work or profession cannot appease. In a way it remains a spiritual calling until we participate in its mystery and work towards shaping it in the material world.

Often it is this question of vocation that brings the client to my consulting room, as astrology invites us to ask questions about our purpose. Solutions and suggestions are embedded within the horoscope, not within me as the astrologer. My role is to facilitate a dialogue between the individual and their horoscope, so that some of the vocational pathways may be acknowledged, brought to light and considered. The client then has more scope to reflect and be involved with the inner voice that calls them.

The horoscope is a map of raw material that can be developed in the laboratory of life. A fulfilling vocation is neither granted nor denied, but is the product of focus, discipline, hard work, effort, passion and consciousness. Chance spins the wheel of fortune, so the vocational path is never linear or certain, but, like the heavens, constantly in flux. In many ways Chance plays her role in our future through opportunities, encounters, appointments and assistance experienced on our vocational quest. By reflecting on astrological cycles and transitions we can enhance our perception of our vocational patterns; then Chance becomes an integral part of the pattern, not something separate from it. Vocation is an inner voice, not one originating in the outer world.

While astrological literature deduces career options from patterns and signatures, vocational pathways in the horoscope are not linear, nor literal. They do not end at a certain profession, point to a creative career or decree a rewarding occupation. But the horoscope does have countless ways to explore talents, money, resources, work, creativity, destiny and direction that assist in giving meaning and insight to our vocation. In the following pages we will explore the symbols and places in the horoscope that address this question of vocation. This book is about the ways that astrology can help us articulate and amplify this question in our life and in others' as well.

This book was seeded in my consulting room where a majority of my astrological clients would ask questions about their life purpose, career and work. It seems inevitable that this question arises. Some were certain about what they needed to do, most were seeking meaning in their work, others were confused, some disappointed, but each had a deeply felt sense of purpose. Together we would attempt to understand the inner voice, their calling. The classroom also revealed many vocational narratives. In the Life Skills module of our *Astro*Synthesis* programme we introduce the astrology of vocation. In these classes we discuss our work and career aspirations alongside the astrological indicators of vocation. Students find this enormously revealing and engaging. I was always in awe of the wealth of horoscope images that contributed to amplifying vocational issues. But I was also aware that while clients and students sought clarity, my task was to engage them in the question of vocation so as to stimulate their own insight and revelations.

The question of vocation is not static, nor fixed, but lifelong. Vocation is more than our work, our activities, our creativity or our career. It encompasses how we make our living, yet vocation is also how we find meaning in living. It is about purpose and what we feel we are meant to do. It is a process, not an end goal.

Alchemists used the word *opus* to capture the entire process of their work through the numerous stages starting from refining raw materials to the final stage. The opus was the process of their lifelong work, not a measured goal or product. To highlight this enduring process they often called the opus, which was this continual refinement and labour on the self, 'The Work'. 'The Work' was in capital letters; vocation is a lifelong work, not just a series of jobs, savings accounts or career bonuses, but a process of expressing Self in the world.

Vocation is how we attend to becoming who we are meant to be.

Tinker, tailor, soldier, sailor, rich man, poor man, beggar man, thief,
Or what about a cowboy, policeman, jailer, engine driver, or a pirate
chief?
Or what about a ploughman or a keeper at the zoo,
Or what about a circus man who lets the people through?[3]

Vocation: Life Work

'Vocation' is a multidimensional word as it can refer to the mundane level of career or profession; yet, at the same time it suggests the spiritual component of what we are meant to do or *called* to do. Vocation is an archetypal concept that transcends race, culture or gender, present in each human being. This common yearning is our quest to discover what we were born to do.

Vocation is spirit in manifestation, the urge to be fulfilled, occupied by our creativity and employed in meaningful ways. It is soulful; a deeply felt longing to be of service, to follow our passion, to be who we were meant to be and to live a meaningful life. It is our lifework; our work through life and how we work on our lives.

Work: What We Do or Who We Are?

When I was a child, adults would always ask me, 'What do you want to be when you grow up?' And like many young children I had my standard answer. Having spent my childhood living on military bases, surrounded by security fences and gates, I was intrigued by the man who would suddenly appear out of a small shed to lift the gate for my father and I to pass through. When the gate lifted, my father and I would continue our way into the headquarters where he worked.

So, when asked this question, I would answer confidently 'A gate-lifter', inspired by the magic and power of that faceless man who guarded the boundary crossing. Was the innocent statement inspired by a pre-existing vocational template? As my life unfolded, I felt called to Mercurial work like guiding and gate-lifting! In a metaphoric way I meet my clients in a transitional space and attempt to lift some gates for them. In our earliest childlike imaginings are images and symbols of our calling.

When teaching classes on vocational astrology I ask students to reflect upon their childhood to recollect what they wanted to be when they 'grew up'. Through active imagination we journey back to childhood memories, summoning up images of what we wanted to do. As youngsters we are relatively free of cultural, gender and familial expectations, still mostly unaware of what work entails. Our memories might seem fanciful, yet as metaphors they are potent indicators of powerful yearnings. Stored in our childhood memory are the first images of what we wanted to be. Like our childhood rhymes, the professions of a doctor, a lawyer, a soldier, a sailor, a tinker, a tailor or a candlestick maker are imaginative, not literal. But they are archetypal and these images are in our horoscope.

After the visualization we focus on the personal astrological symbols of our charts to discover what aspects of the horoscope are compatible with these early occupational images. And we consider whether our present occupations reflect these early images in any way; always a revealing exercise. 'I wanted to be an explorer' was the response from a woman who had a Sun-Mars conjunction on the 9th house side of her MC and Uranus rising; 'A nurse' said another woman with the Moon in the 10th house in trine to Neptune in the 6th; a man with a Gemini stellium and Jupiter on the MC said 'A teacher', while a woman with Uranus rising in Leo and a Sun-Venus conjunction on the MC remembered she had wanted to be an actress. The woman who wanted to be an explorer had travelled widely through her work as a sales representative while the man with the Gemini stellium had developed a very popular blog.

Vocational impressions are inborn and often accessible through early memories and certainly through images in the horoscope, but one of the main obstacles in understanding vocation is literality. Mistaking an internal image or a symbol for a specific indication of a profession puts an end to further exploration or amplification. It also perpetuates the myth that vocation is something that exists outside of us, already established in the world for us to find; not something that emerges over the course of our lives.

Many external factors influence our career choices: familial beliefs, education, financial resources, emotional security, parental support and encouragement from our teachers, friends and community. Role models who we admire as children, experiences that capture our imagination and the breadth of our exposure to the world all have some bearing on career preferences. A major influence on career choice is parental expectation, whether this is overt or not. The horoscope offers ways of thinking about the profound affect that the unlived life of a parent exerts on shaping a child's career.

Throughout the first Saturn cycle, until the end of our twenties, we may be strongly pressured to conform. This contributes to moulding our careers, whether we yield to or rebel against it. We may not yet have the courage, the resources or the wherewithal to be able to forge our own path in life. However, during this period, we may be drawn to certain courses, hobbies and pastimes that help refine our aspirations. Our vocation is like a large tapestry woven with the threads of all our life experiences and choices, not a well-trodden career path with a guaranteed pension.

Vocation is intimately bound up with the course of our lives. Yet because work is how we 'make a living' we often identify work as something we do rather than something we are. Some professions bestow reputation and status, so we may desire a profession because of prestige and security, not necessarily creativity and soul. Some careers offer lucrative financial rewards; however, midway through the second Saturn cycle, in the midst of our forties, it often becomes evident that career bonuses are not fulfilling if our deeper vocational urges are still unmet. The midlife crisis often centres on coming to terms with vocation. Even though all the objective criteria, such as salary, status and security, suggest a successful career, the inner life may be despondent and unfulfilled. It is often at this point that an astrologer meets his or her client who has chosen astrology to help them reflect on the course of their life.

An astrological analysis can be beneficial in contemplating what the individual is called to do. The horoscope does not detail the literal career as that unfolds over the life, but it does offer suggestions as to which work qualities and essences can assist in making the course of one's life truer to one's calling. Vocations include hobbies, volunteer work, activities and courses of study; therefore, they do not always present in the form of a profession.

An individual's career questions are often symptomatic of a larger question about individuation and self-development; therefore it is helpful to listen to the underlying question of vocation which is about who we are, not about what we do.

Work: Finding Meaning in the Mundane

The poet Kahlil Gibran in *The Prophet* speaks of work in a moving way:

> You work that you may keep pace with the earth and the soul of the earth ... When you work you are a flute through whose heart the whispering of the hours turns to music. ... Work is love made visible.[4]

In the midst of our busy lives, worn out by the endless repetition of meaningless tasks, it is difficult to appreciate Kahlil Gibran's poetic appraisal of work as a soul-making sphere. In our contemporary lives, soul and work can seem worlds apart. Our modern quest for economic productivity buoyed by materialistic attitudes numbs the inner yearning for vocational fulfilment. Career objectives such as prestige, status, vacations, bonuses, salary packages and job security eclipse the urge to find meaningfulness in our work. Yet most individuals yearn to be satisfied through their work. In a contemporary culture that has lost its soul we are no longer anchored by values and images that remind us of a meaningful life. This meaninglessness permeates the atmosphere of daily life and contributes to an epidemic of dissatisfaction, depression, illness and insecurity in the workplace.

Our need to tend to soul in what we do in the world is always present. Without nurturing this need, an individual feels empty, incomplete, unfulfilled; an essential aspect of the self feels lacking. Out of this empty place an individual seeks answers. Astrology can address the larger questions of fate, soul and individuation in an individual context, while also honouring transitional changes in the life cycle; therefore, its wisdom is sought in times of crisis. Often the conscious agenda in making an astrological appointment is to be advised of the correct career path, which course to pursue and which choices to make, mistakenly believing that the 'right' career will be the solution to what is missing. However, the answer is not simply a particular profession or a definitive course of action or even pursuing an exciting job, even though that will be helpful. The key is to restore meaning to our work and to nurture the soul through work. Feeling dissatisfied with work, disliking one's job or knowing there is 'something more' motivates individuals to consult an astrologer to explore the realm of vocation. So often in my consulting room someone has described the strong sense of something they feel they were meant to do, yet that same individual does not know what that is or what to do about this feeling. They only know they are meant to be doing something more than what they are doing.

The urge to find soul in the world is often projected onto a profession that seems to address some of the missing components of an individual's current life. The longing to find a soulful connection to the world is prone to becoming inflated and fuelled with fantasy. Archetypal psychologist James Hillman warns that vocation can be a very inflating spiritual notion if we believe we are chosen or meant to do something definite or called to be something special.[5] Vocation is not about being someone, but becoming who we are.

The belief that 'creativity' or a perfect job will appease the soul's hunger is fraught with disappointment since an external position cannot fulfil such a deep aspect of the self. The expectation of the perfect and fulfilling career, whether conscious or not, is often projected onto a literal profession to appease anxiety and feelings of loss. So often our vocation is what we already know or simply what we already do; it is inherently a part of our character that will unfold over time. A literal career or profession, no matter how enlightened, is not the answer to the soul's longing. Vocation is an aspect of the individuation process and its path is not predetermined but forged over time through the relationship of the inner self with the outer world. Vocation demands its own set of rules and insists on its own laws.

Carl Jung suggested it was *vocation* which induced an individual to follow his own soul and become conscious. He affirmed that vocation was 'an irrational factor that destines a man to emancipate himself from the herd and from its well-worn paths. True personality is always a vocation.' To pursue one's true vocation takes courage, as well as the strength to break free from 'the herd'. The herd refers to the well-trodden path of what is socially acceptable to our elders, parents and ancestors. To follow the voice which summons one on their authentic path demands the individual be 'set apart from the others'. As Jung reminds us, 'creative life always stands outside convention'; therefore, vocation demands that we risk being on the margins and in touch with our own need for individuation.

Vocations do not come with job descriptions, opportunities for promotion or a guaranteed income. No doubt work and career are an aspect of vocation, but we often confuse a deeper longing for individuation and self-fulfilment with a literal job. Individuation *is* a job, it *is* a task. It *is* the *opus* of one's life, a reference to the fullness of our 'Work' on the Self. Like an alchemical process, our vocation is continuously refined throughout our lifetime and its success is largely dependent on our ability to be separate from 'the herd'.[6] Following our calling summons the courage to be marginal.

We may over-identify with work to compensate for an unfulfilled vocation, or even de-identify with career in an attempt to try to locate what is missing. A fulfilling career can go a long way towards helping to address the quest for vocation but, as Jung has suggested, one's authentic vocation demands integrity of self and the courage to stand outside the system. Vocation seems to be a healthy synthesis of work and profession, which help to support us on the path of individuation in the world.

Work, Self and Identity

Occupation is one of the ways we are identified. Name, Address, Age, Gender and Occupation are the standard questions we are asked on identification forms. Our work is an integral part of who we are and we are often defined and judged by what we do. We often recognize others by what they do: he works in IT, she's a lawyer, he works downtown, she's studying to become a psychologist, he is unemployed. These are common conversations which help to identify individuals. How often have you been asked 'What do you do for a living'? We continually identify others by their work, are introduced to them by their career, and judge them by their profession.

Some professions attract more status; others command more money. Whether we like it or not there is a hierarchy of professions; hence, some professions are valued more than others and seen to be more prestigious. Those who become a part of these valued professions are often awarded more status and respect. Often these professions are also more financially rewarding and support the sense of self-esteem and self-worth. Heeding the summons of the internal voice that beckons us in our own unique direction is difficult in a culture which has generated a hierarchy of careers and values.

I have witnessed disappointment when an individual's vocation suffocates in an organizational atmosphere of mechanistic models and inflexible structures. I have heard many accounts from nurses whose callings have been crushed by the corporate medical model; those called to psychology have bitterly complained to me of the shift in emphasis to a scientific rational model, abandoning imagination and feeling for empirical evidence. Following a career path often constellates a struggle between corporate and external values and our own inner calling.

Vocational analysis using astrological images can be very beneficial for identifying the vocational template for an individual, what they are called to do. The astrological horoscope does not provide the main course, as that unfolds over the life, but it does supply the necessary ingredients to help make it successful. There are spheres of the horoscope governing vocation and the course of one's life. When analysing a horoscope it is important not to delineate a literal career but to help the individual come to understand their needs, talents and most appropriate course. There are ample astrological images to help with this process.

Over the course of this book we will examine the astrological images that amplify vocation. Vocation is not limited to any area of the horoscope: it is our life course and the outstanding aspects of the horoscope will often seek expression through the vocation. There are many areas to explore and each individual may have many different vocational facets to be realized over the course of their lifetime.

To begin we will outline an overview of the astrology of vocation. Then we will place the three major components of an astrological analysis – planets, signs and houses – in the context of vocation. We will contemplate some of the vocational factors of the horoscope in more detail, such as the Sun, Moon, the lunar nodes, the angles, especially the Midheaven and Ascendant, and the 2nd, 6th and 10th houses. Astrological timing in careers is informative; therefore we will examine cycles and transits in the perspective of career changes and development. As part of this we will examine the transitions in and out of careers. Finally, we will reflect on The Work, our lifework, through some case examples.

Throughout the book there are many descriptions of astrological placements, such as planets in signs and houses, signs on house cusps, aspects to the nodes, angular and ruling planets, etc. Some of these delineations were originally written for the Solar Writer Vocation Report[7] and I have rewritten some and added others. These are only to be used as a guide, a muse to reflect on the inherent possibilities of the astrological situation, not as an explanation. Through reflection and consideration on the astrological statements there is the possibility of insight, revelation and the capacity to greater understand the depth and breadth of psyche.

Astrological imagery is not always well suited to written language, as images can be read as fixed and factual, rather than remain evocative and enlightening. We need to be reflective and imaginative when considering the astrological possibilities.

– CHAPTER 1 –
A FULFILLING CAREER
An Overview of the Astrology of Vocation

In later adolescence, at the beginning of an undergraduate degree in commerce, I found myself in the university counselling office in search of guidance for my vocation. Looking for a different direction, I wanted to volunteer with the union of students working abroad. Clearly, accounting was not my path, but neither was running away from it. People-orientated, creative, helping careers scored much higher than practical, administrative or technical ones on my vocational guidance tests, but I had chosen a course I needed to complete.

We may have an inner sense of our vocation but timing plays an important role in its unfolding. While the horoscope articulates the authenticity of our vocation, it has its own schedule of development. Looking forwards into the complexity of all the vocational possibilities can be confusing; yet, when looking back over the course of our career we can see the vocational motifs and patterns that we were unable to spot when younger.

Vocational guidance can be particularly valuable when young as it often validates the inner calling. The horoscope is a useful guide in exploring choices of schools, subjects, career goals and possibilities. Discussing education, vocation and ambition with parents and their children, using their horoscopes, has proven fruitful and enormously rewarding in my practice. Vocational astrology is also very effective for adults who are questioning their chosen profession, experiencing dissatisfaction in their jobs, contemplating a career change or simply needing to discuss where they are in terms of their vocation.

Reading a chart from a vocational perspective is not static or done just once; it evolves as the individual grows, and becomes more defined as the person becomes more aware of their ambitions and desires. Hence the horoscope can be used in a variety of ways to examine vocation at any stage of the life cycle. While vocation may be the focus of the analysis, its course is affected by the individual's mental, emotional and psychological circumstances. The presenting issue may be a vocational one, yet health or emotional and social difficulties may underpin the question of vocation. Therefore a vocational analysis is holistic in respecting the breadth and depth of the human experience. And, like the vocation itself, it is a work in process.

Let's continue by considering the horoscope from a vocational viewpoint, appreciating that, while there are many techniques and theories of vocational astrology, it is the basic principles that will ground us in developing our own style and approach.

Considering the Horoscope

Since the Greco-Roman era, western astrology has promoted techniques and guidelines for considering the horoscope from a vocational viewpoint. The techniques vary but essentially there are core principles which have remained consistent through time. In the 2nd century CE, when describing the astrological significator for a career, Ptolemy suggested that this was whichever was the strongest planet out of the ruler of the 10th house, a planet in the 10th house or the planet rising before the Sun. In medieval times, Lilly suggested that the sign on the cusp of the 10th, its ruler or its ruler's house position were strong indications for worldly work.[8]

In the 20th century astrologers pointed out the significance of the trinity of Earth houses (the 2nd, 6th and 10th), the signs on these cusps, their rulers and the planets in these houses. The Sun, Moon, Ascendant and Midheaven were also seen to be fundamental to any vocational analysis. Signatures concerning the 10th house have always been assigned importance, whereas earlier notions such as the significance of the planet rising before the Sun have diminished in importance.

Astrological trends come and go; what remain meaningful are the techniques which animate the question of vocation. These I will attempt to outline from my own experience. But first it is important to put a vocational exploration into the perspective of the individual's life stage, because a vocational analysis will be very different for an adolescent than for a retiree, or for someone experiencing their first Saturn return than for someone experiencing their second. It is also important to place the individual's personal history in the context of the vocational analysis: what is their educational background, family environment, work experience, qualifications, motivation and life experience? While it is significant to explore potentialities and possibilities, it is also important to ground the analysis in 'real-life' circumstances.

There are many factors. Therefore, it is important to prioritize the most significant ones. Astrological literature will use many techniques but these are often explored out of context and are secondary, not primary, approaches. To begin we can develop a two-fold attitude. The first stage is to adopt a more general methodology to the vocation, exploring the individual's personality, resources, talents, skills, ambitions, goals and character. While being conscious of the presenting issues, it is also imperative to listen for any mental, emotional, psychological or spiritual difficulties that may be the source of the current predicament. This wide-ranging examination places the individual in the context of their own horoscope and what it vocationally suggests. The second approach is more specific, focusing on the question of vocation by exploring career issues such as the workplace, salary, job satisfaction, co-workers and bosses.

As suggested, astrology can offer many techniques, but what is important is knowing how to use them to open up the analysis, not define or limit it. Astrological symbols are non-judgemental; therefore it is wise to find ways to articulate the images without the involvement of personal opinions. Archetypes also manifest in a multitude of ways. Even though astrology is very reliable in identifying the archetypal energy, the astrologer is not always able to know the countless ways in which it might manifest. Therefore exploration and participation with the images and symbols encourage revelation.

Let's begin with where vocation is placed in the horoscope, or what we refer to as the vocational houses. Also known as the houses of substance, the 2nd, 6th and 10th houses are the spheres where we locate our 'substance': the resources, skills, competence and vision to promote and 'earth' our vocation. These areas of the horoscope are where we are involved with soul-making in the physical, incarnate world:

- The **10th house** locates the goalposts of our lives. It is the public sphere where we strive for authority over the course of our lives and in doing so find meaningfulness in the world. The Midheaven (MC) is the highest point on the ecliptic and is symbolic of what we want to strive towards. It is significant in expanding our understanding of our professional role and what we contribute through our work in the world. Of all the many factors in a vocational analysis, the MC has always been regarded as crucial; hence the MC, the sign on its cusp, its ruler and planets in the 10th house are vital for beginning the exploration.

- The **2nd house** symbolizes the gifts and talents given by the gods, our innate assets and the value we give them. The 2nd house, the sign on the cusp, its ruler and planets in the house reflect how to naturally apply our resources and values. This is the area that tells us which innate resources are valuable and can be exchanged for material security. In a soulful sense the 2nd house may describe how we are able to 'trade' on our resources and assets in order to feel secure in the outer world and wealthy inwardly.

- The **6th house** honours the poetics of an everyday life. The 6th house, the sign on its cusp, the ruler and planets in the house are descriptive of employment and work. This sphere suggests how to apply ourselves to the tasks of an everyday life, how to occupy ourselves. These astrological symbols describe the rituals of daily life that help to achieve satisfaction and well-being. The 6th house is also known as a house of illness; therefore it can often be effective when addressing work-related ills, depression or stress. Workmates and routines can also be explored using 6th house imagery.

All houses are important to bear in mind in a vocational analysis, as each house is an area of our life occupied at different times.[9] A house becomes significant when it accommodates a stellium, the ruler of the Ascendant or the MC, or when it contains the North or South Node. One way to begin taking all the houses into account is to group them into elemental trinities:

- The houses of life (1st, 5th, 9th): this spirited trinity is fiery
- The houses of substance (2nd, 6th, 10th): these three houses of matter are earthy

- The houses of relationship (3rd, 7th, 11th) are based on Air
- The houses of endings (4th, 8th, 12th) are a trinity of soul inspired by Water

A majority of planets in one of these trinities will seek expression through the vocation in its own particular way. Although the houses of substance take priority in a vocational analysis, the houses of life are noteworthy because they locate energies which urge to be expressive, creative and motivated, supportive forces which activate vocation. The houses of life focus on creation, recreation and procreation and urge us to be employed in the conception of the self.

Consider the planetary emphasis by element, modality and in the hemispheres of the horoscope.

- The **elemental emphasis** in the horoscope profiles an individual's temperament, while the dominant element articulates the spontaneous approach to life as being enthusiastic (Fire), pragmatic (Earth), logical (Air) or emotive (Water). Modalities outline the natural way in which life energy is exercised, whether that is through activity (cardinal), stability (fixed) or changeability (mutable).

- **The four hemispheres** of the horoscope are divided into two pairs: above and below the horizon; and east and west of the meridian. Each of these hemispheres supports a particular view on life. Above the horizon is the day hemisphere, which has a more objective focus on the world outside, while below the horizon is the night hemisphere which is more subjective and focused on the inner world. The eastern horizon concerns the more personal aspects of life while the western hemisphere's centre of attention is on others or interpersonal relating.

While it is important to learn to prioritize the planets that are vocationally significant in each horoscope, we can first distinguish each planet's function in the context of vocation.

Being so personal, the inner planets seek expression through our vocation. **The Sun** and **Moon** are core symbols integral to our being; vocation is part of who we are so these luminaries play a prominent role. In a vocational analysis it is vital to take into account each one's zodiacal sign, house position and major aspects. The Sun represents central themes for self-expression while the Moon symbolizes what is needed to feel secure and fulfilled: important concerns for any career.

Mercury rules communication, ideas, versatility and mobility. His presence in any vocational analysis helps to articulate mental attitudes and ways of thinking about one's vocation. When Mercury is prominent, diversity, portability and intellect are significant.

Venus is the archetype which supports the sense of value and self-esteem as well as describing what we like to do, what we appreciate and what pleasures us. **Mars** is the principle of desire, what we want to pursue and the drive to 'go for it'. Both Venus and Mars are erotic in their urge to create life; potent archetypes that occupy and engage us. In essence, Venus and Mars vocationally help us to relate to our vocation and to experience it as a soulful aspect of our life.

Jupiter symbolizes philosophical and spiritual quests in the world. It seeks to ensoul life through wisdom and inspiration. As the ability to extend ourselves beyond an inherited or socially limiting framework, Jupiter brings its beliefs, morals, concepts and ethics to its vocation. **Saturn**, and specifically the MC, echo the calling to contribute to the world in a productive way. These astrological symbols are fundamental to locating authenticity, autonomy and integrity in the world through our vocation. Vocation in a sense demands a relationship with the authoritarian archetype since its success demands that we follow our own laws and pathway.

Chiron and the outer planets invoke more collective energies. When connected to vocation they suggest following paths outside consensus reality, beyond conventional systems or organizations. As a maverick and outsider, Chiron's calling is in the healing arts, mentoring or in socially reformative capacities. His vocational presence invites us to accept our own marginality and wounding. **Uranus**, like the spirit of Prometheus, is culturally rebellious and adventuresome, seeking its career path individualistically and atypically. **Neptune** is the archetype most linked to the spiritual calling and the creative language of the soul. Yet this archetype can also be spiritually inflated and misguided, confusing the personal calling with a calling to be a saviour. Neptune's position in the horoscope shows where we seek the divine and yearn to be creative and soulful. To be creative engages us in the calling to understand ourselves and step beyond the constraints of convention into an 'other' world. **Pluto** is often associated with the 'dark nights of the soul' and brings intensity, depth and power into the search for a fulfilling vocation.

The angles of the horoscope mark out the directions of our lives; therefore they play major roles in the course of our lives. All four angles are equally important and should be differentiated from each other. In a vocational analysis the Ascendant and Midheaven are more overtly noteworthy; however, the Descendant is always counterbalancing the Ascendant while the needs of the IC are naturally embedded in the goals at the MC.

The Ascendant and its ruler both act as a 'driver' on the path of life, the spirited force of personality that enlivens the journey and helps to project the vocational urges into the world. **The MC** and its ruler play a prominent role in assessing the vocational path since they both describe the route into the world. **The IC** and its ruler are foundation stones upon which we can build enough inner security to support our vocation. **The Descendant** and its ruler symbolize both the antagonistic and compatriot inner forces that encourage us to be heroic and conscious of our life's journey. Angular planets seek immediate expression in our lives and demand to be engaged; therefore they often seek to play a leading role in the vocation.

The axis of the Moon's nodes is intimately connected to an individual's path in life. The South Node may point towards the area where we are called to disseminate our instinctual talents and gifts, while the North Node symbolizes what we seek to develop through our vocation. The description of the polarity by sign and house can play an important role in what we are called to do. In a symbolic way the nodal axis and its aspects represent infinite urges seeking expression in an individual's life.

The course of one's life is never smooth and therefore it is important to consider the horoscope's major aspects and aspect patterns, especially if an outer planet forms a prominent angle to an inner planet. These energetic complexes will seek expression throughout the course of one's life and can be a central theme of that life. Integrating these complex aspects into the vocation is an important consideration, although each major aspect pattern needs to be analysed from the individual's perspective. The major themes of the chart need to be considered for how they could be effectively integrated into a 'lifestyle'. When these major aspects or aspect patterns receive transits from the outer planets, the individual is called to extend their self-understanding in the world they inhabit. These periods are significant vocational times or wake-up calls on the path of individuation.

A vocational analysis needs to be considered in the context of the life cycle; therefore it is imperative to recognize the individual's life stage and whether they are at a critical phase of development. These stages are embedded in the planetary cycles, especially their squares, oppositions and returns. However, it is also important to place the analysis in the present time and essential to be mindful of major transits and progressions that refer to vocational issues or times.

When one of the four angles is transited by Saturn, Chiron or an outer planet, an encounter with one's direction and life course is implied. The transits of the nodal axis illuminate the life path; therefore their transits through the houses can speak of vocational development. The transits of Jupiter and Saturn through the houses of vocation are key to understanding vocational shifts.

Vocational awareness can be illumined through secondary progressions. The progressed Moon is the vessel which holds *memoria*, the feeling memory, emotional responses and instincts. The vocation becomes an important focus when the Moon progresses through the 2nd, 6th and 10th houses. The progressed Sun is the development of our ego strength in the world and its aspects to other planetary archetypes suggest how we can identify this aspect of our self through our life experience. Other secondary planets may bring vocational issues to light as they change direction or progress into a new sign or house.

Planetary cycles, transits and progressions are valuable resources for monitoring vocational developments and career chapters. The stages and phases of vocational progress are reflected in the planetary passages.

The Mystery of Vocation
As an aspect of fate, vocation has its own intelligence, timing and pattern. An astrological analysis endeavours to make its mystery more conscious and gratifying by considering patterns and times both within and beyond an individual's control.

The vocational houses focus on three important aspects of vocation: income, employment and career. Ultimately we would like all three to be experienced simultaneously but, realistically, our creative calling is not easily transferred into a profession with a guaranteed salary. Often we can work hours and hours at creative tasks we love, which totally involve our self, for modest money. On the other hand, we can work in monotonous and unfulfilling ways and be paid a secure and good enough wage. Inherent within every vocational quest is the tension between security and freedom of expression, imagination and expediency, dreams and reality. To be true to our vocation we need to be loyal to our calling, patient and prepared to participate in what life offers us. We cannot expect our possibilities to become probabilities without an extensive apprenticeship.

The call to vocation is not limited to a single moment or time but recurs throughout the life cycle and is often synchronous with astrological cycles such as the nodal or Jupiter cycles or life phases such as adolescence, midlife or during the decade of our fifties. However, our first experience of a calling, whether through a vision, inner voice, deep feeling, a dream or our imagination, remains evocative throughout the course of our lives.[10]

An Early Call

Dane Rudhyar was one of the 20th century's foremost astrologers, and he was also a painter, writer, musician and philosopher. His life is characteristic of vocation. As he participated with his calling, the course of his life led him in the direction of people and places which refined and developed his career. But it was his vision at the age of 16 which became the foundation stone and strength for his life work.

At this time he was inspired by two things which would influence the course and direction of his life work. The first was the insight that the nature of time is cyclic and that the Law of Cycles controls all existence. The second was that western civilization was in the autumn phase of its cycle.[11] Both themes were woven into his philosophy, astrological insights, music and art throughout the course of his life.

Rudhyar's Ascendant-Descendant axis is in the 18th degree of the Sagittarius-Gemini polarity.[12] In 1901-2, when Rudhyar was between the ages of five and seven, Uranus and Pluto opposed

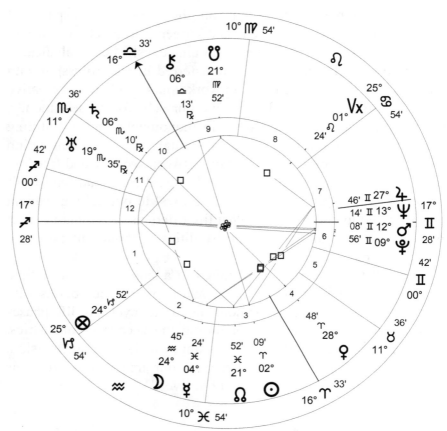

Dane Rudhyar, 23 March 1895, 1 a.m.; Paris, France

each other between 15 and 19° of the same polarity. While Uranus moved back and forth across his Ascendant, Pluto slowly transited his Descendant – a potent astrological image of sowing seeds of awakening and depth realization. During this same period Jupiter and Saturn began a new cycle at 14°♑ in his 1st house.

Jupiter and Saturn reached the oppositional point of the cycle in his 4th-10th house polarity when Rudhyar was between 15 and 16. Saturn had transited Venus, ruler of the MC, while Jupiter had culminated, traversing the 10th house and conjoining Rudhyar's 10th house Saturn. Pluto was also transiting Jupiter, an indication of deep insight and internal fortune. Although transits pass, their power remains. Rudhyar's example demonstrates the potency of the first encounter with the calling that lasted throughout his lifetime.

Vocations are also cyclical and contemporary, in that they emerge out of the spirit of the times, like the technological possibilities that evolved with the digital age. Being archetypal, they have their own intelligence and timing which works through us; therefore they change and develop, often in ways beyond our control. Opportunities, benefactors, possibilities, choices and chances emerge at the right time to direct us forwards on our vocational search. Often this follows a life crisis, but vocation can emerge at any time.

A Later Call

Susan Boyle was 48, having just entered her fifth Jupiter cycle, when she appeared as a contestant on the television show *Britain's Got Talent*. She stepped up to sing 'I Dreamed a Dream', an emotional song encapsulating her own life experience. But how was she to know that the first few chords of this song would change her life and be the key that unlocked a lucrative career.

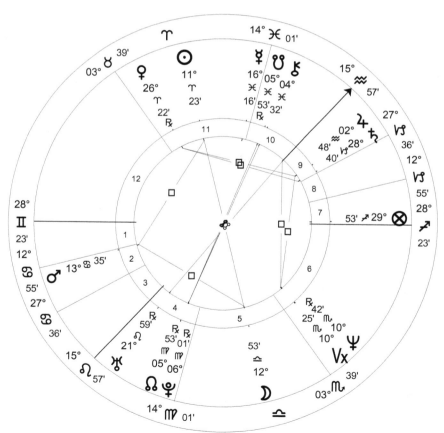

Susan Boyle, 1 April 1961, 9.50 a.m.; Blackburn, Scotland

During 2007, as Chiron approached the MC for the first time and Saturn transited the 4th house and its North Node-Pluto conjunction, Boyle lost her mother. Distressed, she returned to music as this gave her the solace to move through the grieving process. The following year she auditioned for the reality TV show, as her mother had always encouraged her to do while she was alive. Susan was successful; she stepped onto a path that led her to a dream she may never dared to dream.

Chiron was still transiting the MC, preparing to return to its conjunction with the South Node in the 10th. In the lead-up to the show, Jupiter transited the MC, culminating in the 10th house alongside Chiron and Neptune. From that moment, Susan Boyle voiced her calling.

A Midlife Call

Being called can often be quite literal: a voice, a vision, a deeply felt knowing. But it is subjective. And being so deeply personal, it is important not to 'read' it factually but to allow the symbol to reveal its meaning through a more reflective and contemplative approach. The following sketch is of a client who heard a call that changed his direction in a way he could never have imagined.

For a period of three years, Jeff, a young man on the cusp of his third Jupiter return and entry into the midlife passage, consulted me about his career and life direction. He was a solicitor in a high-ranking legal firm and while his work was financially and professionally lucrative, it was emotionally and creatively unprofitable. But for a young man with family responsibilities, it was not easy to take the risk and follow his passion.

Jeff was passionate about writing and had considered journalism, but law was a more secure option. As Mercury is angular, squaring Neptune on the MC, writing fulfils this image of an imaginative thinker and storyteller. And backed up by a North Node in Gemini and a Jupiter-Moon conjunction in the same sign in the 5th house, his enthusiasm to express himself through words, ideas and language felt right. The Sun in the 7th is also angular and to date he had been identified with supporting others.

Throughout our time together, Uranus transited his Ascendant. When it was in its retrograde phase across the Ascendant, Jeff's back pain became severe, which led to an unexpected operation for

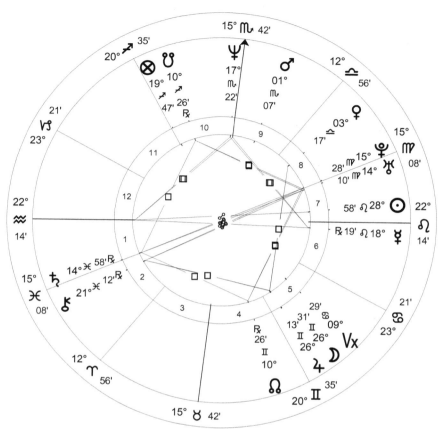

Jeff, 22 August 1965 5.14 p.m.; Geelong, Victoria, Australia

a prolapsed disc. Five days after the operation, on his last night in hospital, he awoke in the middle of the night. The room was filled with light and he heard a man's voice say, 'You are supposed to be a psychologist.' His third Jupiter return would be exact that month and later in the year Uranus would turn direct and pass over the Ascendant for the last time: the chart was indicating a new life phase.

On the phone, Jeff told me that he felt clear and motivated about his vision and was researching how he could become a psychologist. But when he was finally able to come back for appointments, his clarity had faded. We spoke about the voice and its message. Our word 'psychologist' comes from the Greek *psyche* and *logos* which together mean 'a student of the soul'. And perhaps this man's voice was a reflection of Jeff's, an inner calling of his angular Neptune-Mercury square, which Uranus was also triggering as it crossed the angle. Perhaps the voice was the clarity of knowing that he needed meaning in his work otherwise he would continue to feel the weight of the burden on his back.

Jeff had been awoken and had been called. By the next year, when Jupiter crossed into the 6th house and Saturn transited his Jupiter-Moon conjunction in the 5th, his work had changed. Earlier in the year an unexpected opportunity to teach law at an innovative university arose. He followed the lead and moved into a new career, a new state and a new phase of life.

Astrology is a remarkable aid in helping us to understand and track our vocational quest through numerous lenses. We will continue now deepening our study, first turning to examine the planets more completely in their vocational roles.

– CHAPTER 2 –
ARCHETYPES AND VOCATION
Planets along the Career Path

Archetypes

The word 'archetype' is often used synonymously with planetary and zodiacal energies. Coming from ancient Greek, this word combines *arche*, meaning beginning, origin, cause or primal, and *type*, suggesting form, image, prototype or model. Hence, an archetype implies an original form or a seminal image; archetypes portray the determining structures and primal models underpinning our instinctual life.

Archetypes are characteristic of shared urges and desires in us all, advocates for the experience of being human. They are the first principles at the roots of psychic life. Being universal and collective images, archetypes are communal descriptions for psychic life, regardless of what race, culture or gender we belong to. Archetypes can be identified through deeply reflective ways, such as dreams and astrology that allow us to become acquainted with their essence and patterns.

Often archetypes are experienced as luminous and larger than life. They hold a divine quality which is emotionally commanding and possessive. Their power can often modify our conscious intentions or overwhelm our equilibrium. Archetypes are god-like symbols of the instinctual processes that inspire religious imagery, mythic narratives and the storylines of fairy tales and legends. Archetypes are metaphoric, not factual; therefore it is difficult to describe them logically or rationally. They are better understood through images, symbols, feelings and senses. This is why they engage us in an imaginative approach to understanding life. An archetypal perspective is able to organize diverse aspects of human experience under one umbrella; therefore astrology is resonant with this way of perceiving the world, as it is capable of organizing a host of events, correspondences and associations under one planetary symbol.

Archetypes describe common motifs, yet they manifest through an individual's life in very personal and unique ways. For instance, birth is a universal experience yet it is also a personal episode in each individual's life. The process is archetypal – that is, experienced by every human being – but the effects of this experience and the feelings stimulated are personal. Archetypes are common universal symbols; the image of mother is archetypal, yet she is also an individual to us. Often the personal mother is confused or merged with the archetypal mother through expectations and fantasies. Astrologically, this image is evident when powerful archetypes like Pluto or Neptune aspect the Moon. It is also common to project the expectations of the archetypal mother onto the personal mother.

Archetypal figures are awesome, endowed with the power of the ages, mythic and eternal. When a parent is missing or unavailable they may be replaced by the archetypal parent; the missing parent is then mythologized, becoming ideal rather than real. We recognize this astrologically when an outer planet aspects an inner one, as the mythic realm is enmeshed with the personal sphere. When we are in the grips of an archetype we may unconsciously re-enact its myth in a personalized way. We become its surrogate, expressing its voice through us. Astrology enables a way of thinking about archetypes both personally and universally.

James Hillman suggested that 'an archetype is best comparable with a god'.[13] Planets bear the names of the gods embodying their characteristics and patterns; therefore, astrology is well suited to an archetypal perspective, as it helps us to imagine both the individual's personal temperament and the deeper archetypal patterns of psychic life underpinning the character.

Each planet is archetypal in that it represents the similar faculty of soul for every human: what the Greeks suggested was *ousia*, a soul essence. But planets also symbolize a cluster of events and associations, things and people. Each planet suggests correspondences to personality types and traits, literal objects, colours, parts of the body, plants and metals, etc. Each planet can also be aligned with various careers which are worldly correspondences of the archetypal soul essence; hence why an individual may feel driven or seized to follow a particular career or be called in a particular direction.

From a psychological perspective, Carl Jung suggested that archetypes were the fundamental building blocks of the psyche structuring the core of any complex. A system of personal associations and experiences gather round the heart of the complex like a skin or crust. If we think of a planet as being the heart of a complex, we can identify which personal relationships, experiences and events shape its outer layer, thanks to astrology's vast network of astrological associations. Astrology is astute at identifying the archetypal or planetary core of the complex and so, working with its vast set of connections, an astrologer can suggest which course of action may be more suitable or congruent with that archetypal arrangement. From a vocational point of view an astrologer attempts to ascertain the prominent planetary archetypes and then suggest possibilities. However, these are always only possibilities; astrology can be uncannily accurate in identifying the archetypal core but the personal influences and choices remain unique to each individual.

In mapping the landscape of the psyche, Carl Jung first recognized some major archetypal images such as the Persona, the Shadow, the Anima, the Animus, the Hero, the Self, the Wise Old Man, the Great Mother and the Divine Child. At the dawn of modern psychology these were the first archetypes to be identified, acknowledged and amplified. Yet the planets have always been representative of archetypal forces and patterns that shape and govern human experience. When we conceive of the planets as archetypes we might begin with the following images:

The Sun	The self, the father, the Divine Child	Identity
The Moon	The mother, the infant, the caretaker	Security
Mercury	The trickster, the psychopomp, the guide, the lecturer	Intelligence
Venus	The lover, the partner, the sister, beauty	Relatedness
Mars	The warrior, the brother, the entrepreneur, desire	Will
Jupiter	The teacher, the philosopher, the traveller	Knowledge
Saturn	The authority, the senex, the wise old man	Autonomy
Chiron	The mentor, the healer, the tribal outsider	Wholeness
Uranus	The change-maker, the rebel, the humanist	Individuation
Neptune	The illusionist, the magus, the shape-shifter	Transcendence
Pluto	The therapist, the sibyl, the transformer	Death

Each of these planets has been embodied as an ancient god; in antiquity, the gods were often associated with specific vocations. For instance, Mercury was the god of scribes, merchants, messengers and travelers, and Venus was sponsor of the arts. The Moon was associated with midwifery, caretaking, nursing and food preparation, while Pluto was imagined as the undertaker, miner and one who dealt with the riches underground.[14]

Astrologically, each archetype could be seen as being a benefactor of certain professions: the planet is the profession's guiding spirit, or planetary *daimon*.[15] From an ancient perspective the *daimon* was a spirited and passionate force that urged an individual forward along a certain path. When a planet is strong in an individual's horoscope or placed in a house of vocation we might imagine that it will seek expression through a path in life or the career. However, this is metaphoric, not literal, as there may be a host of careers and options arranged under the rulership of the planet, or more than one planet may combine to influence the course of one's career. What we need to note is that archetypes are encountered through one's career and that planets in a high vocational focus in the horoscope may reveal which energies are prone to being expressed through the individual's career.

Underpinning each vocation is a root metaphor, a symbol which succinctly captures the archetypal essence and historical perspective of the profession itself.[16] For instance, a sociologist's root metaphor would be society, while a psychiatrist's would be the psyche. Astrology's root metaphor is the starry heavens. Root metaphors inform our vocation, not because they are well-thought through philosophies or they embrace traditional values, but ironically because they often remain unconscious.

What inspires and draws us to our vocations can often be identified when we look back over the course of life. Vocations are not chosen in a rational way; we might actually feel it is the vocation that has chosen us. Therefore when working with vocational astrology it is necessary to acknowledge the depth of the archetypal presence that informs vocation, and to remember that while the symbols of the horoscope may appear clear-cut, even concise, this is not the felt experience of most clients who present their questions about vocation.

There is often something fated about how we select our careers or courses of action. What remains undefined for many individuals about their occupation is the archetypal background that has shaped their profession. In other words, we might imagine the soul of a profession as a living reality which informs the career we have chosen. Being involved with this profession and participating with its soul might also suggest how we make choices in our lives. I imagine a profession's root metaphor as being analogous to the essence of the profession. Therefore it is critical to reflect on what informs our expectations, urges and choices about profession. Astrology is a valuable aid in this way.

Planetary Archetypes

Planets personify powerful archetypal forces that seek their expression through us. Like gods, they possess and direct us; one of the ways they articulate themselves is through our work and how we become occupied with what we do as pleasure, hobbies, occupation or career. Each planet has its own preferences and persuasions.

From a vocational perspective we could think about a planet in two ways:

- First, each planet has its unique archetypal nature and essence which represents a faculty of the soul. This essence is individualized and uniquely expressed, but can be amplified through the planet's consideration in the horoscope: its sign, house, rulership and aspects.

- Second, each planet signifies certain professions, symbolizes particular occupations and hobbies as well as indicating behaviours and inclinations. Planetary correspondences are the manifested expression of the archetype's essence. As astrologers we seek to find correlations between the horoscope and the individual's archetypal orientation to vocation.

Therefore, we are looking at a twofold approach to the planets: the first is its soul essence and how that seeks to be expressed through the career or life path; the second is that literal professions resonate with certain planets and these occupations may go a long way towards satisfying the vocational urge. These careers can be general, such as an educator, or defined more specifically, such as a primary school teacher or lecturer.

Some planets, such as the Sun and Moon, are closely connected to our vocation through their intrinsic influence on character and we will look at these in more detail in the next chapter. Saturn is also highly influential as it characterizes autonomy, commitment, discipline, maturity, responsibility and structure, which are all important components of a successful vocation. Saturn is also the understanding and respect for ageing which is important in vocational development through the phases of the life cycle. Jupiter, the other social planet, refers to our beliefs, opportunities and visions regarding our vocation and career. The planet also refers to the search for meaning, human values, expansion and exploration through our work.

All planets correspond with certain desires and outcomes, and in a vocational sense these will be sought through work. For instance, Mercury will need to experience connectivity and variety; Venus will want value and beauty; while Mars may desire competition and adventure. Chiron and the outer planets need to be satisfied through work that is cutting-edge, highly creative, transforming and beyond what is known and accepted. A vocational analysis helps to ascertain which planets are more emphasized in the career sectors of the horoscope. To begin, let's consider which planets in the horoscope may take precedence.

When a planet is highly emphasized in a horoscope it will be a driving force in an individual's life; therefore, high-focus planets are important to note because one of the foremost ways these planets can express their potency is through the career path. There are many ways of thinking about which planets are highly focused in the horoscope; the following list is a way of beginning to think about planets that might be accented in a vocational analysis.

- **Angular planets** All planets on the angles are potent indicators of the direction in life. However, it is the Midheaven and Ascendant that are more immediately concerned with profession and direction. Planets on the MC are the forces that call us into the world; these are the urges that want to be applied on our life path and through our vocation. One of the first indications of career is a planet conjunct the MC; therefore, this would be a high priority planet in terms of career and profession. Planets on the Ascendant are life directors and archetypal forces that guide the course of our lives. When a planet is rising in the horoscope it has a major role in steering the life direction and can be one of the first energies experienced in life through the perinatal atmosphere and the birth experience.

• **Ruler of the Ascendant** The planet ruling the Ascendant was often referred to as the lord of the chart or the horoscope ruler. This gives us an indication that this planet plays a major role in the life direction. In terms of vocation we might think of this planet as a guiding *daimon* which infuses the life direction with its energy and characteristically seeks expression through the surrogacy of the individual. This may be through their creativity and how this is expressed in the world.

• **Ruler of the Midheaven** The planetary ruler of the Midheaven helps to direct the course of the career. Its archetypal nature and astrological considerations describe important vocational qualities.

• **Planets in Aspect** A planet in a major aspect to either the Sun or Moon, or a planet that makes a number of important aspects in the horoscope, needs to be assessed for its impact upon the life direction. When planets are in a dynamic aspect to a luminary they seek expression through personal identification with a role or in satisfying a need, often through a chosen career or occupation. Next, consider any strong aspect or aspect pattern. Any major aspect pattern demands to be known and made conscious and the vocation may be a vehicle for this.

• **Planets Aspecting the Nodal Axis** The nodal axis is an important image when reflecting upon vocation; therefore, planets in aspect to the nodal axis may play a role in discovering a fulfilling vocation. Potent aspects are conjunctions to either the North or South Node and squares to the nodal axis. These aspects will be amplified in Chapter 5.

• **Dispositors** Astrologically, a dispositor is a planet that rules the sign of another planet. For instance, if the Sun is in Sagittarius, Jupiter is the dispositor of the Sun, because Jupiter rules

Sagittarius, the sign of the Sun. If Jupiter is in Leo, then this is described as a mutual reception, as each planet disposits the other. This technique will be beneficial when assessing the influence of a planet and becoming familiar with the connections in the horoscope.

A planet which disposits the planets of a stellium (i.e. rules the stellium sign) would be significant to consider. A stellium is concentrated energy; therefore, the ruler of the sign which contains a stellium could indicate an energy that could activate or direct the force of the complex inherent in the stellium. Vocationally it would be important to consider the sign and house position of the stellium in terms of career path and how its ruling planet can help to awaken and actualize the potential of the stellium.

When a horoscope has only one planet ruling its own sign and the trail of dispositors leads back to this planet, it is known as the final dispositor. The final dispositor is an important planet because it is the only planet that is in its own sign; therefore, it is ruled by no other planet. In a way we might consider that all the other planets yielding to this final dispositor are highlighting this planet in the chart.

• **Singleton planets** This generally refers to a planet that is in high focus since it is the only one of its kind in the horoscope, such as:

  – The only planet retrograde
  – The only planet in an element
  – The only planet in a mode
  – The only planet in a hemisphere (north/south; east/west)
  – The handle to a Bucket chart
  – An unaspected planet

Singleton planets may be significant on the vocational path as they may be highlighted due to their marginality rather than their strength. These energies are forceful in seeking to be integrated and participatory in the life purpose.

Assessing planetary potency was always a priority of the ancient astrologers who had many ways to judge a planet's strength.[17] The above list of considerations for planets when considering vocation is from my own experience, and drawn from students and clients who have taught me to consider each individual and each chart in their own way. First we become proficient with all the techniques, principles and considerations of astrology; then we listen to the client and their experience, which helps to forge our unique approach to the horoscope.

Planets in Houses
We also consider planets in the houses of the horoscope, as these spheres represent the spaces and places of our lives where the planetary archetypes are placed. A planet inhabits the space influencing its atmosphere and environment. When placed in a prominent vocational sphere of the horoscope, a planet points to what we may need in our work.

- **The Houses of Substance** The trinity of the 2nd, 6th and 10th houses is known as the houses of substance and also referred to as the houses of vocation. Planets in these houses seek expression through professional talents, resources, work and activities. Because these houses focus on the manifestation of work-related skills and talents, they are generally the first ones to be considered vocationally. Planets here need to be assessed for their vocational urges and attributes and how they may be best employed. As these houses are specifically focused on career we will look at these separately.

- **The Houses of Life** The houses of life – the 1st, 5th and 9th houses – are where life is conceived, born and renewed. These are houses of creativity and self-expression, and support the life direction and purpose. First house planets permeate the personality and the way we reach out into life. These archetypes shape the personality and forge ways to transition between the deeper self and the everyday self. Planets in the 5th house occupy an innovative and self-expressive field; therefore these energies seek articulation through their creative potential. The 9th house sphere influences the vocation through the individual's belief system, travel and exploration urges and the search for something greater. Planets in the 9th infuse the vocation with vision, inspiration and adventure. Planets occupying these houses affect personality, creativity, self-expressiveness and the vision of what is possible.

Other House Considerations

All houses are potentially territories of life that influence the course of vocation. For instance, the 3rd house symbolizes the process of early schooling, learning and communication, all of which are often a major influence on career plans. If any house has a stellium of planets, it may be a place that becomes defined by the career. All the houses may have their own theme or arena of life, and planets in them will seek their expression in that sphere, which may be through work or career.

Whether in the vocational houses or in high focus, planetary energies are articulated throughout the course of one's life, sometimes demanding a prominent role. Therefore if the planetary urge is not satisfied it may become compulsive and driven to express itself in other ways. When these urges are denied they feel powerless and despairing. When these planetary energies are unexpressed, astrology can suggest avenues to help activate and channel the archetypal energy through the vocation. A vocational course need not always be a career or work, but could be a course of study, a creative endeavour, an active pursuit, a hobby or any interests that activate and employ this energy.

Traditionally, planets in astrology have been associated with literal careers; however, from our exploration we recognize that a literal profession is the image of an archetype, or a composite of archetypes, seeking worldly expression. Familiarize yourself with the careers that the planets symbolize as these will be considerations in any vocational analysis. In contemporary times an individual is often destined for many careers, many of which have not yet come into being; therefore, the planetary needs are primary in the vocational analysis.

What follows is an exploration of each planet, its archetypal nature and some of the literal professions that are associated with it. This introduces the planetary symbols in a vocational context. Be aware that many vocations may actually be a combination of two or three planetary energies. This discussion introduces some of the planetary associations with particular careers, but for a more detailed list please consult Appendix 1.

Planets in Vocation

Planetary archetypes are multivalent. Gathered around the core of the archetype are countless associations – whether these are literal objects, psychological patterns or emotional states. Astrological tradition has identified each planet with particular vocational images; therefore let's turn to imagining each planet in context of vocation.

☉ **The Sun**

As the brightest star in the sky the Sun was always aligned with the archetype of the king, who also symbolized a surrogate figure of a god, the father, the ruler, the director or the hero. It personified a powerful leader and represented honours and elevation. Therefore early astrologers equated the Sun with heads of state, high-ranking professionals, leaders and managers of important offices.

In contemporary times, solar qualities of leadership and fathering are still connected with authoritative and executive positions. The person in command of a company or business is still symbolized by the Sun, as they are the focus of the system and everything and everyone revolves around this bright and central 'star'.

From a psychological perspective, the need for the personal father's approval may be high; therefore, father may have influenced or guided the choice of profession. Since acknowledgement and appreciation are keys to the vocation, the individual may be drawn towards careers where support and endorsement are more available, where rank and position are important and one is guided and authorized by prominent authorities. The Sun represents vocations which father and foster others, such as:

- Business manager
- Community leader
- Foreman
- CEO and President of organizations
- Magistrate

Over time, solar occupations have become linked with speculation and risk-taking in entrepreneurial ventures, as earlier occupations linked to the Sun were minting money and working in precious metals. Although the Sun is not psychologically associated with risk, except the risks of self-discovery, the solar sphere of the 5th house rules speculation and gambling. Therefore these contemporary occupations have become assigned to the Sun:

- Commodity trader
- Stock exchange personnel
- Investment banker
- High-risk investor

The Sun is the natural ruler of the 5th house of children; therefore it has been linked to working with children and children's products. Some of these professions include:

- Teacher
- Child counsellor
- Children's recreation or amusement worker
- Making educational toys and products for children
- Designing or selling children's wear

As the Sun is creative and expressive, it has been linked to entertainment professions, amusements, self-improvement, creative expression and careers that involve relating to an audience, such as:

- Acting, theatre and the performing arts
- Motivational training
- Sales, advertising and promotions
- Amusement and fun
- Professions which deal with leisure and recreation

Of all the planetary types, the solar type is one of the most difficult to typify because it also represents the Self, which is not so easily defined or categorized. The solar type needs to enjoy what they do and feel personally identified with their vocation, because often their career is a large part of their identity and raison d'être.

John D Rockefeller, Jr. was born on 29 January 1874 in Cleveland, Ohio. We will use his chart as an example of the archetype of the Sun. As already mentioned, the solar archetype represents father and John Jr.'s father was an American business magnate and philanthropist who revolutionized the petroleum industry. Amassing a fortune throughout his life, he became one of the richest individuals in US history. Therefore, John Jr. was already poised to follow in his father's footsteps, becoming a financier, business leader, patriarch and philanthropist. These images are all resonant with the Sun, but they are also supported by the Capricorn MC, with Saturn in its dignity conjunct three personal planets including the Sun.

In John Rockefeller Jr.'s horoscope the Sun is involved in a stellium with Mercury, Saturn and Venus. All four planets rule the vocational houses: the Sun rules the 6th, Mercury rules the intercepted sign in

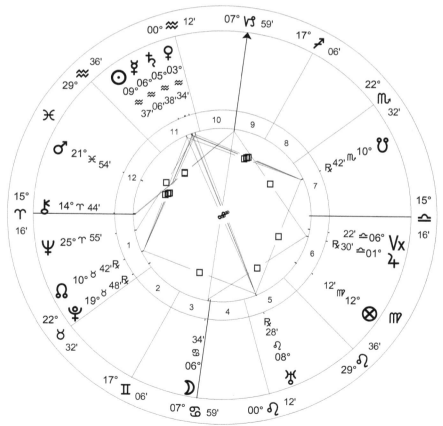

John D Rockefeller Jr., 29 January 1874, 10 a.m. LMT;
Cleveland, Ohio, USA

the 6th, Venus rules the 2nd and Saturn rules the 10th. Therefore all four planets regulate resourceful vocational factors that can be accessed through the career. The dispositors of this stellium are Saturn and Uranus, both of which aspect the Sun. Saturn is conjunct the Sun, adding stability, while Uranus is opposite, highlighting the ability to be innovative and forward-striving. The Sun is also square to the nodal axis, which stretches from its southern pole in Scorpio to its destination in Taurus; both signs address the accumulation of wealth. The Sun aspecting the Nodes identifies with the challenges in the vocational direction.

Aries rising enhances the entrepreneurial attitude already inherent in the horoscope. Angular Chiron brings a maverick quality to Rockefeller's industrial career. While there are many traditional ways to consider a planet's strength, such as rulerships, exaltations and sect, each chart needs to be viewed in its own unique way to assess the potency of any particular planet. This will emerge through practice and experience and in the differentiation of theories and techniques that are helpful in a vocational analysis.

☽ The Moon

As queen of the night, the Moon aligns with mother, the female ruler or heroine. The Moon is associated with women in general, especially women who are attached and influential in an individual's life. Vocationally, this aligns with the moods of the public, women's issues and female power in general. Like the Moon, the archetype is seen as developmental in moving through its phases, being moody and cyclical. The two faces of this archetype embrace the nurturing and compassionate caretaker, alongside its destroying and unfeeling aspect.

The cycles of the Moon are embodied by all women; in a literal way these synchronize with the menstrual cycles and the monthly ebb and flow of moods and feelings. As such, the Moon rules all the professions concerning women's health care, such as infertility, pregnancy and hormonal changes.

- Gynaecology
- IVF research and application
- Maternal foetal medicine
- Neonatology
- Reproduction medicine

Concerned with nurturing, food and beverages, the Moon can be appeased through these occupations:

– Chef, baker and brewer
– Professions dealing with food and agriculture
– Food industry
– Catering, waiting or waitressing, hospitality and hotel management

Astrologically, the Moon has come to represent one's sense of security and safety. When highlighted it suggests that job security, work safety and routine are important considerations. As the main signifier of the feeling life and emotionality, the Moon needs to feel connected and attached to what we are doing or we will feel emotionally depleted and unsatisfied. One of the foremost needs of the Moon is belonging, and this is an important consideration in any vocation. Family businesses, working from home and a familial atmosphere in the workplace are all ways in which the Moon may seek to feel comfortable with work.

As the Moon is concerned with habitat, it is associated with the professions involved with homes:

– Real estate
– Products for the home
– Home design and building
– Domestic and home services
– Furniture and antiques

The mothering and nurturing sides of the Moon are involved in the professions concerned with the care of children, such as:

– Day care worker
– Teacher and early childhood educator
– Counsellor
– Family care provider
– Obstetrician
– Midwifery
– Paediatrician

Traditionally, lunar professions were care-related, such as domestic duties or hospice nursing. Vocations associated with the lunar capacity to attend and care are:

- Health care professional
- Social worker
- Family counsellor or therapist
- Nursing
- Care provider

Traditionally, the Moon was aligned with those who chose the sea as their profession, whether they were sailors or fishermen. Along with these traditional seafaring professions, today there are many others involving the sea, such as:

- Marine biology
- Oceanography
- Marine animal caretaker

Michel Gauquelin's statistical research into vocation and angular planets demonstrated that the Moon is linked to writers. Perhaps in a broader sense we might deduce that professions using the right side of the brain, or those that are highly personal and imaginative, may be symbolized by the Moon:

- Writer and songwriter
- Playwright
- Artist
- Scriptwriter

The sign of the Moon will distinguish the qualities and attributes of the various nurturing professions. In this way these careers can be more closely aligned to an individual's lunar placements. In the following chapter we will explore examples of the Moon in each sign as a way of demonstrating how the elements and signs make distinctions in vocational categories. These are only ways of thinking about how the lunar vocation might manifest and this type of consideration could be applied to all planetary positions.

☿ Mercury

Mercury has many faces, facets and features; as the messenger god he was guide of souls both in and out of the underworld. His dexterity and penchant for variety can be seen in his many roles and functions. Representing many archetypal expressions, such as the trickster god, the shepherd of dreams, the god of thieves and the merchant, the planet named for him came to epitomize many professions. Astrologically, Mercury became known as the communicator, the scribe, writer and thinker; over time he has been associated with the spectrum of occupations from attorney, advocate, clerk and schoolmaster to stationer, solicitor, secretary and philosopher.

As the god of transitions he is encountered on thresholds, on the bend in the road and at crossroads. This suggests that when Mercury is aligned with the vocation there may be many transitions and changes along the career path. His needs are mobility, variety and intellectual stimulation with opportunities for interaction and communicating, which are important in any work under Mercury's jurisdiction.

Foremost, Mercury was the messenger of the gods and his astrological function is to deliver the message and communicate. Therefore, he is associated with careers in communication, such as:

- Lecturing and teaching
- Writing and blogging
- Interpreting
- Journalism
- Radio, television and media announcer
- Social media
- Printing and stationery
- Editing
- Postal work
- The computer and information industry
- Media and news reporting
- Advertising

As ruler of both the 3rd house and the 6th house, Mercurial occupations involve gathering information, as well as the analysis of that information:

- Information technology, Internet, computer analysis and technology
- Statistical analysis and statistician
- Scientist
- Accountancy and economic analysis
- Librarian

The analytical side of Mercury also combines with the urge towards health in these professions:

- Clinical psychology
- Psychiatry and psychiatric nursing
- Dietician
- Health care worker
- Medical analysis

Mercury is also the patron of travellers, their guide, and astrologically rules short trips, neighbourhoods and commerce, so is associated with:

- The travel industry
- Driving
- Courier work
- Tour guide and organizer
- Interpreter
- Flight attendant
- Taxi driver

The Virgo side of Mercury is also important in all service industries and occupations, such as:

- Clerk
- Secretary
- Accountant
- Solicitor
- Attorney

♀ Venus

Traditionally, Venus was associated with beauty, love and peace, and became embodied as the lover, the sweetheart and the romantic interest. If Venus is in high focus vocationally then the sphere of relating and relationships becomes important in a career, whether that be working in a relationship-orientated profession, involved in a partnership or employed alongside equals.

Psychologically, Venus is aligned with values and it is of high priority to feel valued and appreciated, and that the occupation is contributing to the development of self-esteem and personal worth. It is also important that work is valued and the workplace environment is harmonious and peaceful. Venus is highly sensitive to disorder and unpleasantness, and needs the work surroundings to be ordered and attractive.

Venus's affinity for equality, personal development and relating combine to make this archetype a good counsellor. The urge to beautify is not only outer-orientated through careers in beauty therapy, hairdressing and fashion, but inner-directed as well, suggesting that Venus could also be associated with:

- Counselling
- Life coaching
- Psychotherapy
- Mediation
- Arbitration

Archetypally, Venus is the urge to beautify, and over time Venus has become the patroness of professionals such as artists, jewellers, perfumiers, designers, painters and musicians. Venusian vocations often specialize in art or the art of beautification, such as:

- Art museum worker or curator
- Art or beauty therapist
- Model
- Fashion industry
- Perfume or cosmetic industry
- Clothing design
- Music industry (Taurus is especially connected to singing through its correspondence with the throat)

– Interior design and decoration
– Feng Shui and placement
– Gifts and crafts
– Florist
– Ceramicist and potter

Venus is inclined towards the development of social skills, relating, charm and interaction. Therefore, it is linked to professions which highlight these traits:

– Hospitality and hosting industries
– Community relations
– Hotel management
– Protocol and social management
– Receptionist
– Wedding planner and caterer
– Production of social events

It is also linked to professions which involve diplomacy and protocol:

– Diplomat
– Ambassador
– Customer service
– Legal profession
– Social arrangements (wedding planner, social secretary, etc.)
– Personnel manager

Through Venus's connection to partnerships and working in a one-to-one situation or team, professions like the following would reflect this archetype:

– Personal and marriage counselling
– Tutor
– Business partnership
– Personal recruitment
– Personal assistant

As the ruler of Taurus and the 2nd house, Venus can be linked to professions involving finance, money and agriculture:

- Money management
- Banking
- Human resources

Using the senses and the creative flair are also important in vocations like:

- Massage
- Aromatherapy
- Food and wine merchant and connoisseur

When Venus is highlighted on the career path her needs are to be valued and appreciated, so this will become important in any occupation. Her need to beautify and relate is also imperative when considering any career.

♂ Mars

When Mars is in high focus in vocational analysis then occupations that promote an independent and entrepreneurial spirit are important. Goal-orientated occupations encouraging the competitive drive and allowing the freedom to express the self are imperative. If Mars is strongly aspected and the competitive spirit is stifled, the individual may experience displaced aggression in their work environment either through clients, co-workers or their superiors.

As the god of war, Mars is akin to the archetype of the warrior, so is associated with military professions and the armed forces. In traditional astrology his rulership was associated with soldiers, generals and commanders of armies as well as tyrants and conquerors. In a contemporary way he can be linked to:

- The armed services
- The national guard
- Security services and providers

Mars's professions traditionally have also been associated with 'sharp' objects, as well as tools, fire and iron. From a present-day perspective these might be:

- Surgeon and physician
- Dentist
- Acupuncturist
- Any occupations using mechanical instruments, such as machinist, mechanic, fitter and turner
- Handyman, craftsman, artisan, carpenter

Careers involving the sense of danger, adventure and adrenalin are Martian, such as:

- Adventure sports
- Fire fighter and fire brigade
- Police force
- Paramedic and ambulance work

Using physical energies either in competition sports, training or labour:

- Physical education trainer and coach
- Dancer and dance instructor
- Gymnastics, athletics and coaching
- Competitive athlete
- Physical education
- Physical labour such as construction and manual labour

Mars rules the head and has the urge to be first, so administrative and supervisory careers suit, especially in the pioneering fields, through invention and exploration using an entrepreneurial spirit.

♃ Jupiter

Jupiter is the largest planet in the solar system, metaphoric of its outreach in life and its yearning to travel farther afield. Its influence on the vocational path is to bring growth, education, travel, cross-cultural experiences and adventure into the arena of work. The archetype of Jupiter is associated with philosophies, ideologies and concepts. In traditional terms, Jupiter was an educated person often embodied as a philosopher, priest, aristocrat, judge or scholar. Later, careers that involved expanding people's understanding of themselves and the world around them, as well as administering to an individual's religious and soul needs, became associated with Jupiter.

One of Jupiter's strongest vocational urges is to educate and inspire others to a greater understanding of themselves and the world they inhabit. Therefore, vocations that are involved with education, philosophical and religious beliefs and attitudes come under the umbrella of Jupiter:

- Philosopher and teacher of philosophy
- Literature
- Minister and member of the clergy
- Motivational teacher and coach
- Professor
- University lecturer and tutor
- Teacher of higher wisdom
- Educator

A function of education is the dissemination of information and ideas. Jupiter is associated with professions such as:

- Publishing
- Writing fiction and non-fiction
- Advertising
- Telecommunications industry

Jupiter is also connected to cross-cultural affairs, travel and dealing with international matters:

- Foreign service
- Import/export trade
- Protocol including ambassadors and personnel in foreign environments
- Foreign trade
- Interpreter
- Missionary

- Travel consultant and industry
- Foreign affairs and international contacts

Whereas Mars is more aligned with sports champions who compete for themselves, Jupiter is associated with team sports and the sporting industry as well as adventure:

- Horse racing
- Sporting goods
- Team sports
- Explorer and adventure guide
- Coach and trainer

As the chief Olympian, Zeus (Jupiter) was the most influential of the gods and this archetype seeks to influence and impact others with their ideas, generally through some form of education.

♄ Saturn

Jupiter was known as optimistic but Saturn became identified as pessimistic, tending towards more severe and difficult occupations such as tax collectors or ditch diggers. However, Saturn was also associated with age and reputation, so those who had rank or administrative power were seen to embody Saturn. The moral that hard work achieves results and rewards became part of Saturn's ethos. Saturn has been associated with both endings and golden ages; therefore, there can be extremes in experiencing this archetype, ranging from severity to success. The archetype has many layers of associations. While it seeks to be acknowledged through a system and can be highly conformist, its other face can often turn away from convention in order to rebel.

As a standard of excellence, the energy of Saturn seeks fulfilment and achievement, often bordering on obsession or perfection. Often a perfectionist streak or a drive to excel are defensive positions protecting innate feelings of not being 'good enough', a common Saturnine inner voice. This motivates individuals to try even harder, which sets up a demanding performance-orientated cycle. Professions that encourage a need for excellence and precision can direct some of this energy; however, the tendency for perfectionism can be compelling and overwhelming. When this need for perfection becomes compulsive, the Saturn archetype inclines towards the workaholic temperament.

Occupations encouraging a sense of authority are important. The need for responsibility and autonomy is high, so the Saturn archetype is drawn to professions that offer advancement through the ranks and a sense of status and achievement:

- Executive
- Specialist
- Technician
- Scientist
- Corporate manager
- School principal and teacher
- Law-maker, politician, councillor

Saturn is also associated with many trades. especially the building trade, but also may be connected to agriculture, gardening and real estate since it has an appreciation for the earth and its resources:

- Contractor and engineer
- Bricklayer and builder
- Gardener and landscape design
- Architecture and building design
- Construction industry, labourer
- Real estate dealer, land developer and land agent

The need for hierarchy is important to Saturn, as is the need to respect their superiors. With their need for autonomy and authority, a common pattern in strong Saturnine types is to clash with management in trying to resolve and attain a position of influence and control.

By nature, Saturn is autonomous and often works better on its own. As an archetype of reliability, Saturn often attracts issues of responsibility in its work experiences. Vocationally, Saturn learns to deal with responsibility and boundaries. Innately, Saturn strives for competence and high standards, yet ironically in the work experience it often encounters ineptitude and incompetence in its superiors. Often this is the fate of Saturn in the workplace; however, by design it encourages autonomy, discipline and self-acknowledgement.

⚷ Chiron

Chiron's cave on Mount Pelion was the place where young, homeless and orphaned boys were initiated into the vocational ways of the hero, learning skills such as hunting, combat, healing with herbs and navigating by the stars. Chiron's unique tutelage also included the handiness of healing, using plants and folk medicine. With Chiron, the boys were reminded that their birthright was to be heroic and to strive to become the best they could be. In classical myth Chiron is the ancient link to the archetype of the healer/hero/bard and reminds us of archaic traditions which linked the mystical with the mundane, the spirit with the body. It is an archetype of wholeness, not because it is perfect, but because it contains and acknowledges both instinctual and divine life.

In contemporary times Chiron symbolizes this quest for wholeness, individuation and the attempts to heal the split between the body and the soul. Hence in vocational pursuits Chiron leans towards the healing professions that address the need to reconcile the body-mind split:

- The holistic healing professions including naturopathy, homeopathy, osteopathy, herbalism, chiropractic work, Ayurvedic and Chinese medicine and all alternative healing practices which attempt to work with body *and* mind
- Dream therapy
- Spirit channelling and mediumship
- Reiki and other New Age healing modalities
- Astrology and others working with imagery and symbols as a healing tool

Chiron was also a mentor and teacher and therefore is connected with mentoring professions, such as:

- Life coach
- Mentor
- Inspirational teacher
- Educator in marginalized and disenfranchised disciplines

As a foster figure, Chiron is also associated with the marginalized:

- Working with refugees and the homeless
- Caring, supervising and working with the handicapped
- Vocations which aid the underprivileged and the outcast
- Social work
- Working with the disenfranchised and the gifted

♅ Uranus

Discovered in 1781, Uranus was unknown to the ancient astrologers. Its discovery near the advent of the industrial age reminds us that this archetype presides over burgeoning revolutions in the spheres of industry, manufacturing, science and technology. Being up-to-the-minute, Uranus rules technological revolutions, new and cutting-edge expertise, the engineering industry and innovative aspects of electronics and technology. It is an archetype that looks forward to possibilities, not back to traditions; therefore, vocationally it propels one into unknown and groundbreaking spheres of work. Uranian careers are unusual or not yet fully developed. However, at the heart of any of its professions is an urge to revolutionize, liberate and progress.

Like the planet, Uranian occupations were unknown in the ancient world. They represent scientific and logical advancements, such as:

- Computer programming and technical work
- IT
- Internet-based occupations
- Technological advancements in radio, television and social media

Uranus is an altruistic planet and rules humanitarianism and social reforms, including:

- Politics
- Humanitarian concerns and occupations
- Promotion of causes
- Professional and humanitarian associations
- Social services

The innovation of this archetype leads to vocations which encourage inventiveness:

- Inventing
- Science
- Technical work

Occupations which deal with the human condition and the advancement of the individual:

- Psychology (group psychology, Adlerian, Gestalt, Psychodrama)
- Astrology
- Community work and reforms
- New Age occupations (Reiki healing, crystals, channelling)

Extraordinary or non-traditional vocations appeal to Uranus:

- Rock musician
- Metaphysician
- Science fiction writer

As expected, the archetype of the unexpected has many unusual and as yet unknown vocational associations.

♆ Neptune

Wherever we find Neptune in the horoscope we locate the urge to contact the divine. Its house position suggests the environment where an individual seeks the divine and follows its calling. It is an archetype of craving, expecting, yearning, struggling with the gap between the soulful and inner creative experiences and the disenchantment of not locating that in the outer world.

Of all the planets, Neptune resonates with the longing to find soul, since it feels trapped and suffocated by the mundane and its literal and tedious aspects of life. It longs for the connection with soul and/or the divine, languishing in a sense of divine discontent when this cannot be fulfilled or sustained. Its urge to embrace or surrender to the divine is manifest in desire, idealization, fantasy or spiritual hunger. This archetype often finds its expression through the calling to help or serve. Hence, in a vocational way, Neptune longs to be helpful or of service in order to find a way to express the divine through compassion and empathy.

There are two main paths through which Neptune can express itself in a career. The first is through the helping professions where the individual must surrender their own ego needs for those of others:

- Nursing
- Social work
- Hospital work
- Psychology and psychiatry
- Physician and healer
- Working with disabled, physically and mentally handicapped individuals
- The ministry and other spiritual vocations
- Working with the elderly, poor or underprivileged
- Volunteer work
- Intuitive vocations such as clairvoyant, psychic and spiritual healer, dream and image therapist

The other path involves expressing the divine through inspiration, imagination, creativity and artistic calling:

- Poet
- Artist
- Musician
- Photography and camera work
- Film and video industry
- Dance
- Fashion and glamour industries

Neptune is also associated with the drug and chemical industries:

- Pharmacologist
- Chemist
- Working with oils and essences
- Drug and alcohol rehabilitation

Mythological Neptune rules the seas:

- Oceanography
- Aquatic occupations
- Boating

The following chart is that of a client who first consulted me in 2013 to explore his purpose and direction in life. At this time Neptune was transiting the North Node, an image of his longing to find purpose and meaning, yet also the fear that this may never be realized or encountered. This is another short example of the nature of a planetary archetype being prominent in vocation.

This was significant timing, as Neptune is strongly placed in the horoscope on the MC; therefore the Neptune transit to the North Node was synchronous with my client's questions about purpose and direction. While there are no definite rules for assessing how a planet might manifest vocationally, there are ways of thinking about which planets are in high focus in a career perspective.

From a vocational perspective we may first be drawn to Neptune, being conjunct the MC. Neptune is also making a dynamic square aspect to the Sun; Neptune is also opposite Saturn, the traditional ruler of the Ascendant, which is angular on the IC. Therefore, Neptune is involved in a T-square, a major aspect pattern. We might also consider that as Neptune is the modern ruler of Pisces, it disposits the Moon and the North Node, two highly important factors vocationally. Therefore, I would consider Neptune as a strong vocational indicator due to these considerations:

- Conjunct the MC
- Square the Sun
- Involved in a T-square
- Dispositor of North Node and Moon
- Square the nodal axis

The client was involved in film production, which certainly honoured the archetype of Neptune. However, he was disappointed that he could not identify with the profession as he felt it had lost its creativity through corporatization and was now devoid of kindness and meaningfulness. The chart certainly confirmed the client's

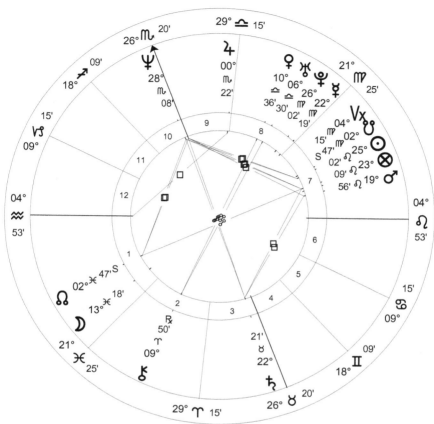

Client, 18 August 1970, 6.05 p.m.; Beijing, China

creative vocation in the field of imagination and image-making; however, it was not the literality of the career that was challenging, but its atmosphere and lack of meaningfulness, a prompt to begin to review his current employment.

♇ Pluto

Pluto's realm is the underworld, which in a mythological sense was a sphere of treasures or riches. As an archetypal presence it evokes what is hidden, is concerned with what is unknown and constellates what is dark and in transition. Pluto's name means riches, from the idea that wealth was in the resources that lay underground; therefore, we might imagine that wherever Pluto is in the horoscope will show where we are drawn to find its buried treasure.

However, this place is also the 'door to Dis'. *Dis* is the Roman name for the underworld god and the location where we metaphorically find subterranean feelings: losses, unexpressed grief, traumatic and shameful feelings, secrets, as well as the myriad of undesirable feelings such as anger, jealousy and envy. In a vocational sense, Pluto often deals with vocations which dig down deeply either into the literal ground or into the psychic ground to locate the truth and encourage the release of the repressed. In this way Pluto rules over research and investigative vocations:

- Psychotherapy and depth psychology
- Analyst
- Doctor
- Loss and grief practitioner
- Bereavement counsellor
- Occupations underground, such as work in the mines, subways or plumbing
- Medical researcher
- Forensic investigator
- Investigative reporting
- Police and governmental undercover agencies
- Detective
- Archaeologist

Pluto oversees the realm of the dead and in a vocational sense deals with this as a literal realm. Since Pluto is also associated with the cycle of endings, demolition and renovation, the archetype correlates with occupations where the cycle of destruction and renewal is prevalent:

- Burials, mortuary work and the undertaking profession
- Coroner
- Wills and legal vocations concerning inheritances, the dead and the rights of the dead
- Insurance agent
- Demolition and renovation work
- Renovation and renewal

The power of Pluto to influence the masses and transform public opinion is reflected in such careers as:

- Market researcher
- Media or other vocations of influence
- Politics

Animating the Archetype

What powers motivate us in the direction of certain careers? What unconscious forces shape our vocation? Many pioneering theorists in the field of psychoanalysis tried to identify an instinct that was the primary motivating force for an individual. Throughout the early psychoanalytic movement different theories were introduced; for instance, Sigmund Freud presented the concept of Eros; Alfred Adler identified it as power; Harry Stack Sullivan as social solidarity; and Erich Fromm as the Self.

Carl Jung's suggestion that humanity's common instincts, drives and urges were archetypes is the model that most successfully resonates with astrological practice. From a pre-philosophical way of thinking, these archetypes were the gods who influenced, shaped and directed our destiny. From an astrological point of view, these archetypes are the planets, each one representing a measure of the human experience, different characteristics, drives and urges, and each one seeking expression in its own way, often through the vocation.

While all human beings are commonly influenced by a spectrum of archetypes, each individual's orientation to a particular archetype functions in a characteristic way. Astrological tradition differentiates how a planet may express its archetypal nature through the use of qualities, elements and signs. Therefore we will now examine the astrological elements and signs in terms of vocation.

– CHAPTER 3 –
ELEMENTS OF VOCATION
Signs and Signals

Facets of Vocation

Like archetypes, planets seek to express their force through us. One of the main channels through which planetary archetypes are uniquely expressed is through the agency of the zodiacal qualities, such as the element and sign they occupy in the horoscope.

Carl Jung formulated four ways or functions that describe how individuals might orient themselves to the archetypal world. These functions came to be known as the four *psychological types* and were termed as intuition, sensation, thinking and feeling. Each individual has their own unique typology or distinctive arrangement of these four types, but one type is generally more dominant in the psyche than the others. Like one of the four points on a compass, an individual's dominant psychological type directs them towards a particular life course. Vocationally this is significant, as the dominant type or element in an astrological sense will tend to manage and inform the career choices.

Jung's typology was not a new initiative because the ancients had also attempted to differentiate character types. In *The Republic*, Plato suggested four temperaments or four facilities of the soul as being imagination, demonstration, opinion and intelligence. Galen developed the Hippocratic theory of the four humours as being choleric, melancholic, phlegmatic and sanguine, which was extensively used in medical practice from Greek medicine onwards. And early Greek astrologers grouped the signs of the zodiac into four categories or typologies known as elements – Fire, Earth, Air and Water.

Chart analysis begins with an overview of these elements. The dominant element of the chart symbolizes the principal channel through which an individual is most inclined to orientate themselves to life. Each element contains three zodiacal signs which characterize its development through the diverse layers of human experience, astrologically represented as the personal, interpersonal and collective signs. Each sign is unique in that it is not only classed by its element but also its quality of cardinal, fixed or mutable energy that initiates, sustains and modifies it. A planet located in an element suggests how the archetype naturally expresses itself.

Mode Element	CARDINAL	FIXED	MUTABLE
FIRE	Aries	Leo	Sagittarius
EARTH	Capricorn	Taurus	Virgo
AIR	Libra	Aquarius	Gemini
WATER	Cancer	Scorpio	Pisces

Element	Personal	Interpersonal	Transpersonal
FIRE	Aries	Leo	Sagittarius
EARTH	Taurus	Virgo	Capricorn
AIR	Gemini	Libra	Aquarius
WATER	Cancer	Scorpio	Pisces

Elements and signs can amplify vocational needs and urges in a variety of ways and we will continue to explore these qualities over the course of the following chapters. To begin, we can consider how the element modifies the archetypal expression of the planet as well as how it might differentiate some vocational choices. But first, it is always important to capture the essence of the element to see how it might influence our vocational nature. If one element is leading or dominant then it is important to be mindful of its qualities and conditions in our vocational search. An individual's temperament may be more introverted than extroverted, and in this case the element becomes more internally focused or reserved, yet is of equal significance on the career path.

Fire

The element of Fire encompasses Aries, Leo and Sagittarius. It is a spirited element, with an instinctive, spontaneous, forthright, energetic, enthusiastic and wilful approach to life. Fire is passionate and, like its element in nature, burns new ground and yearns to move further afield. While individuals with a strong Fire temperament initially approach their job with passion and excitement, restlessness and boredom follow if their need for stimulation is not met. The natural tendency is to suddenly start projects and courses of action with verve and dynamism, yet find difficulty in sustaining excitement and idealism when the blaze of the original passion wanes.

Fire's burning spirit and quest for philosophical perfection and absolute truth meets its shadow in negative feeling, lethargy and criticism. Fire individuals are frustrated when their careers are routine and mundane or lack goals and possibilities. If they feel heavily criticized or unappreciated in their work environment they could begin to act out in a destructive way. Negative feelings are denied by Fire's need to be buoyant and feel the rush of life energy. Denying negativity or depression promotes the projection of these feelings onto co-workers and employers, thereby unconsciously infecting the atmosphere of work with their own unhappiness. Fire builds up the capacity for impulse control by burning off its frustrations and aggravations through physical exercise, movement and exciting activities.

Earth

Earth's approach to vocation is more conservative, traditionally orientated and self-controlled. The three Earth signs are Taurus, Virgo and Capricorn. This element has an appreciation of linear time and letting the job unfold, not wanting to feel rushed or pushed. Unlike Fire, Earth's natural inclination is to move slowly and cautiously. Earth is the element of incarnation and materiality. Resources are important when Earth is involved in vocation. When an innate resourcefulness and an ability to create and sustain resources is combined with a healthy sense of self-worth and self-esteem, the individual feels competent in exchanging their talents and resources for a satisfying income. Without adequate self-esteem there may be a consistent undervaluing of their work or an inappropriate obsession with money, inflating their sense of self-worth, trying to provide that sense through material possessions.

Earth is the element of the five senses, and sharing the sensual world is important: looking at beautiful art, listening to an inspired piece of music, sharing a sumptuous meal, filling the space with fragrant essences or embracing and being affectionate with one another are all images of the important world of earthy pleasure. Since this is an integral part of Earth's character it is important that their work environment or the tasks of their job connect them to the sensual world, allowing them to feel grounded and centred.

Air

The Air trinity of Gemini, Libra and Aquarius naturally wants to communicate ideas and experiences, because Air constantly seeks to relate and reflect. The urge to relate is a vital aspect of their vocational needs. Air seeks a multiplicity of experiences and needs to share its ideas and experiences in work routines; therefore, relationship needs, interaction and the ability to enquire and learn are necessary considerations in a vocational analysis. As a thinking type it is also important that the mind is stimulated in their occupation. A primary need is to use ideas and think things through; therefore the airy type can often feel restless or bored if unchallenged intellectually. This can also manifest in nervousness or anxiety as well as veering off track to pursue things that are unnecessary or irrelevant.

Since Air is the element of relationship, this factor is of prime consideration. The need for a people-orientated vocation may be dominant. Social interaction at work is very important for Air as it works best with others, discussing and working things through with them. Air seeks equality in their relationships so it is important that they feel equal to others in their environment and that the distribution of the work is fair.

Water

The Water element that contains the signs Cancer, Scorpio and Pisces needs depth of feeling and personal involvement in what they do. Water's sensitivity, creativity, compassion and caring are qualities that seek expression though a vocation. There is a strong urge to nurture; however, it is just as important for the individual to feel nurtured, emotionally secure and safe in the workplace.

In vocational terms, creativity, caring, spirituality and imagination are high priorities. Vocational goals are not easy to articulate, nor are they as straightforward or practical as our parents and teachers would like. Therefore, 'What are you going to do with your life?' is a question not easily answered and with it comes confusion and uncertainty. Yet not knowing and ambiguity are invitations to participate with these feelings, as vocational goals and attitudes arise out of the chaos that engages unconscious life. Water flows into mysterious and unfamiliar places and it is from here that the authenticity of vocation emerges.

The element of Water is very enduring and devoted. Professionally it is inclined to wait and see, let things happen, which promotes a sense of strength, yet this might also work to their disadvantage. Water has a difficult time letting go emotionally if they feel insecure; therefore, they must be aware when a work situation needs to change or be confronted.

Vocational Signs: Twelve Career Signposts

The elements can now be expanded to embrace the 12 signs, which contain human qualities, virtues and characteristics. When a planet is located in one of these signs its archetypal expression is modified by the distinctive features of that sign. When these signs are emphasized vocationally, these qualities are important to consider when making career choices and decisions. First, let's review each of the signs separately to establish what qualities they may seek through vocation.

It is important to keep in mind that we are amplifying the signs as qualities, not necessarily as the Sun sign. Even though the signs are personified, it is important to recognize them as qualitative images and descriptions which can be applied vocationally to significant house cusps and planets.

♈ Aries

The spirit of Aries needs to feel free to take action without relating to authority or being bound by rules and regulations. Its calling is to adventure and to be heroic. Aries's need for independence, including the need to make its own decisions, is high; therefore it thrives in a vocation that encourages an independent and enterprising personality. To be free and self-sufficient is paramount, a high priority in any Arian career description. Working independently and instinctively suits this temperament, hence they like to be out front and in the firing line, leading rather than following. However, it is also important for them to be occupied in tasks that are consistently changing, reshaping and presenting challenges. Aries suits occupations that are not fixed or static but have a high degree of uncertainty and risk.

An essential aspect of the Aries temperament is its need for activity, which is often accompanied by impatience. At heart, Aries is an adventurer and risk-taking is an aspect of this. Challenges ignite the Arian spirit. An occupational outlet for their vitality and competitive spirit promotes their sense of well-being. Being a cardinal sign, Aries needs to initiate and move things forward, including itself; therefore, work requiring courage, nerve, adrenalin and stamina suits Aries. The cardinal nature of Aries likes to be first, so it initiates projects but does not necessarily see them through to completion. Aries locates itself at the forefront, on the cusp, at the beginning, not at the end.

♉ Taurus

Being an Earth sign, Taurus needs to employ its sensual nature in its occupation, using the physical senses, whether touch, taste, hearing, seeing or sensing. Taurus is a fixed sign so is grounded in the moment and moves at its own pace. Fast-tracking a bull usually results in them digging their heels in or getting stuck. Hence this type needs time to settle into a routine, find their rhythm and learn the job thoroughly. Taurus types certainly do not want to feel rushed or pushed.

Taurus likes to be attached to what they do, to feel secure in their place, a master of their workshop. But Taurus also needs to value what it does as well as be valued for what it creates. The job needs to reflect a sense of personal value and self-esteem; hence the monetary reward needs to be indicative of their personal worth. The exchange of resources is an important part of the vocational process for Taurus.

In a vocational capacity Taurus is a strong and persistent worker, able to stay with things through to their completion. Its great virtues are patience and perseverance. Taurus can hang on for too long, not knowing when to let go, becoming fixed in an unfulfilling routine. Therefore it is important to recognize when it may be time to leave the present work. While security is a strong element of the career it is important not to let that develop into becoming stuck in work that is no longer fulfilling or rewarding.

♊ Gemini

Adaptability and versatility are Gemini's forte and are great assets in opening doors to an extensive and stimulating world. Fast-footed Mercury is this sign's guide and, with this god on side, Gemini is able to adjust and adapt to many situations, allowing access to new ideas and adventures which develop intellectual strength and moral fibre. In theory, the skills of versatility and adaptability are innate to Gemini, impressed into their DNA and are a strong vocational resource.

Gemini has an open friendliness that draws people into its orbit, lightens their load and animates their mood. They have that knack of knowing the right person for you to meet, which book would be just perfect for your week away or what courses would be helpful. Psychologically speaking, this versatility in human interactions has been born out of a deep-seated quest to discover what is complementary to their nature. Something is missing and this drives them forwards into life, searching for what will balance their restlessness nature. Gemini's totem is the twin. Therefore, the world often seems either like a large mirror reflecting back their movements or the place where they will find the missing other. This search for what feels lost is also part of Gemini's vocational quest, which includes learning curves and translations of ideas but mainly communication and interaction.

♋ Cancer

A safe house, a secure base, a cosy nest, a room somewhere appeals to Cancer's need to feel protected and secure. These needs are part of Cancer's calling, and whatever track the crab takes across the sand it still carries its home with it. Psychologically, Cancer's task is to internalize home, creating a secure foundation. Vocationally, this task is important and a safe and sound work environment is imperative. As there is a preference for a family environment, they often attempt to transform their work environment into a familial one, enveloping their workmates with concern and care. Familial issues can become enmeshed with the vocation in different ways.

Building emotional and financial security is very important. They are intertwined and the more emotionally connected Cancer is in their vocation, the more financially secure they feel. Emotional security in their personal life is a necessity in order to excel in the world; the greater the support systems, the wider the playing field. As long as these needs are fulfilled and they feel emotionally supported and acknowledged there is no need for them to seek acknowledgement in the world beyond.

Providing safety, comfort and care for those in need is Cancer's calling. Yet if they are not emotionally supported or secure, they may feel drained and taken advantage of on their chosen path. Therefore, it is always wise for the Cancer type to seek the shelter and support of those they love and in their vocation to seek the help and backing of those in charge.

♌ Leo

Astrologically, the Sun rules this sign and, like its planetary counterpart, Leo needs to become the central focus of any system they belong to. Leo's calling is to express itself, to be engaged in creative productions. The need for self-expression and self-promotion in a career is important, as is their need for self-discovery through their occupation. Leo wants their vocation to fulfil their desire for self-exploration. In a career it is important to discover their personal talents and skills. Leo is not always a sole performer, but it does need to be identified. Being the producer of their own play, designer of their own label, manager of their own business, pleases Leo. What makes the difference is that their name is attached to their creative output and that it is recognized.

A feature of a Leo's vocation is their encounter with the father archetype whose approval they may unconsciously seek, especially if they did not receive this from their own father. But Leo is a fixed Fire sign and when it feels secure, loved and appreciated, it is loyal and trustworthy, radiating a warmth and generosity into the environment. With support and acknowledgement Leo helps to brighten the worlds it lives in. For Leo, self-esteem and confidence are linked with their vocation. It is important that they feel pride in what they do as well as appreciated by others. Leo also needs to be encouraged to stand back and see the creative results of their efforts.

Specifically, Leo needs to relate to an audience and thrives in professions where they are able to interact with others using their creative skills, not only through entertainment but through play, demonstration, interactions and reflection. Leo needs to have felt a response to their creative endeavours, evidence from the world that their contribution has been valuable.

♍ Virgo

Virgo is represented by the maiden, a complex image that has undergone considerable transformation from its original meaning. Ironically, it implies an image of freedom and independence, a woman in relationship to her internal self, contained and autonomous, in charge of her own desires. Vocationally, this motif is important as Virgo needs to follow its calling into the world, considering its own needs and honouring its desire to be of service.

As a mutable sign Virgo's need to serve may be satisfied through a myriad of careers. However, earthy Virgo can also manifest in many other ways; for instance, there is often an innate technical aptitude that may be utilized in scientific or medical occupations. Their resonance with the instinctual and natural world of plants and animals is often suited to working in nature. Analytic ability is another skill that can be used in a variety of ways. Virgo's goal is improvement; therefore their quest for perfection needs to be recognized in their profession.

A common need for any Virgo profession is to experience their job as constantly improving. Routine and ritual are very necessary to promote a sense of coherence. Disorder and chaos in the workplace feels very unsettling and can result in stress and tension. The thin line between the need to constantly improve and the pressure to be perfect often drives Virgo into over-compensating by working too hard and for too long. Virgo needs to be reminded that its calling towards wholeness needs balance and moderation.

♎ Libra

As the only inanimate object in the zodiac, Libra is the least instinctual or primal of the signs. It has evolved from the archaic and primitive towards culture and refinement. It has strong needs to beautify and harmonize which are vocationally important. Libra often possesses an aesthetic talent, which manifests through art, music, design or fashion. While this may not be their profession, these qualities are often used in their work, as Libra brings its innate sense of space, design and symmetry into its personal sphere. As long as Libra is enveloped and surrounded by beauty it fulfils its desire.

But the Libran scales also remind us of judgement and balance. Through judgement Libra weighs the options and possibilities. It seeks to be fair, yet this might also lead to focusing more on others than themselves, leaving them uncertain as to what they want. Social skills are high and the natural Libran tendency to listen and relate may lead towards the counselling professions.

The need for harmony and cooperation in the workplace is high. Libra also needs the space and the permission for them to feel they can brighten and enlighten their working environment. Without positive interaction and support, Libra will find it hard to concentrate on any task. Yet, knowing it is appreciated and liked, Libra works diligently and productively.

♏ Scorpio

Scorpio desires to be deeply involved in what they do. Vocationally, there is a need to be occupied with what is critical, to feel they can get to the core of their tasks, and to uncover and expose what needs to be changed. Scorpio is adept at the range of therapeutic professions that enables individuals to delve deeply into themselves to uncover negative patterns from the past. Their intimate understanding of the cycle of life and death heightens their ability to work with crisis and near-death experiences as well as dangerous and difficult rescue situations or investigations.

Scorpio's need to be intimate is important in vocation since they need to trust those they work with as well as those they work for. There is a need to feel they can count on others and also be counted on themselves. In a work partnership Scorpio is able to accomplish with their partner something that they could not do by themselves. It is important for this type to recognize its potent creativity in partnership, as there is an innate ability to draw out the resources of others and utilize them for a beneficial outcome. However, the key to any partnership is trust. And if Scorpio can be met on that intense and intimate level equally, then the horizon of possibilities is endless. If their depth is not acknowledged or met, then there is often mistrust, suspicion, even jealousy and intimidation in the work atmosphere.

Scorpio also needs time on their own because a deep sense of aloneness is embedded in this sign. Able to work by themselves to accomplish important tasks, they need to be entrusted by those they work with and empowered by management to complete what they need to do. Their ability to focus is high, being skilled at research and investigative work where their natural suspicion and intuition can be well utilized. Completion is also important and therefore vocations that are highly changeable do not suit this type. Scorpio needs to get to the heart of a situation and transform it.

♐ Sagittarius

Sagittarius is called to adventure, to quest for truth and meaning, seeking answers to the larger questions of life. The image of packing a suitcase or a backpack as preparation for a journey of discovery and education resonates with this sign. Being far-sighted, long-range visions are important in any vocation. Opportunities for growth, advancement and learning, as well as intuitive and strategic abilities, need to be fostered in a career. Sagittarius is a mutable Fire sign and needs to know it has infinite choice, freedom of movement, wide open spaces and limitless possibilities of discovery; anything less is disappointing!

Principles, ethics, morals and ideals are important and their vocational path needs to reflect these. They need to be involved with projects and pastimes that they have faith in, employing their philosophical and humanistic view of the world. The fiery nature of Sagittarius is an enthusiastic energy, which inspires and motivates others to try what they themselves have tried. The Sagittarian ability to enthuse and to weave an inspirational story is a strong talent, which allows them to share their knowledge; however, they must believe in what they are doing.

Sagittarius has an urge to expand their world view and be in contact with ideas and individuals who broaden their philosophy and inspire them to see through the mundane world into a world with meaning. Therefore, professions which foster historical, philosophical and psychological expansion are ideal. There needs to be the sense that work is broadening the mind and spirit, otherwise the individual may be lethargic and off-centre. When Sagittarius loses interest and passion in their work, physical stamina and mental agility are compromised. Roaming around trying to find an answer, rather than focusing on the target at hand, may be the result.

♑ Capricorn

No doubt Capricorn is an 'old goat' as the zodiacal constellation of the goat, either a horned goat or a sea goat, was recognized as early as the second millennium BCE. It is a sign that honours the old order, tradition, hierarchy and ageing. Its respect for structure and the status quo suggests that Capricorn needs boundaries, definition and support from authority figures. However, Capricorn is also highly autonomous and self-sufficient, and over time matures into an authority figure themselves. The 'wise old man' or 'wise old woman' archetype resonates with this sign. Capricorn is associated with age and ageing, so it is over time that the inborn sense of leadership and self-governing emerges. Capricorn wants to be its own boss, writing its own script and following its own manual.

Competence is naturally high; therefore, Capricorn needs to be challenged and fostered in their work, given the space to excel and mature. Like the mountain goat, they need take their time to ascend the mountain. They are naturally aware of the wheel of fortune and that a quick ascent may be followed by a speedy descent. Therefore Capricorn is best taking its time, learning thoroughly and methodically as well as acting professionally and carefully. When there is too much pressure to succeed or there are high expectations, Capricorn becomes anxious and self-defeating, so defining the scope and forecast of the project or job is imperative.

Responsibility is high and often Capricorn can shoulder responsibilities and duties that are not theirs, acquired because others have been irresponsible or immature. It is important for them to try to maintain the boundaries of work as much as possible, having a written agreement or contract that sets out their responsibilities. When pressure is high, Capricorn's self-talk is often damaging and unsupportive, so it is always best for them to find an outlet for their frustrations and injustices in the workplace.

≈ Aquarius

Uranus, the progressive, technological, inventive and forward-looking planetary energy, is the 'modern' ruler of Aquarius. Like their ruling planet, Aquarians are progressive, intuitive and future-orientated and need to feel they are creatively contributing to designing the future. Adept at technological and original research keeps them focused on the future. Their flair for the unusual needs to be acknowledged and considered. Some Aquarians find solace in the New Age movement with its positive and spiritual messages for future peace while others are well suited to the helping professions. However, it is ultimately important that they do not feel tied down or emotionally overwhelmed by these positions, and that they have enough space and ability to promote their own ideas.

An affinity for groups is part of this temperament. Working with associates, friends and colleagues in organizations can be rewarding; however, the need for individual expression and equality in the group is necessary or Aquarius will react, either covertly or openly. Although individualism is important, Aquarius is also tribal and needs social interaction, intellectual stimulation and personal interchange in their work. Aquarius needs to express its individuality in the work sector, feeling unique and independent in what they do, working best in a democratic situation rather than a hierarchical structure.

The key to Aquarius's calling is freedom from following the crowd and the traditions of the past. In many ways their careers cannot be defined as they have not yet been invented. But the symbols of their vocation are known and that leads them into unknown and uncharted territory to discover, reform, innovate and modernize.

♓ Pisces

Two fish swimming in opposite directions, connected by a ribbon of stars, is the image projected onto the constellation of Pisces. The sign's inherent duality is depicted by one fish swimming towards the divine while the other is pulled under into the unconscious. The archetypal urge underlying Pisces is the instinct to dedicate their vocation to something greater than themselves. Often this devotional urge can lead them into one of two directions: surfacing into a path of service in the world or delving into a creative exploration of their spirituality.

One of Pisces's frustrations is bridging their creative world with the literal one. Even though the creativity they aspire towards may not manifest in a literal way, there is the need to take the soulful and creative aspects of the self into their worldly jobs. In this way they find that working is a creative and fulfilling act, and they are able to change and colour the work they do with creative and original designs and images.

The sign of Pisces inspires the 12th house of the horoscope, a sphere connected with institutions and the urge to seek asylum, retreat and healing. Hence Pisces is linked to the sphere of welfare and well-being. For this sign, self-help and care are important, as

Pisces's tendency to give selflessly leaves them suffering from compassionate fatigue. In any vocation the Piscean need for retreat is necessary in order to reconnect with the spiritual energy that underpins their creative and caring nature. As a mutable Water sign, Pisces finds its path through the world by honouring its own time, feeling its own way and letting it be.

Cusps

Every astrological house is entered through a particular sign. The cusp of each house is a threshold opening onto a new sphere of influence; each gateway is opened by honouring the sign at its entry point. When looking at vocation we have already recognized that the signs on the cusps of the three vocational houses are important considerations. As previously mentioned, if there are no interceptions then these signs will all belong to the same element and this element will be prominent in the vocational analysis. The signs are helpful ways to describe which qualities and conditions are important in the area of the vocation that is suggested by the house.

For example, the 6th house is the quintessential house of daily routines; among other things, it can illustrate the working atmosphere best suited to an individual's nature. The sign on the cusp will help to outline conditions that are supportive of the innate temperament. The sign on the 6th house cusp can help us to consider what we need daily in our jobs in order to feel centred and satisfied with our work. Here are some ideas about how each sign on the cusp of the 6th might illustrate a person's workplace needs.

Sign	On the 6th house cusp
Aries ♈	Needs independence, risk-taking, challenges and goals
Taurus ♉	Needs stability, physical comfort, tangible results, value
Gemini ♊	Needs variety, communication, mental stimulation
Cancer ♋	Needs emotional security, a familial environment, safety
Leo ♌	Needs praise, self-expression, play, creativeness
Virgo ♍	Needs order, coherence, efficiency, containment

Libra ♎	Needs harmony, aesthetic surroundings, social interaction
Scorpio ♏	Needs engagement, respect, depth of involvement, trust
Sagittarius ♐	Needs freedom, inspiration, expansiveness, optimism
Capricorn ♑	Needs support, structure, boundaries, responsibility
Aquarius ♒	Needs lack of restrictions, collegial support, progressiveness
Pisces ♓	Needs service, creativity, sensitivity, imagination

The sign on the cusp of the 10th house also has many associations: our relationship to the world and authority figures, in particular bosses and superiors in the vocational sense; keys to our success; our public face; even clues to what career may suit us best. Similarly, the sign on the 2nd house cusp helps to describe which resources and assets are instinctual and need to be developed. The sign helps us to pinpoint what we value and also what is valuable about what we have to offer.

When there is an intercepted polarity in the horoscope then the elemental balance on the cusps of the houses of substance is disrupted. The intercepted signs 'block' the natural flow of energy in the horoscope. Around the intercepted sign polarity is a complex of energy not as readily accessible to consciousness, which could act as a foil in our career. Analyse the intercepted signs to determine whether their energies are unconsciously inhibiting the course of the person's life, i.e. the career. The signs on the cusps of the houses of substance are energetic keys that help to unlock the vocational area. They are energies, which need to be used in pursuit of a fulfilling vocation. The table at the end of this chapter lists some of the vocational needs of each sign and also proposes what may manifest if these needs are not met in the career.

Planets in Signs
The signs of the zodiac differentiate the archetypal urges of each planet and also describe the houses they rule. As we have already explored, planets are associated with various professions.

For instance, the Moon is the archetypal nurturer; therefore, in a vocational capacity it corresponds with nurturing professions. The Moon sign can help to differentiate the aspect or type of nurturing which is appropriate.

For example, the Moon in Libra would suit a one-to-one counselling or caring role, since Libra is concerned with partnering; on the other hand, the Moon in Aquarius would work best in a group or as an independent or alternative helping practitioner. The Moon in Scorpio would be inclined to crisis, or in-depth, therapeutic care, whereas the Moon in Cancer may best suit the nurturing of children or caring for others in their own home. The Moon is Sagittarius may comfort and nurture best in an educational capacity whereas the Moon in Leo could care for the well-being of children. The planetary sign acts as a filter for the archetypal urge when it seeks expression through the vocation and can be applied to any planet that is vocationally emphasized.

When the Moon is vocationally highlighted, the sign helps to differentiate activities and qualities. Let's imagine that the individual is drawn towards lunar professions; the Moon sign can be helpful in discerning what would suit the individual. This will be similar for all the planets, but the summary below focuses on the Moon, as if it were vocationally relevant in the analysis:

- The Moon in Aries is aligned with risk-taking and tasks that demand physical and mental involvement, utilizing quick reflexes and decision-making, such as ambulance work, coaching, paramedics, emergency, trauma and organizational change.

- The Moon in Taurus is instinctually drawn to a hands-on, sensual approach, for instance massage, aromatherapy, chiropractic work, nursing, etc.

- The Moon in Gemini leans towards an amalgam of information, learning and care, for example, speech therapy, teaching, NLP, improving memory, etc.

- The Moon in Cancer gravitates towards caring for the dependent, such as aged care, childcare, becoming a paediatrician or specializing in infant illnesses. Women's issues or family-orientated concerns may also appeal. Nurturing professions such as health care, nursery or day care, primary teaching, nursing, counselling and helpers of all kinds, including family therapists and social workers, are part of this wide spectrum.

- The Moon in Leo is adept at helping to heal the inner child, whether that involves caring for children or working in a creative capacity, such as art therapy, sand play and child psychology. Your capacity for lending a hand comes through your playful ability to radiate warmth, light and laughter.

- The Moon in Virgo is comfortable with clinical work such as psychiatric nursing, clinical psychology, medical research and analysis. Instinctually health conscious, you are naturally drawn to learning about healthy habits and routines. Being in touch with health may be so nurturing that you may be called to a vocation where you can participate in assisting others to feel healthier through diet, preventative medicine, holistic healing, exercising or analytical methods.

- The Moon in Libra naturally inclines towards individual or relationship counselling, marriage guidance and conflict resolution where negotiation and relating skills need to be well developed. Social skills, hospitality and conflict resolution are strong vocational characteristics.

- The Moon in Scorpio may be drawn to critical care, oncology, bereavement counselling, emergency work or in-depth therapeutic work. You are able to honour the dark, recover the repressed and respect the feeling life without judgement or strictures.

- The Moon in Sagittarius is inspirational, a natural educator, coach and trainer. Intuitively you know the role of faith in healing; therefore a contemporary priestly role such as being a pastoral counsellor, a religious advisor, a psychotherapist or a spiritual mentor may appeal.

- The Moon in Capricorn needs to feel constructive and disciplined; therefore you may be drawn to the precision of surgery, the responsibility of being a medical doctor or an administrative role that demands a high level of ethics and competence.

- The Moon in Aquarius leans towards alternative or complementary health care. Naturally drawn to the unusual, and acutely aware of social processes, you work well with groups and for organizational reform.

- The Moon in Pisces is drawn to the compassionate or imaginative forms of caring and healing, such as nursing, caring for the handicapped or underprivileged, spiritual healing and meditation. You may combine your creative skills with care through disciplines such as music or art therapy.

All planets will express their archetypal urges through the signs. While the Moon constellates the nurturing urges, Mercury will express its communicative impulse through the signs; Venus, its value; Mars, its desire; and so on. To complete this chapter, let's summarize the needs of each sign and what might manifest if these needs are not met.

Acknowledging the Needs of Each Sign

Sign	Vocational needs	If needs are unfulfilled
Aries	• Independence and freedom • Spontaneity • Adventure and risk-taking • Entrepreneurial activities • Self-employment	Restlessness, boredom, lack of direction or an inability to commit yourself to the job could result in sudden changes of employment. Frustration and anger may be personally felt or may surface in the atmosphere of the workplace or through co-workers.
Taurus	• Sensuality • Stability • Rewards and compensation • Growth • Financial security	You could feel undervalued and become stuck in positions that deplete your sense of self-esteem. Without rewards from work, the need to be valued could be transferred onto the material world of possessions and finances.
Gemini	• Communication • Flexibility and mobility • Variety and change • Intellectual stimulation	If there is no outlet for communication, you may feel agitated and scattered. Nervous reactions, anxiety or feeling smothered may arise if your routines do not provide enough mobility or variety.
Cancer	• Emotional security • Familial atmosphere • Nurturing environment • Need to belong • Support and closeness • Caring and empathy	If there is a lack of safety or emotional connection to your work or workmates, you may become moody, overly sensitive or over-dependent. Feeling unsupported, you may react negatively to the environment and those in it.

Leo	• Creative self-expression • Feedback and approval • Loyalty • Identification with career • Self-promotion	Without an adequate sense of approval you may unconsciously expect to fail; as a result you do not apply yourself to work, nor attempt to do the best you can. Another defence may be inflation, seeing types of work as being beneath you or not suited for you.
Virgo	• Service • Constant improvement • Discrimination • Containment • Order and coherence	Since the urge to improve is a large part of the Virgo temperament, a perfectionist streak often defends a sense of inadequacy. When lacking discrimination this could manifest as criticism, obsessive needs and an inability to let go until a job is 'perfect'.
Libra	• Harmony in the workplace • Cooperation • Working with others • Equality and fairness • Social involvement	There may be a tendency to blame fellow workers or job conditions if things do not work out. Your difficulty in expressing anger or frustration may lead to an underlying tension in relationships with clients, co-workers or superiors.
Scorpio	• Intense involvement • Trust • Empowerment in their job • Honesty and integrity • Commitment	If you feel disempowered in your workplace, power struggles with superiors or co-workers emerge. Others meet your Scorpio intensity with feelings of envy or intimidation, which leads you to feel isolated and alone at work.

Sagittarius	• Ideals and ethics • Travel and freedom • Learning and advancement • Strategy and insight • Growth and expansion	You are prone to inflation and unrealistic expectations if your vocational needs are unmet. Without focus there is a tendency to drift and 'dream' in an unproductive state. If stuck in a rigid job there is a possibility of lethargy and depression.
Capricorn	• Tradition and regularity • Boundaries • Definition and structure • Possibilities of advancement • Recognition and approval	A compulsion to achieve could manifest as either a fear of success or an inappropriate command of authority. If the need for recognition is unsatisfied you may be overly ambitious or controlling.
Aquarius	• Altruism and uniqueness • Independence and innovation • Social concerns • Stimulation and excitement • Collegial recognition	Without adequate freedom and independence there could be an overt reaction or disrespect for authority and hierarchy. A fear of entrapment could manifest as an inability to maintain regular employment, choosing to remain outside the system.
Pisces	• Devotion and dedication • Creative environment • Service and caring • Appropriate boundaries • Ideals and compassion • Imagination	Without adequate boundaries you may feel overwhelmed with responsibility, feeling you are in 'over your head'. A tendency to absorb negative feelings in the environment or in those you work with or for leaves you feeling drained.

– CHAPTER 4 –
**IDENTITY, FULFILMENT, INDIVIDUALITY
AND FORTUNE**
The Sun, Moon and Ascendant

Character and Vocation

Two and a half millennia ago, the Greek philosopher Heraclitus suggested that 'character is fate'.[18] The integrity of the statement is still meaningful today. The resonant truth is that our fate is sculpted by our character. It is that personal mix of our mannerisms, habits, rituals, values, beliefs, ideals and morals that shapes our temperament and enriches the layers of our personality. Over time these rituals and qualities inform who we are; our fate is then forged from the consequences of our intentions, actions and ambitions. And while we may not be able to alter our fate, we can transform the experience of it through conscious participation with it and an acceptance of its patterns. The future is not fully formed and it is our choices and behaviour that continue to influence its course. Like our vocation, the future emerges out of our actions and decisions.

Character is developed throughout our life journey; therefore, it is an essential aspect of one's vocation. As our character emerges, so does our vocation. The horoscope is a useful guide to understanding the characteristics and patterns that shape our nature and contribute to forging a fulfilling vocation. Astrologically there are three features of a horoscope that are relevant in considering one's individual character: this trinity is the Sun, the Moon and the Ascendant. To ancient astrologers these three symbols were known as the 'places of life'[19] or the basic structure for considering the life purpose. Therefore, understanding the Sun, Moon and Ascendant clarifies what qualities and faculties can be cultivated to assist our vocational development as well as what is needed to mature and nurture character.

The Sun and Moon are known as the luminaries, the lamps of the heavens that light our way. While they are not actually the same size, nor the same distance from the Earth, in our heavens they appear to be equal. The Sun reveals the virtues that are part of the potential character, where we shine and feel confident as well as what is natural to our identity. The Sun is the daylight, so symbolizes what can be seen and known. As the archetypal image of the king and father, astrologers associate the Sun with the conscious self, one's identity, spirit, strength, *joie de vivre* and purposeful nature. It plays a great role in the trajectory of our career, as it is our essential expression and creativity which strive to be identified with something purposeful and enduring. In essence, the vocational urge of the Sun is to encourage the individual to be who they are, for its purpose is selfhood. As a conscious principle, the Sun identifies with the overt messages from culture and family about what is worthwhile and productive.

The Moon suggests those needs that are important to nurture in order to feel safe in the world. Being more receptive and instinctual than the Sun, the Moon distinguishes the unspoken and unlived aspects of cultural and familial life. It is also the vessel of the feeling life and as such contains all the imprints and patterns from childhood, including those that are precognitive and impressed upon the foetus *in utero*. It is instinctive and responsive. The Moon is the reflection of sunlight and the lantern of the night. As such it symbolizes the reflected self, the aspects of our nature that are more illuminated when the conscious self is not dominant. The Moon is the feeling life that underpins the personality, the reactions and responses to life experience and what the soul needs to feel safe, nurtured and content. It is subtle and yielding, often making itself known through unconscious means such as aches and pains, feeling responses, dreams and fantasies. On our vocational path the Moon is the container of all our unconscious memory but also what we need to feel satisfied.

The Ascendant is symbolic of our outreach and how we might travel the road of life. This could be likened to a control panel or helm which guides our ship of life. As the eastern point of the chart, it is the intersection of the ecliptic and horizon, where heaven meets earth and where planets rise out of obscurity to become perceptible. When the Sun is at this point, its rays creep across the landscape to brighten the world. Therefore the Ascendant has become linked with such images as where light enters the horoscope, the first breath, emergence, vitality and beginnings. It is the symbol of the way in which our self emerges through our personality and the face we turn towards the world. We might liken this to steering the vehicle we use to navigate the world, a costume we wear for a day, the way we package ourselves or the mask we wear when we interact with others. The Ascendant is important on the vocational journey because it symbolizes the way we present the self.

Like all astrological images, each of these three symbols can be pictured through their sign and house placements, rulers and aspects. As we explored in the previous chapter, the signs describe qualities; therefore, these will feature strongly in vocation. We could characterize the Sun sign as virtues that seek expression through a career, while the Moon sign suggests what is essential in our vocation. The house placements of the Sun and Moon will direct us to the arena of life where we will focus purposely on developing identity and emotional security. Although the ascending sign is vital to the personality, it is often challenged and moderated by our career choices. In other words, the Ascendant is naturally at odds with the 2nd, 6th and 10th houses that are associated with the career.

Of course, each individual's character is unique, as is the expression of the astrological symbols. The following descriptions will be personalized through other astrological factors such as aspects and house position; nevertheless, this is an entrée into beginning to consider the traits, virtues and needs of your character so you can reflect on how these might shape your vocation and your fate.

The Sun: Virtues of the Essential Self

Sunshine. Essentially, that is the nature of the astrological Sun: to shine. The Sun is satisfied when there is a sense of excellence and fulfilment. Therefore the Sun is a priority in considering vocation as it wants to express itself, be creative, feel acknowledged and accomplished. As a symbol of identity it also wants to be identified with a career or a path in life. From a solar perspective, what I do is an important aspect of who I am.

The Sun is also a symbol of father, the head of state or the boss; therefore, the Sun can often identify, or equally de-identify, with powerful and authoritative figures in its search for acknowledgement. But the Sun is distinctive; part of the Sun's vocational search for identity will be its search for authenticity. The solar journey is often the struggle between recognition and authenticity, applause and legitimacy, and being popular or being true to one's self. While the world may acknowledge our achievements from work well done, our greatest success lies in self-fulfilment and the satisfaction of a life lived authentically.

The Sun symbolizes valour and strength as well as a sense of heroism, aspects of every human who is capable of acting like a god. It also implies action and a conscious striving to act honourably. In a way we might suggest that the Sun is virtuous, of the soul. Astrologically, each sign of the zodiac can then represent a soul state. The Sun seeks to develop the honour of the sign that it is in. As a symbol of the heroic part of the self, the natal Sun sign is a guide to the values and virtues that shape and strengthen our character, which then shapes our fate and contributes to our vocation. Virtue is the garment of character.

What follows are some descriptions of the Sun in all twelve signs. If the Sun is above the horizon then you were born during the day when the career urges may be more apparent and visible; if it is below the horizon you were born during the night when the solar purpose may not be as easily apparent or straightforward.

Astrologically, the Sun illustrates a way to feel confident and vital, and the sign it occupies suggests the qualities and conditions that are supportive of this core sense of self. When the Sun is in Fire it is in its own element, as it rules the Fire sign of Leo and is exalted in Aries. Yet, whatever element the Sun is in, its duty is to find a purposeful way to connect to that element on its life path. The Sun sign seeks development through our vocation; its qualities need to be consciously developed. In a way it is a life task. Therefore when reading your Sun sign and those of your family and friends, you should imagine how the sign's virtues might enhance the quality of your and their careers. Think metaphorically about these qualities and images.

☉♈ The Sun in Aries

Aries represents the stamina to challenge what is not right but also the spirit to forge what is. Aries is the warrior; in a spiritual sense it is the one who has the courage to uphold his or her principles and the one who is the soldier of the true self. Therefore, with your Sun in Aries your labours are to find the courage of your convictions and the strength to sanction them. What is honourable about you is the ability to challenge what is not right, to compete for what is and to find the courage to confront the truth. When you are in touch with your honour, you are capable of summoning the strength to act with bravery and to champion what is noble. You are invigorated when challenged and your spiritually develops by withstanding the moral and ethical trials of life.

Your spirit cherishes its independence and welcomes challenges. You enjoy creative projects, pioneering new experiments and exploring uncharted territory. Being on the starting line, you are animated by the spirit of adventure and brought to life by challenges and possibilities. Innocence and naivety are helpful attributes as you are able to put the disappointments and failures of any project behind you and get on with a new idea or project. Taking a chance, exploring new frontiers and risking the security of what is not known demand this act of courage.

A combination of toughness and affection allows you to be a firebrand on the one hand and an idealist on the other. The compound of these two attitudes creates an advocate who champions the underdog, the conqueror who liberates the oppressed and the hero who scores the winning goal. In an etymological context courage is connected to the heart, the Sun's centre. In an ancient way of thinking, the force of will and character was located in the heart. Like the heart which pumps blood through the body, your energetic spirit vitalizes your soul to be fearless in the world and to claim what is rightfully yours. To find your vitality and spirit, and to feel soulful in the world, you need to appreciate your qualities of assertiveness, bravery, enthusiasm, independence, initiative and inspiration, and apply them on your vocational path.

☉♉ The Sun in Taurus

Patience is the virtue that parents and teachers would always remind us of when we were in a hurry. Yet in our Facebook, iPhone, instant e-world, patience seems a relic from a bygone era. The pace of life is high-speed, everything needs to be available as quickly as possible or else it has no value. As nature and her natural rhythms are replaced by technological and man-made cycles, the understanding of the value of patience has waned.

Astrological wisdom has not forgotten the virtue of patience for it is deeply implanted in the earthy sign of Taurus and it flowers regularly in that sphere of the zodiac. Taurus is the astrological sign most closely associated with the pace of nature and inherently knows its rhythms, its seasons of growth, as well as its natural developmental cycles. Taurus knows there is no sense in pushing when it is time to hold on, nor is it time to move forwards when the light is red. With your Sun in Taurus you are endowed with the basic instinct of common sense, a faculty not so common in a high-tech, artificial world. You innately know when it is time to dig your heels in and wait for the right moment to charge. In the meantime, there is a creative waiting period and this is accomplished through patience. You have a deep respect for quality and worth, and for what can be accomplished through perseverance. You learn to treasure your resources over time, and know that value is added in the long term, not the short. Therefore you are a hardy investor in long-term markets, real estate and any asset that will gradually appreciate over time, being suspicious of get-rich-quick incentives.

Your attachment to the long-term also applies to friends and family, being fiercely loyal and trustworthy in relationship. Any time and effort spent in helping others is returned to you. You may be slow to get to know others but you forge deep bonds over the course of time. Once formed, these bonds are almost indelible. You have the patience to handle the most difficult child, the most demanding client or the most annoying neighbour, able to remain calm and present in most situations, not backing down or giving in, but allowing the problematic situation to pass.

Eventually it is this pace of being able to slow down, stop and smell the roses that supports your success in life. There's no rush, as internally you ultimately know that you need to build one layer at a time. Your building plan is from the ground up, a floor at a time, season by season. It is this gathering of strength over time that becomes a powerful ally and contributes to your resourcefulness. With the Sun in Taurus your secret to success is your steadfast pace and your innate virtue of patience. To feel vital, spirited and soulful you need to recognize the value of loyalty, perseverance, consistency, stability, solidity, reliability and trustworthiness on your vocational path.

☉♊ The Sun in Gemini

With your Sun in Gemini you have the ability to mimic. Your wit, quickness of mood, intonation, accent and facial contortions all combine to amuse and make us laugh. Your versatility helps you to defend against unwanted overtures, but also is useful in getting you accepted into the group. Adaptability is your forte and a great asset as it opens doors to a wider world. In theory, the skills of versatility and adaptability are innate, impressed into your DNA. It is in your early relationships with siblings, cousins, childcare chums and playground pals that you first recognized your dexterity. Later, your adaptability developed into a useful ability to solve puzzles, open locked doors, expand ideas, write, teach and widen your social circles.

You have an open friendliness that draws people into your orbit, lightens their load and animates their mood. Your totem is the twin. In this archetypal icon is the image of a copy of one self, a double, a soulmate, a reflection. In this search for what feels lost you experience contact with others and the vastness of the human experiences. But sooner or later you will realize that the quest for what is absent is an inner calling to guide, direct and teach others to understand and read the map of life.

Duality is your bonus, as you are capable of commandeering a host of tasks simultaneously. You can accomplish more in a short space of time than most people. This versatility comes in handy in a fast-paced world where dual, treble, even quadruple roles all at the same time are more the norm than the exception. Whether coaching, teaching, tutoring or training, you have the great skill of being able to read others. Through their speech or body language, you are very astute at helping others to understand themselves better. You can explain how to get from A to B along the best possible route; you could write the how-to manuals or design diagrams to increase the understanding of how things work. You help to articulate the world and make it easier to navigate. It is these qualities of eloquence, flexibility, friendliness, perception, versatility and wit that help you find your calling.

☉♋ The Sun in Cancer

While kindness may not be exclusively the domain of Cancer, this virtue is shaped from the bonds of kinship first experienced in the home. Family values such as doing good rather than harm, being friendly, compassionate and helpful, are the tender-hearted acts that promote the virtue of kindness. Deep inside, these are virtues that inspire you. Even if your family upbringing did not provide the stability you needed to feel safe, nor the thoughtfulness, you are still drawn to nurturing and acts of kindness.

Like crabs that dwell on the threshold of the ocean, Cancer is sensitized to the shape-shifting seas and their tidal cycle. It secures its home regardless of the fluctuation in fortunes and alternating tides. For you, this instinctual truth suggests that you find stability within the daily tides of feelings, which swell, ebb, flood and retract. You feel compelled to find a secure place on the edge of life's upheavals and live in the world without being swept away by emotional complexity. You build a strong enough shell to contain your feelings so that you are able to love and care without harm to your tender heart.

When you feel safe and protected you emerge from your shell to demonstrate your caring, affection, warmth and kindness. You are vulnerable and tender, slow to trust and warm up, but when you feel securely attached then your heart opens to care and nurture others. Your instinct is to protect the vulnerable, shelter the homeless and care for the sensitive. Being so responsive to others, you are finely attuned to what others need. Moved by the plight of those less fortunate, those in distress or people who feel hurt or rejected, you are able to demonstrate kindness and compassion. You are strongly influenced by the maternal archetype whose natural instinct is to nurture, protect, shelter and foster those who are vulnerable.

Charity begins at home, which is your domain. Therefore, one of your labours of life is to find your home, where you belong, and your ancestry. This might take some time. In the meantime you will have different places where you settle in your search for home. Along the way you bring warmth and character to your tasks. Caring, helpfulness, protection, sympathy and tenderness are qualities that you can develop on your vocational path.

☉♌ The Sun in Leo

Being constant, enduring and warm-hearted are attributes of the Sun in Leo, a fixed Fire sign. Fixed Fire calls to mind images where the power of fire can be contained, whether raging in a fireplace or softly twinkling on a candle. Similarly, you have the ability to emanate warmth, personality and charisma when your passionate feelings are tempered and focused. These fires are your creativity and your creative act is to explore and discover the self. Being affectionate, tender and hospitable, you are endowed with generosity and originality.

Being loyal and protective are your strong virtues. You demonstrate these through your allegiance to those you befriend and a fidelity to those you love. Astrologically, Leo is associated with the heart, a central focus in the body. When you are focused on the heart of the matter you have an ability to radiate warmth for yourself and others in your atmosphere.

As the archetypal father, king of the pride or queen of the parade, you'll often find the Leo Sun at the centre or occupying the seat of power. While you might fantasize it is a throne, it is more likely that yours will be the teacher's seat at the head of the class, the director's stool in front of the action or the psychiatrist's chair opposite your client. Your vocation inspires others to become their true self, encouraging creativity and playfulness, because you can embody both the serious professional and the playful child. Ironically, although you can be dignified and powerful, you also have a healthy inner child who balances the serious sides of life with amusement and frivolity. It is your lion heart that knows how to play, find amusement in the humourless and irreverence in formality. Therefore, while you might aspire to greatness you don't want to be precious. Wisdom without humour, truth without wit or status without integrity is antithetical to your nature.

You are responsive to others but in your own heart you know that you cannot remain true to them without first being true to yourself. You instinctually know that being true and constant to others begins with the difficult task of creating an honest relationship with yourself. This often means you need to be candid about your vulnerabilities, sincere about your fears and straightforward about your motives. Hence your honour in being genuine allows you to shine. Your heroic journey begins with acts of self-disclosure, a vulnerable gesture that softens your heart so as to express love easily and authentically. The possession of the heart light is your gift, but your task is keeping it alight through acts of loyalty and fidelity. When creativity, generosity, joy, loyalty, affection, playfulness and an optimistic spirit are included in your occupation, you find pleasure and satisfaction in your vocation.

☉♍ The Sun in Virgo

In contemporary astrology, Virgo is associated with the sacred acts of an everyday life that promote health. With the Sun in Virgo you respect the holistic approach to life, aware of the need for moderation in the holy trinity of body, mind and soul. As an archetype, Virgo represents the instinct for wholeness embedded in every human soul and with your Sun in Virgo you strive to consciously express this. This might manifest as your need to be healthy and achieve balance in the chaos of an everyday life. It could also call you to become involved in the improvement and betterment of others.

You need to experience feeling centred in your daily routine. In your busy world the repetitiveness and simplicity of domestic tasks is a mantra for stabilizing and grounding your spirit. Completing simple tasks enables you to find a sense of fulfilment and well-being. While meditation, yoga, walking the dog or reading the paper may be the rewards of an everyday life, other routines such as paying the bills, cleaning the kitchen or mopping the floors are monotonous. But your task is to find the synthesis between the extremes so the cadence of the everyday life is free of stress and worry as much as it can be.

As it is imperative to be health-conscious, you need to systematically order health rituals to promote a sense of well-being. Having a great respect for the body, you are able to apply its wisdom through a healthy diet and lifestyle, regular exercise and work. You have the ability to concentrate, focus on detail, follow instruction and be consciously involved with repetitive tasks, which combine to make you skilled at handicrafts and detailed work. Work is an important aspect of your ritual and no matter how mundane that work may be you can find soul in being focused and attentive to the task at hand.

Instinctively you honour the quest for purity of mind and soul. The psychology of Virgo suggests that this may be achieved through discrimination, analysis and orderliness. Hence you respect these qualities and try to revere them in your own life. The power of discrimination allows you to know what is important to pursue and what needs to be rejected. Analysis contributes to improving your world through identifying what works and what doesn't. Orderliness is very important too, as a tidy environment promotes your state of calm and reflects your inner need for order and organization. Your vocational quest will include health and well-being, whether it is your own or that of others. When you strive for self-discipline and order, the qualities of moderation, diligence and service support your vocational well-being.

☉♎ The Sun in Libra

Balancing, weighing, judging and reflecting are all attributes that Libra has become known for in astrological symbolism; the scales epitomize the longing to experience balance. With the Sun in Libra, you may be called to bring opposing factions into a peaceful alignment by mediating in disagreements and arbitrating disputes. You have a vision of a peaceful world, free of conflict; no wonder you are skilled in mediation.

This quest for peace is deeply embedded in your psyche. Your internal image of peace and your innate ability to see the goodness in both the individual and the world at large calls you into diplomatic, social- and relationship-orientated professions. Pursuing peace for you might have begun in your childhood relationships with your siblings, schoolmates, team members and friends. The Libran child is often fated to be in the middle, appeasing the aggressor and comforting the victim. In victory you might sympathize with the team that has lost and in defeat you boost the sagging spirits of your own team members. You have the grace of being able to see past the faults in others into their potential, allowing you to be sympathetic to those who have been offensive and supportive to those who have been discouraging. You give confidence to the underdog, hearten the loser and make friends with the unpopular, being blessed with the innate skill to bring opposing factions into alignment and include outsiders.

Part of your strategy for peace is to create an attractive environment so that the outer landscape inspires inner thoughts and feelings of beauty. By creating picturesque surroundings you are hopeful that unsettled and angry feelings will be calmed and peaceful thoughts will be restored. You need to create an environment that inspires you to feel at peace, both at home and in your workplace. Your urge for harmony, symmetry and peace needs to be reflected in your vocation, whether that is through your relationships with others or by beautifying the environment.

Having an innate respect for humanity and empathy for every individual, you appreciate what is refined and developed. You strive to create a better atmosphere, not through conquering or chastising, but by revealing a better option. To you this option is peace, the inclusion of all, harmony and understanding. You know that a civilized world begins with harmony and that your fate is to be an architect of the peace proposal. When using the qualities of cooperation, diplomacy, gentleness, idealism, peacefulness and tactfulness in your vocation, you feel satisfied and fulfilled.

☉♏ The Sun in Scorpio

The eighth sign of the zodiac is the most enigmatic of all and has a reputation for being mysterious and powerful. In the northern hemisphere, Scorpio heralded the ending of the year and the sign became associated with fermentation and decay, as death stalked the countryside and announced the time for withdrawal. Astrologically, this realm locates the deepest layers of the human psyche, the forge where integrity is fired and shaped through self-analysis. With the Sun in Scorpio you learn to trust your instincts and emotionally differentiate between truth and falseness from an early age. Your emotions can be intense, your feelings deep and powerful, suggesting that in your life you need to experience passion, honesty and intimacy in all walks of life. Vocationally you need to be respected for the power of your feelings and the truth of your convictions.

In Scorpio we encounter the hidden and unexpressed aspects of the self as well as the negative impulses that we learn to control and direct. Therefore with your Sun in Scorpio you are challenged to summon the psychological strength to contain your compulsions and create space for unwanted feelings. You have the emotional capacity to control these impulses and the integrity to act honestly and authentically. Therefore you may feel drawn to working with others in difficult situations, dealing with crisis or helping in transition. Your innate capacity to summon inner strength in the face of emotional adversity and loss means you are unafraid to acknowledge the reality of your feelings, mourn for what has passed or grieve for what cannot be. Your emotional integrity is therapeutic and transformational, helping others to heal and move forwards through the dark. You have a powerful gift of being able to confront the most difficult truths and feel unashamed of your humanness.

Therefore you might feel called to use this in your vocation, whether as a therapist, healer, counsellor or in any other profession where you can combine the complex amalgam of love and honesty in your life work.

Integrity is your virtue, that ability to be painfully honest with those you love, to disclose your own vulnerability and face the truth about what has happened. You have the emotional courage to face the disappointments and anger of others. You also have the capacity to trust in yourself and to know that when others let you down, you can forgive yourself. It is this integrity that allows you to know the depth of intimacy and the power of love. Knowing how to be trustworthy, you are able to contain the fears and vulnerabilities of others. Your integrity inspires others to be honest and open. Through this open exchange trust can be built; honesty is the key to self-mastery and a clear conscience. When you strive for sincerity, trust and truth using your intuitive and resourceful faculties you feel close to your calling.

☉♐ The Sun in Sagittarius

In Sagittarius we encounter the human virtue of faith that encourages each soul to know the continuity of life through its darkest moments. With your Sun in Sagittarius you are blessed with this gift of faith. Your positive spirit can soothe the troubled soul and your innate wisdom can guide the weary traveller. Your zodiacal emissary is an archer whose bow is taut, ready to release an arrow towards the heart of the galaxy. This arrow suggests your power of perception and your ability to penetrate to the heart of the matter. With your Sun in Sagittarius you are a positivist and you urge to act according to the highest values and principles possible. You constantly question in order to civilize the uneducated aspects of yourself that keep you bound to an unexamined life. You flee from futility by focusing your arrows on a faraway target, one that is preferably unknown. Whether this is an overseas locale or a philosophical ideal, you are on a quest to make the foreign familiar and to participate in broadening your horizons in life.

Your instinct for the religious and philosophical as well as your urge to spiritually develop and to civilize the primitive will call you away into many different cultures, beliefs, ideas and places. Your task is to discover meaning in the world around you; in order to do this you search for the answers to metaphysical questions. Being naturally far-sighted, both your inner and outer vision can extend far beyond what the naked eye sees. Intuitively orientated, you work best when following your instinct and sensitivity, even in the face of scepticism and statistics, trusting in the reality of internal perceptions. Buoyed by your faith you are confident in the power of positive thinking and spiritual insight. Protected by an armada of affirmations you can always be optimistic, even at the darkest hour. Your ability to conceive of a more worthy life, to know the existence of something greater and the urge to search for a higher purpose in life require your courageous spirit and open mind. You need to explore cross-culturally and journey beyond the safety of what is familiar. Therefore you are highly motivated by adventures into the unknown, whether that is through physical travel, intellectual discoveries or educational opportunities. Vocationally, you are well suited to any sphere that offers you the opportunity to educate, administer, publish or inspire others.

What is moral and right is of great importance to you. You live by a code of ethics that inspires you to do what is noble, non-discriminatory, honourable and just. You seek temperance, moderation and balance in order to find the middle path and distinguish between right and wrong. For you, right action is not imposed by an external moral code but spontaneously springs from your inner respect for all of life. When you act ethically you feel closer to the divine and therefore closer to your goals in life. Your capacity to search for meaning and establish your own belief system, free from the prejudices and opinions of others, is your vocation. But one of your greatest initiations is the experience of having faith in the process of life. When you are armed with a reason you can face anything. To find your vitality and spirit and to feel soulful, you need to strive for justice and temperance and to remain enthusiastic and optimistic about the world. When your ideals, ethics and positive nature are your companions you feel gratified with life.

☉♑ The Sun in Capricorn

From the beginning of your life you may have felt responsible, not just for yourself but for the people and environment around you. With your Sun in Capricorn you have a heightened sense of what is right and wrong. Like the mountain goat whose gaze is on the pinnacle, your peak represents the summit of excellence so you are always striving to reach the highest point in yourself. Being so acutely aware of what should be done and what constitutes an offence, you endeavour to always do the right thing. Even though you may feel inadequate or ill equipped to succeed, nothing could be further from the truth and over the course of time your success is revealed through hard work, dedication and commitment. Time is your ally.

Most present-day portrayals of Capricorn suggest they play by the rule book. And this is true to a certain degree. Ultimately the rule book that you want to adhere to is your own, yet often you may end up with a weak authority figure who is steering the organization in an impossible direction. One of the motifs that may show up in the tapestry of your life is woven by a string of unskilled or inefficient authority figures – teachers, bosses and managers, even paid professionals! Often you are more proficient, with a higher level of comprehension of the job, than your boss or service provider. If so, your challenge is to become your own boss and strive for excellence without the impediment of a system that does not share similar values. Yet this takes time to figure out.

Time, quality, excellence and distinction are hallmarks of your character. You preserve and contain things of value. Responsibility is your great virtue; this suggests response-ability or the ability to respond. In other words, you need to support yourself authentically from within, becoming the authority or author of your own life script, not living out of someone else's programme. Capricorn is old in its wisdom but youthful as well, since it has the time to grow into itself.

Your honourable traits, such as commitment, dedication and perseverance, help to support you in gaining autonomy from the system to which you feel bound. You are born with a strong work ethic and responsibility to whatever you are doing or whomever you are with. Therefore, you are never free of a system, but hopefully free from the systems that no longer support or acknowledge you. It is important to be self-reliant, but not exclusively so, as you need to be responsible to something in the world, be it a project, a task, a baby or a book! Therefore it is not uncommon for you to find yourself as the managing director of your corporation, the president of your golf club, the principal of your school or at the top of the ladder. But your satisfaction comes not from being the supervisor of others, but being the boss of yourself. Having learnt the lesson of inner authority and personal responsibility you can be liberated enough to feel acknowledged within the system. Commitment, reliability and your respect for tradition are qualities that help you to shine in your vocation. Your efficiency, practicality and work ethic are your guiding lights.

☉≈ The Sun in Aquarius

In contemporary astrology Aquarius's image has been transformed from its ancient counterpart through the discovery of Uranus, the first planet sighted beyond antiquity's seven classical ones. As Uranus joined Saturn as this sign's modern ruler it brought the collective values of parity, liberality, consensus and social equality to the zodiacal territory of Aquarius. With your Sun in Aquarius, you sense the winds of change and want to be carried away by the new spirit of freedom and equality for all. Aquarius is the archetypal essence that reminds us that world peace and equal opportunity are not only ideals but also human values that can be achieved through a humanitarian spirit.

Your Aquarian virtue of freedom is not only the urge for unity in your external environment but your inner experience of independence, which inspires you to strive for the rights and liberty of others. It is the freedom of your spirit that strengthens you to be liberated from the herd, to make your own choices, create an unconventional lifestyle, assess a situation independently, evaluate freely and be politically incorrect. All these are essential to your lifestyle and vocation.

You are drawn to feats of humanitarianism that lessen mass suffering, improve living conditions and help in time of crisis and catastrophe. You celebrate the communal spirit that forges trustworthy communities and establishes socially responsible organizations. While you embrace the individuality of each person, it is important that exclusivity does not detract from building community. It is the community where you encounter your spiritual siblings; they are your friends, allies and colleagues, kindred spirits who share your inner drive for freedom, individuality and human values. Your freedom of expression for your shared passions and enthusiasm is your link to your friends and colleagues. Friendship and the experience of being accepted for just being who you are is like returning home to a sense of congeniality and an enjoyment of the shared spirit of life. You need to experience the sense of belonging to a larger family and have your individuality acknowledged within the larger collective.

Your task is to learn the value of inner freedom, no longer being enslaved to wanting what others have or feeling the need to be like others. You yearn to be valued as an equal individual within the group, but equality does not mean having the same as everyone else or being like everyone else: it involves embracing your individual needs, desires and tastes. Freedom to be outside the herd, to broaden your perceptions and admire your own uniqueness, is your vocation. In making every effort to be fair, broadminded, friendly and original you are a step closer to feeling that you are on the right path.

☉♓ The Sun in Pisces

Piscean virtues are numerous because this sign is attuned to the spiritual. Therefore you are familiar with heavenly qualities like compassion, sympathy and thankfulness. While you might become enraged at being 'ripped off', you do accept it as the way it was meant to be. As Mahatma Gandhi suggested, forgiveness is an attribute of the strong, not the weak. Forgiveness is one of many soul states you are experienced in, so no wonder you are drawn to the realm of mystics, healers and prophets.

In a personal way your imagination is what allows you to access soul and give meaning to your life. When you have no room for the imaginative process then everything that is mysterious or unknown becomes projected onto matter and begins to happen outside you as confusion and chaos. Imagination allows your soul to breathe and brings you back in touch with your own mysteries and unconscious processes, restoring meaning to your life. You are fluent in the language of the imagination, which speaks through images, dreams, symbols, signs, omens, oracles, hunches and feeling responses and is also the medium through which the spiritual realms are made accessible.

The unconscious realm is the phantasmagoria where colours, shades and sensory experiences are alive with meaning. You know this realm of creativity and spirituality well. You may be an artist who seeks this expression on a canvas, in a song, through movement or in a sonnet. Or you may be the care-giver who helps, heals, guides and shelters others. In creating an impressionistic and meaningful atmosphere you are able to escape from the banality of an ego-driven life and to feel embraced by something much greater. Your imagination is the gear that takes you to someplace higher.

Without imagination you are a fish out of water and life becomes soulless, dull and meaningless. You have the ability to re-inspire your life through acts of compassion or creativity. Whether you are expressing the music of your soul through helping others, volunteering at the local hospital, dancing in the dark or journaling your dreams, there is a great necessity for you to be actively engaged with your imagination. Your great gift is the ability to lift the veil of illusion by activating your imagination and allowing the compassionate act of serving others to legitimately flow out of you. Along your vocational path the qualities of compassion, forgiveness, sympathy and understanding contribute to your feeling whole.

The Moon: Caring for the Soul
The Moon is the archetype of care and nurturing, and to care for the soul requires that we pay attention to our daily needs. Therefore the Moon plays an important role in our vocation, as success depends not just on our worldly achievements and outer life, but on how we take care of our personal needs and our inner life.

From a general perspective the Moon reveals those needs that are important for us to feel comfortable in our vocation. The Moon sign can help to identify what basic requirements are necessary to care for the soul at work. Because its nature is reflective it can also help us to consider and contemplate our vocational drive and ambition. Planets are multidimensional so they also can signify certain professions, and the Moon is often associated with caring and nurturing professions. If an individual is drawn to one of these professions, the Moon sign helps to differentiate what kind of caring occupation could suit its temperament. The planetary sign acts as a filter for the archetypal urge when it seeks expression through the vocation.

What follows are some ways of thinking about the Moon sign in the context of your path in life.

☽♈ The Moon in Aries
You need independence and adventure in your vocation. Stimulation and challenge are basic requirements, as is being free enough to

make your own decisions. Therefore in caring for the soul you need to find the courage of your convictions to follow your own course. Being active and physical is important as well, as you feel more alive through exertion and drive. Instinctively you respond quickly to situations. Able to think on your feet and be in the moment, you are well suited to work in critical or dangerous situations where quick action is needed. These handy responses may allow you to be adept at a variety of mechanical, technological and electrical trades. If not, they will support you in being spontaneous and responsive to whatever blocks or challenges are in your path.

Your fiery spirit needs to push itself, so physical work or work which requires nerve, adrenalin, stamina and courage is well suited to your need to be heroically engaged. Occupations, including sport and business, which have goals and deadlines, as well as risk factors, could also encourage your driving spirit. However, at the end of the day what is important is that you have tended to your soul in work; this needs to trail-blaze and be a pioneer, preferring to be out in front rather than at the back of the queue. Without this stimulus you may feel bored and restless, craving thrills and stimuli which could be unsafe.

☽♉ The Moon in Taurus

In your daily life you prefer a stable environment where you can settle and not be rushed or surprised. It is essential for you to know what you are required to do. Having a job description is important; therefore, at work it is necessary for you to take care of these structural needs. You also need to feel valued and know that you are providing an essential service through your work, no matter how routine or repetitive it may be. Income is a core consideration, as it is necessary to feel not only valued in what you do but secure enough to support yourself financially. Therefore it is important to speak up when you feel it is time for a raise or promotion. As you are committed to the long-term, you need to proceed along the career path step-by-step. You need tangible results in what you do and to be able to monitor your own development.

From an early age you were instinctively drawn to nature and content to be surrounded by natural beauty. To care for your soul in everyday life, you need to be secure in what you do and comfortable where you are, involved with the sensual aspects of life. You need to nurture yourself through your occupation; if you do not discover this security and pleasure in your daily life, you may find yourself compensating for this through food, by spending money or with other pleasures.

☽♊ The Moon in Gemini

Mobility and diversity are important in any vocation. It is quite natural for you to often be involved in many tasks at the same time and to have an uncanny ability to be able to apply yourself to each one without losing your momentum. Being quick and agile you easily make connections, thinking best when you are on the move or in between two places. It is when you are crossing the road, answering your mobile or falling asleep that you may have your best ideas. Therefore it is important for your vocation to give you flexibility and fluidity in managing your time and the freedom to communicate. You naturally prefer a range of tasks; at heart you are a born communicator and messenger, with an abundance of ideas.

From an early age you were active and inquisitive, ready to explore the sights and sounds of the surrounding neighbourhood. Curious and enquiring, you wanted to report back what you saw. Instinctively, you are a reporter and at some time might have thought of becoming a journalist, writer, lecturer, teacher, translator or blogger. Even though your path might have meandered off in another direction, you can always care for your soul though communication and connection. You love to learn in your own way and figure things out. Soul can also express itself through your hands, making you a natural at drawing, graphics, playing the guitar or piano, or using them to heal. It is not easy to express your feelings, but through your vocation you find ways to express them through words and images.

☽♋ The Moon in Cancer

Like the Moon, you are aware of your constantly changing phases, the fullness of feelings and the letting go of attachments. Therefore you are highly sensitive to the subtle textures and nuances of the feeling life, especially when you are in a closely-knit group. You respond to others in your environment and can easily feel hurt when they are unresponsive or withdrawn. Therefore, in your daily work and rituals, it is important to feel emotionally safe and secure. You prefer your work environment to be like family and instinctually might try to recreate a familial environment. It is important to be aware of your security needs and strive to have those met, or to protect yourself when you feel unsafe at work. Building both emotional and financial security in your vocation is important.

Early on you recognized your tender touch. You might have imagined being a nurse, a vet, a carer or a teacher. While your life path may have veered away from your childhood images you still need to feel engaged and attached to what you are doing. Much of your need to care can be fulfilled through family and parenting; however, if you do not choose this path then you might find yourself drawn towards professions where care is highlighted. To care for your own soul, however, you first need to feel supported by close friends and to provide a safe nest for yourself.

☽♌ The Moon in Leo

Who you are and what you do are intertwined; hence it is critical to have a sense of certitude about your work. What you do needs to be creative and self-expressive. Therefore you might find yourself drawn to professions that allow you to be expressive and innovative or careers where the products are your designs, ideas or creations. With the Moon in Leo you have an innate presence and intensity combined with warmth of character. You can naturally light up a room and make others feel better about who they are. Being passionate and playful, it is important that your vocation gives you enough scope to express your personality.

When you were a young child you felt the urge to perform and to make the right impression. In your own mind you might have been a celebrity, as your soul is drawn to celebrating life. To care for your soul, your mood needs to be positive and upbeat. The identification and use of personal talents and originality is important. It is necessary for your identity to be a central part of your vocation, even if you are helping or serving others. Your creativity needs to be identified and demonstrated through what you do.

☽♍ The Moon in Virgo

Your feelings and moods inspire your life search to understand the nature of health and well-being. To care for your soul you need to provide enough structure and coherence to contain the natural chaos and disorder of life. Without order or consistency you are prone to worry, anxious about what might happen. You are so acutely aware of what may possibly go wrong that your body often bears this stress, making it imperative that constancy is created through your work and health regime. This characteristic calls you to your vocation to analytically understand the complexities of life. Being industrious, hard-working, disciplined and precise is inborn and can be directed through your career.

As a youngster you felt the urge to attend to others, to cultivate, prepare and improve situations. Instinctively you are drawn to be of service through figuring out the problem. Whether your vocational path has led you into the service or technology industries, healing, repair, labour or improvement occupations, you have a great need to be productive and helpful. Work and labour provide you with the means to feel productive and meaningful.

☽♎ The Moon in Libra

To feel safe in the workplace, your environment needs to be peaceful, uncluttered and orderly. If your external world is messy and in disarray, this affects your mood and ability to feel well. You are naturally polite, welcoming and gracious, but in an unpleasant atmosphere you can respond by being rude and disengaged. Therefore, to care for the soul, you need to surround yourself with what is pleasing and calming. Your need to beautify and place things harmoniously could be a feature of your vocation. Even if you do not choose a career as an interior designer, Feng Shui practitioner, professional artist, beautician or stage designer, you will bring your innate urge to harmonize into whichever career path you choose.

You were always aware of differences; whether that was the delicate balance between the sexes or the way someone else was behaving. Your natural tendency to judge others assisted you to know what you liked or didn't like. This instinct to judge and weigh up situations is high; therefore you have a natural ability for detailed and considered appraisals when asked to make a judgement. However, making choices is never easy if there is an emotional content to the decision; therefore when working in close proximity to others you need to call on your ability to detach when emotions run high. With your keen awareness of others and an urge to relate, relationships will naturally become part of your vocational path. First and foremost, your own personal relationships are important to help you feel secure and validated. This urge to work in a partnership or in close cooperation with others might be reflected in a close business partnership or working in one-to-one situations with clients.

☽♏ The Moon in Scorpio

Rather than breadth, you need depth of contact. You feel deeply, intensely and passionately, often preferring to contain your feelings rather than express them. You often feel that your own emotions are too intense or destructive to express; at other times you prefer to be private. Yet, when you do share your feelings, they are often transforming and liberating. In these instances you are a witness to the power of honesty. Depth of feeling is natural for you, and you have an acute awareness of the intensity of human feeling, such as grief and loss. Because of your urge to get to the root of the matter, destiny often provides you with critical situations in which you experience the transforming power of your feeling life. You care for your soul through acknowledging the intensity of your feelings.

When you were young you did not have the full capacity to understand your intensity and power. You may have experienced this in your need to be private, keep a secret diary, your interest in all things hidden and mysterious, your sexual curiosity or through intimate friendships. However, as you have matured you have recognized this need. Trust, integrity and honesty are paramount for you to open to be intimate with another. Your need to be personal is important; this highlights your need to trust those you work with and for. Ultimately, power is an issue you encounter on your life path, as your intensity and integrity may threaten others. However, you cannot hold yourself back because of others' insecurities and you need to dig below the surface even if that is confronting to others. This need for emotional authenticity and intensity are hallmarks on your vocational path.

☽♐ The Moon in Sagittarius

Even though you might be a natural student, the schoolroom is where you can feel bored and restless. But in the university of life, where you can be engaged in understanding other cultures, other languages and other ways of being, inspires you. It might be quite natural for you to travel, even to spend some time living abroad, in your quest for answers. The Moon reflects your home and in Sagittarius this implies that your home is beyond the familial horizon. To care for your soul you need to venture further afield and to search for meaning. You love freedom, whether it is being in nature, a wide horizon, open spaces or travel, because being involved with other cultures or with nature is conducive to your temperament. Both travel and study are important for you. If you are not explorative then you will not have the marriage of knowledge and experience, so that dry theory and opinions replace wisdom.

You may have always imagined journeying to faraway and exotic places; whether you do this physically or intellectually, you still feel stirred by the urge to adventure. Human values, ethics, morals and ideals are important and you need to become involved in pursuits you believe in and can recommend to others. Your positive and optimistic nature inspires others and often draws you towards social education and reform.

☽♑ The Moon in Capricorn

Instinctively, you are receptive and responsive to rules and regulations. Your natural response is to always do the right thing, because your need for approval is strong. But how do you define what is right? The amount of love and support you received when growing up plays an important role in your sense of security. Without adequate support, guidance or nurturance you may feel compelled to be dutiful. In doing the 'right' thing you may hope to get the acknowledgement you never received as a child. Therefore, in caring for the soul it is important that you author your own rules, become an authority over what you need and nurture your own ambitions, not those set out for you. You need to be industrious, so work and productivity are essential for your well-being.

As a child you may have felt the weight of responsibility, feeling that your chores and duties stood in the way of being playful. You might feel you have missed out on childhood; however, the good news is that the weight of obligation lifts as you mature. It is important to feel that you are in control of your environment, even of those in it; therefore, you thrive in managerial and parental positions where you are able to be a director. But when you feel insecure, your need to control others may surface. Therefore, to tend the soul you need to create the structures and autonomy to support what you need.

☽♒ The Moon in Aquarius

Although born to be a humanitarian, you may often struggle with the difference between personal and impersonal relationships, preferring to remain disengaged rather than be involved emotionally. Ironically, you feel safer in the future than the past and therefore are intellectually agile in understanding progress and social development. You need to be involved in the making of the future, so are often drawn to science, technology or alternative avenues that help to shape the times to come. Therefore, it may be difficult for you to feel connected or involved in emotional, sentimental or traditional ways, as your soul is in touch with tomorrow, not yesterday. You are unique and need to express your individuality in whatever you do. Vocationally, independence and the lack of rigidity and hierarchy are important. This may lead you into discovering your own tribe of radicals who are able to work in a more egalitarian and self-affirming way.

When you were younger you might have stood out by being different. Your lunch box contained different foods, or liking different styles may have marginalized you from the core group. Eventually you were able to find your own friends, who probably were one of a kind as well. As you matured you needed to express your individuality and differences, as these are important features of your character. Your flair for the unusual and unconventional needs to be acknowledged and considered. Individualism, along with social interaction and intellectual stimulation, is important. To care for your soul you need to be moved by the spirit of being human and to strive for the ideals that are inherently a part of who you are. No doubt you need a progressive, inventive and forward-looking career path, in which you creatively contribute to designing the future.

☽♓ The Moon in Pisces

Your natural disposition is to merge with your surroundings; therefore, your frame of mind is strongly influenced by the atmosphere around you. On the one hand you are given the gift of being sensitive, attuned to the environment, intuitive, even prophetic. Yet, on the other, you may struggle to set appropriate boundaries, have difficulty in leaving emotionally unfulfilled situations or struggle to articulate your needs. You may be hard to pin down as your moods shift and change depending on the atmosphere. To care for the soul you need to be aware of this tendency to be a medium to others and choose when and how you want to express this gift. Your urge to serve is important; therefore you may feel the need to dedicate yourself either to a service or to a cause. Make sure that this is what you need to do, not what others need from you.

As a young child you were surrounded by wonderment. From an early age you would have recognized your capacity to imagine, to create, to dream, to envision. As you matured you were challenged with knowing the fine line that separated the imagination from delusion. But to nurture your soul you still need the contact with the other world of dreams and images. Vocationally, this suggests you are able to draw on something much larger than yourself to inspire and inform your work. What you need in your daily life is contact with the dream world where imagination and human ideals are valued. Hopefully your creative, intuitive and artistic temperament can find an outlet through your vocation. If not, you need to provide a place where you can go to be in contact with the imagination.

The Ascendant: Steering the Soul through Life

As one of the four angles of the horoscope, the Ascendant plays a major role in the course and direction of one's life. The Ascendant faces the world and is first met by the world. It has been known as breath, life, birth, spirit; all words that lead us back to the beginning of the life force. In the horoscope, birth is generally equated with the Ascendant because the eastern horizon is where planets actually rise into view. While life exists long before birth, it is birth that marks the beginning of life. Birth acknowledges our separateness, independence and individuality and marks the transition between the divine and the secular worlds. Similarly, the Ascendant carries the aspects of our individual self, the way we greet life and conduct the soul's vital energies. It is the personality of the vehicle that carries us, often the first visible qualities that others see in us. Therefore, others whose personal planets connect with our Ascendant respond to us immediately.

The sign on the Ascendant, its ruler and angular planets convey images about the atmosphere of birth and this includes the family condition at the time. Astrologically, the Ascendant can reveal many things about perinatal conditions as well as how we instinctively confront the world.

Planets that are on the horizon, especially conjoining the Ascendant, symbolize not only conditions surrounding the birth but how this energy is called upon every time a transition or new beginning occurs. The life force that is channelled through the Ascendant and spills into the 1st house is indicative of our early environment and the energy that is able to be channelled and focused towards the growing and forward-moving personality. Our immediate environment is our physical body, which transports the self. The Ascendant is representative of how the vital life is channelled and how the body conducts energy.

Howard Sasportas suggested that birth and early family experiences are connected with the Ascendant. He described the Ascendant as how we might hatch;[20] in other words, how we opened the shell of our self into the world. Any planet on the Ascendant might tell a birth tale or a family story.[21] However, it is also a theme that is awoken in each life transition because we constantly look through this archetypal lens at the world as we approach it. Therefore it is often very revealing to obtain the story of our birth, as the feelings, reports, images and anecdotes that surround it often reveal early images of our personality and the way in which we later approach life.

The sign on the Ascendant symbolizes the outer personality, often constructed as a way to 'house' the self. It is the image projected out onto the world and initially apparent to others. In older texts there is often a physical description of the rising sign; however, the sign refers more to the characteristics that help the individual to navigate life.

Planetary aspects to the Ascendant also modify personal expression. As an analogy, let's think of the Sun as the protagonist of the story, the essential self, and the Moon as the inner feeling life and soul. The Ascendant could then be likened to the eventful course that the character takes through life.

To the ancient astrologers, one of the most important planets in the horoscope was the ruler of the Ascendant. In vocational astrology this planet assumes importance because it animates the individual's purpose and direction. It is also an image of what directs the life course and helps to steer its course of action. The ruling planet describes an important temperament that will oversee the vocational path: its sign position describes the qualities of the archetype, while its house position locates themes and issues and its aspects encourage dialogue with other archetypes in the horoscope.

We will look at the Ascendant again in a following chapter but for now let's look at the seven traditional rulers of the Ascendant and the characteristics they bring to our vocational path. Each ruling planet is unique for each individual, as it will be in a different sign and house as well as have different aspects, but its underlying essence will be the same. Here are the seven traditional rulers of the rising signs; the ruler was known as the lord of the chart in traditional astrology.

The Sun as Chart Ruler (Leo Rising)

When the Sun is the ruling planet of the personality, vitality, confidence and an air of self-assurance are important characteristics that assist in developing the vocation. With an optimistic attitude and a flair for creativity and performance, the Sun guides the individual towards the path of self-expression and originality in their career.

The Moon as Chart Ruler (Cancer Rising)

With Cancer rising, the personality is highly sensitive to their atmosphere and how they interact with the environment. The Moon at the helm describes how the protective instinct will be engaged to shelter the personality. However, it is also an indication that the nurturing, sustaining and caring instincts will be drawn out on the vocational path.

Mercury as Chart Ruler (Gemini or Virgo Rising)

When Mercury rules the Ascendant its mutable nature operates the control panel. Variety, curiosity, dexterity and changeability are the hallmarks of this pathway through life. When Gemini is rising, Mercury steers the individual more in the direction of a guide, the disseminator of ideas or communication. As ruler of Virgo, Mercury is more circumspect and the vocational path may be more orientated towards vocations that record, serve and analyse, or towards craftsmanship that includes detail and precision.

Venus as Chart Ruler (Taurus or Libra Rising)

Venus is associated with values so it targets vocations that provide a sense of worth and self-esteem, whether that is physically, financially or psychologically. When Venus is the director of the Ascendant she leads the personality in the direction of their values, both sensually and spiritually. With Taurus rising this might be towards the appreciation of physical and earthy beauty; as the ruler of Libra it might be towards beautification through divine ideas and fine art.

Mars as Chart Ruler (Aries or Scorpio Rising)

With Mars as the driver of the Ascendant, the course of life points towards an innovative and independent route. Confrontation and challenges are integral to the vocational search as these clarify where the individual wants to invest their energy. With Aries rising the career path is entrepreneurial and pioneering, while with Scorpio rising Mars is more directed towards the investigative and mysterious, to what lies beneath the surface.

Jupiter as Chart Ruler (Sagittarius or Pisces Rising)

Jupiter points towards understanding and wisdom, and as the executive managing the Ascendant he leads the individual down a wide pathway through education, travel, cultural awareness, philosophy, spirituality or other forms of expansion. With Sagittarius rising, Jupiter's path heads beyond the familiar horizon towards new discoveries in education, knowledge, travel and culture. As the ruler of Pisces the vocational path exposes the individual to creativity, spirituality and compassion.

Saturn as Chart Ruler (Capricorn or Aquarius Rising)

As the guide of the Ascendant, Saturn's influence stabilizes the personality to focus on its life direction. Saturn provides the personality with a sense of tradition, timing, competency and a work ethic that can be developed through the course of life to maximize a fulfilling vocation. When Capricorn rises the qualities of dependability, organization, autonomy and integrity can be employed to assist along the vocational path. When Aquarius is on the eastern horizon the progressive skills to reform, liberate and evolve are helpful assets.

Fortune and Your Lot in Life:
The Alchemy of the Sun, Moon and Ascendant

Astrologically, the Sun, Moon and Ascendant can be combined into one point known in modern astrology as the Part of Fortune. While 'fortune' has come to mean money and wealth, it also refers to chance or luck. The word is also synonymous with destiny or fate. All these ideas come together in one point which contains some clues about our quality and share of fortune. Ptolemy, one of astrology's first authorities, suggested that the Part of Fortune was primary to the circumstances that regulate the 'fortune of wealth'. While he only endorsed one formula for its calculation, other Hellenistic and medieval astrologers suggested alternative calculations, depending on whether the birth occurred during the day or night. Differentiating day and night had significance to ancient astrologers who made planetary distinctions, known as 'sect',[22] according to a nocturnal or diurnal birth. The Sun above the horizon signified a diurnal birth, while the Sun below the horizon was nocturnal.

The Part of Fortune is also known as the Lot of Fortune. In ancient Greece, the concept of fate suggested a lot, which is a portion or part of what we are allotted in life. The Greek word for fate was *moira* and the Moirai were the three weavers of fate: those who measured, allocated and cut the threads of one's life. With this lot, the ancient astrologers recognized that the tapestry created by weaving together the three threads of the Sun, Moon and Ascendant could be fortunate. In modern practice the Part of Fortune is recognized as a mathematically derived point in the horoscope, but in ancient times it was generally perceived as a geometrical concept. The arc between the Sun and the Moon is symmetrical to the arc between the Ascendant and the Part of Fortune. For diurnal births this arc moves clockwise from the Ascendant, while for nocturnal births the movement from the ascendant is counterclockwise.

As the lunar phase or distance between the Sun and Moon is measured from the Ascendant, the Part of Fortune occupies a certain house of your horoscope depending on your lunar phase at birth. Therefore the Part of Fortune is intimately tied to your lunation phase, as follows:

Lunation Phase	Sun–Moon Separation	Approximate house for Day births	Approximate house for Night births
New Moon	0°-45°	1st or 2nd	11th or 12th
Crescent	45°-90°	2nd or 3rd	10th or 11th
First Quarter	90°-135°	4th or 5th	8th or 9th
Gibbous	135°-180°	5th or 6th	7th or 8th
Full Moon	180°-225°	7th or 8th	5th or 6th
Disseminating	225°-270°	8th or 9th	4th or 5th
Last Quarter	270°-315°	10th or 11th	2nd or 3rd
Balsamic	315°-0° (360°)	11th or 12th	1st or 2nd

Diurnal (DAY) Formula: Ascendant + Moon – Sun
Nocturnal (NIGHT) Formula: Ascendant + Sun – Moon

Whether ancient or modern, the Part of Fortune is fashioned from three highly significant aspects of the horoscope: the Sun, the Moon and the Ascendant. This zodiacal point represents an amalgam of astrological characteristics that forges a symbol of our personal fortune. Being constructed from the luminaries and the Ascendant, the Part of Fortune is a symbolic combination of body, soul and spirit; no wonder this horoscope point was highly valued by the ancients as representing an area of life where good fortune and happiness could come by chance, independent of an individual's will or action.

As the Ascendant represents our physical environment, personality and levels of vitality, it is a primary gauge for well-being, both in terms of health and wealth. The Sun represents vital force, the spirit of health and heart, while the Moon symbolizes the emotional and soulful aspects of being secure in the world. Since the alchemy of all three created the Lot of Fortune, it came to be seen as an image of well-being, happiness, connection, security and being well-placed in the world. This was considered to be prosperity: that ability to be supported by the world around you and to be able to access its abundant resources.

As an ancient symbol in a contemporary context we might see the Part of Fortune in the horoscope as a metaphor of prosperity or where we might align ourselves with the seed potential of our fortune. However, it is wise to remember that fortune is connected not only to wealth, but chance; therefore we have to activate and participate with this aspect of our nature in order to maximize our chances in life. And the choice of the right gods or archetypal patterns is necessary. Therefore the Part of Fortune's sign position will amplify innate qualities that are destined to be prosperous, while its house position will identify which area is important to focus on to increase our chances in the game of life. Confucius is credited with saying 'When prosperity comes, do not use all of it', perhaps a reminder that the wheel of fortune is forever turning, sometimes up, sometimes down.

The Part of Fortune does not necessarily mean literal finances or fortunes, but rather where we are able to gain from opportunities and circumstances. As a metaphor, this position is where we might locate happiness, feel fortunate or blessed, even lucky. In a way the Part of Fortune is like our lot in life and gives us ways of thinking about how we might best maximize our chances of winning the lottery, symbolically and perhaps even literally. In this way it is an interesting point to consider in our vocational analysis.

What follows are some descriptions of the Lot of Fortune in each house. This position will also be tempered by planetary aspects and other influences but it is a good place to start contemplating this part of your horoscope. Reflect on its position in terms of how and where you connect with prosperity and how you might best maximize your chances at spinning the wheel of fortune.

The Lot of Fortune in the 1st House

Much of your wealth is derived from your own personal effort, ingenuity and distinctiveness. Your unique personality brings its rewards and the more you extend yourself out into the vibrant marketplace of life, the more that life brings a variety of possibilities to you. It is necessary to project yourself into life and summon the courage to pursue your dreams, as it is this spirit of exploration that guides you towards your destiny. Therefore it is in developing your distinctive character, your individuality and your ability to be self-sufficient that you create your own luck. Opportunities are born out of your initiatives, self-determination and ability to heed the advice of others but not be dependent on it.

If you were born during the day, a New Moon cycle was just starting and your spontaneity, enthusiasm and naturalness are godsends for you personally. If you were born at night, the Moon was Balsamic, in its final phase of the cycle, endowing your personality with insight, intuition and perception for the future. Whatever time of the day you were born, the Moon was dark, overflowing with instinctual creative urges that seek expression through your personality. Your fortune has its own personal stamp on it and increases the more you feel free enough to pursue your own pathways in life. You are fortunate to be one of a kind, able to have an independent lifestyle and a personality that animates life, bringing its own rewards.

The Lot of Fortune in the 2nd House

You are instinctively fortunate with money, but it is important to note that the fundamental spirit of this house aligns money with values. An important question is 'What do I attach importance to?' On a material level you do very well, appraising what is of value, finding a bargain, negotiating the best deal, improving the net worth of your assets and estimating the cost of projects. But on a psychological level, money is the reflection of your self-esteem and your estimate of worth. To secure your fortune, be aware of what it is that you value and appreciate, what it is you like and how you can best support your sense of worth. In a way you are what you possess; therefore it is best to find out who you are and what you treasure before you spend your money. You have a great head start by being lucky with money, but by respecting your self-worth, your fortune increases.

The 2nd house is known as a house of substance. Having the Part of Fortune here is substantial in locating a focus for your destiny. Money is important as a way of securing your future and satisfying your need for comfort and safety. When you invest in what you value and appreciate, as well as in those you love, you find your net worth increasing. When you bring that sense of worth and value into the heart of your life, you are blessed with fortune. No doubt money is gained from your personal endeavours. But the secret of success seems to be that as you improve your sense of self-worth and value your assets, the wheel of fortune turns in your favour.

The Lot of Fortune in the 3rd House

Since the 3rd house has a variety of rooms, there are many fortunate opportunities within your immediate surroundings. Your ability to forge links and connections within your family and a wider social circle assists in creating relationships that can be advantageous to you. Your siblings and school friends may still be close by and they can be supportive when you are planning and launching your ideas and projects. You are fortunate in that close friends, associates or neighbours may also lend a hand on your journey towards financial security. You benefit from close kinship and being actively involved with others in your immediate environment.

However, one of your best assets on the road to success is your ability to be considered, to access information and news about trends, and to keep a clear head in managing your affairs. Multitasking and being busy are beneficial, but what is fortunate is your knack of thinking things through. You succeed in the sphere of communication, information, transportation, news, teaching and coaching. Metaphorically, you are in your element when you are able to connect, interact and network. Your wheel of fortune is busily turning with many balls in the air and many projects on the go; therefore you improve your chances when you are moving, talking things through and making connections. Fortune is keeping your money in circulation, as this is the way you spread the seeds for future financial fortune.

The Lot of Fortune in the 4th House

The 4th house represents the family of origin, so some of your keys to fortune rest under the foundations of the family home. Fortune may well come through your parents; however, this might not necessarily be in the form of cash or material assets, but in terms of what you may have inherited emotionally or psychologically. What is your attitude towards prosperity and how has this been shaped by your parents' experiences of money? Was the emphasis on physical possessions or centred on the felt experience of home and family, the sense of belonging and the gift of place? Your inner sense of security is the platform on which you can build up your fortune. It is probably when you have the feeling that you are settled in the right place that you are able to begin building your wealth. The weight of your familial past and your own depth of security become the counterweights that secure your wheel of fortune.

With the Part of Fortune placed in this sphere, the family or current home may become wellsprings of capital for you. However, you may also have a knack at real estate, so you gain from investment in land and property. Or this could suggest that you gain through a family business or family investments. Symbolically, this indicates that your prosperity is entwined with feeling grounded and settled, able to feel that your roots are firmly planted in home soil. With a solid foundation your family tree can flourish and your particular branch can reach out towards success.

The Lot of Fortune in the 5th House

Developing your originality and creative flair will encourage prosperity. Traditionally, this might be read as gains through children, perhaps projects or industries that centre on children's needs. Or, more simply, it could refer to the joy of being a parent or re-experiencing the enchantment of childhood. On a soulful level we might think of this as the enjoyment that comes from being creative and giving birth to new ideas, projects and activities. Approaching life through the eyes of a child, protected by innocence and enthused by possibilities, is rewarding. Although setbacks are part of the process, you triumph by not complicating your creativity with feelings of disappointment and disillusionment. You are fortunate when you approach life wide-eyed and animated about the outcome, like that first time you broke open that Chinese cookie to find your fortune inside. This is not blind optimism but a deeper knowing that the outcome will be positive. Something fortunate is embedded in the heart of your inspiration, enthusiasm and creative talent.

When we enter the 5th house we enter a theatre complex, an amusement ground, a sports and leisure centre, a casino or a quaint inn. Perhaps inside these arenas you find your fortune but, more likely, it is when you allow yourself time to play and be amused that you feel lucky and privileged. It is not luck that brings your fortune, but your persistence at being positive, your creative involvement and your attitude towards life. Destiny will repay your generosity through creative opportunities and risks that pay off.

The Lot of Fortune in the 6th House

You are fortunate when you are able to feel successful with your work and happy with your health. With the Part of Fortune in the 6th house, these are the main concerns and when these are satisfied you feel prosperous. In a traditional sense this placement suggests that gains will come from work or through those you work with. However, the rewards of hard work are not all in the payslip or salary bonuses, but in being occupied and focused. You are rewarded by your service; advancement opportunities come through your ability to be thorough and accurate in what you do. Your best assets are your self-discipline, ability to follow a plan and manage the details of life. Success emerges from your attention to detail and management of the everyday life. Fortune is found in this consistency and continuity of life.

This sphere is also concerned with well-being and maintenance of the physical body; therefore, you will gain from taking care of yourself with a proper diet, exercise and relaxation. You feel like a million dollars when you are fit and healthy, and this is an indication of how significant health is to your fortune. With this focus you might find that you are drawn to the fields of health and well-being; time spent here is time well spent for you. The 6th house is also connected to service but in essence it is more the service to the self that is important. When you find the best ways to stay healthy and as stress-free as possible, you also find happiness. Your investments are in the everyday; therefore, what you value and give importance to will become profitable for you.

The Lot of Fortune in the 7th House

It is through your involvement with others that you are able to find more meaning and purpose in life. Others help to initiate projects which are worthwhile and expose you to different approaches and values that are rewarding. Traditionally, this placement would show gains from marriage and partnerships; in essence, whenever there is a contractual agreement, a verbal commitment or an equal exchange you are in a position to profit from the relationship. This is the potential of your relationships, but you need to choose wisely who will partner you on the wheel of fortune. You are supported and encouraged when a partner is able to hold up a mirror so you can see the reflection of your own worth and value. Metaphorically, it is not the money that is your fortune, but the processes of relationship such as sharing, equality, conversation, altercation, empathy, caring and loving that bring pleasure and wealth.

If you were born during the day you were born just after the Full Moon, which signifies that others are able to illuminate your path forward and partner your goals and aspirations. Being born at night implies that you were born just before the Full Moon and it is through your openness and responsiveness to others that you develop ways and means to become resourceful. Since others are important on your path to prosperity it is important to develop the skills of negotiation, the art of compromise and the ability to read character. But it is also vital to know how and when to stand up for your rights and your share. Fortune comes through equality and a transparent, open relationship, even if that relationship no longer exists. Vocationally, there are many trades and professions that work with others and you have the opportunity to gain from any of these, but it is when you are in an equal, committed and evenly balanced partnership that you find your fortune.

The Lot of Fortune in the 8th House
You may need to descend below the surface to find how to unravel the threads that connect you to your wealth. Literally, this might suggest unseen resources, but since this is also a place where money is exchanged with others, gains are made through honest and clear contractual agreements, sound financial management and reliable partners. Metaphorically speaking, fortune is the integrity of your inner and private life. This is the natural house of inheritance, and inheriting generally suggests that something has ended or someone has died. While your lot here may not always signify a monetary legacy, it does suggest that your birthright is to gain from what has been passed on, unfinished by others or bequeathed to you. You are fortunate as you know the deep secret that whatever ends is reborn. While there may be grief in an ending, you certainly gain by renewing, remodelling and transforming what has been left to you by others.

The 8th house is where you exchange resources with others. With the Part of Fortune here you can profit from your involvement with others when there is a straightforward and trustworthy partnership. When the relationship has trust and integrity it blossoms. Even if it ends in an honest way, there are gains. As already stated, it may not be monetary, but it is emotional. And when there is deep healing through sincere and truthful interchange then you mine deeper resources that lead you to prosperity. This is the house of other people's money so it is wise to reflect on how much debt you need in order to be prosperous: you will gain through borrowing capital to fund your business, your home or worthwhile investments, not for monetary gain but for emotional security. And even though you may not think it, there is a legacy that you will inherit and gain from.

The Lot of Fortune in the 9th House

The quality of this cross-cultural environment suggests that your quest for meaning will be enriching and rewarding. Fortune is gained in the escapades of life; it is through life-changing travels, inspiriting guides or educative adventures that you find the riches of life. While they may not be bankable or saleable, they are soulful. And it is in the soulfulness of life where you find your wealth. You may not find value in conventional religion but you can be prosperous through your spirituality. You understand the well-quoted passage from Mark 8:36: *What does it profit a man to gain the whole world yet lose his soul?* You profit from exploring both the outer and the inner worlds, journeying through foreign landscapes as well as psychic ones. Fortune comes from extending your opinions, widening your horizons and tolerating differences.

Prosperity is embedded in your beliefs; hence the more restrictive and prejudicial these are, the poorer you feel. Therefore, your fortune lies in open-minded philosophies and attitudes. On a literal level this suggests that you do well with groundbreaking projects, foreign development, cross-cultural assignments or any vocations that endeavour to reach beyond familiar boundaries and entrenched traditions. But your most fortunate asset is that you believe in the possibility and are willing to pursue your ideals and dreams. You are disheartened by negativity and buoyed by positive affirmations of what is possible. Therefore it is wise to invest in your own vision and potential by embracing a philosophy of success and adopting an imaginative mandate.

The Lot of Fortune in the 10th House

Finding your role and place in the world is beneficial for you; therefore you are fortunate when you are able to feel that you have a job to finish, a role to play or a goal to achieve. You gain from being ambitious, having a plan and focusing on getting to the top. But success for you is not always being in control of your direction, but in the challenges and responsibilities along the way that contribute to shaping your character. Gaining a sense of autonomy and control in your life is important for your fulfilment. Although business success, money and reputation are also important, the nature of commerce has many targets besides money. It is fortunate for you when you are able to feel satisfied with the amount of money you earn and fulfilled by the many other rewards of life.

Being a leader is also important to your success. When you are in the role of fostering and mentoring others, you are in a privileged position. It is providential for you when you are called to take a commanding position, whether that is in your business or personal life. You often have a responsible role to take in life, even when you were younger; therefore your attitude towards responsibility is key to your success. Accepting the function as part of your lot in life, rather than feeling resentful about your duty of care, brings its own opportunities. Your attitudes towards life and its challenges are paramount to success, because being successful always has its rewards and its responsibilities.

The Lot of Fortune in the 11th House

The indications are that you are already in a fortunate position. Surrounding you are friends of the family, schoolmates and team members, colleagues and co-workers who might all have keys that open up some doors to success. Perhaps you need to take better advantage of the position that you are in so as to reap the rewards. Your networks, associations and organizations are where you find the right contacts that can help you to take the next step to success. It is through your colleagues or friends that you might find out about a new venture or project that you want to be a part of. Therefore all around you, in your community, your social circle and your groups, are opportunities to increase your fortune. Again, this might not solely refer to investment opportunities, financial gains or material increases, but to finding a tribe to belong to and a place where you feel at home. With this sense of belonging you are in a much better position to feel fortunate. Because of the 11th house's emphasis on community, humanitarian projects are opportune for you. Whether your social work is salaried or through volunteering, you are rewarded in different ways for your contributions. There may not be a lot gained financially but what you reap emotionally and achieve collectively provides you with a sense of well-being.

The 11th house is where science labs, computer programmers and technological corporations are located. The space is adventurous, explorative and future-orientated, so when you step into any of these spheres you are likely to be in a better position. Opportunities lie in areas of reform and change. This house is also where democracy and the voice of the people want to be heard. When you align yourself with greater communal causes for human and animal rights, equality and freedom, then you find yourself in the fortunate position of being part of a wide circle of compatriots who share your spirit and support your vision.

The Lot of Fortune in the 12th House

You are fortunate in ways that are not readily visible to others. The wellspring of your resources is not easily evident or knowable, but it is there, an anchor entrenched in the deepest part of the soul. It is in the quieter moments of reflection or in solitude that you find an inner reserve that sustains and supports you. But it is also in these moments that you receive the inspiration and guidance that leads you on the right track towards success. Your destiny might be that you make your fortune in a non-traditional way, be that through a spiritual, creative or sacred avenue, via an ancestral legacy or through your dedication to what you deeply believe in. Traditionally, this might suggest that fortune is hard-earned; therefore it is your deeper beliefs about the soul that bring good fortune. Prosperity is encouraged through your acceptance of your lot in life.

If you were born at night, a New Moon cycle was just starting and your spontaneity, innocence and naturalness are of great benefit in activating your creativity and imagination. If you were born during the day, the Moon was Balsamic, in its final phase of the cycle, bestowing insight, intuition and perception for future prospects. The Moon is darkened at birth, but it is in the dark that you find the treasure, whether that is through a dream, an intense feeling or a premonition. Since your fortune is deeply embedded in soul, your true worth is unable to be estimated. How do you put a price on deep conviction and enduring beliefs?

The Sun, Moon and Ascendant are the principal spokes on the wheel of life and come together to forge a potent trinity in the horoscope.

But the Sun and Moon also create another significant vocational factor in each horoscope: the axis of the lunar nodes. We will now examine this axis in the horoscope in the context of our calling.

<hr>

For students who would like to learn to calculate the Part of Fortune manually, please consult Brian Clark, The Lunation Process, available from Astro*Synthesis at: http://www.astrosynthesis.com.au/student-astrology-e-booklets/

– Chapter 5 –
DESTINY
The Lunar Nodes

Astronomically, the nodes are the two points where an orbit crosses its reference plane; in astrological language, where the plane of a planet's orbit intersects the ecliptic. The lunar nodes are the two points where the Moon's orbit around the Earth crosses over the apparent path of the Sun. These two intersecting points are nodes, the lunar nodes being the two sites on the ecliptic where heaven meets earth and where an interconnection between our spiritual purpose and worldly vocation is symbolized.

All planets have nodes. However, in contemporary astrology it is the lunar nodes that have become widely accepted as being essential in understanding a holistic horoscope. Most astrologers include the nodal axis in horoscopes, but the delineation can vary considerably. The North Node is also referred to as the Dragon's Head or Rahu, which comes from Vedic astrology; the South Node is also called the Dragon's Tail or Ketu. 'Node' is derived from the Latin *nodus* or knot, which is a multifaceted symbol. When a knotted cord is looped, it can symbolize an enclosure, a closed ring of power, a psychological container or an alchemical alembic. The knot is also associated with magic through its association with binding and attachment. In the heavens the nodal knot signifies the complex intermeshing of the divine and mortal where the bonds between the planes of heaven and earth are joined.

Other definitions of the nodes also exist and in English we find interesting classifications that help us to understand the intricacy of the astrological nodes. Each definition shines a different light on their complex meaning: for instance, a node is the joint or knob on the stem of a plant, from which leaves, buds and shoots grow. Similarly, along the nodal axis there is the potential for new life to emerge out of the system. The nodal axis suggests places where reconciliation between the past and the future is possible, and from this new growth emerges.

A node is the point which curves across itself. Nodes are the horoscopic sites where the great planes of spirit and matter intersect, becoming vessels for the spiritual life. Each node or nodule is a container of life energy: the South Node has the accumulated wisdom from past experience while the North Node contains the seeds for potential growth. Both nodes have an intimate connection with destiny, being significant markers on the vocational path. A node has also come to mean the plot of a story or drama, and the nodal axis in the horoscope symbolizes the spiritual drama which unfolds through this lifetime. In family therapy, nodal points suggest defining moments or critical times in the family life cycle, and the lunar nodes map critical 19-year phases in the life cycle. It is at the first nodal return, between the ages of 18 and 19, that the individual may first hear their calling to vocation.

The Sacred Geometry of the Nodes

The nodal cycle lasts between 18 and 19 years or, more precisely, 18.6 years. Its cycle retrogrades through the zodiac; its direction is opposite to the planets' movement, which highlights the nature of the lunar nodes as being distinct from the archetypal nature of the planets. The nodal cycle also has an interesting harmonic, highlighting the 18-19 year cycles of our lives:[23]

- On average, the mean lunar nodes cycle though the zodiac in *18-19 years* (the 'node year')
- On average, the mean lunar nodes transit one zodiac sign in *18-19 months* (the 'node month')
- On average, the mean lunar nodes retrograde one zodiacal degree in *18-19 days* (the 'node day')

The lunar nodes are intimately connected to the Sun and Moon;[24] it is fascinating that the tarot cards of the Moon and Sun are also numbered 18 and 19 respectively. Each card represents an important sequence of resurrection in the Fool's archetypal journey through the 22 initiations portrayed by the Major Arcana cards.[25]

In most ephemerides the lunar nodes are listed as either the *mean node* or the *true node*; many ephemerides list both. The mean node is the average daily movement of the node, which was traditionally used by astrologers before computers were able to accurately measure the nodal position. The mean node retrogrades regularly through the zodiac at an average of 3.2 minutes per day.

The true node is the precise astronomical position. This began to appear in ephemerides in the last quarter of the 20th century. This node turns direct in its retrograde cycle and moves through the zodiac irregularly. It reaches a plateau every 4-5 months for 2-3 months, stressing a particular degree of the zodiac. When traced through the zodiac, the true north node makes a serpentine movement through the signs, synchronous with its dragon symbolism.[26] The true north node will accentuate nodal transits to certain degrees of the zodiac for nearly 2-3 months at a time.

The question then becomes, 'Which node should I use?' I differentiate it this way: in looking at the nodal cycle from the perspective of the fullness of the life cycle, I use the mean node, as its movement illustrates the patterning of the nodal cycle. But when looking at the natal chart and specific transits, I use the true node. In certain cases when the mean node is on the cusp of a sign, the true node may actually be in the neighbouring sign.

A Rendezvous with the Dragon

The modern understanding of the lunar nodes has been greatly influenced by the work of Dane Rudhyar.[27] He proposed that the nodal axis is one of destiny and individuation, suggesting the south node was past work and the north node is the work to be done, firmly aligning the lunar nodes with the vocational path. Early Hellenistic astrologers mentioned the lunar nodes, but these did not come to be known as the Dragon's Head and Dragon's Tail until the 4th century CE.[28]

A mythological motif in most western mythologies is the hero's battle with the dragon. However, it is the Vedic myth of the Churning of the Milk-Ocean[29] which recounts how the dragon-snake Vasuki became associated with the points on the ecliptic known as Rahu and Ketu. In Vedic astrology, Rahu and Ketu are venerated like planets. The myth also explains the phenomena of eclipses. The legend says that Rahu and Ketu lie in wait on the ecliptic to swallow the Sun and the Moon if they venture too close, because they were furious at the Sun and Moon who were responsible for their downfall.[30] The nodes are not planets, but they are found on the ecliptic. Rahu is the ascending node while Ketu is the descending node; solar and lunar eclipses occur when the Sun is near either pole of the nodal axis. There will always be at least two solar eclipses a year; one near Rahu and one near Ketu. A lunar eclipse may precede or follow the solar eclipse.

Rahu is the head of the dragon; here is where destiny is magnetized through divine intervention. Like the Sun, the desire is to be active and to battle the impulse to regress. Ketu is the tail of the dragon, the southern pole of the axis, and is likened to the Moon where instinctive knowledge from our past accumulates. The nodes's retrograde movement and their crisscrossing of the ecliptic represent where there is an aperture to spirit, an opening between the world of spirit and the mundane.

Its retrograde movement in the horoscope also suggests that the transit of the nodes coerces us into engaging with the sacred aspects of our life experience. Therefore, the nodes's transits to the angles of the horoscope every 4-5 years are significant in terms of vocation. Rahu and Ketu are divine and belong to the same system as the planets, presenting us with the task of understanding what the dragon-serpent represents in us, as it is a systemic part of who we are. The poet Rainer Maria Rilke said: 'Perhaps all the dragons of our lives are princesses who are only waiting to see us once beautiful and brave. Perhaps everything terrible is in its deepest being something helpless that wants help from us.'[31] Rilke reminds us of the archetypal nature of the dragon battle and that the monstrous may be a vulnerable, forgotten or unexpressed aspect of our own nature. Embedded in each horoscope is the archetypal image of the dragon battle and, as myth reveals, the hero encounters the dragon on their life path. This encounter with the dragon is allegorical, symbolizing the battle with the dark sides of our own nature.

Jungians call it the shadow; Freudians nickname it the Id. By whatever name it is known, the struggle with the dragon is a psychological reality, one that the ancients always scripted into their mythic epics. Long before St George killed the dragon or the chivalrous knight rescued the distressed damsel from the jaws of the monster, this phantasmagorical motif was embedded in the mythological stratum of most cultures. Ancient wisdom knew that the heroic aspect of each human being had a rendezvous with the dragon at defining moments in their life journey.

In psychological terms, the battle with the dragon is the clash with regressive forces that can devour our strength and motivation. To overcome the dragon, the hero must reconcile the serpent's destructive force to draw strength from it. Along the nodal axis we encounter this symbolic dragon; the tail is the regressive pull into the shadow, while the head is the ego striving to gain strength and move forwards.

In considering this axis we can envisage the North Node or Dragon's Head as the invitation to be heroic, to develop an identity in the world and pursue our calling. The North Node points to what can be developed by valuing and cultivating our innate faculties. The South Node or Dragon's Tail is the container of talents, skills and aptitudes gleaned from the past, lying untapped and undifferentiated. Without recognition or consciousness these abilities remain stagnant, unable to be directed advantageously. The heroic act is consciousness, which dislodges and distributes the energy at the South Node so it can be of service. In releasing and circulating this energy, the potential at the North Node ripens. When we are mindful of the South Node, destiny is petitioned and vocation becomes more apparent. The South Node is a vital key to unlocking the treasure chest of untapped talents and potentials that can be focused and directed at the North Node.

An Axis of Destiny
The northern pole of the Moon's nodal axis is often aligned with the Sun, as its inclination is to promote the conscious understanding of one's vocation. At this node both desire and destiny are magnetized through forward striving and movement. Like the head, which is the seat of consciousness and the container of the brain, the North Node is the rational pole and the one facing towards heaven. Yet its mythic image is a severed head, disconnected from the body, symbolic of its disassociation with the earth and incarnation. In its lower manifestation it is the serpent brain, unanchored intellect or a head without a heart. It is the pole that takes in and devours yet, being severed from the body, is unable to digest the contents. Therefore the labours of the North Node need to be mindful and conscious. North Node experiences are illuminating and awakening, but are unable to be developed without conscious intent, mentorship and divine intervention. Without the awareness and will to continue to develop

the North Node, the individual may regress to the instinctual comfort of the South Node.

This southern pole of the axis is homeostatic; instinctively at the South Node we return to stability. It is the counterweight that prevents us from capsizing, the ballast on our life journey. Therefore the nodal axis can feel like a game of snakes and ladders, because once we have experienced the enlightenment of the North Node we slide back to the familiarity of the South Node.

The axis's southern pole can be likened to the Moon and the past. At this node we experience instinctive knowledge developed from our understanding of what went before. The South Node is a point of release and any planet conjunct this node seeks release in the service of the self. In its lower expression the South Node is overwhelmed by the past, as here is where the retraction into unconsciousness is most likely. Yet within this familial place are the souvenirs and endowments necessary to make our destiny a success.

Like a tail, the South Node is a relic, often seen to be of little use, but ironically brimming with wisdom. Having been severed from the body, the tail holds what has been digested from the past, yet, to be of any use, its contents must be disgorged or they ferment and become toxic. By nature the South Node is a homeopathic riddle, as its contents are potentially helpful yet at the same time may be toxic. It takes a heroic act to dislodge the contents and employ them in the service of the individuation process. No wonder the hero emerging from the belly of the dragon is a common motif in mythological narratives.

We could also reflect on the North Node as a summons to participate and cooperate in our life journey. The North Node is where effort must be exerted to learn what needs to be developed and made conscious. For vocational purposes we could view the North Node as a symbol of what demands to be anchored and directed in the world. Unlike the South Node it is not instinctive and therefore needs to be recognized before it can be applied.

The South Node is in the opposite sign of the North Node. Both signs are innate qualities needing to disseminated and used freely in pursuit of our destiny. It is providence, a gift of inherited qualities from the past, that can be used as resources for the future. It symbolizes what must be utilized in the conscious attempt to fulfil one's purposefulness. The South Node acts as a dissemination point for what is becoming conscious at the North Node. In a way the South Node brings to mind the need to contribute this energy to the familial and social realms, the world at large. Since this energy is instinctual, it is not necessarily always consciously directed or purposefully used.

The lunar nodes are important to consider in a vocational analysis because this polarity in the horoscope represents an axis of destiny. The polarity of the signs embraced by the North and South Nodes describes important qualities in the vocational expression of our lives. The house position of the nodes will illustrate the environmental factors that shape and influence our destiny. The North Node's house position directs us to consciously participate in this area of life where inner and outer worlds collude with our destiny. Since the North Node is the place where we momentarily may experience the transcendent and spiritual aspect of the self, its house position maps the place where these experiences may happen. The North Node does not have a cumulative effect; in other words, experiences at this place are not sequential, but more arbitrary. Due to its subjectivity and entanglement with the paradoxical world of spirit, revelations at the North Node seem to happen out of the ordinary. The house position of the North Node suggests the setting where the encounter with the spiritual self may occur.

The South Node in the opposite house describes a familiar place, an area of safety, and a comfort zone which supplies an anchor. However, it is also a place where we can become caught in the safety zone of our complacency. It suggests an area we must leave in order to develop and explore our pathway in life. Another metaphor we could use to define the nodal axis is that it is similar to a tramline: the North Node is the destination, the station where the tram is headed, while the South Node is the departure point, the station where we embark.

Combining both factors of sign and house establishes a more individual profile of the essence that needs to be to recognized and developed so as to actualize an individual's potential pathway. What follows is an examination of the lunar nodes by house and sign to help you reflect on your own vocational pathway. Although the nodes in a sign polarity will have a similar expression when placed in the natural house polarity that is associated with these signs (such as the North Node in Aries being similar to the North Node in the 1st house), it is important to remember that the signs suggest qualities embedded in the character. Therefore, the sign position of the nodes will speak to an essential aspect of the individual's destiny that is experienced as part of themselves. The house position of the nodes illustrates environmental factors that impact an individual's path. These factors can be literalized in the environment, encountered in the physical body, the emotional atmosphere or through psychological states. Combining both factors of sign and house establishes a more individual profile of the essence needing to be developed so the individual can put their vocation into action.

For instance, the North Node in Aries suggests the need to consciously develop the independent and entrepreneurial aspects of the self because there is an inherent concern for others, suggested by its South Node partner in Libra. The house positions of the nodal axis point to the arena where this task will be experienced. Imagine this that North Node is in the 6th house; then this suggests that the independent, active and pioneering approach to work and employment will support the individual's personal development. The South Node in the 12th house implies that there is a well developed compassionate concern for others, an insightful ability to tend to the human condition; but the focus needs to be on the independent development of satisfying the daily life (North Node in the 6th house) or the individual will become enmeshed in the chaos and unexpressed expectations of others.

Before we consider the themes of the lunar nodes in both the signs and houses of the personal horoscope it is helpful to have a picture, metaphor or key to reflect on the nodes and what they may reveal through their natal placements. In considering the Dragon's Head we might begin to envisage the North Node as the calling to be heroic, to develop the ego strength and identity to be able to master and assimilate the regressive and destructive forces of the past. At the South Node is the dowry, the gift that needs to be made available. To begin, reflect on the northern pole of the axis as being the invitation while the southern is the gift; the sign polarity will help to bring this to light. Here is a short summary of the twelve polarities and a discussion of the nodal polarity by sign.

The Lunar Nodes: The Invitation and the Gift

The NORTH NODE ☊ The Dragon's Head What needs to be developed **The invitation**	The SOUTH NODE ☋ The Dragon's Tail What needs to be disseminated **The gift**
☊♈ Risk-taking, adventure and initiative promote success; therefore, you are invited to be courageous and daring. The heroic battle is to fight off the regressive instinct to keep the peace and please others.	☋♎ Relating skills and mediation expertise are well developed. Being involved with others is natural, yet becoming more self-focused will add to your vocational success and personal relationships.
☊♉ Feeling that you can rely on your own assets and skills is essential. Your invitation is to develop self-worth and value in yourself and your assets. Depending on others' security and capital triggers the dragon battle.	☋♏ You understand the emotional motives and desires of others and are successful at partnering and sharing. However, your maximum potential is realized when you feel valuable and allow others' resources to promote your talents.
☊♊ You are invited to widen your network and disseminate your knowledge through communication. Fight the instinct to understand, because this will emerge through your learning and application of data.	☋♐ Born with a breadth of understanding and intuition, you have the gift of knowing what is right. As a natural educator and instructor it is important to apply what you know to your own projects.
☊♋ A successful vocation involves interdependence with those you love and protect. You are invited to stay close to home in order to be fulfilled, fighting off the dragon's need for acknowledgement and approval.	☋♑ You have a natural ability to structure, build and be responsible for yourself and others. Having inherited a strong tradition you are in the position of initiating others into the clan. Your gift is your ability to lead and take charge.

☊♌ Your invitation appeals to your inner child who seeks expression through playfulness, spontaneous expressiveness, innovation and creativity.	☋♒ Inherently, your gift lies in knowing how to be a team player, supporting and encouraging others. Your personal creative projects will be productive and beneficial to the group at large.
☊♍ You are invited to create daily routines to promote wellbeing. You are fighting the dragon of selflessness, but to be heroic you must make sure your service is acknowledged and that you are rewarded for your work.	☋♓ It is natural to know what others feel and to try to fulfil their longing. But your task is to follow your yearning to disseminate your creative, imaginative and original talents through your work.
☊♎ Your invitation is to be mindful of opposing viewpoints. The warrior needs to be gentle; the crusader needs diplomacy. Your dragon battle is against the tides that pull you back to an independent and individualistic point of view.	☋♈ You have inherited a fiery and independent will, knowing what you want and how to get it. But to know yourself means you need to forge relationship and a cooperative spirit of equality, becoming a warrior for others as well.
☊♏ Your invitation is to trust that you will do the right thing by yourself and others. Your dragon fight is with the urge to become possessive and controlling by reining in your emotions and your resources.	☋♉ You have an inherent sense of worth that is expressed through your generosity of spirit. The spiritual law of getting back what you give certainly applies to you in both emotional and mundane matters.
☊♐ You are called to make information meaningful and inspiring through education and mentoring. You battle the dragon of facts and statistics by using your intuition, farsightedness and perception to make a difference.	☋♊ You have accumulated a tremendous amount of information, facts and data. However you are not just an apprentice and learner, as your destiny will pull you towards becoming an educator and a visionary.

☊♑ Your invitation is to be responsible and authoritative in the leadership of others. You might like to slip back to being cared for; however, destiny decrees it is your turn to be the parent in the driver's seat.	☋♋ You have the gift of support, whether that is from a wide family circle, a clan of colleagues or a tribe of friends. Your vocational path may lead away from home, but your sense of belonging enables leaving to find your destiny.
☊♒ You are called on to develop your humanitarianism. Stepping away from singular creative pursuits into communal ones provides the best venue possible for your talents and creativity to flourish and mature.	☋♌ You are an original; a classic, as they say. Ironically, you become the star of the show when you focus on the needs of the group. You find your heart's desire through the lighting of communal fires, not solely your own.
☊♓ You are invited to let go of all the details so that a larger picture may be revealed. You may struggle with the dragon of perfectionism and self-criticism in heeding the call to service.	☋♍ You have a knack for detail but are prone to becoming obsessed by perfection until you recognize that you are part of a bigger picture and in the service of a much larger mission.

☊♈ The North Node in Aries

Your tendency to avoid altercations or confrontational situations means you may compromise your own desires, leaving you feeling angry and unfulfilled. It is important to recognize that your difficulty in putting yourself first actually ignites the tension between yourself and others in your workplace. Therefore, it is important to know that co-workers appreciate decisiveness and clarity. Ironically, you are complimented and supported when you take the lead, as those around you know they can count on you to do the right thing by everyone.

At the South Node, the Libran scales remind us of this sign's propensity towards judgement. Psychologically, this is the path of discovering how to value and appreciate through comparison with others. Vocationally, this instinct to judge can be utilized in professions where arbitration, a keen perception or clarity of thought is important. Libra is also skilled in conflict resolution, negotiation, relating and communication, which suits professions that involve personnel recruitment, adjudication, political negotiation, counselling, consulting and judging. You are fulfilled when you can negotiate a truce, resolve an awkward situation or introduce the right person into the right situation. It is this instinctive counsellor and mediator who needs to be used in your vocation in an entrepreneurial and active way. You like to be in accord with others yet you are called on to be identified for your personal thoughts and ideas. This is part of the paradox of your vocational quest: in order to leave the herd you need to confront the displeasure of offending others.

☊♉ The North Node in Taurus

Vocationally, there is a need to be occupied with what is crucial and important; to feel you can get to the core of your tasks and uncover and expose what needs to be changed. You have inherited a knack of being able to manage crisis and to repair what has become ill or damaged. You could also be adept at enabling others to delve deeply into themselves to uncover negative patterns, and are astute at healing and in therapeutic situations. Now these innate skills need to be focused and one of the best ways is with a hands-on approach. Your sensual nature needs to be harnessed in your vocation, and whether that is through building, gardening, singing or massage, your depth of connection with the physical world shines through.

You need to be able to trust those you work with and for; therefore, you could hold yourself back for fear of being misjudged or misunderstood. Although you know you are able to accomplish something with your partner that you could not achieve on your own, your destiny suggests building up your own strength and security. Once you have accumulated your own resources and assets you will be in a better position to be met on the intense and intimate level that you desire. Developing patience, substance and a core of integrity helps you to feel successful. Wealth lies in the depth of soul and intimacy that you are able to provide for others.

☊♊ The North Node in Gemini

You are innately scholastic yet, ironically, schooling may never have brought this out because it was too limiting or uninspiring. It is your own courses of study, adventures and travels that have educated you. Through your own personal experiences and training you have accumulated a large library of resources and you will need to draw on these in your vocation. By nature you are a teacher, an educator and a trainer, and your vocation is to inspire others, not convince them of your beliefs.

Your invitation is to be a correspondent with larger ideas. Since you have an innate knack of seeing the larger picture and the underlying meaning of what is going on, you are called to impart these concepts to a wider audience, becoming a practical dreamer, an everyday philosopher. Communication is a necessary part of your vocation. How you express your creativity is not as crucial as your need to articulate your scholarly and creative ideas. Any medium that can offer a venue to exchange ideas, thoughts and information is vital if you are to be vocationally content. Flexibility and the freedom to communicate are paramount. Having an instinct for education and knowledge, you are able to marry this with facts, statistics and information. This opens up occupations that involve telecommunications, the Internet, sales, specialized information, maps, atlases, books, magazines, news, reports and statistics. Your vocation may find you in many ways but it probably will be when you're on the move, in between two jobs or asking the larger questions about life.

☊♋ The North Node in Cancer

Having inherited a strong tradition, you are in the position of initiating others into feeling that they belong, whether as a parent to your child, a counsellor to your client or a helper to a person in need. Vocationally, your task is supported when there is a secure working environment, preferably one that you control. The North Node in Cancer is drawn to vocations which involve the family and its dependants, as there is a pull towards the archetypes of mother and family. This could manifest in multiple ways but the most obvious is having a vocation as a parent. However, this vocation may also be expressed through the caring and helping professions, working with children or the elderly, or creating comfort and safety through the products you create. As long as you find an outlet for your sensitive feelings through work, you feel fulfilled.

Building emotional and financial security in your vocation is very important. Both are interconnected and the more emotionally connected you are to your vocation the more financially secure you feel. You may feel anxious about your economic security, but it is always there. You have an innate ability to provide and manage your finances; therefore, it is also important to develop emotional security through your work. As your personal life becomes settled your professional life becomes more gratifying. An important symbol for you in the world is your home. Metaphorically, this is your security on all levels and also where you will experience financial gain and emotional solidity.

☊♌ The North Node in Leo

Feeling recognized, and receiving feedback and applause for your achievements and creations is highly fulfilling and propels you further along your career path. Your solid network of friends, colleagues and acquaintances will be on hand to acknowledge you if you let them. This is important as you need others to celebrate your creations and admire your performances. Self-expression and self-promotion are intrinsic to your career; you find that self-discovery and self-knowledge are forged through a creative occupation. Taking pride in what you do is important because your sense of self-esteem and confidence are linked to your work.

While you instinctually know how to be a friend it is important to develop your own identity through your vocation. As a colleague and friend you are able to listen to others but your personal creativity needs to be identified and demonstrated. So whether you produce your own play, design your own label or manage your own business, what makes the difference is that your name is attached to the creative output and it is recognized by others. Specifically, you thrive in such professions as promoter, teacher, entertainer, instructor, motivator, author and actor, where you interact with others using your creative skills and expressive talents. You need a response for your creative endeavours, a reflection from the community that your contribution has been valuable. You are learning to become your greatest support, having been a friend and champion to others in the past.

☊♍ The North Node in Virgo

Your deeply felt sense of compassion and empathy longs to be of service to others. However, this will need to be realistically focused on a career or you might risk falling into the fantasy of 'might happen', rather than the reality of 'what can happen'. Your urge for self-improvement and self-understanding opens doors to a wide range of service occupations, including health care, psychology, veterinary science, social services and holistic healing. You can excel in service industries because you have an innate creativity that brings kindness and organization into your work. While there are many possible paths you can take, your need to be in touch with the natural world is a significant part of any vocation.

You need to develop your discriminatory faculties, not as a defence against chaos but as a container for your imagination. Learning to deconstruct the whole into its various parts so it functions better is your goal, so whether this deconstruction is done through dissection, editing or criticizing, your objective is improvement. Routine and ritual are necessary in promoting a sense of coherence because confusion in the workplace is unsettling. You have an intrinsic ability to see through things, to be highly intuitive and perceptive, but your task is to organize and arrange all these possibilities into a coherent life work.

☊♎ The North Node in Libra

The spirit you have inherited needs to feel free to take action without relating to authority or being bound by rules and regulations. Its need for independence, including the need to make its own decisions, is high, so therefore you thrive in a vocation that encourages an enterprising personality. When you trust your own integrity and motives, your entrepreneurial spirit is a boon for everyone. Vocationally, this independent spirit is a vessel for others, and when you join in partnership you help your partner and colleagues to become successful and fulfilled. The classic storyline may be that your partner is recognized for his or her success, but make no mistake that you have played a leading role. Your need to act independently in the world is paramount, yet your destiny is that you must learn to temper this in relationship. Therefore, you are successful at being out front when you have another's interests at heart.

Self-image and personal identity need to be a focus in any career path. Being self-motivated, you are driven by competition and challenges from others, so you do well when you have equals and competitors. When you utilize your innate pioneering spirit you will find yourself initiating projects that help others. You have the knack for working in a managerial capacity where your vision and motivation can inspire others. Life may lead you in a direction where your gift for relating leads you towards counselling professions. You can develop the capacity to listen to others, a skill you use successfully in counselling and training. This, along with your ability to reflect, draws individuals out of themselves and motivates them to get what they want.

♋♏ The North Node in Scorpio

Your patience and perseverance can see projects through to their completion. This faculty is important in your vocation, as you may be drawn towards work that has an intense focus or depends on critical judgement. As you have an innate understanding of the relationship between body and psyche, you may be drawn to healing professions. Other avenues leading to an engaging career may be crisis management, repair or renovations, or other occupations where rebuilding and transforming the old is central. An understanding of the cycle of beginnings and endings heightens this ability to work with crisis and near-death experiences as well as in frightful and difficult rescue situations or investigations.

When you are defended or guarded you are unable to develop what you really want, which is sharing on a deep and intimate level. Your inherent sense of worth is uncovered through a spirit of generosity and sharing. Your innate resourcefulness means that money and assets will be there when you need them, and it is often by letting go of your belongings that you find they are returned to you in other ways. Hanging on to what is no longer useful or valuable inhibits your vocational development. You can never lose what you truly own; this is important to remember whenever you need to move forward and liberate the past.

♋♐ The North Node in Sagittarius

What pulls you towards your destiny is your quest for meaning, a deep desire to understand life. To discover your pathway in the world you need freedom of movement and lots of opportunities to be mobile to activate your journey. Opportunities for growth, advancement and learning, as well as your intuitive and strategic abilities, need to be fostered no matter what career path you choose. You need to know that you have an infinite range of possibilities, a freedom of movement, wide-open spaces and a limitless promise of discovery in your career.

While you might feel comfortable in your familial environs, destiny lies outside. You are called to be more visionary and far-seeing than you may feel comfortable with. You are called further afield from where you began, learning in a cross-cultural milieu that expands your understanding of life. Your idealism and interest in social education and reform may require that there is a degree of social involvement in your occupation. But philosophical and humanistic views of the world also need to be utilized; then, an enthusiastic energy that inspires and motivates others emerges. Vocations involving the dispensation of knowledge, sales, motivation and encouraging others to perform beyond their limits are natural for you. Your need for freedom and the necessity to fully express yourself to pursue your goals openly and honestly is important.

☊♑ The North Node in Capricorn

Unconditional qualities like caring, sympathy and empathy are second nature to you. Vocationally, tradition and the past need to be honoured, yet not to the extent of hindering a new order which needs to emerge. Organization, structure, boundaries and discipline are imperative on your career path. A professional approach is important, backed by training and qualifications. Even though you may be naturally competent and capable, you need to recognize the importance of investing time and energy into developing your career. Setting realistic goals within a reasonable time frame may help to appease your perfectionist streak and tendency to demand a lot of yourself. You need to battle the dragon of feeling parental for the whole system, as this will impede your own ability to succeed.

The possibility of advancement and reward for dedication and hard work is vital to you. Being identified, responsible for your own area, having a title, approval and feedback, and having regular reviews and mentoring help you to find security on your vocational path. If too much pressure to succeed was placed upon your young shoulders you may recognize that the path you have taken into the world was designed by others' needs and expectations, not yours. Your invitation is to develop autonomy and authority, knowing you will support and nurture yourself in the right direction.

☊≈ The North Node in Aquarius

Underpinning your personality is a self-assurance that you are loved, but to deeply know this truth your vocation leads you into the community. Humanitarian ideals are an important aspect of any vocation; however, your vocational ideals may lead you into involvement with humanitarian pursuits or organizations sympathetic to charitable, ecological or animal concerns. While individualism is of high importance you also need social interaction, intellectual stimulation and personal interchange. It is of prime importance for you to express your individuality in the work sector, to feel unique and independent in whatever you do; therefore, vocations that are different, even marginal, are the ones that catch your attention. With your innate confidence, you are not afraid of being on the fringe. If your working atmosphere is too rigid, authoritative or emotionally demanding you rebel either through shock tactics, acting out or simply leaving. You need to feel unrestrained in your occupation and work best in a democratic structure, not a hierarchical one.

While you need social involvement to feel successful, this does not mean you need to feel attached to what you do; in fact, you are probably happier at work when you are separate from others. Therefore, in a work environment you appreciate the social interaction but do not necessarily develop intimate emotional bonds. The more space you have in your working life, the more successful you become, because without space you may feel frantic and suffocated. When you draw on your reserves of self-confidence and conviction in your talents, you create opportunities in your vocational pursuits.

☊)(The North Node in Pisces

With the North Node in Pisces you may face confusion and disorder; yet when you realize you are instinctively systematic, your fear of chaos subsides and you become more relaxed. Being centred and organized helps you to construct appropriate boundaries. Your career needs to incorporate creative and spiritual aspects; however, this is often difficult to achieve in day-to-day work. Hence your creative work may be done behind the scenes, emerging in its own time. To do this you need to fight the dragon of self-criticism. You have aspects of yourself that are ordered, centred and contained, and being critical corrodes these resources. Being careful, at times meticulous, is what can support your magical and spiritual labours.

In any vocation the need for privacy is high because you need the opportunity to get lost in creativity. Unless you can consistently tap into your internal spiritual springs you feel drained by the demands of life, confused and directionless in your work, disappointed that the world does not reflect your compassion. Therefore, being alone gives you the timeless possibilities you yearn to develop. Your invitation is to apply boundaries and control in service of your creative and spiritual vocation.

The Lunar Nodes: Destination and Departure

When considering the nodes through the houses, I use the metaphor of a tram track. The well-worn grooves of the South Node will be in the house that is the departure point, while the destination of the North Node is the house where we are heading. Below is a brief summary of the nodes before we amplify their house position in your horoscope.

The North Node: The Destination Point	The South Node: The Departure Point
1st House A focus on the self to increase vitality and develop the personality	**7th House** Placing the needs and desires of siblings, partners and friends before our own
2nd House To value the self, honour and develop skills; to build and maintain our own resources	**8th House** Emotional, psychological and financial support from others; debt and emotional control
3rd House The clarification of ideas, attitudes and thoughts; to be active socially and in relationship	**9th House** Intuitive concepts, outdated beliefs, innate understanding and the eternal searching for answers
4th House Home is where the heart is; to travel to what is familiar and safe	**10th House** Knowing that the world is within you and that you take it wherever you go
5th House Taking a risk; the playground and the recreation centre are the stage for self-expression and creativity	**11th House** The support and backing of friends, colleagues and community who await the announcement of your success

6th House The everyday, workaday routine provides continuity, coherence and well-being	**12th House** The chaos of doing it all and being everything to everyone is left behind to creatively live an ordinary life
7th House Relationship and partnering in an equal way; sharing and working together	**1st House** The single life, focusing only on your own needs, independence and individuality
8th House An intimate understanding and being involved in something larger with someone else	**2nd House** Your dependence on possessions and assets, fear of change and need to be self-sustaining
9th House A cross-cultural exploration through travel, literature, study or spiritual realization	**3rd House** The complexity of ideas, the significance of details and the constant need for stimulation
10th House Your vocation is your intention and the target for your steady aim	**4th House** Leaving home allows you to meet your destiny in the world; belonging is intrinsic to your nature in many ways
11th House The community, the circle of friends and the company of colleagues	**5th House** The solo performance, the soliloquy, the lone performer and the need to be centre stage
12th House The creative and spiritual life; an imaginative and compassionate way of being in the world	**6th House** The fear of confusion and complexity, the need for order and control of the environment

The North Node in the 1st House

There is a delicate balance between being focused exclusively on yourself and on someone else. While you might be very comfortable compromising your position to please others, it does not work to your best advantage. As the scales may instinctively tip to the side of others, your task is to know your own mind and become clear about what you want. It is necessary to construct your own game plan, forge your independence and know that your life partners are naturally supportive of you, no matter what you decide to do.

You are discovering who you are on a very individual basis. Personal development becomes vital in feeling that you are fulfilling your life purpose. Using your inherent understanding of others and your fluency in social situations to focus on your own goals will help you to reconstruct relationships in a renewed and more fulfilling way. Vocationally, you need to strike out on your own, knowing that significant others, especially your partners, friends and siblings, are backing you. Ironically, the more you assert yourself and voice your point of view, the more you gain in terms of partnerships and relationships.

The North Node in the 2nd House
You may get entangled with others' assets before clearly defining your own. This could simply suggest that you are adept at handling other people's money and investments but need to be more aware of building your own wealth and capital. On an emotional level this could indicate that you become deeply involved with others. However, being therapeutic and intensely aware of others' needs may deplete your own emotional reserves. Professionally, this suggests that your capacity to successfully build up others' capital resources must be aligned with your own needs. Vocationally, this hints at a resourceful career in the healing, research, financial or investment sectors.

'What am I worth?' is an important question to ask on your road to enlightenment. Finding the answer to this question, along with developing your self-esteem, is the invitation offered by your nodal axis. Your task is to develop your own resources, skills and wherewithal. It may be tempting to rely on the emotional, financial and material resources of others but security is not there; instead it lies in your values and the journey towards finding your own resources. With a well developed sense of self-esteem and value you are more likely to find the intimate relationship in which to share your self and not feel ripped off. But until you have developed that sense of self-worth there may be a risk of counting on others who are not skilled emotionally nor financially. Therefore it is wise not to trust or rely on others until you know you can rely on and trust in yourself. The course of your path in the world echoes the theme of trust, security and value, learning to respect your innate sense of worth. Once you learn to manage your own power and abilities you will find that others will want to invest in your resources.

The North Node in the 3rd House

Knowing how to coordinate and collate information so that it can be communicated effectively to others is one of the tasks suggested by this aspect. You need to know that the world around you is not haphazard and that you are not pursuing pointless connections or unnecessary detours. This suggests that you need to be aware of your immediate environment and its boundaries, exploring its environs before you are confident enough to travel around further. Curiosity and interest expand your territory and push the boundaries, but it is important not to be sidetracked by impossible schemes, vague philosophies or charismatic ideals. Finding your place in any system is important. Originally, this may have been with your siblings or friends; however, vocationally, it is important to be aware of your place in the corporation and with co-workers and colleagues. The culture of the workplace is an important consideration for you and therefore you might take some time before you settle into a routine. Your early work experience is broad and you might have to exhaust some wanderlust before you can establish yourself professionally.

You have a worldly intelligence. You instinctively understand cultural and philosophical complexities and are more comfortable than most with the bigger picture. You might feel like a citizen of the world, not bound to your place of origin. Vocationally, you may be challenged to express and disseminate this understanding, whether that is through written or oral communication, the creative arts or another form of dissemination or broadcasting. One of your developmental tasks expressed through your vocation will be to challenge yourself to be articulate about what you know. Like a journalist, you may find yourself expressing the complexities of human nature to others who do not have your level of understanding and far-sightedness. Your nodal invitation is to express your vast understanding in a succinct and everyday language, translating the imaginative into the practical.

The North Node in the 4th House

Your private and public lives are in focus and the contrast between the inner and outer worlds invite you to lead a balanced life in both. Your natural tendency might be to find it easier to be in the world, being public and focused on your career trajectory; hence a career theme might be an ongoing encounter between the stress of the outer world and finding enough time and space to engage with the needs of the inner world. In real terms this might be the tug of war between your career and your family, outer achievements and inner peace, or the feeling of being successful versus the feeling of being settled.

Destiny points to the need to consciously create a strong and secure base before launching yourself professionally. It is important to recognize where your foundation stone is located, as you will need a strong rock upon which to build your career. Interestingly, the effort involved in stabilizing yourself, delving into your feelings and maintaining a supportive family life will promote your vocation. Ironically, your outer world opens its arms as you make the effort to develop your inner nature. Taken literally, this might suggest being successful at a career involving family, such as a family business, working from home or the promotion of familial products or values. Another variation on this theme might be in real estate, homeware or even a nurturing profession. Regardless of how fate weaves her pattern, the two threads of career and family are primary. Innately you have a successful relationship with the world and what it has to offer when you secure your nest and family life.

The North Node in the 5th House

Individual imagination and self-expression are contrasted with group participation and communal creativity. The pole of collectivism may be innately more comfortable than personal expression and creativity; therefore, your vocation may bring you to a crossroads to promote your own creations and innovations rather than having your originality used for corporate ends. Destiny supports the development of your own unique, original designs and suggests that when you find the courage to be self-motivated, the voice of the community will encourage and egg you on.

The emphasis in your career is on personal self-expression and creativity, encouraging you to learn new creative art forms and skills. When you liberate yourself from being concerned about what others think or feel, your playfulness emerges. Some name it the inner child, others spontaneity; whatever term is used the mood describes the playground where you can explore and participate in your imagination and creativeness. Destiny provides the audience; you need to do your best with your spontaneity, creativity and optimism. Whether this is focused on the theatre, the creative arts, production, entertainment, sports or children, you belong in the spotlight. It might not feel comfortable, but it is where you need to head. If you draw upon your own experiences as a child – what it felt like being a child or just your own vulnerabilities – you will be inspired. Hence your vocation is coloured with innovative and novel ideas, and when you let yourself be stimulated by them you find community support. Metaphorically, you are like an artist demonstrating your art to a welcoming public.

The North Node in the 6th House

Order versus chaos is thematic, suggesting that the process of ordering, sorting, discriminating and focusing are important themes in your everyday experience. Since work is an aspect of the everyday, you will encounter these matters in your occupation. One of the first considerations of any vocation would be that it supports your need for coherence, direction and productivity. An open-ended job description or an undefined work schedule with no budget or goal is not suited to you. You need to know what you are doing. Being in the moment, mindful of what you are working on and supported by the techniques and structures that you are using is important. Without this, you might feel pulled back into the rip of confusion or lost in a hazy fog which keeps you from applying yourself to a useful outcome.

In terms of work, you are suited to tasks that demand your attention, details that involve you in the moment and routines that can be managed. Innately, you have an understanding of health and well-being and may even feel pulled to this professionally. You also have a knack for bringing order out of chaos and therefore may be drawn to jobs that need overhauling, improving, even perfecting. Deep inside you know you have a fertile imagination and depth of understanding, yet you are invited to use this to solve the complexity of disorder and the riddle of mismanagement. Development of your managerial and business skills will always be useful. Having the gift of inner sight and depth of feeling, you are invited to use these in a pragmatic and constructive fashion.

The North Node in the 7th House

The focus on the self and the other is an embedded feature of your vocation. While your chart suggests that you may be more inclined to follow your own desires than to compromise, the life task focuses on relationships, be they intimate or business partnerships. Therefore, to feel that you are an independent soul, free of the need to be involved with others, becomes an unhappy deception. You have a strong spirit and a well developed independent streak, but to find fulfilment these now need to be directed towards relationships.

Time invested in others will be rewarded because focusing on others will bring out your true nature. Relating and the interchange with others become satisfying; therefore, in your vocational quest your partners, associates, colleagues and workmates play a significant role. You love a contest and the challenge now is to master relationship. Even when facing your adversaries, your challenge is to find the middle ground by developing reconciliatory strategies. This suggests you are well suited to managerial and leadership roles, as you have an innate sense of being able to take risks and confront difficulties. Effort is needed to remain focused on others; however, when this is accomplished your mix of entrepreneurial skills and enthusiasm contribute to you becoming a leader in your field. Independence, freedom and adventure are the innate aspects you bring to your vocation.

The North Node in the 8th House

You may find it easy to be self-made and independent, but you feel that others do not meet you equally with wealth and resources. You might be able to trust yourself with your feelings and bank account, but are not so sure that you can trust anyone else. Your challenge is to trust yourself enough to be open and intimate with others. The task is to merge your skills, resources and hidden aspects with another's in order to feel complete. Trust, loyalty and integrity are challenges that await us in the 8th house and these are encountered through a deep emotional bond that confronts our vulnerability. The invitation of the North Node is to face this challenge and not get fixed in the safety zone of your own assets, where you are able to be generous, giving and resourceful. Your kindness and generosity may be your defence against being vulnerable. You might be asked to risk losing in order to take a chance on loving.

Vocationally, your assets are better invested in working with others and forging deep and trustworthy connections. You have an instinct for what is valuable and when you share this talent with others you find that you become even better off. Call it luck or fortune, but providence has blessed you with an innate sense of resourcefulness for the purpose of helping others to feel secure. Your vocational path intersects with the spiritual, emotional and financial needs of others.

The North Node in the 9th House

This nodal dilemma contrasts the sphere of ideas and information with meaning and imagination. You instinctively gather statements, pieces of evidence, figures, statistics and information, and in your vocation you will be called upon to make these facts meaningful. With the North Node in the 9th you are called to expand your horizons, remove yourself from your familiar surroundings and look further afield. There are broader issues, wider social parameters and cross-cultural attitudes that want to be developed vocationally. Therefore, you might become involved in travel and adventure that exist outside the normal bell curve; you might find yourself drawn to the study of different religions and cultures so as to understand other people's philosophy of life; or you might be challenged to learn human values and ideals by becoming educated in the ageless traditions of human aspirations. Your soul urges you to take flight into the search for meaning and the pursuit of higher values. To do this you need to develop a vision and not get trapped by the details of the smaller picture.

Your comfort zone lies in getting involved in detailed information and ideas, rather than exploring the larger picture. However, your vocation probably calls you away from the safety zone of all its familiar connections. Vocationally, you might be challenged to step away from your schoolmates, your friends and neighbourhood to find what feels as though it is missing. What you need to discover lies outside these familial and cultural safety sectors. While your career may lead you into information technology or the world of ideas, your destiny will be to infuse these areas with significance and imagination, educating and awakening others to greater meaning. Your nodal invitation is to become an educator, inspiring others to become more of who they are. Your gift is that you have an instinctual way of expressing this in a language that others understand. Your strategic capacity provides maps for others to follow on their journeys through life.

The North Node in the 10th House

The disparity between the inner and outer worlds forces you to find a meaningful alliance between them throughout the course of your life. Your natural tendency might find it easier to be at home, private and involved with your family; however, the importance of your role in the world encourages you to focus on your vocational pathway. Meaning will be found outside the familial environs, not inside them.

Even though you may find it daunting or uncomfortable, effort is needed to develop your career path. If you reflect on it you will realize that you have an innate sense of feeling safe and grounded, therefore it is time to take your sense of self out into the world. Ironically, when you manage this task you are met with acknowledgement and acclaim. Your ambition is strong and you will not be satisfied with underachievement. The unlived life awaits you in the public sphere but you need to know this will not interfere with your need for privacy; recognize your innate ability to be public without compromising your integrity or privacy. Although you may be comfortable with your familial roles it is necessary to find your social responsibilities: you may know your place in the family, but it is time to know your place in society. Astrologically, career is a focus of your life and one that can provide stability and completeness in being.

The North Node in the 11th House

Although you may be more comfortable being personally involved with your own creativity, it is necessary to become more aligned with community concerns. Vocationally, your path leads towards being involved in group projects and undertakings. Therefore you need to strive to integrate your originality with the social climate in the environment. Ironically, although you are passionate about your own ideas and beliefs, your path takes you into the political arena where the voices of the people and the community need to be heard and supported. You have the capacity to be a voice for a larger collective; therefore it is important to know that others will respect your views and beliefs.

It is valuable to know that you will be well received and admired in the community when you heed the call to become more involved in organizations and group efforts. Turning the spotlight away from your own need for acknowledgement and applause to follow your strong humanitarian impulses will be beneficial for your career. You need to be involved in a cooperative so you can exchange ideas and information and bring your unique enterprise into the public domain. Your creative talent is both exclusive and original, finding colleagues through like-minded associations which are often marginal or out of the mainstream. It may be through your participation in communal action that you find a greater purpose and direction. No doubt others will acknowledge your social role; therefore it is important to consider others' invitations to speak publicly about your creativity, join the executive of the society or represent the group in some way. Vocationally, your creative expression is ultimately tied to the wider community of artisans, healers, visionaries and entrepreneurs. Your voice adds weight to the acceptance and respect of your creative endeavours.

The North Node in the 12th House

For the ancient Greeks, chaos was a different concept from the way we understand it today. Chaos was the void through which creation emerged and therefore it was honoured as the seminal moment in cosmology. In this respect, your 12th house North Node suggests that it is important for you to face your own creative potentials, because they appear limitless. It invites you to make an effort to understand your own psyche, the soulful part of you which is as deep and mysterious as the ocean, called to learn how to swim and navigate the depths of your inner world. It is comforting to know that your discriminating instincts are well developed and it is important to find the courage to understand your own limitations that inhibit your exploration into the inner goldmine of your creative possibilities.

Vocationally, you may feel drawn to the rich world of the imagination, wanting to utilize it to express your artistic talents, your healing abilities or your creative ideas. However, you may get caught up in your own self-criticism and scepticism, or become so involved in details and routines that you abandon your own ingenuity. At this juncture a deep sense of grief or loss calls you back to explore your own inner depths and fears. Your vocation is not something you can know; however, it is something that can be. It exists outside conventional structures and limits. In fact, you are more inclined to know your purpose when you step out of your routines. When you are on holiday, taking a risk, away from your routine or trying something different, you might hear that voice that beckons you towards understanding the mystery of yourself. That voice is the call of vocation.

Aspects on the Nodal Journey

Planets aspecting the nodal axis demand our attention, especially if they are conjunct either pole. When a planet is conjunct the North Node its archetypal energy pulls us towards our destiny. It invites us to consciously apply this archetype to actualize our life goals. At the South Node a planet may be regressive, holding onto the past or undervaluing the resources in our life. At the South Node it takes a concerted effort to focus the planet in the service of the self. Through disseminating the natural energy stored in the planet, the life direction becomes more apparent.

Planets that square the nodal axis suggest the need to incorporate this energy into the destiny. A time-honoured way of thinking about this square was that the planet was at its bending, a moment in the cycle when a change of direction occurred. From a traditional point of view, planets at the bendings present critical issues that change the course of one's life. Planets at the nodal bendings mark turning points in emotional situations, changes of attachments, transitions of home and belonging. But from the dragon's point of view they are archetypal challenges that the hero must encounter. These planets are vital keys to understanding our habitual behaviour, instinctive responses and compulsive patterns, and they summon us to excavate the depth of the self to find the treasure. In terms of the vocational path this planetary archetype at the bendings is a challenge that needs to be consciously integrated and acknowledged. It is key to the changing fortunes of life.

Here are descriptions of the lunar nodes when they aspect planets in these powerful arrangements in a natal horoscope.

☉☌☊ The Sun Conjunct the North Node

Your profession is integral to your identity. Whether you are identified for your passionate views, your leadership, your creative output or even your name on a designer label, the focal point of your vocation is you: your creativeness, your ideas and your imagination are your trademarks. With the Sun close to the nodal axis, you were born during an eclipse season, highlighting your sensitivity to cycles associated with the nodes and eclipses. These cycles occur every 18-19 years; therefore it would be wise to pay attention to this pattern in your life. Thematically, your life course encourages you to be valiant and courageous, to champion your spirit and creativity in the world by becoming the central actor on this stage of your vocation.

Example: Donald Trump was born a few hours before the Full Moon, with the Sun conjunct the North Node in the 11th house. The Sun on a node signifies an eclipse season and Trump was born under a lunar eclipse with the Moon conjoining the South Node in the 5th. The Moon on the South Node in the 5th is a strong image of his innate ability to speculate and take risks in the property market; yet it is his Sun conjunct the North Node that distinguishes his drive to be identified and be known for his creative and life-affirming powers.

☉☌☋ The Sun Conjunct the South Node

You have a strong sense of your own capabilities and potential. Instinctively, you are confident and courageous, undaunted by the competitiveness and criticism of the world. And even though you have a unique talent, your task is to express it, because you may feel complacent about your creativity. Unless you strive to be expressive and confident you could become lost in the daydreams of what might be. This placement suggests you already have an inherent, well developed ingenuity that needs to be disseminated in the world in order to find its full expression. Projecting your creative self wholeheartedly into the world can open doors you never imagined.

You were born during an eclipse season, highlighting your sensitivity to the cycles of the nodes and eclipses every 18-19 years. Having inherited an abundant life force that seeks to be expressed, the challenge is to believe enough in your own talent and creativity to keep discovering its limitless potential. You do not need to be fearful of losing contact with your creativity; the only way that can happen is by never expressing it.

☉□☊☋ The Sun Square the Nodal Axis

The challenge is to continually be aware of your need for recognition. As a young person this could be fuelled by a lack of parental applause or encouragement, exacerbating the need to be seen. Destiny's challenge lies in how you handle acknowledgement. Ultimately it is your own creative fulfilment and ability that seek recognition, not yourself; therefore the most effective way to guarantee this is to respect your own talent and foster your own creativity. Along the course of your career you might feel overlooked or unacknowledged, but this is a catalyst for success. Ultimately it is difficult for you to find your own way if you are only mirroring what others want; therefore, you might need to venture away from the spotlight to find your authentic vocation. Integrating your creativity and strong identity into your career are the challenges; however, it is also important not to let the adoration or adulation of others lead you off course.

☽☌☊ The Moon Conjunct the North Node

Lunar vulnerability and sensitivity are not always comfortable in the outer world. Therefore you need to build your nest in a safe place where you feel comfortable to pursue what you need to be successful, not what others value or demand.

You are called to develop tenderness and compassion, as well as nurturing abilities which can be incorporated into your work. You may be drawn to vocations that involve caring for others, healing, personal development and growth, education or counselling. These are emotionally demanding professions; therefore, it is imperative to know that this is the right direction for you. While this may not be an easy decision, you can be open to experimentation. Your need to care for others and to express this in the world could be satisfied through volunteer work, hobbies and of course as a parent, coach or teacher. What is important is that you find the place where you feel attached to your work and those you work with and for.

☽☌☋ The Moon Conjunct the South Node

Vocationally, this could indicate that you have an innate ability to care for others, be empathetic and understanding, as well as to provide a nurturing environment in which others can develop and prosper. It is important to know that you may underestimate these values, because they come naturally to you. These are talents that could be used vocationally; by disseminating these qualities you feel fulfilled.

Your capacity to understand the complexity of feeling and the emotional nature could be applied in endeavours connected with child and family development, education, counselling and healing. Having an innate regard for the human condition is an asset in management and in creating healthy workplaces. Literally, vocations involving childcare, food, health and home are suggested. Your instinct for understanding security suggests you would be able to use this in a therapeutic and practical way. While empathy, depth of feeling, the understanding of security issues and the importance of home, place and family seem natural to you, it is imperative that you use these skills and insights in your profession. In fact you will be surprised by how much better you feel when you take the risk to support and nurture others.

Example: In ancient Rome, Diana was the goddess of the Moon. Diana, the Princess of Wales, had the Moon conjunct the South Node in Aquarius. Her North Node was in the 8th house conjunct Uranus, Mars and Pluto. Diana's Aquarian Moon-South Node reflects her epithet 'the Queen of Hearts', given to her for her humanitarian care and concern, especially for causes that were not mainstream such as AIDS and injuries from landmines. With Uranus ruling the South Node and conjunct her North Node she endeavoured to do it her own way, risking her status and security within the system of the Royal Family.

☽□☊☋ The Moon Square the Nodal Axis

One of the major challenges on your vocational path is feeling secure in your work. Therefore this aspect poses the question, 'How do I find security in the transitional nature of work?' Ultimately it is your attachment to your vocation and what fulfils you that offers security, not the external workplace or your literal job. Growth and change are inherent in your career. While you may feel that this destabilizes you, it actually helps you to discover your true place. Through the changing landscape of your jobs you find an inner security in your work. Therefore it is vital to reflect on whether your particular line of work is offering you the sanctuary you really need, or have you become stuck in a routine? If you are getting caught up in others' needs this may lead you down a path that detracts from your vocation.

☿☌☊ Mercury Conjunct the North Node

As Mercury is associated with all forms of communication, information and exchange of data, the archetype plays a busy role in both your life and in the fast-paced technological era. Unable to sit still for too long, it is important for you to keep moving, therefore you are drawn to occupations that permit mobility and flexibility.

It is important to keep learning on the job, otherwise you become bored and restless. You may find that you want to go faster than the others around you or to explore ideas that no one else seems interested in. Your passion is different and seeks its own expression; your destiny is to express the thoughts, words, stories and information that are your passion. Finding the courage to convey your ideas and communicate information will work in your favour. Your fluency, whether that is articulated through writing, lecturing or communicating, is a great asset. Developing your communicative skills, expressing your ideas and becoming competent with computers and data resources is worthwhile. Ultimately, the urge to connect, share data, distribute ideas or spread the news needs to find its own medium of expression.

☿☌☋ Mercury Conjunct the South Node

You have access to an inbuilt instinct that intuits the right time to change direction or connect appropriate people and situations. It is important to recognize that the intelligence of change and the ability to link all your different experiences together in a coherent pattern exists in you. This allows you to be one step ahead of the others, adapt to a variety of situations and think things through while on the move. The trick is to activate this legacy and to do that you need to be mobile and inquisitive.

This suggests that your instinctive facility to communicate is inbred. Because it is natural you may overlook your own talents: use your ability to communicate, write, instruct and share information and facts in your vocation. Whether you use your expressive ability to market yourself, promote others, sell products, disseminate information, collect data or deliver goods, your mercurial nature needs to function freely for you to feel satisfied. It is imperative that you are able to talk, move and think freely in your work, and as you move or talk about your ideas your pathway becomes much clearer.

☿□☊☋ Mercury Square the Nodal Axis

We meet Mercury at crossroads, on thresholds and in transitional zones, disguised as the gatekeeper or border guard. His presence is felt in airport lounges and bus terminals, between leaving and arriving. His presence identifies the necessity of movement and travel in your vocation and the many different ways and opportunities in which these may materialize. You may be asked to juggle many different tasks or roles, manage diverse groups of individuals or projects, be a go-between or regularly travel for your employment. While these may challenge your natural direction or what you feel comfortable doing, they are necessary to incorporate if you are to feel fulfilled. The trickster element is an essential aspect of your vocational destiny and at important junctions you will be challenged to go in a direction you had never imagined possible. At the same time, be aware of tricking yourself into taking the wrong path. Double-check, be reflective and ask questions to help you ascertain if this is really the right track to be on.

As Mercury also challenges us to articulate and express ideas, it is not surprising that many writers including George Bernard Shaw, James Joyce, Gertrude Stein, TS Eliot, Robert Louis Stevenson, Edna St Vincent Millay, Thomas Mann and Alfred, Lord Tennyson have this aspect.

♀☌☊ Venus Conjunct the North Node

Reflect on how you work with others: through partnerships, alongside an associate or equal or as a consultant, counsellor or team leader. Venus calls you to develop the skills of cooperating with others towards common goals and objectives. In doing this you will glimpse the potential to collaborate, perhaps as a mediator, relationship consultant or service provider. Cultivating social skills is also indicated; therefore, career opportunities and directives in the hospitality, hotel, catering or other social avenues are possible.

As the lover of beauty Venus wants to be creative and artistic. Areas that appeal are design, décor, colour, fashion, entertainment and art. These avenues might be expressed through a range of careers from beauty therapy to interior design to museum curator. Venus's sensual quality can be applied to the design of gardens or food, concerts or theatrical productions. Physically, she is astute at massage and redecoration. As you can see, Venus has many avenues of expression but one thing is for sure: the urge to create works of beauty wants to express itself through your life.

Example: Ricky Martin has Venus conjunct his Aquarian North Node in the 8th house, an apt reminder of the artistic talent, charisma and creativity waiting to be directed and focused in his career. However, it is also a significant symbol for his humanitarian work and his personal romantic life. True to the nonconforming symbol, Martin came out as gay and fathered twins by employing a surrogate mother.

♀☌☋ Venus Conjunct the South Node

Venus's expansive understanding of love, beauty, symmetry, desire and value is both multicultural and profound. These resources are available to you near the southern pole of your nodal axis. Venusian resources are best utilized vocationally in a social or artistic way. You have inherited a great appreciation of culture and art and this could be disseminated through many channels, whether that is art collection, the history of fine art or through beautification. Inherently you have a developed sense of taste, knowing the value of things as well as how they are best showcased.

Design and placement are natural, as are symmetry and harmony in the environment and the knack of brightening the atmosphere. Being adept at social interactions, protocol, hospitality, etiquette and fashion, these threads of culture and beauty will weave themselves through the tapestry of your vocation. Your instinct for understanding the complexity of human interaction and partnership is another attribute you are able to use in your vocational development.

♀□☊☋ Venus Square the Nodal Axis

When on the bending, Venus strives for connection, acceptance and value, but sometimes these needs are not found on your path. Therefore it is important to recognize that self-worth and value need to be acknowledged. To be appreciated and valued in your work you need to recognize your own merit. While it may be difficult to put a value on yourself, this is necessary in the marketplace. You may also be challenged to bring social skills and aesthetic qualities into the work environment, as you may have to integrate these into your vocation. Ultimately, it is on the vocational track that you discover your creative talents and social skills; however, it is also on this path that you are likely to experience the tug-of-war between career and romance. Creative men like Vincent Van Gogh, Rudolph Valentino,

Marlon Brando, Nathan Lane and Michael Hutchence share this aspect.

♂☌☊ Mars Conjunct the North Node

You might feel drawn to take an independent and risky path, yet at the same time feel unable to initiate your life adventure. Mars on the North Node challenges you to be courageous and adventuresome on your vocational path.

You have a strong desire is to be independent in your vocation; therefore, you need to assert your opinions and goals without being held back by trivial rules and meaningless traditions. You have a pioneering spirit which needs to venture into the unknown to discover what works and what doesn't. Boredom is the dragon that you fight against, because it drains your energy and dampens your spirit. When you lose your enthusiasm for your job or profession, your will and drive are weakened; therefore, you need to set goals, take risks and be challenged in your career. It is important to keep your occupation alive and challenging and to be stimulated by the goal of what you are trying to accomplish.

Example: Lance Armstrong was born on 18 September 1971 in Dallas, Texas. His birth time is unknown, but Mars will still be conjunct the North Node. Mars in its affirmative face is ambitious to be the best it can be, highly motivated and a champion. Armstrong was a national sprint-course triathlon champion when he was diagnosed with a potentially fatal metastatic testicular cancer. Overcoming this, he went on to win seven consecutive Tour de France titles. But he was stripped of these titles after a protracted doping scandal; in its negative appearance, Mars can be scheming and underhanded.

♂☌☋ Mars Conjunct the South Node

Deep inside is the instinct to explore and be engaged in exciting activities; however, at the same time you may be ambivalent about initiating anything new. With the warrior archetype on the South Node it is best to recognize that perhaps the only choice is action. Abundant energy is available to assist you on the vocational trail and this is summoned when you are ready for action and determined to win. Activities and occupations that are challenging and demand you to be vigorous and forceful help to shape your destiny.

Discovering the venue where you can compete, take risks and be adventuresome is imperative. The gymnasium, the sports field and the marketplace are training grounds where you can learn to express and focus your power. You've inherited the thirst for adventure, so you become effective when you frame your life as an exploration. No doubt, once you push yourself forward, a strong personality emerges to lead you on an adventuresome journey in the world. This might be the inner entrepreneur, the savvy investor, the sports champion, the pioneering explorer or the inventor.

Example: Mark Spitz has Mars on the South Node in Libra in the 2nd; therefore, Mars rules the North Node in Aries. As a vocational indicator Mars aligns itself with competitive and adventurous careers such as sports. Mark Spitz is one of a handful of Olympians who has won nine gold medals in both personal and team efforts. Being in the 2nd house, the Mars-South Node is a powerful inner resource and drive for Spitz. At the 1972 Munich Olympics, when Spitz won six of his gold medals, the massacre of Israeli athletes took place (an ancient image of the amalgam of war and sports connected to the archetype of Mars).

♂□☊☋ Mars Square the Nodal Axis

To act independently and be free from authoritative regulations and directives is a major challenge on the life path. As Mars is associated with conflict, it is prudent to be aware of your reactions when you feel restricted. You are challenged with the delicate balance of respecting tradition and authority but not compromising your own integrity in the process.

How your competitive instincts could be constructively integrated into your profession is an important consideration. To have a vision, an objective and something to strive for drives you into action. Knowing this means that you can be proactive rather than reactive, setting challenges for yourself, harnessing your power and focusing your ambition. Denying your competitive urge renders you impotent and angry, reactive to the restrictions others are placing on your time and energy. Destiny challenges you to be enterprising, more independent and self-motivated. Accept the challenges along the way because they provide the tension that helps to engineer your success, but take care not to be diverted by conflict that cannot be resolved or desires that cannot be fulfilled.

♃☌☊ Jupiter Conjunct the North Node

From a young age you may have recognized your yearning to explore ideas and beliefs and find meaning in the larger questions of life. You urge to quest for something greater and leave behind the details and dreariness of an ordinary life. What you seek lies beyond your culture of origin and family of origin. Your destiny might be beyond the shores of your homeland or away from what is familiar and natural. What calls you is beyond what is known to you.

You have an urge to share your vision with others; therefore, skills like coaching, instructing or teaching are waiting to be developed. You are also able to inspire others with your passions and guide those who have not yet travelled the roads you have. Therefore education and travel, and any other forms of learning, are in your best interests. Whether you take up a foreign language, study ancient history, become devoted to a different religious point of view or travel the world, you are destined to shape a life that is multicultural. In front of you lies a wide horizon of possibilities so it does not really matter which one you choose as long as the chosen path allows you to be unlimited and expansive. Ultimately, Jupiter is a social planet, and what you are destined to do will contribute to the society around you.

♃☌☋ Jupiter Conjunct the South Node

Deep inside you see the big picture. You are able to understand the complexity of the human experience, therefore you can find meaning and order in the chaos of life. Innately you are able to contact a deeper wisdom which informs your philosophy of life. This understanding and knowledge needs to be disseminated through your work for without this abundant spirit you may feel unfulfilled, seeking satisfaction in the material world where you are susceptible to excess and inflation. Acquiring more is not the answer, nor is accumulating more knowledge; motivating and sharing with others your instinctual understanding of life is the key. Consistent with his Jupiter South Node conjunction, Cecil Rhodes established the Rhodes Scholarship, the world's first international study programme.

Your faith in the process of life can encourage others to understand themselves and the world around them. In this way you are a genuine motivational teacher and coach as well as a spiritual counsellor. You have a flair for education and the dissemination of knowledge and may find you are drawn to the sphere of tertiary education, writing or publishing. Your far-sightedness brings you into contact with other cultures and ways of being, and you are able to integrate this into your chosen career. You have an inborn sense of justice and will be called on to judge certain situations and bring insight and wisdom to them. Wherever you find yourself in life you will want to engender that place with hope, faith and meaning, seeing the greater purpose in what is being asked of you.

♃□☊☋ Jupiter Square the Nodal Axis

The nature of Jupiter suggests that your challenge is never to put limits on yourself, to imagine that all appropriate dreams are possible and to continue searching until you feel satisfied. You are called to challenge the assumptions of your everyday world, forge your own beliefs about what is important and step beyond what is familiar.

A restless feeling calls you to explore what is beyond your well-known world. Vocationally, you are asked to integrate a more cross-cultural approach and be more educated on social and political issues. This education can be formalized, although that is not always necessary. The point is to continue to learn and grow, as without this continual sense of development you feel disinterested and unchallenged. Your journeys into understanding other religions, your travels abroad or your love of literature are important threads in your vocational tapestry. Others may have been able to guide you about how to become educated in a chosen career, but it is up to you to become wise.

♄☌☊ Saturn Conjunct the North Node

Saturn sets a standard. It is that faraway goal of excellence, and when Saturn is so close to the northern axis of destiny it suggests that your invitation is to become purposeful in your life direction, become aware of your objectives and understand the nature of your ambition. You aspire to professions that encourage a need for excellence and precision. However, it is also important to keep your ambition in perspective as otherwise your need to excel might take over the course of your life.

Facing a future in which responsibility and duty are vocational challenges suggests the need to be structured and discerning, aware of the expectations from others. Occupations promoting autonomy and authority with clear-cut rules, standards, boundaries and hierarchy are highly compatible. However, systems are not always as efficient and reliable as you would wish, nor are the elders in the system as honest or competent as you imagine. Ironically, this helps you to see your own professionalism and competence. When you are able to acknowledge these attributes in yourself, others will as well. It is highly likely that you will be called on to father, lead and direct others as part of a management team.

Upon any emperor's shoulders is placed a heavy responsibility consistent with Saturn conjunct the North Node. Akihito the reigning Emperor of Japan has this placement as did British monarch George V whose great-great-great grandson Prince George of Cambridge also inherits this signature.

♄☌☋ Saturn Conjunct the South Node

An innate professionalism, integrity and being able to set boundaries is inborn; deep inside you understand quality and excellence. Innately responsible for yourself and others, you naturally understand how to take leadership and structure the situation for the best possible outcome; therefore, these attributes can be supportive of your career goals.

Inherently, your drive for excellence can guide you towards projects and courses of action where you can become masterful. Work and being occupied are essential for you but it is important not to be too concerned about the nature of your work, as you will be led in the right direction through involvement in what you do. Once you apply yourself and work hard, the rewards are there. Having an innate flair for management, planning, building and structuring could lead you in many directions. It is important not to get caught in seeking others' approval, as this may not be available no matter how hard you try.

♄□☊☋ Saturn Square the Nodal Axis

One of your main challenges is to discover your autonomy and authority. With Saturn you will encounter conventions and systems, yet ultimately how you find your own set of laws is the key. In a way, Saturn demands specialization, but the speciality you need to master is yourself.

This suggests that you will be acutely aware of the many different forms of rules and regulations and your reactions to them. While you might feel a strong need for guidance and mentoring, your experience is often quite different; not all managers are competent, not all systems are effective and not all structures are solid. Therefore, you often feel your integrity and values are at odds with the organization. Your strongest ally is time and over time you become acknowledged and respected for your integrity and hard work. Remaining true to your own values and standards is integral to your success; therefore, you are challenged to value your time and energy.

⚷☌☊ Chiron Conjunct the North Node

You are called to healing. One way in which this is possible is through your own wounds, whether those are energetic, physical, mental or emotional. Chiron's placement is an indication that you are drawn to understanding the complexity of healing and are able to develop the capacity to read symptoms and diagnose discontents.

A serious disease or difficult prognosis is often the voice that leads us into a more meaningful pathway. What is important to recognize is that you are summoned onto a healing pathway because of your own need to understand. Vocationally, it is important to consider how you might integrate education, well-being and self-understanding into your career. The amalgam of both traditional and complementary methods is necessary as this archetype bridges the instinctual with the cultured. Chiron is the archetypal force that initiates us into understanding and accepting the misshapen and marginal aspects of our self, and it is through these disenfranchised parts of our self that we find our calling.

Example: Oprah Winfrey has Chiron conjunct the North Node in Capricorn with Uranus conjunct the South Node in Cancer. Inherently her urge is to be concerned for others and she found her own unique way to satisfy this. Among her many accolades, *Time Magazine* listed her as one of 100 people of all time who changed the world. Certainly her influence brought issues into the open for healing, whether that was homosexual acceptance, co-dependency, sexual or substance abuse. Oprah's calling led her to express the healing and accepting powers of Chiron through her vibrant personality.

⚷☌☋ Chiron Conjunct the South Node

Deep inside you may feel connected to the wisdom of the ancestors. Many ancestral lines may have been severed so there is no way to confirm this except through your own feelings. This might be the source of your feelings of marginality. In this life your feelings of estrangement also arise from knowing your vocational place is not in the corporate or traditional world, but more on the margins of these worlds.

This placement suggests you may have an instinct for understanding the source of illness and wounding; therefore, it is important to respect and cultivate this in your career. While your call towards the healing and therapeutic professions may be strong, you may resist it because of your own wounds and disorders. Yet, since antiquity, healers have understood that they are called to their profession because of their own wounding. It is through the acceptance of your own troubles that you find the courage to help others. Whatever course this takes, you are able to understand the depth of human suffering because of your own.

⚷□☊☋ Chiron Square the Nodal Axis

The vocational turning points of your life are when you might find yourself on the margins or a foreigner in the system you are working in. It is at these critical periods that you forge your destiny, realizing that you feel more comfortable on the fringe or edge of your profession than in its centre.

This aspect suggests that your calling involves integrating something more subjective and intangible into your vocation. Your challenge is to embrace what has been relinquished and integrate it back into the system. You are an advocate for approaches that are not purely mechanistic, economic and based on reason; therefore, it is possible that this will lead you into an 'alternative' discipline, one that complements what is generally accepted, such as areas of unorthodox healing or therapy, unusual education or alternative philosophies. Your challenge is to integrate these with your chosen profession without the stigma of feeling like an outsider.

♅☌☊ Uranus Conjunct the North Node

Being familiar with the pull towards the unusual and non-traditional, you are invited to take the road less travelled. While it may not be the easiest or the best known path, nonetheless it suits your calling. Imagine your career path as being like a fast-moving conveyor belt, with you being uncertain about where or when it will stop. But when it does, it will be with a jolt and unexpectedly; so using strategy to plan your next career move may not always be wise because life's roller coaster has many surprises in store.

Your vocation is never static, but always growing and changing. As a spokesperson of the future you may be involved with new ideas that reshape the world around you, innovative technologies that take you beyond the limits set down by previous generations. Whatever your chosen path you put your own individuality and uniqueness into whatever you do. Although you work best independently, you seek your tribe in like-minded revolutionaries. Uranus's invitation is to step outside the box and explore, because what is outside convention is where you will hear the call. As a visionary you are called to modernize your world with your innovative, inventive and original ideas.

♅☌☋ Uranus Conjunct the South Node

You know that you cannot accept rules that have no truth, or boundaries that are unfair. However, with integrity, truth and the spirit of reform you are a natural trendsetter and voice of the future. It is this spirit that is needed in politics. You are democratic at heart, an egalitarian and moved by the plight of the underprivileged. Therefore, in your profession you are unable to tolerate rules for the sake of rules and will speak out against any injustice or unfairness in the workplace. In this way you are highly political; however, you are also very independent and need a lot of freedom and space to do your own thing in any career.

Vocationally, you are called to help liberate the workplace but first you must feel free enough not to get enmeshed or trapped in work politics. You have a gift of being able to do your own thing in the corporate world; therefore you could be the independent consultant, the self-employed IT expert, a clever scientist, innovative writer or the unconventional rock star. Find the place where you feel free enough to express your ideas and beliefs and you will find yourself making a difference. The more you are able to be independent in your vocation, the more you feel you are contributing.

Example: Germaine Greer has Uranus and the Moon conjunct her Taurean South Node, and the North Node in Scorpio in the 10th. Greer innately understands women's rights and freedom; from an early age she was compelled to write and speak on these issues. Her groundbreaking opus *The Female Eunuch* was written at her first Saturn return; at her second Saturn return, she wrote *The Whole Woman*, a sequel to her breakthrough book from the previous Saturn cycle. Throughout her adult life Greer has been a potent voice for women, but from a personal perspective she has described her greatest sadness as not being a mother. While the capability of her Moon-Uranus-South Node has been to capture the free spirit of woman, it has also remained a symbol of disconnection and a soulful ambivalence that expressed itself through her.

♅□☊☋ Uranus Square the Nodal Axis

Change for Uranus is natural, often surprising and sudden, but nonetheless an essential aspect of this archetype; therefore you may be challenged with sharp turns, unexpected detours or sudden accelerations along your career trajectory. Needless to say, your vocational path is never dull; however, this is not always comfortable. Thematic to this arrangement is your ability to be able to follow the call of the unforeseen, take risks and act independently. Your test is to embrace the unusual in your career and not fear being the one out on a limb. At critical moments you will be faced with a choice: follow the traditional trail or take the road less travelled. Your challenge is to welcome the unpredictable. Destiny demands that you create enough space in your life for what is extraordinary, cutting edge and revolutionary, and then those unexpected turns along your vocational pathway truly become roads less travelled.

♆☌☊ Neptune Conjunct the North Node

Your invitation is to make your inner world a part of your vocation. In a soulless world this is no easy feat, because it is a struggle to value what is invisible to others and honour what is subtle. Therefore it takes a great strength of spirit to pursue your artistry and vulnerability and not collapse under the sheer weight of the task.

But there are many routes to your creativity, such as through the imaginative arts of music, poetry, photography, literature or engaging in compassionate pursuits. Your task is to become one with what you do; therefore, at times you may feel lost and uncertain. The goal is never clear and constantly shifts but more than anyone you know that you want to find meaning and soul through your life work. Whatever road you take, you have a deep urge to be connected with your compassion and your creativity. It is not the easiest route as the world does not provide a lot of avenues for this archetype to be acknowledged in an authentic way. With Neptune conjunct the North Node, musicians Bob Dylan, Joan Baez, Madonna, Neil Diamond, Paul Simon, Placido Domingo and Prince all heard the Muse's call.

♆☌☋ Neptune Conjunct the South Node

You have a deep connection to the spiritual world, whether you are conscious of this or not. Feeling misunderstood, you might retreat or draw back, yet your invitation is to invite others to know your feelings and inner images. While you need time to meditate and be still, it is important that this does not diminish your capacity to be creative. Your challenge is to reveal your compassion for others, communicate your creative potential and express your spirituality.

You have many avenues available to disseminate your innate talent: nursing, social work, the ministry and other spiritual vocations, volunteer work and intuitive vocations such as a clairvoyant, psychic and spiritual healer, dream and image therapist, to suggest a few. Poetry, music, photography and camera work, film and video, dance, fashion and glamour, painting and design are also ways that the innate creative ability of Neptune can find its way into the world. These careers are not the goal, but a process which helps you bond to a deeper part of the self.

♆□☊☋ Neptune Square the Nodal Axis

This suggests that you will be challenged to continually re-imagine your vocation in order to feel fulfilled by what you do. While it may be difficult to inject some creativity or spirituality into your job, it is necessary for you to introduce this into your life or you will feel haunted by feelings of purposelessness. This can be achieved in numerous ways: a few suggestions might be volunteer work for the needy or underprivileged, a drawing or design class, playing music, dancing, dream work or tarot, or an engagement with the soul through a form of devotion. When you feel fulfilled in this aspect of your life you are better able to know how to infuse your work with meaning. Once you are able to invite the creative spirit you turn a corner in your life, bending towards feeling more authentic and satisfied. It is important that you channel your creative imagination, as without a structure for it you may find that you are bypassing your vocation.

♇☌☊ Pluto Conjunct the North Node

You are curious about what lies under the surface of things, probing for answers to the nature of life or drawn to life's mysteries, acutely aware of your depth of feeling. While you may be more inclined to withdraw into the silence of your own thoughts or find sanctuary in your own world, you are invited to integrate your passion for mystery and intrigue with your career path. You might be surprised by how many different vocations could capture your attention.

Metaphorically, your vocation is like being an archaeologist who can dig to find the buried treasure or a miner who finds the minerals embedded in the rock. Psychologically, your terrain is the unconscious and you may develop a great interest in fields like psychology, medicine, research or any other variation on the theme. Investigative vocations, medical research, agriculture, ecology and recycling are all well suited to this archetype. Pluto also suggests the power to influence the masses and transform public opinion; therefore, areas where you can make an impact on the human condition may also be of interest. What is always of prime consideration is that you remain true to your own calling and never shy away from the truth.

Pluto represents the power of persuasion for good or ill. On the North Node this can place us at important crossroads in our vocation where we are called on to make a difference. For instance Polish activist Lech Walesa piloted Poland's revolution from a communist to a post-communist state. In contrast Joseph McCarthy used his power to incite fear and hatred towards communists.

♇☌☋ Pluto Conjunct the South Node

You have inherited a powerful ability to delve into the depths and it is important that you use this ability to shape your vocation. Also crucial is that you learn to trust your instincts and be honest about your motives. When you are sincere and straightforward about your intention, the path ahead is less cluttered. The pull towards the past is very strong and all the while you keep yourself identified with feelings in the past you are unable to move into your vocation.

You need to be intensely committed to what you do, challenged to look underneath the surface of things and dedicated to finding the truth, bringing your passion and devotion to what you do. Others whose motives are dishonest or manipulative may experience you as threatening or intimidating. Because you are clear about your motives you may also feel the envy of others in your working environment. There is nothing you can do while these feelings are unconscious except be true to your integrity. Like a therapist, you naturally draw out shadows, untruths and secrets.

♇□☊☋ Pluto Square the Nodal Axis

Pluto challenges you to let go of outmoded ways of thinking about your vocation. What is past its use-by-date needs to be relinquished so that something new can replace it. This suggests that you will be challenged to leave no stone unturned, for your vocational direction reveals itself through research, digging deep and overturning what is on the path to find new clues. You need to call on the investigative and self-probing aspects of yourself for assistance. No matter what it is you do to occupy yourself, you will always be aware of the urge to go deeper, unveil the truth, probe the mystery or crack the code. This drive will come in handy for researchers, investigators, scientists, archaeologists, psychotherapists and all those who know that there is more beneath what they can see. Denying the call to look under the surface casts a black cloud across the vocational horizon; however, honouring this vocational urge to dig deeper will uncover some priceless treasures. Therefore, it is wise to heed the call to the unknown. The more you tend to this calling, the stronger you become. In this way the descent into knowing yourself is intimately entwined with your vocation; therefore, it is wise not to sidestep what appears to be difficult and demanding.

– Chapter 6 –
DIRECTION
The Angles of the Horoscope

Angles on Life
At the moment of our first breath, our personal horoscope exists. After a long and arduous migration, a child awakens to life, inhaling the spirit of the new world and beginning to live a new dream. The ancient Greeks imagined three goddesses presiding at birth. They spun, measured and cut the threads woven into the fabric of one's being. These three divinities were called the Fates; the first was Clotho who twisted the raw filaments, Lachesis assessed their length and finally Atropos severed the cords to free the spirit on their path. Embedded in each soul are these strands of life. The Fates's design, impressed upon the child's spirit at birth, is the eternal horoscope.

Astrological tradition suggests that your genesis is your life map. We think of the horoscope's outlines as a template for the life journey, a vibrant multilayered blueprint of character, potential and persuasions. The horoscope unites the earthly birth with the heavenly one. But while the child is embodied, the horoscope is not. It reflects possibility, not literality. The threads of the horoscope are given but it is the individual who becomes the weaver of their own life fabric.

The moment of birth identifies your orientation to life through four directions known as the angles of the horoscope. The horizon and meridian are the two planes that intersect with the path of the planets, or the ecliptic, to create the four directions that fasten us to the wheel of life. Along the horizon is a tightrope that separates what cannot be seen from what can. This horizontal axis is the Ascendant-Descendant angle; above is the visible sky, underneath is what is concealed. On the eastern horizon, the rising sign distinguishes qualities that are embodied through our personality; to the west, the opposite sign is setting, offering us a glimpse into inner attributes that can be seen through the reflection of others.

The meridian is the vertical line that separates the individual from others, but it also draws the spirit down into the depths of itself. The meridian intersects with the ecliptic at its highest point. The sign that culminates portrays the self in the world; the opposite sign on the lowest part of the ecliptic symbolizes life's foundation stones and represents a private and familial place. Like a compass, each one of the four angles marks out the life direction. Vocation and direction are entwined and astrologically the angles are guideposts along the course of our lives.

Your four angles form two planes of experience. The first plane is an individual and personal orientation to the world detailing personality, the spontaneous outlook on life, vitality and the natural inclination and orientation towards partnership. This is the angle of the Ascendant and is marked by the sign and degree of the zodiac rising at birth, a metaphor for one's personal motivation and therefore what personal characteristics can be brought to the vocation. Its polar position is the Descendant, the zodiacal sign and degree setting on the western horizon when Atropos cut the cord. An astrologer might read these patterns as potentials for relationship; however, in a vocational analysis this axis is important in terms of personal motivation, the ability to cooperate with others and to steer the personality along the course of one's vocation.

The second plane of experience is an inherited view of the world, shaped by ancestry and familial lines. Along this polarity the impact of the family of origin and familial expectations and influences are experienced. Embedded along this axis are ancestral patterns that shape career direction and choice. The angle of the IC reveals the atmospheric conditions of early home life and family while the opposite angle suggests one's destiny in the world, which is strongly influenced by parental and societal expectations. The natural axis of the MC-IC is perpendicular to the Ascendant-Descendant axis, suggesting that the inherited world view may not always be aligned with the personality. Where these axes cross is the centre of the horoscope, the place which may generate a third option or an amalgam of both points of view which is more individually authentic. It is here that we find a sense of balance in our lives. However, as these angles are naturally at odds with each other, this is a lifetime project.

The Ascendant-Descendant Axis: Self and Other
Birth, both literal and metaphoric, is located at the Ascendant, because the eastern horizon is where planets first rise into view after their night journey underneath the horizon. While life exists long

before birth, it is birth that marks the visible beginning of life. Birth acknowledges our separateness, independence and individuality and commemorates the transition between the divine and secular worlds. Similarly, the Ascendant identifies the perceptible personality, the way we greet life and conduct the soul's vital energies; it is the first visible qualities others see in us.

The sign on the Ascendant, planets conjunct the Ascendant and the Ascendant ruler all convey images about the atmosphere of birth, and this includes the family condition at the time. Astrologically, the Ascendant can reveal many things about perinatal conditions as well as how we instinctively confront the world. Birth is also metaphoric of the natural pattern of how we meet the world and how we operate in transition. Planets that are on the horizon, especially conjoining the Ascendant, symbolize not only conditions surrounding the birth but how this energy is called upon every time a new beginning or transition occurs. Therefore, the Ascendant plays a key role in our vocation as this is where we begin reaching out into the world, forming personality and striving forward.

Example: Angelina Jolie (see her horoscope on the next page) has Cancer rising, infusing her personality with warmth and feeling. With Venus on the Ascendant, her persona is blessed with charm, grace and beauty. The Moon, ruler of the Ascendant, is conjunct the MC, bringing the alluring personality along with qualities of caring into the public domain. Venus is the ruler of the IC, suggesting that family values and ideals are an intrinsic part of her personality. With Capricorn setting, she will discover the more pragmatic and responsible parts of her character through interaction and relationship.

If how we approach life is characterized at the Ascendant, then what we attract from life is met at the Descendant, the gateway to relating. Being opposed to what is ascending this angle is often experienced as muted, shadowy or foreign. The Descendant represents 'other', generally an equal other involved in a contract or a commitment. However, 'other' can also refer to the poorly lit aspects of the inner self, qualities that are seeking consciousness. As we are more inclined to identify with the qualities of the Ascendant, the polar qualities described by our Descendant are left to drift into the world, finding a safe harbour with those we feel drawn towards. The Descendant is symbolic of qualities attractive in others, yet perhaps still unconscious in us.

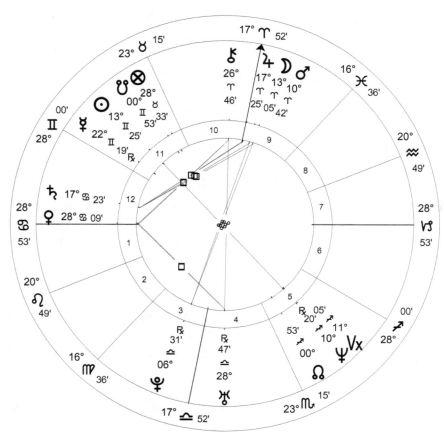

Angelina Jolie, 4 June 1975, 9.09 a.m.; Los Angeles, California

Vocationally, it is imperative to take note of the sign on the Ascendant, its ruler and any planets on the horizon which are conjunct or opposite it. These will be key factors in a vocational analysis.

The MC-IC Axis: Private and Public

Unlike the plane of the Ascendant-Descendant, the MC-IC axis runs up and down, creating a spinal column that supports the horoscope. At its base is the IC which is rooted in the instinctual self and the familial gene pool; at the top is the MC, opening out onto the world at large. From earliest times this was the parental axis, the mythological pair of opposites that foster, shape and socialize the self in the world.

The horizontal axis of the Ascendant-Descendant implies being side by side, suggesting equal relationships between the self and other, whereas the vertical nature of the MC-IC suggests top and bottom: therefore, hierarchy and authority. A power differential exists along this axis. The IC is private space; the MC is the public arena. The IC is base camp; hopefully a well secured base from which the summit is visible and reachable. The IC anchors the self to its inner and private world so that the door to the outer and public world at the MC is securely hinged. The ruler of the IC is both a guide and resource to developing internal strength and support, while planets on the IC are the archetypal forces impacting upon our sense of safety and sanctuary. When outer planets cling to the IC, forces beyond the familial and personal affect our security systems.

Example: Angelina Jolie's MC is in Aries, an entrepreneurial, adventuresome, independent and self-motivational path leading out into life. Its ruler, Mars, is in the 9th house in its own sign, supporting the pioneering and motivational urges that seek creative expression in the world. Jupiter on the MC opens up a cross-cultural meridian of possibilities. The angular stellium ruled by Mars, which also rules the MC, suggests a dynamic and forceful spirit in the world. The IC is in Libra, ruled by Venus conjunct her Ascendant, confirming that her personality and love of family will help to settle her inner life and add to her sense of privacy, safety and security.

If the IC is the touchstone for our well-being then the MC is the touchdowns of our lives, the symbol of achievement and performance in the worldly sphere. I often visualize the MC as a path continuing out into the world. It is our career, not just in the literal sense of a field of employment, but as a course through history. The MC is the access to the unfolding path of our life. I like to think of it as 'professional' or what we profess to be. It is the soul's vow in the world, anchored by the IC. Astrological intelligence helps us to maximize the potential of this axis through understanding the images constellated here. Even as children we carry the image of what we want to be when we grow up; this is not a literal image but a soulful urge to be as creative and content as we can be in our own world.

Familiarizing yourself with the influence of each angle will add to your understanding of vocation. The Ascendant marks the birth point and is metaphoric of natural disposition and outer image. This describes natural outreach and personality traits that are spontaneous; in fact, this is the person we first meet, the face turned out towards the world.

But the personality needs to find a conscious way to be with work. As the elements on the cusps of the houses of vocation – the 2nd, 6th and 10th – are naturally at odds with the Ascendant, this is never easy, nor straightforward. As a more integrated self begins to emerge, we become more conscious that what we do in the world is often in conflict with our self-perception or image of our self. A human challenge is learning to adapt the personality to the vocation. What follows are descriptions of the signs on the Ascendant-Descendant axis, recognizing that the personality needs to accommodate differing vocational demands and energies.

The influence of the sign on your MC will be amplified in Chapter 10. Any planet on the MC-IC axis plays a major role in vocation. Each angular planet could be seen as a guiding force, a *daimon* or soul force seeking expression through vocation. If there is more than one angular planet, each will have different needs and these may conflict with or contradict one another. The key is to find the right time and venue to be able to express them as fully as possible.

Rising and Setting Signs

Here are some ideas about the rising and setting signs or the Ascendant and Descendant signs. As always, these are generalized and need to be seen in the context of the full chart; however, they are a way to think about how we might reach out in life and what we might attract along our path.

Vocationally, the sign on the Ascendant is important in terms of its relationship with the houses of substance or the houses correlated with vocation. In the natural wheel, the 2nd house is semi-sextile the Ascendant; therefore, it is elementally incompatible with the rising sign. Similarly, the 6th house is quincunx the Ascendant while the 10th is square to it. This arrangement suggests that the personality emerging at the Ascendant is often challenged along the vocational path, whether that be through interviews, work routines, co-workers, bosses, promotions or any other facet of career. Therefore, while personality is a great asset on the vocational quest, it is confronted with disparities, adjustments and challenges along the career path.

Aries on the Ascendant, Libra on the Descendant

Aries rising endows you with a heroic personality, one destined for adventure and exploration. It is your spontaneity and enthusiasm that are liable to lead you to the next green pasture. While you are a restless spirit who loves to wander, a knight on a quest or a heroine with a mission, when it comes to work you may be engaged in a different story. The world of work helps you to become conscious of a more stable, detailed and traditional part of yourself. When it comes to vocation you might need to temper your enthusiasm and direct it towards more tangible results. Your personality is too fiery to be managed simply by rules and regulations, so it is important to choose a path that allows some self-determination and freedom for your restless and competitive nature.

Setting was the sign Libra, concerned with equality, fair play and relationships. Ironically, your independent spirit and urge for freedom will meet its greatest challenge in relationship. Relationships teach you that your independence and fiery spirit are at risk when trying to please others; therefore, being yourself in all encounters is the key. Part of your great vocational challenge is to find the balance. On the surface of things you appear to be an independent spirit, open to relationship and interchange, yet through work and life you find a more conservative spirit that becomes emotionally initiated through relationship.

Taurus on the Ascendant, Scorpio on the Descendant

In your perfect world nothing would change, but if it had to it would change slowly and deliberately. You are an individual of substance enjoying the beauty of nature and the pleasures of the world, seeking to share your life with others who are engaged and passionate. You need time get accustomed to anything new and time to let things settle down. It is important for you to proceed cautiously, step by step, so you can think things through; yet your work in the world may be very different, challenging you to be multitasked, interactive and visionary. It is as if you are asked to do a quick step when you are more comfortable with a slow waltz. While your personality may not be comfortable or familiar with taking on too much, your work draws you out of yourself to discover many ways of being improvisational. Your personality needs stability and structure. It is important that your choice of career assists you in being secure and stable while working in a fast-paced world.

With the Scorpion setting you are attracted to the qualities of honesty, integrity and intensity in others, seeking out partners who relate to you profoundly and passionately. However, while you want to be deeply engaged, you do not want to be possessed. Freedom and independence to explore your own beliefs, passions and studies is ultimately important and ironically you might discover this through the intense feelings that relating ignites. You are deeply committed and intensely involved, yet close to the surface is a curiosity and impatience that wants to get moving to explore the wide world. Vocation supplies you with this opportunity.

Gemini on the Ascendant, Sagittarius on the Descendant

From birth you've probably always been active. You wanted to start moving even before you knew where you wanted to go. Curious and inquisitive, you might ask a lot of questions without waiting for the answers, as these are always too slow in coming. You want to find out for yourself. Your genes may have equipped you with long legs to be as mobile as possible, a highly charged nervous system to manage everything all at once or a brain that remembers all the facts. Like the sign Gemini, your personality is mutable, changeable and able to be in two places at once. A born messenger with ideas to share yet, ironically, to feel satisfied in your lifework you are drawn into a world of feeling and complexity where you cannot think your way out or change direction when you want. Vocationally, you need to be attached to what you do, involved and emotionally secure. It might take some time to exhaust your restlessness to settle into a career path, but ultimately you do know where you are going and what you want to be, so no matter how varied your career path may be, it is meandering towards its goal. Vocationally, your path may be more involved than your personality is accustomed to; therefore, it is important for you to make sure you have your hobbies and interests which allow you to get away from the emotional demands of work.

Sagittarius setting suggests that you are attracted to the enthusiastic qualities of others, especially their independence, passion for life and search for truth and meaning. You will meet a lot of wise ones in your life, as well as a lot of know-it-alls. But you can't find the truth without running up against its shadow. Ultimately, what relationship teaches you is to find your own truth and believe in yourself. At the end of the day you are the authority and will be invested with a lot of responsibility. Curiously for someone who seems so carefree and light-hearted, your vocational path helps you to discover the more attached and responsible sides of yourself. Ironically, it is through feeling, emotional involvement and commitment that you find success and satisfaction.

Cancer on the Ascendant, Capricorn on the Descendant

You may have tentatively arrived in the world; while you still might be a bit hesitant about stepping out, you've probably matured enough to find an inner sense of safety and security. You have a knack for making others feel safe and secure in themselves. Once you have a safe nest, a support group or a place to call home, you can do almost anything. And this is how the world will challenge you to come out of your shell, because your work will immerse you in your creativity and self-expression. While your personality might be more inclined to stay at home, vocationally you are called to be adventuresome and explorative. In fact, many of your jobs might call on you to reach beyond your comfort zone and cross a cultural line into new ideas, new beliefs and ethics. So it is wise to remember that, while you like to play it safe and maybe stick close to home, life beckons you further afield from your home base and familial attitudes.

Capricorn setting at your birth suggests you may attract authoritative and capable people. Being attracted to others' qualities such as worldly wisdom and competence, you learn how to manage and structure your life more successfully. On the other hand, you could be inclined to surrender your vocational quest in order to care for others, especially those who might seem to navigate the world better. This could be self-defeating, as the qualities of authority and competence are the ones you need to develop to become more independent. Ironically for someone who would like a traditional and family-orientated life, your vocational pathway might be more innovative and entrepreneurial than you imagined. Along the way you help others to find more worth and security in themselves.

Leo on the Ascendant, Aquarius on the Descendant

With Leo on the Ascendant we might imagine you entering the world with fanfare and applause. The world needs to take note; if you want, you could walk into a room and light it up with your charm and self-possession. Creative and self-expressive, you have a knack for commanding everyone's attention, sometimes through your warmth and magnetism, sometimes your humour, but essentially simply by being you. Your personality is a natural gift that wins friends and influences people. Ironically, when you show up for a job interview the prospective employer is more interested in your diligence and discipline than your personality and charm. Herein lies the paradox. While you have an expressive persona and vital image you might have to check it at the reception room before you enter the world of work. Vocationally you are called on to develop your competency and authority. No doubt you need the passionate fire to burn at the heart of what you do, but it is more of a steady flame than you might have imagined. Satisfaction in your working life comes through your well earned accomplishments, patience and commitment. Your vibrant personality needs to support your vocational search, not stand in its way.

Aquarius is the setting sign, which suggests you are attracted to the qualities of fairness and equality in others and appreciate their differences and uniqueness. Through friendship and relationship you learn to respect the individuality of others, their different opinions and viewpoints. This is helpful as you might be called on to be a supervisor, a boss or authority. Ultimately, the world offers you the recognition and praise that you seek. When it does so you know you have earned it, not because of your charm or popularity, but because you were disciplined and committed.

Virgo on the Ascendant, Pisces on the Descendant

Virgo rising suggests an ordered approach to life. Before you venture into the world of work it is important to have a plan, a programme, a list or a map; at the very least, an idea of where you are going. You need to be prepared; once you feel you have taken all the considerations into account, you are able to relax and let it happen. Feeling relaxed is not spontaneous unless you are composed and surrounded by order. Although others might see your attention to detail as worrying, you see it as a necessary preliminary. While you have innate organizational and structural skills that will come in handy, it is likely that your vocation will involve working with others who may not be as fastidious or as ordered as you. Your workmates may not be as inclined to tidy up or be as thorough as you are; therefore, it is important not to be drawn into the chaos of others. Vocationally, you are invited to develop your social skills and can earn your living in this way. Whether this work takes you into personnel work, human resources, hospitality, counselling or a range of other people-orientated professions, you are called on to be more adaptable to others, open to changing your mind and not letting routine override variety.

Pisces is setting in your horoscope, which implies that even in your personal relationships you meet chaos and a lack of clarity in others. Your partners and close friends help you to accept that life does not run on schedule, nor is it as ordered as you might like. No doubt you are in touch with nature's rhythms and cycles; it is others who are the challenge. No wonder you may feel more akin to the animal kingdom than the human one. But this is your vocational challenge: to work with others in a capacity that informs them of the possibilities of improving their lives. And improvement is something you instinctively know how to do.

Libra on the Ascendant, Aries on the Descendant

Libra rising at your birth graces you with an attractive and welcoming personality: perhaps a bright smile, twinkling eyes or open expression. It is not these physical features but your aura of friendliness and inquiry that appeals. You are ready to be in relationship with others, listen to their trials, share their triumphs and just be together. You strive to make your environment as pleasant and peaceful as possible, being cordial and warm-hearted to everyone. And you have the knack of tolerating and appreciating the most difficult and unpleasant people. Your social skills and pleasing personality will come in handy in your vocation. However, your idealism and innocence about others will be challenged in making your living. Not everyone is as fair and just as you are, nor are they as open and considerate. You may need to toughen up when it comes to work, as your good nature is vulnerable to being taken advantage of. Vocationally, you might be called to work with others in very personal or intimate ways, so it is necessary to create emotional boundaries, be firm and professional. Your work might take you into territory that is critical and intense, where emotional strength will be demanded of you. Your natural people skills and 'bedside manner' become great assets, but on your vocational journey they need to complement a more discriminating and critical part of yourself.

On the opposite side of your birth horizon is Aries, suggesting that through relating you will find the ability to be more independent and self-willed about what you want. You are attracted to the autonomous spirit and competitive drive in others and naturally can complement their independence. You learn from others about your own will and desire, and this comes in handy when you want to break out on your own, have a tough decision to make or need to stand up to an intimidator at work. Your personality is designed for relating but through your vocation you also learn that others not always share your justice or values or have the same good intentions at heart.

Scorpio on the Ascendant, Taurus on the Descendant

Scorpio rising brings a quality of power and gravitas to the forefront of the personality. Perhaps you are fiercely private, having no time for small talk. If so, you may be characterized as being intense and unapproachable. The truth is that you are wary of becoming too close or overly engaged too quickly. Trust is important to build over time and when it is established you are loyal and true. Sincerity and honesty are priorities and you have a knack of knowing when others are phony or inauthentic. Therefore, you may be intimidating to others, yet paradoxically they are also drawn to your depth and charisma. Ironically, in your vocation you may be called upon to share your insights and beliefs, be challenging and self-expressive. Satisfaction in your working life comes not through being private and insular but through the acknowledgement of your identity and the forging of a good approval rating. Vocationally, your challenge is to be creative and popular in the world without losing your soul. Therefore, you need to retreat from time to time. A sabbatical, not a full-time retreat, is a better option.

On the other side of the horizon is Taurus, acknowledging that you need to be balanced by a stable and grounding partner. Therefore you are attracted to others who can help you to build your life but who are self-contained enough not to interfere with your vocation. These qualities of stability, durability and reliability are developed in yourself through relationship. Ironically, once you find your own inner rock of stability you are free to enjoy a variety of relationships and friendships. Therefore, while you might feel more inclined to closet yourself away, your vocation is found through exploration, expression, learning and developing. And when you are not looking, praise and recognition come your way.

Sagittarius on the Ascendant, Gemini on the Descendant

Optimism and faith are innate and permeate your personality. In some ways you are a born idealist, as you can find a positive meaning in every circumstance. Everything has a reason if you look hard enough, and you do. As an imaginative thinker you are able to see what others can't see. You have the knack of seeing a metaphor in each situation and reading signs and omens that bring meaning to life's experiences. Buoyed by your enthusiasm and certainty, people are attracted to your ideas, innate knowledge, intuitive flair and the way that you view the world. Your personality is well suited for inspiring others, educating and bringing consciousness into the world. Vocationally, you are asked to structure and document your ideas, be more disciplined and grounded and become more discerning and analytical. When you marry wisdom with hard work your beliefs and ideas take on a more pragmatic form that can be applied and utilized. In some ways your career experiences help you to channel and express what you already know. Since your personality may take some time to adjust to routine and structure, the earlier phases of life might be filled with wandering, travelling, experimenting and studying, all in the spirit of your finding your niche in the world.

Along the way, with Gemini on the Descendant, you will meet others who help you to find the missing pieces of your theories, lend you the right book, teach you important information, introduce you to the right teacher; all assisting your vocational path. You are attracted to other people's turns of phrase, their ideas and stories, their brightness. In interacting with them you are better able to shape your own ideas. Interestingly, you might find that you become a colleague and friend to the teachers who inspired you, becoming their equal in the world of ideas and understanding. Your vocational path forges and shapes your instinctive knowledge and improves the way you express your ideas, which in turn contribute to a greater understanding of being human.

Capricorn on the Ascendant, Cancer on the Descendant

Capricorn rising bestows an innate sense of reserve and control. Structure and tradition are important and this is evident in the way you reach out in life. Convention and the law are also strong pointers on your path. You may choose to rebel against strictures and regulations. An encounter with authority is inevitable, but at least you do it on your own terms. The Fates have determined your role as the elder, the responsible one; therefore, duty and obligation are characteristic features of your life experience. But when it comes to your vocation you are encouraged to be more risk-taking and adventuresome, more cooperative and flexible. Behind your life experiences you may have always felt responsible for others, so it is a welcome relief that you need only to focus on being responsible for yourself in your career. No doubt your natural managerial skills, your autonomy and maturity will be a bonus, but you are challenged to stretch yourself into becoming more of an independent thinker on your career path. You are ambitious to do the best you possibly can and your great challenge will be to find your own standards and goals. You are sensitive to other's expectations, guidelines and ambitions for you, but you need to respond to what is right for you, not others.

On the other side of your birth horizon is Cancer, which draws you to the caring, empathetic and sensitive qualities of others. Through your relationships you learn not to be so tough on yourself and find a place to belong. It is important to nurture a sense of belonging and familial experience in order to feel secure in reaching out into the world. Relationships help to instil an inner sense of security so you can be anchored in the world, where your individuality and flexibility will be keys to success.

Aquarius on the Ascendant, Leo on the Descendant

Aquarius is the sign of both the nonconformist and the humanitarian; therefore, these qualities permeate your personality right from birth. Your birth bestows a sense of uniqueness and differentness upon you. You don't do things just because you are supposed to but because they are the right thing to do. Whether through circumstance or character, you have always been independent and experimental and this has given you an ability to feel separate and non-attached. From an early age you were used to change, especially sudden changes in atmosphere and security, leaving you feeling that it was best not to get too attached to the way things were. But vocationally this may be quite different, as you might discover your urge to be involved and deeply connected, whether that is through your creativity or your compassion. While you might have to confront your urge to be separate in your vocation, being different and one of a kind adds to your rate of success. On your career path you are challenged to not let your independent spirit and rebelliousness interfere with being devoted to what you do.

When Aquarius is rising, Leo is setting, so the other half of the equation suggests that you are attracted to the confident and creative qualities of others. Relationships help you to become connected to your own self-expressiveness and to highlight your unique talents. It is important that you do not get stuck being the admirer of others' talents and skills, but be inspired to discover your own. Others will help you to find your own creative flair as well as the urge to improve and work with it.

Pisces on the Ascendant, Virgo on the Descendant

Pisces on the eastern horizon implies that the veil between the incarnate and heavenly world is thin, imprinting the newborn with sensitivity to their surroundings. Being so tuned in and receptive to the atmosphere suggests that you are vulnerable to being influenced and taken advantage of by others. Sometimes it is difficult for you to figure out where you end and someone else begins, because the boundaries between you and others get easily blurred, leaving you feeling confused and lost. Like a chameleon, you can shape-shift to suit the environment, which is good for hiding and not being seen, but not all that helpful for being visible. Ironically, your path into the world will confront all that, because vocationally you are called on to be much more direct, identified and opinionated. Satisfaction in your working life will not necessarily come through being accommodating and sensitive to others, but in being more challenging, entrepreneurial and adventuresome. You may even find the courage to strike out on your own; therefore your challenge is to use your idealism and vulnerability in service of yourself. No doubt you need to be employed in an environment which respects the human condition and is sensitive to its employees; however, you do not want to lose yourself in others' expectations.

On the western horizon is the opposite sign of Virgo, which suggests that it is through relationships that you will be able to learn the art of discrimination and how to order the chaos that arises in your life. This also suggests the importance of relationships with workmates and colleagues in helping you de-stress and debrief.

Relating to and communicating with others helps to prioritize what is important. You are sensitive to the critiques of others but it is important to recognize that these are probably not as tough as your own. It is by feeling equal and communicative with others that you are able to find the depth of relationship.

Angular Planets: Planets on the Horizon

When a planet conjoins an angle it acts as a sentinel, guarding the threshold between one direction and another. It can also act as a guide or master of the direction that it faces. Its influence permeates this life direction because the sign's qualities are impacted by the presence of an archetype. We could imagine this planetary archetype taking over, exerting its strength over the life course. Being so dramatically placed, highly visible and apparent means that angular planets can dominate the horoscope's terrain. We might imagine that they are in the driver's seat, like a powerful *daimon* affecting our life path.

A planet on the Ascendant shapes the personality, making its presence known through behaviours, mannerisms and characteristics of that planet. It expresses itself through the personality and body. Being a surrogate for the planetary archetype, the individual expresses its nature in the immediate environment. A planet on the Descendant is a mirror for the fading light, finding its expression through projection and identification with others or through events that reflect back unconscious characteristics. The Descendant is dusk, when elongated shadows expose what was unseen in the daylight. A descending planet is a guide into the mysterious, unrecognized qualities of the self. Being highly erotic in its urge to connect and relate, it manoeuvres its way into other people's lives.

From a vocational point of view, angular planets are a high priority as they seek overt expression through the individual's life direction. Here are some ideas about planets on the angles; however, these would need to be considered in the context of the whole horoscope. You may also find it helpful to refer to the planetary correspondences to career as discussed in Chapter 2. Use these ideas to muse and reflect on the potency of angular planets and how they may reinforce certain directions in life.

Sun Rising

You were born when dawn broke; the Sun was rising in the east and radiating its first light of day at your location. Another day was reborn. This is a powerful moment of transition symbolizing youth, vigour, charisma and power. The Sun infuses the personality with warmth and vitality, which becomes a great asset on the vocational path. Self-will and self-assurance are instilled as well, although when confidence or self-esteem is lacking these qualities may be used defensively. With the Sun on your Ascendant, your strong and vibrant personality needs to be harnessed to serve your creativity and passion. Natural leadership and fathering skills can be developed through your career, as you will probably be asked to take a leading role in whichever direction you choose. Your confidence, optimism, courage and resilience are vital keys to finding and maintaining a fulfilling vocation.

Sun Setting

At sunset, dusk brings a more settled and quieting atmospheric change. You were born as the Sun descended in the west on the threshold change between day and night. While you might be more inclined to notice creativity, confidence and self-assurance in others, these are also well developed in yourself. Perhaps it is wise to remember that you may see both positive and negative qualities in others before you are able to see them that you have them too. The creativity and identity seen in others reflects your own back to you. Relating is important to you and the many creative and animated people you befriend become systemic to your life. Relationship and partnership will be keys to feeling fulfilled in the world and will play a role on your vocational path.

Moon Rising

When the Moon comes over the eastern horizon, feelings are close to the surface. You entered the world at this point, inhaling the spirit of that moment. It is difficult to hide feeling uncomfortable, insecure or upset; equally, you cannot hold back your joy or excitement. Being highly sensitive to your environment, you unconsciously take on the emotions of others or feelings in the atmosphere, and are easily swayed by other's opinions and concerns. Therefore, you might be moody or reactive when your own feeling life gets entangled with others who are unable to express their true feelings. Your intuition and instincts are heightened and you are gifted with being able to read others; therefore, with adequate emotional protection, you are helpful and caring in all endeavours. The lunar archetype is out front in your horoscope, suggesting that your feelings, instincts, hunches and reactions are your best guide to the world.

Moon Setting

The Moon setting on the western horizon suggests that you are drawn to the sensitivity and gentleness of others. However, this could lead you into becoming caught up in their dependency, needing you to take care of them. It is imperative to reflect on your own needs and how you might best fulfil these yourself, as you are vulnerable to enmeshment with others who you unconsciously depend upon. Therefore, it is necessary to nurture yourself; part of this challenge would be to find what you need to do for yourself in the world. The Fates have given you a sensitivity and concern for others, but you need to figure out how to best utilize this in the direction you are heading.

Mercury Rising

At birth, Mercury appeared in the east. It was probably difficult to spot; likewise, your personality may be difficult to pin down or be seen for long. Like Mercury's elemental nature, you were born with the insight to know when conditions are hot or cold or if the current situation is about to boil over. You sense it in your nervous system, which often feels exposed and vulnerable. Yet it is your nervous energy that helps you to accomplish a great deal. You move around quickly enough to do what you want. Highly-charged and unable to settle, you need to keep moving if you are to find where you need to be. It is your quicksilver personality that helps you to find the right direction easily. Communicative and flexible, your character is geared to communicate, deliver the message and connect people and ideas. These are vocational traits that are natural for you. Mercury is in the driver's seat so it is best to get accustomed to his quick turnabouts, changes of mind and sudden interests expressed through your personality and physical movement.

Mercury Setting

Mercury was in the evening sky when you were delivered. With the god of transition on the western threshold of your horoscope, you will experience important passages and transitions throughout life, especially in the sphere of relationship. Whenever you are at a crossroads in your life you will be fortunate enough to meet the right guides, mates and friends to assist your passage. This also implies that you have an uncanny ability to counsel and communicate with others when they are experiencing their own rites of passage. It is likely that your instinctual ability to communicate will be utilized in imparting knowledge, information and guidance to others. When Mercury descends, he shepherds the initiate into their dream world. Your gifts of imagination, listening and counselling can be beneficial to your vocation.

Venus Rising

Venus rising is a blessing from the gods. But each blessing, if not used in the way the gods ordain, can become complicated. Venus, the planet associated with value and beauty, is prominent in your personality and life direction; therefore, qualities of beauty, grace, charm, fair play, equality, justice and interchange are principal features that play a major role in shaping your life course. It is wise to use the gifts of the gods to promote the values of equality, cooperation, exquisiteness and fairness. You have the potential to open many doors with your engaging personality, so it is wise to realize that you may have an advantage when suitably presented, available and interactive. Your social skills can become well developed and are assets on your vocational path. Your values are visible, so make sure you present to others the ones that you want to be known for.

Venus Setting

From the time of the earliest records, Venus on the western horizon was considered to be a favourable omen. In contemporary thinking this still is so, especially in the realm of relationship. With Venus descending you are more attuned to the goddess's favours. In a sense, this is Venus's angle as she is concerned with the sphere of relating, its pleasures and comforts. Values of equality, fair play, justice and sharing are important to you, as is the enjoyment that relationship can bring. Your life path challenges you to value relationship, strive for equality and be part of a team. It is through your relational experiences and what you offer to others that you find self-esteem and personal worth.

Mars Rising

From earliest associations, Mars has been connected to the gods of war. Mars rising at your moment of birth brings this archetype out into the open. This suggests that your personality is strongly impacted by a forceful energy. Psychologically, it is not necessarily war or conflict, but certainly competition, ambition and drive that are the hallmarks of his presence in your personality. Hence the correlation of Mars rising with sports champions. His urge is to act, to initiate and trail-blaze. Therefore, it is imperative to channel your drive and energy towards the goals that you desire. Knowing what those are or what you want to do might be the problem. The question up front is always 'What do I want?' Adventure, action and physical exertion will help to bring this into focus. It is important for you to act, to be challenged and to go after what you want in your life.

Mars Setting

Mars on the western angle of your horoscope indicates that you meet the nature of this archetype through your experience of others. Through relationship you are challenged to get what you want, be independent and assertive. The more you deny your own desires, the more that aggression is noticeable in the atmosphere. Therefore it is important to acknowledge your competitive skills and ambition, whether that is in yourself or others. Who you challenge or who challenges you is not the issue. It is that you compete: the task is to find healthy ways to be competitive. Your task is to unleash your drive and initiative so that it can energize what you want. Your independence and entrepreneurial skills need to be recognized and directed. As a vocational image, Mars on the descendant suggests that you will be challenged to be genuine in all your encounters.

Jupiter Rising

Jupiter's reputation is to be expansive; therefore, with his eastern appearance he brings a disposition that is generous and visionary. We might imagine an extrovert with a big personality or an introvert with an engaging and profound nature. Qualities of enthusiasm, open-mindedness and optimism infuse your personality, contributing to you being positive and having faith in life. Your birthright does suggest an innate trust in life and faith in the future. Your belief that everything will work out right generally proves itself to be true and offers you protection on your path through life. Grace and good luck are guardians for you. Others can see your prodigious knowledge and ideas; these are sometimes a bit inflated, but that creates enough fire for you to get moving in the right direction. For you that direction will be connected to your beliefs, ideals and human values. Vocationally, your optimistic personality and philosophical character are a boon to your employment prospects.

Jupiter Setting

Jupiter was the sovereign Roman god associated with justice and supremacy. When the planet is setting, this implies that you might find the experience of this divinity through others before you find it in yourself. Therefore, the knowledge, insight, perception, acumen and spiritual perspectives you are attracted to in others are partially a reflection of your own good judgement. You are challenged to find your own beliefs, morals and ethics in your relationships with others. This is important, as no doubt you will be called upon to be a teacher or guide for others as well. What is most important on your path is that you find your own faith and beliefs that help you to feel part of the larger picture. These principles will assist you on your vocational path.

Saturn Rising

With Saturn rising, your mother's labour may have been drawn out or stressful. The process of arrival is complicated or delayed in some way, be that physical, emotional or psychological. Not only your birth but all the other entrances of your life may be unhurried. Saturn rules time, which is essential for you to understand. It takes time for things to mature and be born at the right moment. Therefore, you are tested to be patient and tolerant about things you cannot control right from the beginning. The Fates have also given you a high degree of responsibility, and this permeates your life. Personally, you may feel short-changed in that you did not get enough opportunity to be independent and wild, yet on the other hand you are well ahead vocationally. You have innate qualities to be successful and authoritative. Match this with your ambition and endurance and you have an advantage in applying yourself to the leadership roles that are destined for you in the world.

Saturn Setting

With Saturn on the western angle of the horoscope you are probably attracted to successful people who are structured and disciplined. However, you might not be aware of the time, control and dedication that these qualities demand, leaving you feeling that there is not enough attention or time for you. Essentially, your task is to learn to become more structured, self-sufficient and masterful in your relationships. It is through relating to others that you develop your authority and find your own competence. You have a knack of befriending, even partnering, your superiors, as you are learning how to differentiate hierarchy from equality and how to delegate and lead. Vocationally, your management and people skills can be used on your career path. In later life the roles of leadership and mentoring become much more fulfilling for you.

Chiron Rising

When the Centaur rises on the eastern horizon its maverick qualities permeate your personality. While this brand may literally be a birthmark or birth scar, it is psychologically evident through feelings of marginality, foreignness and separateness. Abandonment and exclusion are often facets of this symbol; for instance, you may have been literally separated from your mother at birth, or feel alien to the familial and cultural system you were born into. Like mythological heroes you are set adrift to find your true calling to be heroic. While it may feel painful to feel separated from your tribe, your direction leads you to your adopted home. In terms of your vocation, you are a maverick, a champion of the underprivileged and a wise soul drawn to healing and the betterment of others.

Chiron Setting

Chiron on the descendant influences the realm of relationships. Part of the pattern will be the recovery and healing of emotional wounds through relationship. You may be drawn to those who are emotionally in need. Through these relationships you understand how your wounds inhibit emotional intimacy. Vocationally, you have an aptitude for working with others in a therapeutic way, empathetic to the addict, compassionate to the bereaved and nurturing of the homeless. With Chiron angular your destiny engages the complexes of others in order to facilitate healing.

Uranus Rising

Unexpected Uranus endows you with a unique perspective on life and an independent will that seeks its expression through your personality. Your originality and ingenuity, along with your need for independence, are high priorities on your life path. The highly-charged nature of Uranus stresses the physical body; therefore it is important to channel your nervous energy towards practical goals. To feel successful you need to find enough space to be able to do your own thing, feel free enough to express your radical views and feel comfortable being different. The Fates have mapped a road that few will travel; therefore, you need your adventuresome and independent spirit as a guide.

Uranus Setting

When revolutionary Uranus is setting it suggests that you may be attracted to those who are unique, one-of-a-kind, complex and highly original. That's because you are, too. This also suggests that your relationships will be out of the ordinary and that chance encounters and unusual liaisons will help you to discover and explore your true self. It is these atypical encounters that also bring opportunities on the career path. While you might not consider yourself to be unique, you certainly have a lot of unique relationships which contribute to your depth of self-understanding. Friends, colleagues and acquaintances are equals who contribute to forging your unique pathway through life.

Neptune Rising

With Neptune rising, you probably have been described as wearing rose-colored glasses. No doubt you are idealistic and imaginative, yet sometimes this is a defence against reality. For the most part, your optimism and romanticism are essential and genuine aspects of your personality; therefore, creativity, sensitivity and hopefulness are second nature. This also suggests that you may wander about in some confusion before you find the right path to take in life. But what is certain is that your direction needs to provide enough spiritual sustenance, meaningfulness and imagination in order for you to feel fulfilled vocationally.

Neptune Setting

Neptune on the western angle of your horoscope implies that you are vulnerable to projecting your idealism and romanticism onto others, becoming their redeemer. You see potential and possibilities in others, often sacrificing your own creative potential in order to develop their talents. When you relinquish your own creativeness for the sake of others your path in life becomes immersed in fog. When the romantic projection fades and the person you loved goes missing, you awaken from your trance. Vocationally, your task is to rein in your creative potential and direct it towards either being creative or helpful. The soulful qualities you see in others are the reflection of your own, which want to be channelled towards your own self-development and possibilities.

Pluto Rising

Pluto, the archetype of life and death, symbolizes your birth struggle. The impact of birth is often profound: the possibilities of life lie alongside the reality of endings. You are deeply aware of transition and what must be relinquished so as to move forward, mindful of what needs closure. Endowed with a perceptive and penetrating personality, you are acutely conscious of whether others are being genuine or not. This could intimidate others, especially those unable to be honest with themselves. At the same time it also inspires trust and loyalty, and allows you to be met openly and truthfully. Your charismatic personality can befriend you on your vocational pathway as it helps you to discriminate what is right or not for you. Being true to yourself and honest about your feelings opens doors to power and influence.

Pluto Setting

With Pluto setting at the time of your birth, you are drawn to the intensity and passion in others. You seek to be engaged and be met honestly and openly. However, it is through relationship that you begin to know the darker and repressed aspects of your nature.

Themes of trust and betrayal, love and honesty, sex and power are confronted in your relationships. No wonder you sometimes feel that relationships are like therapy. Intense encounters with others allow you to be strong in crisis, attending to those in grief, containing difficult and negative feelings and enduring difficult interchanges. Through relationship you find your emotional strength and resolve, which are useful tools on your vocational path.

Angular Planets: Planets on the Meridian
Planets on the MC influence the vocational path and authoritatively insist on being used in the world. They generate strong influences on the career as they seek expression and application on the vocational pathway. Planets on the IC are at the lowest point of the chart, securing the foundation of life communicating through dark and instinctual forces. They are experienced in the atmosphere of the family home and through the emotional attachments of our lives. Planets on the IC are the ballast of our life journey, stabilizing, de-stabilizing and re-stabilizing the course of life.

Sun Conjunct the MC
You were born near midday as the Sun reached its highest peak. Like the bright Sun you are called to shine in the world, suggesting that your destiny is to be identified through your career. Your vocation is a call to know yourself through your job, identifying strongly with your work and profession. Your career may even have you as the focus or luminary, the CEO, director or producer. Developing the solar qualities of leadership, fathering, fostering, creativity, self-expression, confidence and courage is important for you throughout your career. It is helpful to understand that, as with all vocations, there will be peaks and troughs, successes and failures, as well as critical moments of transition. The wheel of fortune rises and falls; therefore, it is imperative to be as aware of the times when shadows fall across your career path as you are of the times of light. Understanding these patterns helps you to capitalize on timing in your career.

Sun Conjunct the IC
With the Sun conjunct your IC, emotional and psychological security are your foundation stones. The quality of your father's

acknowledgement and support may have influenced the way you feel about yourself. Favouritism may also have played a key role in the family. However, it is from your family origins and inheritance that you can forge your separate identity, and this becomes the bedrock for your worldly experiences. A sense of emotional stability and the feeling that you belong both provide a supportive platform for your career.

Moon Conjunct the MC

The Moon is at the uppermost point of your horoscope, bringing a strong lunar influence to your vocation. This suggests that you may be drawn to care, protect, cultivate and nurture. While this caring will mainly be for others, especially children or the aged, it could also imply your concern for animals, plants, antiques and artefacts. You feel called to provide through a caring capacity or service. You are a born historian and collector, probably happiest when surrounded by souvenirs and mementoes that connect you to your past. Your vocational path challenges you to express your sensitivity, empathy, intuition and imagination in the world.

Moon Conjunct the IC

At your birth the Moon was at the lowest part of your chart, suggesting that you have a strong attachment to your family. However, this astrological statement does not describe how this bond feels for you, except that it strongly influences your feelings of belonging. For success in your vocation you need to feel nurtured, cared for and secure enough to feel that you are a vital part of the system you work in. Therefore, you may feel best suited to working from home, joining the family business or even working in homes or real estate. Wherever you find your vocation, the foundation stones need to be secure and firm.

Mercury Conjunct the MC

As messenger of the gods, Mercury's astrological function is to deliver the communiqué. Mercury is at the highest peak of your chart, so this task is apparent through your vocation. You are a born communicator, helpmate and guide. From an early age you have been curious enough to explore a range of paths and career opportunities. You are not limited to one because you bring your multidimensional interests to any role you play in the world. Whatever career you choose, mobile Mercury challenges you to express your ideas through one of his many channels of communication and information. This signature suggests a range of professions: lecturing, teaching, writing, information technology, statistical analysis and wherever words, outlines and movement are strategic in the industry.

Mercury Conjunct the IC

When Mercury is anchoring the base of the horoscope, mobility and communication are important aspects of family life. To feel secure you need to communicate and interact with others. Having a moveable anchor in your life allows you to feel secure when dealing with change and variety. Your sibling relationships, early schoolmates, neighbours and friends may have influenced your style of relating, impacting the way you forge friendships and express yourself. To feel secure in the world you need to express your ideas and speak your mind. Your inner initiatives and deeper thoughts are strategic to your vocational success.

Venus Conjunct the MC

Luminous Venus is at the pinnacle of your horoscope, suggesting that her values of beauty, pleasure, form, balance and proportion are woven into the fabric of your vocation. Vocationally, this suggests you are well suited to careers where design, décor, style, fashion, hospitality, diplomacy, mediation, pleasure, partnership and counselling may play a major role. You are interested in beautifying and harmonizing the environment, and whether you take an artistic, economical or social pathway to satisfy this yearning, you feel called to enhance and improve your surroundings. As the archetype of sexuality and relationship, Venus here also suggests that partnership and career may be entwined at some point on your vocational journey.

Venus Conjunct the IC

With Venus at the lower angle of your horoscope you are nurtured by beauty and need harmony and agreement in your home to feel secure. Your family of origin had a great impact on your self-esteem and personal worth, as well as helping to shape what you like and dislike. Therefore it is important to recognize and respect your authentic values so as to create a congenial and supportive base. Your attitudes towards relating were shaped in the family and these patterns may again appear at work. Feeling appreciated and valued enables you to feel worthy and creative, but it is essential that your personal values and self-esteem anchor your pathway in the world.

Mars Conjunct the MC

Mars, being at the summit of your horoscope, suggests that the entrepreneurial archetype is in high focus in your vocation. Your independent and competitive spirit needs to be recognized and fostered, along with your drive and ambition. You need challenges, direction, goals and tough training to focus your forceful instincts towards successful outcomes. Therefore, it is probable that you will be a pioneer, an intrepid explorer or a challenging voice in your chosen field of endeavour. Your vocation is your invitation to adventure and by following its path you can find the stimulus you crave to feel fully alive and satisfied.

Mars Conjunct the IC

The Mars archetype leans more towards going out than going in, independence rather than dependence, and risk, not security. Therefore, it feels ambivalent when placed on the lower meridian whose landscape is domestic and family-orientated. The interchange between individuality and belonging is highlighted in your family and a strong focus on self-determination may have permeated your upbringing. Consciousness is needed to assert the self. Self-sufficiency, standing up for yourself, being tough, and striving ahead may have been emphasized. On a positive note you have a strong base from which to launch yourself into the competitive world. Yet patterns of repressing anger, rivalry, desire and frustration may be contributing to a fearful approach to being in the world. As an adult it is important to recognize that you need to be secure when dealing with negative feelings and that they are part of the human experience and not a deterrent to being loved and accepted.

Jupiter Conjunct the MC

Jupiter, the archetype associated with philosophies, ideologies and beliefs, is at the pinnacle of your chart, suggesting that fate has placed these matters in a prominent position. You are a born educator and visionary, drawn to the dissemination of ideas that foster understanding and expansion. Your search for truth and meaning is at the forefront of your investigations, leading you down a path of cross-cultural discovery and learning. Both a pilgrim and a professor, you can gather and disseminate wisdom to help expand human understanding. Whether teacher, explorer, guide or publisher, optimism, faith and vision are the necessary virtues of your vocation.

Jupiter Conjunct the IC

Jupiter at the base of your horoscope suggests that this archetype brings the poles of familiarity and foreignness, home and the world, feelings and concepts, instinct and culture, together in your life. The urge to explore and question was shaped in the family environment. Religious and cultural beliefs, academic and innovative education, human values, hope and optimism in the future play a large role in your security. How this was accomplished in the family will influence the degree of safety you feel in the world. As an adult, your personal convictions, opinions, ethics and morals play a central role in feeling anchored enough to be yourself and to strive for what you believe in. Your beliefs and faith are the touchstones of your life.

Saturn Conjunct the MC

Saturn's tendency towards perfection and excellence is highlighted in your horoscope, as this planet was near its culmination at the time of your birth. Professions encouraging the need for quality, responsibility, autonomy and precision can channel some of this energy. However, it is imperative to consider your own standards of excellence and not be driven to overachievement as a compensation for not feeling good enough. Focus your critical faculties on work, not the self; discriminate between your personal ambitions and the goals that others might set for you. Destiny has given you the role of the elder and called on you to be an authority and a model for others. The Saturnine archetype is concerned with time and this is fundamental to your life pursuits; therefore, it is imperative to recognize that the developmental process takes time. Your vocation builds from the ground up, starting small but ending large.

Saturn Conjunct the IC

With Saturn at the lowest part of your horoscope, your home may have been full of rules and regulations. In this atmosphere it might have been difficult to know what you really wanted or needed. Therefore, leaving home, moving interstate or emigrating abroad might be necessary for you to hear your true calling, away from the expectations and traditions of your upbringing. Whether the family atmosphere was strictly constrained or had porous boundaries, you have inherited a deep sense of responsibility and duty. Your life task is to make sure that this does not become a sense of obligation towards others or a feeling of being duty-bound, but an inner sense of duty and responsibility to yourself. Your task is to set down secure enough foundations and boundaries in adult life to be able to support your vocation. Ultimately, you are your worst critic, but also your best advisor.

Chiron Conjunct the MC

Chiron's culmination on the MC of your horoscope suggests that you will be a maverick on your life path. The Fates have woven the theme of wounding and healing into your vocational sector. This might manifest as being drawn to a career in complementary medicine, non-traditional healing or unorthodox education. You are called to be heroic in your search for a fulfilling vocation. It is important to recognize that while you may be marginal and foreign in the system, you can be a significant contributor and find fulfilment and freedom. You may feel called to work with the underprivileged, the handicapped, the outcast or the orphaned.

Chiron Conjunct the IC

The Centaur Chiron is conjunct your IC, bringing his archetypal presence into your life through your early experiences of home and family. Often this suggests there may have been a schism in the family, an adoption, step-parenting, or a single or missing parent. Regardless of how fate has arranged the scenario, the common element is that you may feel foreign or estranged in your family or country of origin. A wound in the family ignites a crisis of healing and it is through your own experience of feeling disenfranchised that you are able to bring a deep and empathetic understanding to the plight of others. At the core of who you are is a legacy of healing and mentoring. Your life work is enhanced, not impaired, by being an outsider.

Uranus Conjunct the MC

Uranus, the archetype of unexpected change, is at the summit of your horoscope, suggesting that destiny has some surprises along your vocational pathway. As well as sudden twists of chance, the planet also symbolizes the urge for independence and nonconformity. It is concerned with innovation, future possibilities and virtual reality, and these can all feature in your vocation. Whether your destiny is cutting-edge technology, new and innovative aspects of the electronics industry or future-orientated science, the road ahead will be unique and very different to what you can imagine. The world is interested in your extra-ordinariness and uniqueness, so it is important to follow the bends in the road because these are the paths that lead you into the opportunities and possibilities of your career.

Uranus Conjunct the IC

At the foot of your chart is the planet Uranus, whose urge for freedom and separateness is rooted in the family. Disengagement and separation are themes that resonate when Uranus is on the IC. The possibility of a fractured or dislocated family atmosphere, or the lack of an unconditional bond, is suggested, whether perceived or real. Individuality and independence are important hallmarks in your family experience. An urge to adventure, take risks and be emotionally self-sufficient is valued; surprises and unforeseen changes were part of your familial landscape. As an adult it is important to reconcile your urges for separateness with your need for closeness, as this is a theme that will overshadow your feeling safe and successful in the world. Your independent and unique attitudes support your creative urges in the world.

Neptune Conjunct the MC

Neptune, the planet of creativity and spirituality, is atop your horoscope, suggesting that these ideals are an important feature of your vocation. From an early age you may have been aware that your calling was to be spiritually active in the world. While you may not know what this actually looks like, you feel deeply moved by the urge to be of service. In any vocational pursuit you long to find a way to express the divine. Generally this will be either through being a helper or an artist. Your path in life is never clear-cut; therefore, you need the courage of your convictions and faith in your beliefs to sustain yourself in the world. Confusion, uncertainty and not knowing where you are going are common feelings when you reflect on your career. Your vocation is a constant work in progress, but in the meantime it is important to bring the creative and spiritual aspects of your nature out into the open.

Neptune Conjunct the IC

With Neptune on the lower meridian, the ideal of the family is important to you. However, the reality may have been quite different, because enmeshment, sacrifice, relinquishment or illness could have dominated the familial atmosphere. Whatever your experience of the family, it is important to remember that emotional understanding, compassion for others in the family and for the community at large, as well as the urge to serve others, are all part of your inheritance. To build a solid nest in your adult life, you need the foundation principles of creativity, spirituality and imagination. When you have this strong base you are better equipped to support your vocational longing in the world.

Pluto Conjunct the MC

Vocations which dig deep down into literal, financial, emotional or psychic terrain, such as mining, archaeology, detection, investigative journalism, surgery, psychotherapy, taxation expertise, forensic specialities, pathology or working as a funeral director, come under the jurisdiction of Pluto. Being intensely private and contained, Pluto is uncomfortable in the public spotlight. You need to learn to contain your private life in the public spotlight and be mindful of having strong emotional boundaries between your personal and professional life. You are emotionally and psychologically involved with your career but you need to protect your own privacy. Fate asks you to channel your intensity, perceptiveness and depth of understanding into the transformation of other people's lives without exposing your own personal biography.

Pluto Conjunct the IC

Pluto, the mythological lord of the underworld is on the foundation stone of your horoscope, implying that power and influence were issues that affected the family integrity. Your family system may have had to deal with powerful issues of loss and grief, as well as taboos and secrets. Your need for truth, trust and cohesion is strong but ancestral denials and unexpressed grief in your family may complicate honest expression. To feel emotionally secure, your privacy must be respected. In adulthood, honesty in your intimate relationships and attachments support your equilibrium. Honesty, trust and integrity are cornerstones to your success in the world. When you are trustworthy, genuine and honest with yourself, you become well respected and trusted in the world.

Chapter 7

CREATIVITY AND TALENT
The Houses of Life and the Houses of Substance

My experience has been that clients seek assistance, clarification, conformation, direction and insight into their career and vocational experiences due to a lack of meaning in their job, a conflict in the workplace or feeling undervalued by their industry. In my work with clients I have experienced that deeper insights are more readily available when discussing complexities, ambiguities and uncertainties, rather than giving definitive answers or direct advice; therefore, I have become more counselling-orientated in approaching the horoscope, listening carefully to my clients and consciously suspending my need to get it right or know the answer. In participating with the client's contradictions, confusion and despair, deeper feelings behind the astrological images and symbols are revealed.

The most common motifs voiced by clients in vocational consultations are the desire to be creative and the quest for creativity. But what is creativity? And why do many feel that creativity is the resolution to their vocational dissatisfaction? It is a word often used by counsellors and astrologers in an all-purpose way. But what is meant by creativity and what is it in us that responds to this feeling?

Carl Jung imagined five main groups of instincts from a psychological perspective. These were creativity, along with hunger, sexuality, activity and reflection.[32] In discussing the creative instinct, he preferred to categorize it as a psychic factor, one more akin with the soul. Perhaps it is this soulful, deeper, resonant quality that creativity arouses in us. Creativity is like an 'X' factor that many feel will bring them a more meaningful life, yet at the same time it is mysterious and unknown.

A common perception is that creativity is akin to being artistic. Many clients feel that if they were a writer, artist, actor, poet, painter, dancer or musician, this would bring them the meaning and contentment they are seeking. But creativity is not a product; it is a process. Neither is creativity limited to the arts. Science, engineering, commerce, technology and human resources can all be creative fields; physical and mundane work, as well. The work on oneself, development and maturity also involve the creative process. Engagement in the process, not the focus on the product or end goal, is vital to creativity.

Like alchemical work, there are stages in the creative process. The initial struggle with the creative urge is followed by an interval of incubation where the pain of creativity surfaces through self-doubt, anxiety and despair. It is during this phase of anguish that seeds are planted and, if they take root, the consequence is inspiration. The final phase grounds the creative process in the world of form where it is given shape and substance.[33] The process requires both ego strength and surrender; receptivity and activity. Therefore, it is evident that creativity is not a commodity to be obtained, but a deeper psychic process that requires the ability to be open to complexities and ambiguities. Imagination and symbolic thinking are valuable, along with the capacity to be fluid and accepting. While many clients felt that doing something other than what they were doing would be meaningful, ironically it is the involvement with their current vocational process and working through its stages and troubles that becomes creative.

Being creative requires sensitivity and empathy. Its nature involves the capacity to give birth to ideas and activities, to play and imagine as well as to search for greater meaning. The instinct to create is at the heart of each vocation. Being erotic by nature, it is life-giving, fuelled by fantasy and filled with possibility. It deeply touches the core of oneself and in this way it also stirs the darkness of melancholy and depression. Our vocational development engages us in the duality of creativity: inner and outer, personal and collective, and conscious and unconscious.[34]

Astrologically, each planet could be seen to have its own special creative qualities. When locating the creative process in the horoscope, I explore the 1st, 5th and 9th houses as embodying creative development. Each of these houses addresses an aspect of the creative process, whether that is birth, self-expression, play, inspiration or the search for meaning. And each house in the trinity leads to a house of 'substance' where the creative process can be grounded and then expressed in the world. The dictionary defines 'to create' as bringing something into existence or being. Creativity is more than imagination and inspiration; it implies incarnation. This truth is embedded in the astrological wheel, because the houses of matter and substance follow the houses of creativity, play and inspiration.

The Houses of Life

In the houses of life, creation, procreation and recreation occur. These are supplementary houses to consider in a vocational analysis because they locate vitality and creativity. The 1st house contains the primal and initial urges to express the self from the inside out. It is where the self is birthed and symbolically where creativity stirs and wants to be expressed through the personality. In the 5th house we explore the interests and activities that enliven us; we play, imagine and perform, developing our ego-identity and its expression through us. In the 9th we search for meaning beyond ourselves, expanding and discovering our personal creativity in a larger sphere. Creativity and development of the self are now tempered with ethics, principles, convictions and human values.

Therefore, it is sensible to analyse these houses in terms of what creative resources support the vocation. Personality, ego-strength, the capacity to see beyond the self, along with self-expressiveness, vitality, plus an ability to recreate the self, to honour ethics and beliefs, are all aspects of these houses that enhance our understanding of vocation.

The 1st House

The sign on this cusp symbolizes the way you enter into your life experiences. These are the visible traits of your personality and the window through which you naturally view your life experience. The cusp of this house is the Ascendant, which indicates birth, the first entry into life. While the Ascendant can describe the literal birth, it is more suggestive of the births throughout the course of our lives; therefore, this angle characterizes how we give birth to our Self and our personality style that transports the greater Self into the world. This sign represents the way you meet life, and visibly how you embody these energies. The sign is a conductor of vitality and has an important role in your identity, as we have previously discussed with the Ascendant.

The ruler of the Ascendant is traditionally known as the ruler of the chart, symbolizing the helmsman, the one at the controls. Therefore, the ruler is a significant force in directing the vocation. Its placement in the horoscope shows what additional resources are available to support the personality. Planets in the 1st house are the archetypal energies encountered in the development of personality and through personal interactions. These energies are embodied in the persona, defence mechanisms, physical vitality and the way you present yourself. These energies need to be mobilized in order to steer the personality along its life course.

The creative process of the 1st house engages the personality and the developing ego in giving birth to aspects and qualities of the self that seek to be valued and appreciated. How we initiate and continue this process is our originality. The 1st house describes how we face the world, so it is here where we begin cultivating a persona that supports our vocational quest.

The 5th House

The sign on the cusp of the 5th house symbolizes natural qualities inherent in your creativity and self-expression. It suggests how you can access the joy of life and find inroads into feeling imaginative and alive. It also suggests how you might separate from your familial attachments to be free enough to express your own ideas, opinions, beliefs and world views. This cusp is the separation between the 4th house familial security and the world beyond; therefore, reflect on how you cross the threshold into your own self-exploration.

The ruler of the 5th house contributes to your self-expression. Consider the additional resources that are available to express your creativity and inspire your inventiveness and originality. Planets in the 5th house suggest unique and original aspects of your creative being. These planets are tools, resources and supplies for your adventures into self-exploration, needing to be utilized in your projects, hobbies, amusements and activities. When their potential is accessed, you feel more alive and happy because you feel closer to your natural spontaneous self. They are also important in your quest for creativity, self-expression and ingenuity.

The creative process of the 5th house involves play: not being carefree but being imaginative and animated. Play promotes personal growth, amusement and fantasy; it is motion and activity that stir both the inner world of ideas and the impulse to construct them in the outer world. When clients are struggling with being creatively stuck or feeling their handiwork is flawed or unrefined, I encourage them to pretend, like a child, that their project is play, not performance. Play engages the imagination and allows feelings of freedom and spontaneity.

For instance, Cate has Cancer on the cusp of her 5th house. Her creative project of building a glass atrium in her house was stalled. In her natal chart, Jupiter is in Cancer in the 5th house; also by transit, it was returning to begin its fifth cycle. Cate was still fixed in her ideas about what she wanted and how to be creative. So I asked if she was willing to be playful and childlike in approaching the project. I invited her to pretend that the project was starting and she was gathering together the materials that were needed. What would she do? The first step was to visit old building sites to collect unique and colourful glass windows from houses that were being demolished. When I saw her next, she had started the process. We often mistake being stuck, uninspired or self-deprecating as something being wrong, whereas it is an intricate and early part of the creative process. Play helps us to relax into the joy of creativity.

The 9th House

The sign on the cusp of the 9th house symbolizes the way you search for meaning in your life. It suggests how you approach life's adventures, such as journeying into cross-cultural experiences, what you might be interested in studying to broaden your understanding of the world, as well as your natural inclination to travel, study or even live abroad. However, it also suggests methods for finding meaning in life as well as how you might formulate your beliefs, philosophies, morals and ethics. Your faith and confidence in life is impressed by the qualities of this sign.

The 9th house ruler broadens the influences that affect your search for meaning. The ruler brings another dimension of inspiration and enthusiasm to your search for a meaningful philosophy. Planets in the 9th house underpin your quest for meaning, your philosophical search and travels into foreign territory, as well as forging your life beliefs, ethics and principles. These planets are the forces that promote your philosophical and spiritual adventures. They encourage truth and meaning, uphold human values and strive for higher principles.

They are also valuable resources in the university of life that can be used to infuse your career with faith and human values.

The 9th house creative process is searching for meaning in the wider context, philosophically and spiritually. With meaning we develop confidence and faith in the course of life. Having this perspective encourages our imagination and self-expression to flourish as we begin to be capable of recognizing a larger picture and become conscious of the duality and ambiguity embedded in the creative process. Faith, wisdom and acceptance help us tolerate the personal disappointments and vocational setbacks of our lives. The 9th house contextualizes disenchantment as a learning curve.

The 9th house is the territory preceding the Midheaven, where the career goals of our life become aligned. This 9th house sphere of the horoscope is vocationally significant since transiting and progressed planets move through here before reaching the MC. This is the 'finishing school' or the 'postgraduate' period before we become identified with our vocation in the world. When planets transit this area there is often a training, preparation and conscious movement towards the vocation. The 9th house is also where we experience being foreign and outside our familial culture in a way that supports self-development, so we become better prepared to take on our role in the world.

The Houses of Substance
The three Earth houses – the 2nd, 6th and 10th – are known as the 'houses of substance'. 'Substance' refers to the material world of matter and the ability to stand firm. It is in these houses where we become a 'person of substance' and anchor ourselves in the world. The signs on these house cusps and the planets in them play a major role in turning our creativity into talent and shaping a fulfilling vocation.

The trinity of the houses of substance represents where we inhabit the physical and worldly spheres of life. These houses symbolize both psychological and literal aspects of an everyday life, including work, routines and rituals, resources and rewards for our efforts. These are earthy environs which support and maintain our well-being. Therefore, these three houses are important in helping to amplify the unique aspects of vocation natural to each individual.

The element on these house cusps is naturally incompatible with the element on the Ascendant. If the horoscope has no interceptions then the following grid shows the relationship between the Ascendant and the houses of substance. An intercepted polarity disrupts these combinations.

Element on the Ascendant	Element on the 2nd, 6th and 10th Houses
Fire	Earth
Earth	Air
Air	Water
Water	Fire

This suggests that these houses are at odds with the Ascendant, or the way we reach out in life. Another way to think about this is that the houses of substance represent tension that shapes and modifies the personality. Accessing the resources of these houses requires consciousness and an applied effort to bring the personality into line with our physical and practical needs. The nature of these houses emphasize our ability to find ways to balance our monetary needs and income potential (2nd) with work (6th) and aspirations in the world (10th). We may be able to earn a living with our work but it may not be a fulfilling vocation. We may give everything to a vocation but it may not be able to provide an income. These areas of our lives seek to find their natural sense of balance.

To begin working with these houses in a vocational framework, take into account:

• The element or elements on the cusps of the 2nd, 6th and 10th houses. If there are intercepted signs in the horoscope there may be a combination of elements on these cusps. Note the element or elemental combination on these house cusps.

• The signs on the 2nd, 6th and 10th house cusps, and note their rulers. What signs and houses do the ruling planets occupy and what aspects do they make? Each ruling planet shows other resources, assets, needs and responsibilities that influence the house in question

- Planets in the 2nd, 6th and 10th houses. Consider their assets and liabilities.

The signs on these house cusps are the natural qualities, characteristics and experiences that support the individual in maximizing their vocational potential of each house. They also point to which energies are encountered as we cross the threshold into the atmosphere of the new house. The sign's planetary ruler is an accompanying presence in this vocational sector. Planets in the house are the archetypes that we meet on our vocational quest. They seek to express themselves through us in this area of our lives.

Elements of Substance

To begin to imagine how these houses may assist in amplifying your vocational needs and concerns, we can begin by contemplating the common element on these house cusps, or the combination of elements if there is an intercepted sign. These are not meant to be character descriptions or facts about your work, but ways to begin contemplating your natural approach to vocation. Whether you are in agreement or not, it is more important to honour and stay with this image of your chart to see what it might reveal about your vocational temperament.

Fire on the 2nd, 6th and 10th House Cusps

Fire approaches vocation in a courageous, competitive, animated and inquisitive way, empowered to know its capabilities and with an enthusiasm to fulfil its dreams. Career is a vital component of your life, especially since it complements experimentation into the self; therefore your vocation includes a sense of investigation and adventure to satisfy your urge for travel and learning. Your natural sense of exploration could be expressed through physical, creative or conceptual activities, leading you into the arenas, theatres and universities of the world. Physically, your risk-taking spirit could be expressed through sport, adventure treks or competition. Creatively, this might manifest in entrepreneurial, communicative or theatrical ways, while scholastically this could be employed through education, travel, religious or philosophical pursuits. The planetary rulers of these houses – Mars, the Sun and Jupiter – are dynamic and energetic energies that govern the vocational sectors. This vibrant triumvirate suggests you can tap into abundant energy, confidence and foresight, and bring 'oomph' into your chosen profession.

Fire demands its freedom and needs to explore new territory, which may result in many changes and moves in your career. While the initial spirit of commitment to a new job is there, enthusiasm fades in the tediousness of daily tasks, so change and a lack of routine are important vocationally. Fire needs to inspire and empower others in what they do. With Fire it is important that your vocation either provides enough competitive stimulation and challenge or you are actively engaged in exciting and adventurous projects that demand physical and mental exertion; hopefully, you have both. Five important constituents of your career are:

- **Conception** Your creative spark conceives of many ideas; talents are best utilized in envisioning and promoting future projects and goals.

- **Vision** Faith and optimism in the future, along with your prophetic talents and abilities, suit a forward-moving career in an upwardly mobile industry.

- **Intuition** You work best in an environment that respects your instincts and gut feelings, allowing you to be spontaneous and natural.

- **Enthusiasm** Your energetic and optimistic approach to life seeks its outlet in the sphere of work by inspiring and motivating others.

- **Freedom** Work that allows a freedom of movement in mind and body, travel and mobility matches your temperament.

Earth on the 2nd, 6th and 10th House Cusps

Being self-controlled and pragmatic in what you want to achieve in the world, it is important not to feel hurried or pushed by others into a career trajectory. Rushing into certain courses or careers due to stress or insecurity is not you: your natural inclination is to move slowly and cautiously. Job security is a high priority and you need to know that there is coherence and continuity in your job.

You are serious about your career and invest this with emotional and material resources, as well as the devotion of your time. The planetary rulers of these houses are Venus, Mercury and Saturn, all adept and accomplished energies. This skilful triumvirate suggests that you have abundant ability, dexterity and authority to bring to your chosen profession.

In the work environment you value fidelity and devotion, and are serious and focused at work. This is also evident in taking your work duties and obligations earnestly. Hopefully, your earlier experience of rules, responsibilities and tasks in the familial and school environments helped to forge awareness of the necessity to provide secure structures and routines in your vocation. Reflect on your attitudes to authority, commitment and structure. Rebelling against being in the world may be defensive due to the severity of rules and regulation in your early life so it is important that these defences do not inhibit your natural inclination to be comfortable in the world.

It is also important for you to define boundaries at work, having clear objectives and plans. You need to focus on your responsibilities without cutting off the life force in your job. Your routines need to be stable and committed without becoming overly fixed and rigid. It is important for you to find a balance in the constantly changing atmosphere of the work force, as it might be moving at a faster pace than you are comfortable with. Tangible results are important, but it is also imperative not to become fixated on being in control when things are not going to plan. Relaxation and taking time off are imperative because you are sensitive to somatizing work stress.

With Earth highlighted in your vocational sector it is important that your career path has a constant horizon with possibilities of growth and opportunities for advancement. Five important constituents of your career are:

- **Manifestation** Your forte is to bring creative ideas into manifestation through persistence, hard work, application and concentration.

- **Application** Being positively engaged in hands-on projects, working with details, organizing and structuring.

- **Sensation** Your instinctual connection to the five senses, the physical world and your physical well-being are important aspects to be considered in your vocation.

- **Practicality** You need to remain down-to-earth in your profession, thriving best with work commitments that are practical and have specific guidelines.

- **Stability** To be fulfilled and successful in your vocation you need to feel secure and stable in your work routines and habits.

Air on the 2nd, 6th and 10th House Cusps

Having open channels of communication and appropriate outlets to engage in a variety of interests are priorities in your vocation. You need to relate to others, so relationships are a vital element of your vocational needs. You seek a multiplicity of experiences in your career and need to share your ideas and skills in work routines; therefore, it is necessary to take into account your inquiring, reflective and interactive manner when considering vocation. The contemporary planetary rulers of these houses are Mercury, Venus and Uranus, all vigorous and independent energies that govern the vocational sectors of your horoscope. This scholarly triumvirate suggests you have abundant dreams, style and innovation to bring to your chosen profession. Saturn, the traditional ruler of Aquarius, brings autonomy and conscientiousness into the house it rules.

Even though you may enjoy the social interactions and culture of relationships at work, you also need a great amount of space, emotionally, physically and psychologically. Change is natural for you; therefore, you need an atmosphere that is not static but open, allowing you to set your own routines and schedules. Without enough space or distance between you and your colleagues, you feel stifled, unable to breathe freely. Even though you might not be aware of it, your levels of anxiety rise as more restrictions are placed upon your mobility. Stress accumulates when you feel stifled at work or when you are not given enough freedom or independence to do your own thing. If the atmosphere of work feels oppressive, the urge to separate is triggered. Therefore, it might be wise to experiment with different avenues before you settle into a work routine.

Communication on all levels is important; besides it being a function of the job, there needs to be an open line of communication between you and your co-workers, superiors and clients. While you consistently attempt to be lucid and logical in your conversations, you can become unclear when there are hostile feelings or grudges in your workplace or if you feel hurt or betrayed.

With Air highlighted in your vocational sector it is important that the career path offers a variety of possibilities and opportunities for exchange. Five important constituents of your career are:

- **Reflection** Air's ability to reflect, be impartial and detach from emotional situations are assets that seek expression through work. Your ability to theorize and perceive what is taking place in your environment is a positive feature that can be utilized to your best advantage.

- **Thinking** Your facility to stand back from the situation and rationally think the process through from conception to its completion gives you an advantage over others. Your capacity to grasp an overview of the situation is instinctive.

- **Communication** To be able to communicate, share and discuss ideas, relate to others and be social in your work environs is essential in your vocation.

- **Mobility** You need movement and freedom in your job and are fulfilled when your mind is active with many ideas, projects and a variety of tasks.

- **Space** Your need for physical, emotional and psychological space must be taken into account in both the environment and nature of your job routines.

Water on the 2nd, 6th and 10th House Cusps

Water flows towards the mysterious and mystical, and you long to use this energy in your vocation. This implies that you are capable of deep connections and are moved or motivated by an instinct to nurture, fuse or merge with others. Boundaries may become confused; therefore in the work sphere it is important to be conscious of setting appropriate limits to what you are willing to do for others. You may be attracted to the helping professions. If so, you need to be separate and pragmatic enough to be aware of how much you realistically can help. Because of high idealism and a strong compassionate streak, you may be forced to learn the difficult task of discrimination and drawing boundaries in the work sphere. Once aware of this, you have a vast canvas on which to vocationally project your creative possibilities. The contemporary planetary rulers of these houses are the Moon, Pluto and Neptune, all sensitive, profound and potent energies that govern the vocational sectors of your horoscope. This thoughtful triumvirate suggests that you have abundant warmth, charisma and insight to bring to your chosen profession. Mars and Jupiter are the traditional rulers that also bring their energy and spirited beliefs to the vocational sector.

Your power to obliterate emotional separateness engages you with your work colleagues on a deep level. This could lead to an enmeshment with others in your work environment. This arises from your ability to feel others' feelings, to serve others' needs and to care for others' insecurities. While this may come naturally to you, in a work environment others may experience this as smothering or invasive. Or, if you try to recreate a familial environment or an intimate atmosphere with your co-workers, they may not be as responsive as you might wish. It is important to consider whether you are transferring your intimacy needs onto the work sphere; however, it is also essential to reflect on how you can professionally harness your depth of feelings and emotional intelligence in your vocational aspirations.

Sensitivity, creativity, compassion and caring are qualities you bring to your vocation. You may have a strong urge to nurture; however, it is equally important to feel nurtured, emotionally secure and safe in your work. With your high degree of sensitivity you might absorb negative feelings from your work atmosphere, which can weaken and dull your spirit. Therefore, it is imperative that you create enough time to be able to disengage from the demands of your job, having moments alone to recharge and focus once again. Even though you may not yet have mined your creative potential, it is there and it inspires others. Several channels are possible: they include music, art, photography, dance, imagery, design, writing, poetry, literature, classics, myth, fashion and the theatre.

With Water in your vocational sector, opportunities for engagement, expression of feelings, spirituality and creativity are highlighted. Five important constituents of your career are:

- **Attachment** It is important for you to feel a part of your work environment and to feel connected with your workmates. The need to be needed, to belong and feel familial is important to consider.

- **Comprehension** Your ability to grasp the deeper layers of meaning and understand subtleties is a great gift that can be utilized in your career.

- **Feeling** Your sensitivity and impressionability, as well as the depth of your feeling life, needs to be acknowledged.

- **Nourishment** A strong urge to nourish and care, and to be nurtured and cared for, seeks fulfilment through your vocation.

- **Soul** Your depth of understanding and your tenacity in the artistic aspects of life seek to be engaged through meaningful and imaginative work.

Interceptions and Duplications

When using an unequal house system, the continuity of the signs on the house cusps can be broken due to seasonal and latitudinal influences, at times resulting in one or more polarities of signs not being represented on the house cusps. As well, there will be cusps where one or more polarities of signs are duplicated on the subsequent houses. This disrupts the flow of elemental energies through the houses that are naturally trine one another, bringing two elements to bear upon the nature of these houses.

If this occurs on the cusps of the houses of substance, the management of these two elements will be important to consider vocationally. Generally, the mixture of elements will be naturally incompatible. Here is a summary of psychologically divergent elements and their differences. Although we are focusing on the cusps of the Earth houses, we might also imagine these scenarios whenever these elements are combined in the horoscope.

Fire and Earth are psychologically incompatible, as Earth strives to be realistic whereas Fire is idealistic. Fire faces the future and the possibilities of what can be, while Earth is located in the present with the realism of what is. Therefore, it is this predicament that needs management in your vocational goals. Astrologically, the tension of this combination can produce high achievers and good results, as there is both vision and pragmatism. However, the tension needs to be managed so that one way of being does not override the other. Somehow you need to find the right mix of being able to dream the dream, as well as to produce the product.

Fire and Water are also unsuited; in nature, water can put out fire. To bring a more conscious attitude to understanding their differences, reflect on what they have in common. First, both elements are highly passionate; therefore, reflect on what you feel passionate about doing, not what you think you should do or what is expected of you. Secondly, both elements are idealistic in their life view. This suggests that they are creative and involved when applied. Thirdly, both are warm and engaging elements. It is necessary to be involved with what you do or restlessness develops. On the strength of these three points it is important to recognize that in order to be fulfilled in what you are doing you need to be passionately involved and free enough to express the creative elements of your being.

Earth and Air also require a conscious effort for their natures to be coordinated. In nature, we know that air scatters the earth. While Earth is comfortable being contained and stable, Air needs distance, space and mobility. This is a dilemma for these two elements, as they are focused in different directions and are often on different time schedules. Therefore, it is important that you are able to manage your time efficiently, setting schedules and making appointments but also leaving enough space in between. In your career you need to find the balance between structure and freedom, making things happen but also letting them happen. Striking the right chord between following traditions and obeying rules is necessary. Therefore, one of the tensions in your career is how to remain true to yourself in the system or organization. The mix of these elements can also produce aridity and dryness; therefore, outside work, you need support systems where you are able to feel connected and involved.

Air and Water also have a difficult time co-exiting or inhabiting the same space. Air is inclined to be objective; Water tends to be subjective. In terms of relating, Air is separate, Water is engaged; Air needs space and distance, Water needs closeness and support. This is a difficult dance; one element approaches, the other avoids. When the balance is struck you discover that you have a well developed sense of understanding the human predicament. Ironically, both elements combine to work together well in the fields of relationships, human resources, management and personnel. The key is not to feel pressured or claustrophobic in your working environs. With enough space around you, you are able to become attached to what you are doing.

When an intercepted sign is in one of the houses of substance, then the house space is larger than the others and also has three signs within its sphere: the sign on the cusp, the intercepted sign and the subsequent sign which appears on the next house cusp. This suggests that this house may be more complex and may demand more attention in the vocational mix.

Summary

Creativity, passion, adventure, artistic, entrepreneurial and caring qualities are all vocationally evident in Angelina Jolie's horoscope (see page 182). Let's recap the houses of life:

- Water signs are on the cusp of the 1st, 5th and 9th houses
- The traditional rulers – Moon, Mars and Jupiter – are conjunct in Aries in the 9th house
- The modern ruler of the 5th house is Pluto, which is opposite Mars, while the modern ruler of Pisces is Neptune, located in the 5th house
- Although there are no planets in the 1st house, Venus is angular; Neptune is in the 5th house conjunct the Vertex and widely conjunct the North Node, all in Sagittarius; the Aries stellium containing Mars, the Moon and Jupiter are all in the 9th

Similarly, let's recap the houses of substance:

- Fire signs are on the cusp of the 2nd, 6th and 10th houses
- The ruler of the 2nd house is the Sun in Gemini in the 11th opposite Neptune; the ruler of the 6th house is angular Jupiter

in Aries conjunct the 9th house Mars, which is the ruler of the MC

• Chiron is in the 10th house

The houses of substance play a major role in the vocation process. Over the next three chapters we will examine each house separately as well as the signs on the house cusps and the planets in these houses. Let's now turn to the 2nd house to explore its roles in our career.

– Chapter 8 –
VOCATIONAL VALUES
The Rewards of the Second House

Traditionally, the 2nd house is associated with money, possessions and the accumulation of assets. In a vocational sense the 2nd house profiles our earning capacity, income potential and attitudes towards resources; it is the site where the first foundations for stability and security in the outer world are laid. When astrologers are asked such questions as 'Will I be rich?' and 'How will I make money?', the 2nd house of the horoscope is the first place to consult. It is in the analysis of this house that the images of money, earning capacity, income and resources first take shape in the astrologer's mind.

The 2nd House	• The nature of your innate resources, talents and strengths • What you like to do, what you value and how you need to be valued • Your assets and resources, both psychologically and materially, as in self-esteem, personal values, income, assets, money and financial rewards
Keywords	Artistic values; Appreciation; Assets; Capital; Income; Money; Pleasure; Possessions; Resources; Self-esteem; Self-worth; Sensuality; Sharing; Stamina; Talent; Wealth
The Sign on the 2nd House Cusp and its Ruler	• What you need in order to provide a sense of security and reward • Instinctive attitudes toward possessions and money • Ways to enhance your self-esteem and self-worth • Innate strengths and resources • How you judge and value yourself • Key to psychological and financial worth and value
Planets in the 2nd House	• Need to operate in productive activities • Need to be utilized resourcefully • Support personal worth and values • Need to feel rewarded for their efforts • Value beauty and symmetry in the atmosphere of work • Create psychological worth and monetary capital

As the second house from the Ascendant, this sphere sustains and maintains the emergent personality. In context of the natal chart, the developing personality begins to be grounded. Like its natural sign Taurus, the 2nd house represents incarnation or inhabiting one's self, literally the body, its senses and its physical environment. The house is also connected to the pleasure principle. In our post-modern world, what is pleasurable often seems to require money, which is another aspect of the 2nd house. But 2nd house pleasure can also be experienced through apprenticeship and the mastery of skills and talents, not necessarily only through economic management or sensuality.

Psychologically, this is the sphere where self-esteem and personal values are shaped by family attitudes and early experiences. The 2nd house phase of child development is when the child senses taste, becomes attached to objects, responds to what they like and dislike, discerns how to voice 'mine' and develops the capacity to share, trade and exchange articles of value. Self-worth and self-esteem, the impact of familial values and the substance and significance we place upon our efforts all underpin the structure of this house and have an effect on our internal sense of value. The earliest messages about our sense of worth, skills and talents are located here. If the personal sense of being valued was unsupported, then self-esteem may be impaired, contributing to shame and/or disrespect for what may in reality be innate talents and skills.

This house locates where innate resources can be developed and valued. These resources can be physical, intellectual, emotional or spiritual; however, they need to be expressed through an everyday occupation or activity. In a literal sense, our resources are 'traded' for income or remuneration; therefore, it is sensible to recognize the natural resources and supplies situated here. Our inner reserves sustain us in our careers but, when manifested through our work, these assets materialize into rewards and revenue. A 2nd house talent not only refers to natural abilities, but in ancient times a talent was a weight of gold or a monetary unit. Traditionally, the 2nd house has always referred to rewards reaped from our talents.

Money is an archetypal reality and the horoscope provides many ways of thinking about possessions, resources and prosperity. While we can attribute many of our difficulties to money, it is our approach to and participation with it that are problematic, not money itself.

Being archetypal, money troubles are always nearby and potentially overwhelming. Our impasses with money are often reflective of our difficulties with sharing, being split between spiritual and worldly matters or our struggle with being in the world. Yet, wherever there are oppositional beliefs, there is a middle position. James Hillman supports a detached perspective towards money: 'I see money as an archetypal dominant that can be taken spiritually or materially, but which is itself neither.'[35] As he says, money is 'devilishly divine'; the trick is how we break free from being fixated in its complexities.

In a way, money is an aspect of fate. As a psychic reality we can consider our relationship with it by reflecting on its archetypal nature through an astrological lens. Traditionally, the 2nd house of the horoscope, its derivative sign of Taurus and its ruler Venus are all associated with money and the accumulation of assets. The natural 2nd house is ruled by Earth and is the first of the three houses of substance. Astrology reflects how we might deepen this area of our life and endow it with meaning by honouring the authenticity reflected in the horoscope. Money becomes the living gauge of how we share ourselves, our resources and our passions.

The 2nd house also describes what we like to do. Consider what it is that you enjoy and value: how can you create more space and meaning for this in your life? The key to the 2nd house is in valuing and appreciating innate talents and skills. In turn, these bring wealth and reward. Wealth is multifaceted and not only applies to money; for some, it is health, peace, family, security, freedom, relationship or spirituality. The 2nd house describes what we invest with value and what we appreciate.[36]

Let's look at the signs on the cusp of the 2nd house as ways to think about our resources, talents, gifts and merits, as well as ways we might learn to appreciate these. In a vocational sense, the sign on the cusp of the 2nd and its ruler(s) are important in terms of our feeling valued and satisfied in what we do. Imagine the sign as being the key that opens the door to the 2nd house, its resources and its wealth.

Signs on the Cusp of the 2nd House
The sign on the cusp of the 2nd house symbolizes personal assets that need to be valued and utilized to become resourceful and prosperous.

The sign suggests what is essential to value, the natural style of earning an income, as well as innate attitudes towards income and money. This sign offers us a key to becoming more aware of our attitudes and approach to self-worth and personal values.

In the natural wheel of the horoscope, the sign on the 2nd house cusp follows the Ascendant. As previously mentioned, the element on the 2nd house cusp is organically at odds with the rising sign. Psychologically, this proposes that our personality traits may actually conflict with our attitudes towards money, the way we earn our income and how we assess our own values. Ironically, the skills, talents and values that are resourceful could be eclipsed by the personality. One way to imagine this conundrum is as being a job interview. When your personality is in charge, your talents and worth might not be well represented, hence not promoted adequately. It is always insightful to reflect on the differences between how we present ourselves personally and professionally.

Another way that we might think of this is that the 2nd house cusp invites us to develop qualities and responsibilities that may be obscured by the personality. For instance, a client with Aries rising who was accustomed to being mobile and impulsive discovered that he became much more resourceful and affluent when he was committed, permanent and fixed in work routines. Similarly, a Gemini rising man told me that when he finally had children, emotional responsibilities and a home, he was wealthier than he had ever been when he was single. He was perplexed, as his salary had not increased and ironically he had more outgoings. A Capricorn rising woman reported that when she managed to let down her guard and be less defensive and controlling of her environment, her ability to take risks, be forward thinking and unconventional allowed her to become more appreciated at work. This is the secret of the 2nd house cusp: when we honour its essence, it becomes bountiful.

To contemplate your relationship to financial security, your innate resources and earning potential, let's consider the 2nd house sign on the cusp in its own right. Reflecting on the 2nd house is a way to consider what is authentic about your attitudes and relationship to money. The 2nd house cusp suggests ways to enhance your sense of self-esteem and personal worth. The sign may also point to what you value and appreciate, which encourages strength and stability in your work. This sign may also describe how you access your personal resources and assets, as well as the instinctive attitudes towards your possessions.

Aries on the 2nd House Cusp

Being innovative and spontaneous shapes your attitudes towards money and your relationship with it. While you may not see yourself as fiercely independent or daring, nevertheless you value these qualities. One of the most courageous things is to challenge your passivity and timidity and risk taking a chance. When you do, you discover your skills and talents. To find your own innate worth you need to cut through the confusion, challenge the chaos and proceed in spite of all the odds. Your assets are built on being free enough to explore opportunities, take risks and learn from your mistakes.

While you may not necessarily be aware of this, your relationship with money needs to have that element of risk and challenge. When your heart is in it, you feel anything is possible. As your income is commensurate with being spontaneous and courageous, you need to initiate projects in order to be successful. One of your greatest resources is your independent spirit and bravado in the face of adversity. Therefore, the best way to enhance your self-esteem and self-worth is to act on your own initiative and learn to trust your instincts. Income is not as important as the freedom and potential scope of your work. Ironically, the freer you feel, the wealthier you are.

The sign also points to what you authentically value and appreciate. Qualities you value include assertiveness, bravery, enthusiasm, initiative and inspiration. Action is the key to monetary success. You do well with a challenge; there is nothing like a global financial crisis to bring out your entrepreneurial streak. Your efforts and ability to get going are ultimately rewarded. Don't be surprised if you have an immediate response to and return for your efforts; just don't bank on this as a given. Your instincts and intuition are good guides to helping you source the right investment and the best value for money. With Aries on the cusp, investment in sport, competition, adventure, start-up, entrepreneurial and risky businesses might be worth trying.

Taurus on the 2nd House Cusp

Qualities that are helpful in securing your financial future are loyalty, perseverance, consistency, stability, solidity, reliability and steadfastness. These are the virtues that help build a strong economic future for you. You need to stick with things, see your tasks through to their conclusion and progress slowly but surely, fighting off the restless urge to cut your losses and run away, as your adventuring personality might demand. Although you may be impatient or bored, anchoring yourself in the present stabilizes you and pays off. You need long-term investments, not the short returns. When you are on the move, so are your finances, but money responds to you when you initiate something.

From an early age your aptitude to use one of the five senses in a creative and productive way was evident. One or many of these five senses may play a leading role in earning your income. Sensually, this might manifest in many ways; for instance, you might have 'healing hands', chiromantic ability, the Midas touch, even a green thumb or be able to build and construct. So whether you are a masseur, potter, arbourist, financial wizard or architect, you utilize your innate sensual skill and practicality. There are numerous other ways you might apply this skill, such as singing, cooking, gardening, banking or construction, but the bottom line is that you have common sense and earthy talents which pay off. These would be worth investing in. Even if you don't feel connected to this sensual quality you know value when you see it, and part of your investment portfolio might include a beautiful painting, a sculpture or a collection of perfume jars.

Pampering yourself is also a good investment because the more relaxed and in the moment you are, the more successful you become. Being grounded and seeing the job through to the end works best for you. Wealth is built with a sensible and long-term approach. While you might like to make quick money and throw fiscal caution to the winds, this does not suit you. You need to be pragmatic and certain about your finances and security. When you take a more realistic approach you feel more in touch with your authentic resources. Innately, you mistrust things that come too easy; somewhere inside you know the satisfaction of a job well done when it is completed with integrity and hard work.

Gemini on the 2nd House Cusp

Your curiosity and keenness to learn are great resources and could lead you into considering earning your living through communication, travel and reportage. If not, these are avenues of investment where money can be generated, because your fate with money is bound up in your communicative skills. Your ability to be a strong communicator provides your living. Whether it is writing or demonstrating, teaching or coaching, it is about communicating important information that helps others to become more conscious of who they are and the world they live in.

Emblematic of Gemini is the image of twinship or duality. On one hand, this could suggest that your earning power is increased or developed when working side-by-side with a partner, sibling, friend or soulmate, especially if you share a vision or goal. Another possibility is that you manage two jobs, tasks or projects that provide income. Your relationship to money may not be as stable as your personality would like, but changing and trying new things does work well for you in the money sector. Security is not really based on fixity or longevity, but in valuing the constant changes in your life. When you feel the freedom to be more mobile you will also feel more secure and more financially competent.

Learn to value your social skills. Success lies in connecting and networking all the different personalities under one umbrella. Another quality is your intellect. Language, ideas and communication skills are all talents worth capitalizing on. You learn on the job and prosper by sharing your know-how and ideas with others. It is no surprise that you might work as an advertising agent, promoter, publicist, speech writer or salesperson. Sharing information and earning a living or making money are bound up together.

Cancer on the 2nd House Cusp

Attachment and bonding, plus feelings of emotional security and safety are resources that translate into wealth and assets. Your financial security and material success depend upon your level of emotional involvement, not your annual salary or earning power. This is a fairly radical concept to consider but, simply put, you become financially confident when you are emotionally secure. Your relationship to money is a barometer of feeling protected and valued.

It is curious that someone who feels that they need a lot of space and mobility might actually become well off through emotional attachments and family responsibilities. Once you settle, you are able to be economically prosperous. When you begin to nest and have emotional responsibilities, you start to financially flourish. There is something quite uncanny about this reality, as your qualities of caring, nurturing, providing and being emotionally present are the keys to economic security. When you care and provide for others, you are making sure that there is enough financial security for everyone to feel safe. Quite literally, you may earn your income in helping or caring professions or in a profession that provides security, nurturing or protection.

However, this does not always mean you feel secure. You may often worry about money and feel vulnerable and insecure about your ability to provide. Yet the reality is that you are able to get what you want, you have enough savings to buy what you need and you manage quite well. It is just that money is the object onto which you project your insecurity. Your talents are your capacity to care and connect with others, and when you care for others and their needs, the cosmos provides for you. It gets easier as you age because you begin to see at long last the rewards of your work.

One of your best investments is your home. Alongside that are your loved ones and then those precious mementos that you have collected over time. What you may not realize is that other money will come from other investments that you are not counting because they have not yet hatched! You may have developed an insecurity or cautiousness about money, but it is through your conscientiousness in intimate and business relationships that you become more secure and confident. Resources are not only materialistic; value lies in your nurturing and how you allow yourself to be responsible and respected in these relationships.

Leo on the 2nd House Cusp

Personal creativity, charisma and self-expression play leading roles in your feeling satisfied when earning your living. Whether that is as an educator, spokesperson, trainer, entertainer or entrepreneur, there is something about you that makes a difference. What makes your contribution unique is not as simple as following a formula, a map or a job description. To value your personal resources and yourself may feel awkward, because personally you might be self-conscious, reserved or prefer to be behind the scenes.

The qualities necessary to maximize your resources are confidence and self-expression. Vocationally, you are in a position to capitalize on entrepreneurial projects, technological advancements, educational reforms or corporate changes if you can find your own creative expression and confidence. You need to stand out and be seen. If you are self-employed or an independent practitioner, your pride in what you do, warmth and generosity are the assets that will secure and enrich your place in the world. You need to feel comfortable selling your product, publicizing your talents and displaying your creativity. As an artist you need to promote yourself. Innately, your generosity of spirit, your geniality and charisma are great assets that you bring to your tasks.

Psychologically, it is imperative to come to know the self and what you desire. If not, you might be prone to inflating your sense of self and being out of touch with what you do; equally, you might underestimate your sense of creativity and then feel undervalued. Earning a living can be fun. Tap into your playfulness and spontaneity. Work and fun need to be aligned for you to feel good, and once you find the rhythm of being engaged in the creative self you find joy and pleasure in what you do. Having a healthy attitude to money is a game and you need to find a way to enjoy playing it.

Virgo on the 2nd House Cusp

From our earliest records, Virgo has been the harvest maiden, associated with the value of the land and its ecosystem. This is the landscape where resources, money and assets are revealed. Metaphorically, your abundant resources need to be cultivated and tended before they can be disseminated. Like the agricultural maiden, you might need to honour the process of time and be aware of the order of the seasons so you know when to reap and when to sow. Virgo appreciates stability and consistency and these are valuable concepts, even though they may not always fit easily with your personality.

Your innate industriousness and analytical skills are central to your relationship with money. You have an abundance of renewable resources that, if tended carefully and respectfully, can become profitable, such as a talent for recycling, renewing and making things better. While you have a vibrant personality and presence, it is your unassuming and focused nature that is rewarded. Details, small designs and what has been overlooked by others are profitable to you.

Your discriminating faculties, precision, analytical skills, self-reliance, containment and orderliness are prime resources. Whether these take you into the business world, an artisan workshop, a medical clinic or a veterinarian surgery, you trade on your detailed and analytical skills when earning your living. Vocationally, you are suited to earning your living in the health and service industries, but any area that provides you with the feeling of improving and developing will be satisfying to you. Whether that is working with animals, crafts or healing medicines, you need to feel that you are improving a situation in order to feel valuable.

When you start to ruminate about the lacks rather than what you do have, you undermine your greatest asset which is your unshakeable knowledge that all things are cyclical. The time might not be right now, but it will be soon. Like the goddesses who cultivate the fertile fields of Virgo, you have a range of resources that provide a secure living. Your pleasure is derived from being in tune with the natural cycles of life. Virgo here reminds you that the harvest is seasonal and that there are cycles in your economic stability.

Libra on the 2nd House Cusp

Appreciating your skills in diplomacy and tact, your sophistication and refinement, as well as your relational skills, will go a long way towards being successful and valued. Your innate skills in dealing with others suggest that you have an instinct about what is right. Being able to compromise, see all sides of the situation and negotiate a fair outcome are valued skills and they might lead you into vocations working alongside others or where negotiation, diplomacy, communication, bargaining, mediation, reconciliation or teamwork are vital. Your diplomatic skills also come in handy in hospitality and creating pleasant and friendly professional atmospheres. All these are possibilities where you can earn income.

An even-keeled approach to making money and creating your lifestyle is important, as money is less available when you become unbalanced or out of sorts. You have an appreciation of beauty and value the refined things in life; therefore, investing in art and works of beauty add value to your life. However, having beautiful things is not important enough to risk being in great debt because you also value your independence and ability to make the right financial decisions. If you find yourself spending lots of money on beautiful things, yet still feel unvalued, this is a clue that you may feel dissatisfied with your work and direction.

Success and feeling valued come from developing solid relationships, being part of a team, a partner's other half or an intimate friend. You may derive your income from a partnership or have investments with others; either way, you have the knack of knowing how to make money for and with others; therefore, it is necessary to be clear and contractual in your financial dealings. Justice and fair play are important aspects of your portfolio and you need to remember this when signing work agreements, mutual investments or contracts. When you clearly negotiate your own values and share these with others, you feel free enough to be wealthy. You may be humble, but money is important because you value quality and class and these cannot be discounted.

Scorpio on the 2nd House Cusp

Pluto, one of the rulers of your 2nd house, metaphorically brings the mysteries of the underworld into your financial and vocational awareness. This might suggest that you have hidden talents and resources that are revealed through your working life; perhaps you are adept at investigating and appraising financial mysteries. It certainly means that you need to consider what riches you do possess and how you may best maximize your potential. Your talents and resources may still be unacknowledged, because others may not see your skills and talents clearly.

The value of the underworld is that this is the place where seeds germinate and begin their growth. It also was the resting place for disembodied souls, suggesting that your resources rest in knowing what lies beneath the surface of things. You have a knack for coping well in crisis and one of your great skills is dealing with critical passages, whether they are in individuals' lives, in organizations or projects. Whether you are helping to rebuild someone's life, a company or a house, you have an ability to transform situations. Some may need to rebuild their lives in their relationship to money; therefore, you may be drawn to working with money, whether that is as an advisor, an investor, a banker or an arbitrageur. Using therapeutic skills as a psychoanalyst, doctor, healer, caretaker, bereavement counsellor, fertility specialist or in situations where life and death are in high focus also are resonant with this image. Being a forensic, archaeological, medical or financial researcher searching underground to find the truth – herein lies your talent and your fortune. But is fortune money?

Wealth is not just a fiscal reality. You find pleasure and riches in the deep connections with others in life, whether that is helping someone in distress, being a witness to another person's transitions or feeling respected and appreciated. However, there is a cautionary side. Power and money are aligned; therefore, beware of money being used as a power tool to manipulate others or yourself. Money is a potent symbol in your life and your path may lead to corporations where there is a lot of wealth or you may encounter wealthy business people or clients. But the secret in your life is that integrity, honesty and presence are the sources of transformational power, not money. Your greatest asset is your character.

Sagittarius on the 2nd House Cusp

You value education, vision and philosophy, and feel financially secure when these interests are incorporated into your occupation. Another aspect you must value about yourself is your ability to give meaning to other people's life experience. When this is coupled with your intense and charismatic personality you are able to craft your living in meaningful and significant ways. In modern jargon you are a life coach, best suited to making your living inspiring others, encouraging their beliefs and attitudes about themselves in order to improve the world they live in. You have your own philosophy about money and you find it works best when you are not attached to pursuing the dollar, but are free, spontaneous and adventuresome. As you say, believe in it and it will happen.

Your capital worth is intimately bound up with being true to your beliefs. Ethics play a large role in your sense of wealth and investments. When you marry your own philosophy and principles to your understanding of money, then you released from having to follow the herd. On one extreme you might have lofty ideals about money and end up feeling ripped off when others do not aspire to such ideals. On the other hand, you could exaggerate and inflate your resources to cover up a meaningless life. You need a valid way of thinking about money, assets and possessions so you feel satisfied and supported in doing the things that you value, such as travelling, studying and learning.

Unfortunately, qualities like truth and knowledge, vision, far-sightedness and optimism are not valued in a share portfolio. So you need to find a way to value these. The freedom to explore, be involved in cross-cultural projects, travel and learn is key to your sense of satisfaction. Vocationally, this suggests that you will need to be expansive in your ideas, your principles and your opinions, remaining open to all possibilities. You learn on the job and opportunities are always on the horizon for you when you let yourself have faith and confidence. Jupiter, the ruler of Sagittarius, knows that when you believe in yourself and your abilities, the world responds.

Capricorn on the 2nd House Cusp

Your attitudes towards economic opportunities and financial security are bound up with your sense of self-esteem and personal worth. While qualities like responsibility, duty, conservatism and pragmatism shape your approach to money, you are just as likely to rebel again traditionalist views of wealth if these feel restrictive and authoritative. Hence your parents' attitudes to money play a role in shaping your own. You may have inherited strong morals and conservative messages about how to earn a living, or cautionary tales about extravagance; therefore, you may feel as if you are battling an inner demon when it comes to your relationship with money. However, the truth is that you have your own economic rules and need to reflect on what these are.

Capricorn is a sign of authority and embedded in its psychology is the awareness of consequences; therefore, it brings its consciousness of rules and regulations to the sphere of earning an income. This methodical and more serious approach to money matters may conflict with a side of your personality that wants to feel free and unconstrained by rules and duty. Work and career are lifelong processes and over time there will be many conflicting needs to attend to, but time is Capricorn's domain and it feels safest taking its time. This might free up some of your time to have your adventures, coming back later to the serious business of earning an income. It is easier to be disciplined, responsible and authoritative as life develops. Perhaps it is wise to recognize that you will grow into these qualities and develop these resources as you mature, so that you do not hold yourself back from experimentation and adventure.

Your innate strengths and resources are best supported in a system where you feel you can be in charge or in control and are satisfied when you have jurisdiction over your own territory or are self-employed. Respect is important, and you thrive when you find the right place where your talents and skills are respected and validated. The secret of your success lies in knowing that you have worked hard for what you have accomplished and that you are secure on the wheel of fortune. Debt does not fit the traditionalist view of money and you are challenged to look beyond the money models given to you to find the one that suits you and of which you are in control. Vocationally your discipline, dedication, management skills, responsible attitude and organizational expertise are guaranteed to contribute to your success.

Aquarius on the 2nd House Cusp

Even though Aquarius is traditionally ruled by Saturn, it is progressive and future-orientated, looking to what is ingenious and cutting-edge to establish a sense of worth and value. Therefore, you need to capitalize on your progressive, electric, altruistic and technological talents in whatever way you can. It also suggests that you feel satisfied and valued when you are able to be both inventive and individualistic. With this combination it is likely that you may find yourself earning your living in a radically different way from what you had ever imagined. This might be difficult to picture, as you may feel your personality is too conservative.

Your self-esteem is intimately connected with your independence, so your personal opinions and beliefs will support your values. They may be marginal to the system but nonetheless sympathetic to you. It is important to recognize that being your own person is more of an asset than following tradition for the sake of it. This could suggest that you might at times be embroiled in political manoeuvres and changes, but it is also important to know that you can detach from these when there is nothing in it for you. Money is going to be earned on the road less travelled, not on the well trodden path of conservative values. Sometimes you are ambivalent about money; at other times inspired, occasionally disinterested.

Vocationally, you are well suited to a variety of innovative, scientific, technological and/or intellectual endeavours. You do well when engaged in humanistic and political reforms because your social and personal skills are an asset. Ecological, environmental and humanitarian pursuits can bring your skills to the forefront. When it gets too hard you may disengage from the material sphere and escape into an altruistic one. Astrologically, you can be of two minds about money but in the big picture your personality needs to be grounded and secure in this area.

Pisces on the 2nd House Cusp

The two fishes on your 2nd house bring their magical and chaotic energy into the sphere of financial stability, economic management, earning ability and resources. When we analyse the combination at face value, it appears to be a mismatch; therefore, the secret of this combination is to recognize your distinctive resources and different approach to cash flow. First, your income and cash flow may not be earned in a predictable way. Second, you have an intuitive knack for making money and third, you seem to have more resources when you are investing your money and talent creatively or compassionately. You might feel that money is mysterious: there one minute, gone the next. One part of you feels 'I should be saving, doing something realistic and practical'; the other side feels inclined to let things happen.

You may feel confused about money; sometimes you don't know what you have or how much you have spent. You do not need to transcend wealth or your desire for it; it is best to find a meaning for money in your life. You can make money artistically, either through your creativity or by recognizing that in others. Living creatively also suggests a unique experience of worth and value. It is these spiritual and creative qualities that need to be valued in order to provide yourself with a sense of personal security, self-esteem and reward. Vocationally, this could also suggest that it is your artistic or mystical side that you value most. Called to a caring or creative vocation, you may struggle with feeling valued or rewarded, either psychologically or financially. But your talent, artistic and imaginative faculties provide you with enormous pleasure and when you participate fully with these you do find that life provides exactly what you need. Your struggle is to make your skills and talents visible.

Planets in the 2nd House

A planet in the 2nd house reveals your earning style; literally, this may suggest how you earn your income, as well as your patterns and attitudes towards money, possessions and security. These are the archetypal urges that need expression in a skilful and resourceful way. Planets in this sphere shape your sense of worth and value and tap into your natural resources; therefore, these skills and resources support your self-esteem.

Planets here may also be invested with patterns from the past, be that through family, culture or race. Through reflecting on this archetypal design in your life, damaging patterns from the past can become conscious. An impoverished sense of self, low self-esteem or a disapproving attitude towards money may originate from the past, not present. Being mindful of 2nd house planets helps to change our inherited pattern.

Forging an alliance with the 2nd house planets creates a sympathetic and positive approach to your sense of worth. It is through these planetary energies that you can begin to deepen your relationship to money and economics. We could liken the 2nd house planets to the complexes we have about self-esteem and money; therefore, to name them helps to build a relationship with them and supports our vocational journey.

The Sun in the 2nd House

The Sun has a storehouse of supplies, such as confidence, brightness, positivity, self-assurance and leadership, which are sources of security. Assets and income are important and your identity is shaped by attitudes towards ownership and possessions. Prosperity and a healthy bank account are signs of achievement but to what degree are you identified with the material world? This does not suggest that you are money-orientated, but it does suggest that money may be identified as important in your feeling successful. Therefore, it is essential to prioritize the importance of money, material goods and capital in a realistic and honest way, so you feel comfortable with your relationship to the material world.

The Sun builds self-image, character strength and identity in the world; when in the 2nd house this suggests that confidence develops when you express your individual skills and abilities, especially when it comes to turning your innate talents into income. Building a successful career and having disposable income are intimately tied to feelings of confidence. When you are connected to your purposefulness, authority, power and authenticity, you feel rich. Yet when you feel immaterial, you compensate for your inferior feelings through finances and possessions, finding power in money, rather than in the self. Displaying wealth or boasting of your properties or stock portfolio is a sure sign of overcompensation for feelings of inadequacy.

Financial security is realized through strength and courage. You have a natural potential for a high degree of creative ability, flair for self-expression and for placing yourself in the right circumstance. But to be successful in building assets and income you need to express your uniqueness and creativity in the job. The secret to feeling financially successful is not necessarily the amount of money you have in the bank, but the amalgam of confidence and creativity you experience in what you do.

You need to put your own mark on whatever you do; therefore, it is important to speak up, find your voice and express your talents. On a personal level, your relationship with your father may underpin your feelings of worth and value. If you felt unvalued you might be at risk of carrying these feelings into the world of work. However, you can rebuild your confidence and self-worth by being present and expressing your skills and talents in the creative sphere. Acknowledgement and approval contribute to your feelings of worth and value; however, they are not a given.

There are many ways in which your talents could be profitable, but the bottom line is always to put your creative self at the centre of what you do. One sure way of knowing if you are on the right track is your level of vitality and energy. When you are in the right position and expressing your skills and talents, your energetic level and vitality will be high, but when you are in the wrong place you will feel drained. Make sure you are able to shine in whatever you are doing.

The Moon in the 2nd House

As the eternal symbol of change, the Moon brings her waxing and waning rhythms to the financial sector. This suggests that it is important to recognize that there will be tides in monetary security; at times abundance, at other times austerity. Like the tides, this is controlled by the lunar tempo which is naturally cyclic. When you are feeling emotionally assured, you feel financially confident, but when you are feeling vulnerable, a negative assessment of your finances is reflected back to you. Since finances are intertwined with emotional currency, money becomes the transitional object that you need when you are feeling unhappy. Some need chocolate, a cuddle, a reassuring smile; you need cash flow.

Emotional and financial security are intertwined; you can't have one without the other. The 2nd house Moon personifies your mother and her financial instincts, uncertainties and worries, all of which may have affected your sense of security. Wealth is very much bound up with feeling safe, having a home, family connections and familial possessions around you. Being susceptible to this cycle, it is important to have a strategy about financial security. Certainly, having a home base, whether that is a piece of land, a caravan, a rental property, an apartment or your own home, is most important. This is generally everyone's biggest asset and this is definitely the case here.

You could also invest this instinct in your career. You may have a knack for collecting valuables, antiques, coins, stamps or any other objects that have emotion, history or sentiment attached to them. You may have a keen eye for property ventures, the wherewithal to start a restaurant, or you may be interested in child care. Once you get attached to the idea of a project, it is hard to talk you out of it. You may earn your living in one of the caring professions, whether that is as a nurse, teacher, child or carer of the elderly. Your home is of great importance and you have a knack for knowing value when you see it. These are the skills that can be turned to real estate or property development. Working from home in your own business or family business may also be a possibility. In fact, you might have inherited a family concern or be the administrator of a family trust. Home and family play a major role in your financial affairs and lifestyle. Another way this might manifest is working in homes in a multitude of capacities, from handiwork to decoration. It is important for you to recognize the large roles that safety and familiarity play in making your living.

Becoming accustomed with the changing phases of the Moon helps you to remember that there are times of growth, times of inflation and times of recession. Resources fluctuate. Protecting your resources as much as possible secures your sense of well-being. Worrying about fluctuations in currency, the stock market or interest rates is disturbing; therefore, it is best to ensure that you feel as protected as possible by investing in stable commodities. A strong family, a warm home and a familiar routine are your most valuable resources.

Mercury in the 2nd House

Mercury is not known for his constancy or permanency, but he is the divine patron of commerce, the god of the marketplace, trade and the exchange of money. He is also known as the trickster god and brings his fondness for deceit and theft into the marketplace. Therefore, although Mercury in the 2nd might be flexible with cash flow and adept at trading, it is important to recognize that his sleight of hand may also be in play.

All archetypes have dual faces and Mercury is no exception. One side supports an analytical and consistent attitude towards money, but the other is more fickle and changeable. Consider both sides of the coin in all financial dealings: is this a serious long-term investment or one for fun, with potential for short-term gain but carrying a big risk? Mercurial images shape-shift so what may seem a sound investment could turn out to be a sham; on the other hand, what appears to be dodgy could really be beneficial. With Mercury in the 2nd your relationship to money is like quicksilver. It is never dull and always changing. However, if you are interested in saving for the future, superannuation or long-term financial goals, be very aware of the unsettled nature of Mercury, who prefers the open road to the stable home.

One of your resources is that you have an innate capacity to read people and situations in the marketplace. You can be flexible with communication and can be known in a variety of ways. You are at home in the world of commerce, bargaining, buying or selling, trading, importing and exporting, even communicating about financial markets. If Mercury were given a portfolio in the government he would be the Minister for Communication and Transportation, the Minister of Information or the Minister for Commerce.

Therefore, you could make a living as a trader, salesperson, commercial investor, financial writer, and/or in IT. You can also thrive in areas where there is a lot of anxiety, movement and change. Whether you are on the floor of the stock exchange, behind a shop counter or purchasing the latest fashion line in Milan, you are at your best when there is lots of activity, challenge and things to do. Your great skill is thinking on the hoof, being swift-footed and mobile. As the divine patron of writers, Mercury in this sector indicates that you might have a knack for earning your income by storytelling, writing, lecturing, journalism or educating. Whether you are a scriptwriter, songwriter, speechwriter, screen writer, journalist, novelist, columnist or you just write in your journal for pleasure, you are satisfied when you are exchanging stories and information. Through communication you find your worth and value. And where there is an exchange of values, there is also currency exchange. Mercury inspires you to use your intellect, your ideas and your ability to communicate in earning your living. Whether you write it, think it, speak it or draw it, you need to express it to feel satisfied.

Mercury in myth was rarely depicted as growing old. So it is important to recognize that you might be instinctively handy with money when you are young and fit, but that as you age you may need a different set of guidelines to deal with your funds.

Venus in the 2nd House

Being in its natural home, Venus appreciates a highly developed sense of taste, life's sensual pleasures, form and design. Money, the domain of Venus, is important because it can provide a cultivated lifestyle or whatever you judge as being worthwhile. Personal worth and value are bound up with money, bridging your inner worth and value with material acquisitions. Do you compensate for any feelings of lack by spending money or buying things? Today, this is known as retail therapy, which is a great pastime but not helpful in the long term if it covers up insecurity and low self-esteem.

Being susceptible to inherited attitudes towards money, it is worth reflecting on your family's attitudes towards money, power and values. Venus connects money and love: in your family experience, when love was lacking was it replaced by money? Or were money and love tangled up in any way? Consider how feminine values were appreciated and respected, because Venus, the doyenne of feminine values, needs to be respected and appreciated.

A peaceful and attractive environment contributes to your self-esteem, as ultimately the aesthetics of the outer world reflect an inner feeling of harmony. Therefore, you might enjoy investing your income in what pleases you, such as clothes, furnishings, art or music. When beauty and taste surround you, you feel well. Inherently, you have a knack for pleasing and attracting others. Venus encourages you to be partnered; but with this placement money, sex and relationship may all be intertwined. Sorting out what you value in the material world, as opposed to the emotional and the spiritual worlds, will be helpful.

Consistent with this astrological placement is often a talent for art, music or social skills. Many fine singers, including Patsy Cline, Edith Piaf, Elvis Presley, Maurice Chevalier and k.d. lang, with this placement have been blessed with rich and pleasing voices. While this may not be your destiny, it is worthwhile considering what skills and resources you value about yourself and how you might earn your living developing these, or at least expressing these talents through a hobby.

Most consistent with Venus in the 2nd is earning income through the urge to beautify. Or you might be inclined towards pursuing a profession where the development of social skills and hospitality is a priority. People-skills are resources that can be developed in order to feel satisfied and successful in professions where diplomacy, protocol and relating are important. Whatever path you choose, the archetype of love and beauty wants to be honoured and acknowledged. One way might be to save money for the things that you really value, investing in something beautiful, sensual or exquisite. Venus is about valuing the self and in the 2nd house it is important that you find the resources that encourage and support your self-worth.

Mars in the 2nd House

Mars values adventure, independence and individualism; therefore, you may prefer to earn your own living and pay your own bills, rather than relying on others to provide. Being self-governing and free to make your own choices around money is a question of vocation. As an archetype, Mars equates with danger, intrigue and excitement. It values autonomy, risk-taking and courage, needing to be stimulated and challenged. Therefore, like this warrior god, you find value through your independent spirit and, when it is activated, money follows. Happiness is finding the way to be gainfully employed while doing your own thing.

Livelihoods where danger and adrenalin are high, such as working in an emergency unit, the police force or the fire brigade, would also appeal to action-packed Mars. Given the entrepreneurial streak, you might also be fired up by working in high-risk positions such as the stock market, financial trading and investing or property development. This energy also yearns to be active, so physical or sports-orientated jobs might suit you. It is also common for individuals with this placement to earn their living in trades such as electricians, plumbers, builders or carpenters, or any occupation where there is goal and a deadline. Even though these jobs may be masculine in temperament, they are not always the exclusive domain of men. I have often seen female clients with Mars in the 2nd who excel at fitting and turning or are highly successful in the military. Mars in the 2nd is not gender-biased, because its strength and passion are archetypal drives.

Your resources are your entrepreneurial flair and bravado, and your willingness to take risks, confront obstacles and be challenged. You need to be challenged and stimulated by what you do; therefore, your competitive nature needs guidelines and objectives. It is wise to set goals for accumulating resources; not rigid or fixed ones, but ones that you can strive for with all your heart. Challenge yourself with realistic goals for savings rather than allowing them to be enforced by others.

In your background there may have been arguments over money; perhaps anger or low self-esteem because there was not enough. Money is a contentious commodity and Mars in the 2nd links money with aggression; therefore, it is important to know what you want. You don't want or need resentment because you have lent or given money away indiscriminately. When consulting others, it is important to recognize your own instincts and hunches and to feel you have been heard. If you let the financial 'experts' take the lead all the time you may become frustrated. When Mars is irritated or blocked, it can turn against the self, becoming depressed and discouraged. It is important that you encourage your own voice in your fiscal policies and plans.

Mars is also the planet of desire, and depending on your background you either have a strong desire to go and get what you want or you are ambivalent, still caught in the wash of earlier attitudes which do not support your sense of self-esteem. Make your wish list and work towards acquiring what you would like and reflecting on what you value.

Jupiter in the 2nd House

On one hand, this placement suggests a positive and confident approach to making a living, as well as an ability to be financially prosperous, yet, on the other, it hints at a sense of entitlement and superiority. The key to being successful is finding the right balance, such as using Jupiter's abundant spirit without getting caught up in its inflationary certainty and false hope. Perhaps it is best to take stock about what is valuable to you; for instance, travel, spending money on learning something meaningful or developing your career prospects might be a good investment. Money allows you to stretch yourself beyond the boundaries of your upbringing.

Lady luck is often personified as Jupiter's partner; in the 2nd house this suggests that you too might be partnered by wealth. At the very least, this might suggest that there are more times when the wheel of fortune is rising than falling. Again, that is the promise, but Jupiter often promises more than it delivers. Therefore, you need to take advantage of the good times, as they can be very lucrative. It is during thriving times that you can build your wealth. Two of your great assets are your faith and optimism, and when you project this positive attitude onto finances it works its spell. You have the Midas touch when needed, able to turn around difficult situations to make them work in your favour. But let's remember what happened to Midas: everything he touched turned to gold, even drink, food and water. Turning everything to gold can be both a blessing and a curse.

When you feel dispirited or depressed you may overinvest or become blinded to realistic possibilities. It is important to differentiate between when you are in touch with an authentic sense of possibility and when you are inflated. Let's take an inventory of your most resourceful assets; these will include spontaneity, insight, vision, faith, optimism, generosity and enthusiasm. These and your confidence and leadership abilities will pay off.

Jupiter is associated with philosophies, ideologies and concepts. The search for meaning is entwined with making a living and it is very important that you feel your job is meaningful and purposeful or you lose spirit. Money-making projects involved in expanding people's understanding of themselves and the world around them, or administering to an individual's religious and soul needs, could be successful. You may feel drawn to educating and inspiring others to a greater understanding, to work in travel or to deal with international concerns. Your great skill is in sharing knowledge with others and there may be many ways that this manifests in earning your living. When you lose this spirit and optimism you also lose touch with your innate resources and capacity to be successful. Finding meaning in what you do is optimum. In the corporate world the search is more focused on money than meaning, which makes it difficult for you to be confined by corporate philosophy, even though you strive to be part of the system.

Metaphorically, we might describe Jupiter in the 2nd as a prophet of profits. In other words, you could be successful as the advertising manager of a bank or financial institution, thrive at educating people about their investments or coaching others on using the markets. You have a wide range of resources but ultimately you need to feel inspired and find meaning in how you make money. There are two kinds of profits in your life. One comes from being engaged and happy in what you are doing; the other from searching for something meaningful.

Saturn in the 2nd House

When placed in the sector of resources and finances, it is important that the archetype of Saturn can support your innate attitudes towards self-worth and value. This suggests that tradition, caution and security in your approach to money and finances will be important. With the planet of consequence in your financial sector it is best to follow the letter of the law. Creative accounting, tax dodges and money laundering are not for you; if they are, then there is an above average chance of being caught and fined. When rules apply it is best to follow them, even when these rules do not suit you. Destiny has bound you to the economic system and it is in respecting the system that you find your wealth. This does not mean that you cannot be creative, but Saturnian creativity lies in being well prepared and trained in your area of expertise.

Saturn is connected to time and ageing, as if time is the key to wisdom. In this sense it is important to be a long-term investor rather than a short-term one. Saturn does not value what is transitory or impermanent but finds worth in what builds up over time. As time goes by, your assets will appreciate and grow. You derive great satisfaction when your investments mature, your mortgage is paid off or your assets are sold after they have been of value and service to you.

Similarly, when it comes to making your living you will be cautious and hard-working, because value is what has been earned through effort and conscious application. Therefore, your attitude towards material possessions will also be the same: valuing what is of good quality and well made, mistrusting what is cheap and readily available. You value employment when there is a strong, well established structure and room for advancement. Saturn rules what is durable, long-lasting, hardened and structured, like lead or concrete, as well as industries such as building, agriculture and those with long-range goals that are traditional and enduring.

Saturn can be highly self-critical. This may have begun in your family of origin, with strict policies and austere attitudes about feelings of self-worth; perhaps you internalized a feeling of disapproval. If you were criticized for your values or chastised for what you liked, you may still be rebelling against these standards and participating with a negative version of your worth. Saturn in the 2nd suggests that the road to recovery lies in authenticating your own worth and value.

While you may seek approval and feedback in your handling of money matters, investments and savings, you might not attain them. The reason is that you need to find your own way. Even though you would prefer to be mentored, fate has placed the responsibility for financial success in your own hands. This might make you feel anxious and on your own when handling money matters. Potentially, you have what it takes to find the successful economic route. Projecting expertise onto others may not suit you because their agendas for financial gain may not be compatible with yours.

256 Vocation: The Astrology of Career, Creativity and Calling

Take a personal inventory and you will find a wide array of valuable resources that support you, including organizational skills, professionalism, self-discipline, competence, responsibility, trust and dedication. Sound management of your resources makes it likely that you will earn your income in an executive or managerial capacity. Like the mountain goat, you are adept at starting at the bottom and slowly climbing to the summit of your success. However, the key to this is maintaining your integrity, self-respect and valuing the process of time.

Chiron in the 2nd House

Your experience of financial and material security may not be mainstream. In fact, money may feel alien to you because others' values, and especially the familial values you inherited, feel distinctly separate from yours. In your earlier years there may have been financial hardship or insecurity that might have left its wound on your sense of being resourceful or valued. Chiron can point to an ancestral wound; perhaps there may have been difficulties with money in the family history or a loss of possessions and resources in the past. Or, you may have been wealthy and prosperous, but this left you feeling an outsider. However we portray this image, it suggests that your attitudes and experiences of money will be atypical.

In the realm of finances, money, income and resources, you feel outside the system and this may feel like a wound that you need to heal or a pattern that needs addressing. On a psychological level, this suggests that familial values may have damaged your sense of personal worth and value, influencing the way you think about earning your living and your attitudes towards wealth. Yet, ironically, this part of your healing process will come through earning your living and finding financial security in the world.

Chiron suggests that you will be masterful at helping others to recover their sense of personal power and self-esteem. You will also be skilful at helping others to find the right ways to invest their money, tap into their own resources or earn a living in their own way. When you realize that you do not need to follow the herd, you do well at accumulating assets and building wealth. Psychologically, Chiron in the 2nd may suggest a wound to your sense of self-worth, value and ability to sustain yourself in the world. One reaction to this might be that you compensate for this feeling through the acquisition of money and possessions. Ownership might dull the feelings of a lack of worthiness for a while; however, the healing journey comes through facing the demons so as to become authentic and supportive of the self.

While you may feel handicapped when it comes to resources or making money, destiny will place you in the path of others who need your guidance, wisdom and support. Therefore, it is possible that you could earn your living working with refugees, the homeless, the handicapped or in social work vocations which aid the underprivileged and the outcast. Vocationally, you could also be drawn to a myriad of holistic healing professions or alternative healing practices, which attempt to work with the integration of the body and the mind, or at some point you might earn income using New Age healing modalities, channelling or Reiki. Traditions such as dream therapy or astrology, using imagery and symbols as a healing tool, are also possible. Chiron was a mentor and teacher and is connected with mentoring professions such as life coaches, inspirational teachers and guides. Healing comes through earning your income and developing an authentic and appropriate relationship to money and the material world.

Another pattern with Chiron in the 2nd can be the renunciation of material goods and money, because emotional and financial security may be polarized. There may be a feeling that money has damaged the well-being of the soul; therefore, to reject money is to stay clear of its wounding. However, the split only grows wider, because the key to understanding Chiron is that the source of the pain is also where the cure is found. If financial control or money has been the wounding agent then you must find a way to relate to it in order for the pattern to be healed. With Chiron here you need to be less factual about the pains or the gains of money and better able to see it as an agent of change and awakening.

Uranus in the 2nd House

Your approach to money and possessions could be quite unconventional, as Uranus is known for its defiance, nonconformity, unpredictability and surprises. In the 2nd house this might suggest sudden changes of fortune, the fluctuation of material assets and financial security or feelings of being out of control when it comes to finances. Whatever the accepted consensus is towards money, yours will probably be different; however, you might also unexpectedly receive money. With Uranus in the 2nd, financial security can be erratic, highly influenced by your intuitive and forward thinking abilities.

You might find that you have an uncanny knack for picking the right shares, making astute investments or being clever at financial planning. Reflect on original ways to make money, because your resources are your inventive streak. Discover how this might work best for you. Ultimately, you have the ability to be detached from the material world and this helps you to relax. Reflect on what stocks you might consider valuable. Are these futures? High-risk? Energy or technology?

Consider how you might use your unique skills and specialized talents for making money in order to feel comfortable on the unpredictable wheel of fortune. Your question might be 'How can I maximize my return on my distinctive talents to feel financially secure?' Perhaps you might forge your own independent route, choosing to make your living in an unconventional way. Or are you destined to make money in an environment that is futuristic, cutting-edge, non-traditional or ahead of its time? Another possibility may be earning your income in a humanitarian way, working to improve the human condition or the state of the earth. Whatever financial road you take, it needs to be a road less travelled.

To find your own distinctive untrampled path you need to tap into your uniqueness and inventiveness, using your ingenuity and imagination to forge your way. Workwise, you are well suited to unusual jobs, ones that have not even been discovered yet. Being comfortable on the edge of change, helping to forge new directions and advancements, suggests that a career in cutting-edge technology might suit, especially if you are helping to revolutionize attitudes to work or helping to create solutions for the future. Or politics, if you can bear it, is another sphere where you might use your vision and protest to create change. Whether you are attracted to science or the liberal arts to earn money, your need to advance human understanding and equality is your valuable asset. You have altruistic, ingenious and intelligent resources that seek expression and support.

Neptune in the 2nd House

At face value, this placement could suggest that your perspective on money and possessions is not well grounded in reality. On the other hand, it reveals that your earning capacity and resourceful nature are fluid and creative and that you value the more refined, spiritual and artistic aspects of life. The god of the seas is creating waves in your financial sector; sometimes you might feel you are riding the waves, at other times being thrown about by angry and stormy economic conditions. Either money is earned through creative, artistic and/or spiritual endeavours or your relationship to money is vague. Living in a material world, the question might be 'How can I be creative and spiritual yet still feel financially secure?'

Being in the workaday world may be painful and soul-destroying unless you are able to reconcile the two worlds and incorporate your creative longing in the everyday experience of earning a living. Your talents and skills are collared by the archetype of transcendence; so, however you earn your income, you are satisfied when your spiritual beliefs are acknowledged. Your task is to not let your creativity or spirituality be held back by a lack of money. This suggests that you need to bring your artistry, your compassion and your magic into how you earn your living.

It is wise to reflect on your attitude towards money. Is it misshapen by any spiritual beliefs or driven by fantasy? You may have a tendency to confuse the material and spiritual worlds, leaving your ability to handle money matters in chaos. If this is the case, it is best to seek practical, reliable advice about how to manage your money. It is also important that you do not unconsciously collude with sacrificing or surrendering your talents. You could offer your creative talents to organizations or groups that use them without acknowledgement or reward for you. Yet, you also need to recognize the enormous potential of Neptune in your financial sector because it means that almost anything is possible. Neptune governs dreams, visions, magic and the unattainable, and in the 2nd house it may transport you into an economic situation you might never have imagined.

Re-enchanting the way you earn your living in a disenchanted world may not be easy. However, it is not impossible and it is the archetype of Neptune that inspires you to make your living in a creative and spiritual way or in one that is compatible with your inner urge to be imaginative and valuable. In fact, this is a necessity, as it is in the mundane world where you find the magic. Rather than turning away from the traditional, physical and mundane world of commerce and industry, it needs to be embraced in a new and inspired way.

Neptune needs meaning, imagination, art, music and love to bring it to life. Therefore, in your 2nd house it could suggest that your struggle with money is soul-making. For you, soulfulness lies in the everyday world of making a living. Although the material world might not feel soulful, it is your task to make it so.

Pluto in the 2nd House

In ancient Greek, *plutus* meant wealth and this association with riches was transferred onto the archetype of Pluto. These riches were not what was in the bank, but were what was buried. Psychologically, the deity reminds us that wealth lies in our untapped resources and riches that are awaiting release. Literally, this might mean the riches excavated from mining, sunken treasure, archaeological ruins or an heirloom. When in your 2nd house, Pluto suggests that you have innate wealth and power to be mined. First and foremost, it is necessary to know what feeds your desire for wealth, because money will confront you with intimate and personal issues. Money might be therapeutic as it forces you to assess what you value and respect on the deepest levels. Perhaps the greatest asset you have is the ability to trust yourself in times of decision-making about resources and to know that you have made the right choices. Over time you can eliminate what is not necessary; however, you will also bring the hidden treasure to the surface.

One of your best resources is your ability to work therapeutically with crisis and change. Part of this pattern is that you will do well in emergencies where you are called upon to go with 'gut feelings'. And this is your best approach to wealth creation. You will do well when you use your deeper instincts about what is of value. Anything connected to alterations and renovations, therapeutic interventions, cycles, endings and getting to the truth is a boon to you. Income could come in mysterious ways. Vocationally, professions involving research, medical or psychotherapeutic work, crisis management and consulting or with any underground link could also be lucrative. What is important to know is that you have depth perception, integrity and honesty. When you invest in the things that are of worth to you, although not necessarily to others, you understand that you are able to see value where others cannot. What might be discarded by someone else may contain the seeds of fortune for you. Wealth is a subjective experience and while others may objectify money and possessions, prosperity engages you at a deeper level. Remember that Pluto had his invisible helmet and when he surfaced he could not be seen. He only ascended to obtain what he desired, or to seek healing for what had been damaged. Like Pluto, you need to bring your intentions to the surface when you are passionately interested in something you value.

You may fear losing your money or be haunted by images of not having enough. One recurring pattern I have seen with the 2nd house Pluto is that money and the accumulation of assets confronts one's sense of worth and power. There is often a fear of lack. It is important to know that these feelings are not prophetic but psychological, forcing you to confront your worth to find the resources that promote a valued sense of self. The question then might be 'Does money reflect my worthiness and sense of success in the world?' Another pattern is that the accumulation or loss of money is enmeshed with crisis. In other words, you may lose your assets due to a crisis, but then rebuild and regain your resources. In the process you find out how resourceful and powerful you are. However, you do not need to lose everything to know that you have the power to restore and rebuild your capital. You have a powerful sense of wealth creation which will work for you when you recognize that you would like to be more critically involved in your work and that what you do is valuable.

– Chapter 9 –
MAKING A LIVING
The Sixth House Lifestyle

The 6th house is an eclectic territory associated with many facets of daily life, all of which focus on everyday routines.[37] These rituals of daily life are necessary to maintain order and sustain coherence in our lives; therefore, the 6th house reveals personal ways to remain focused and centred. When we lose touch with the threads of continuity in our day-to-day lives, chaos fills the empty space and is often experienced as stress, loss of direction and purposelessness. This is the house of daily living, how we make our living; therefore, in essence, it reveals our lifestyle.

As a house always associated with illness and more contemporarily with health, the 6th house tradition signifies areas of the body susceptible to carrying stress. When work is not nurturing or fulfilling, we are reminded of our distress by the complaints in our body and mind. In the 6th house work and health come together; hence, the often heard phrase 'my work is making me sick'.

The 6th House	• The nature of your technical skills and ability to focus on tasks • What routines, responsibilities and activities you need to perform daily to feel centered • How to achieve satisfaction in the course of your everyday life • Dealing with chaos, life crisis and illness
Keywords	Body/mind; Centring and focusing; Coherence; Co-workers; Crisis; Daily rituals; Diet; Duty; Eating rituals; Everyday reality; Health; Hygiene; Illness; Jobs; Pets/small animals; Service; Stress management; Well-being; Work

The Sign on the 6th House Cusp and its Ruler	• What daily rituals help me maintain a sense of order and coherence in life • How do I focus and apply myself to the task at hand • What part of the body may be sensitive to carrying stress • What do I need in my daily atmosphere to be organized • How I deal with the daily crises of life • My relationship with co-workers and others in my everyday life environment
Planets in the 6th House	• Need to be consistently employed in developing and sustaining a balanced lifestyle • Urge to be productive in day-to-day tasks • Allies in times of crisis that help to concentrate on and manage the situation at hand • Archetypes which may be personified by co-workers, bosses or those who assist us in our daily lives

Vocationally, the 6th house describes our occupation or how we are best occupied; therefore, it can illustrate the routine conditions of the job and the daily responsibilities and activities involved in performing job tasks that contribute to our personal satisfaction. It also profiles the working atmosphere, environment and those who share the workspace with us. This house symbolizes what is natural to feel fulfilled; therefore, to feel less stressed.

Astrological wisdom implies that work and well-being are companions; in order to be well we need work that suits our soul. However, 6th house issues can become confused. In our workaday world, duty can replace satisfaction, quality can be sacrificed for quantity and the focus on perfecting the end product corrupts being involved in a process. The work instinct is to be productive; however, when this turns to rigidity or perfectionism, the enjoyment of work is lost. Rituals can become obsessions and, rather than contributing to our well-being, they become compulsive. Perhaps this is why traditional astrology often suggested this house was 'malefic' and early Hellenistic astrologers labelled it as the house of 'bad fortune'. Like the 2nd house, its elemental nature is at odds with the Ascendant. As the Ascendant is vitality, the ancients saw the 6th house as what conflicts with this. Therefore, conscious effort needs to be applied to the 6th house in order to maintain our well-being and manage the tensions of daily life.

Analysing the 6th house reveals the most satisfying work environment and routines as well as the most rewarding way that an individual can be employed. The 6th house is often referred to as a house of service. However, it is where we best serve ourselves through the quality of our employment and the organization of our everyday life.

What follows is an analysis of your 6th house as described by the sign on the cusp and any planets that occupy this sphere. We are focusing on the 6th house in the context of our daily routines which are largely work-related. Descriptions of literal occupations might also resonate with 10th house placements. You will be able to maximize your fulfilment with work by recognizing the routines and tasks that are incompatible with your temperament and contribute to stress. By becoming aware of the daily rituals that support your natural disposition you will feel more satisfied and rewarded by your job. We do not always need to change our job to be content; perhaps we need to change our attitude and approach to it instead.

Signs on the Cusp of the 6th House
In the natural wheel of the horoscope, the sign on the 6th house cusp is quincunx or 150° from the Ascendant. This may not be so when using an unequal house system, but using the natural wheel suggests that the element on the 6th house cusp is naturally incompatible with the rising sign. Psychologically, this suggests that the 6th house may be at odds with the vitality, spontaneity, outlook and temperament represented by the 1st house and its personality. Therefore, the 6th house cusp becomes the conscious striving to maintain stability and consistency in daily life. While the Ascendant is birth and the thrust into life, the 6th house is how we manage life on a daily basis. The sign on the cusp helps to articulate how to do this.

The 6th house cusp invites us to develop rituals and practices that support the personality. As already stated, the sign on the cusp is generally quincunx the Ascendant, an aspect that combines two inharmonious elements. Yet there is often a secret affinity between signs that are quincunx one another which we could contemplate, as follows in the table over the page.

It is apparent that in being mindful of the sign on the 6th house cusp we can find ways to bring equilibrium into our daily life. Without a conscious effort to do this, the chaos of daily life intrudes.

We can contemplate the affinity between the sign on the Ascendant and the sign on the 6th house so as to maximize their relationship potential. We can also be aware that stress and illness gather round the 6th house cusp, symptomatic of what might be out of balance at work or in the daily life.

Signs	Affinities	Both signs share a quality of
♈–♍	Self-determination	*Independence* Aries is self-governing; Virgo is contained
♈–♏	Both signs are ruled by Mars	*Exploration* Aries is outer-orientated; Scorpio is inner-orientated
♉–♎	Both signs are ruled by Venus	*Form* Taurus is sensual; Libra is intellectual
♉–♐	The natural world	*Nature* Taurus loves the earth; Sagittarius cherishes the great outdoors
♊–♏	Contact	*Relationship* Gemini communicates; Scorpio communes
♊–♑	Systems	*Logic* Gemini prefers the proliferation of ideas; Capricorn systematizes them
♋–♐	Place	*Home and Away* Cancer is home land; Sagittarius is foreign land
♋–♒	Care	*Human Regard* Cancer is familial; Aquarius is universal caring
♌–♑	Power	*Authority* Leo personally commands; Capricorn is public autonomy
♌–♓	Creativity	*Imagination* Leo is self-expression; Pisces is inspired and collective

| ♍-♒ | Self-government | *Autonomy*
 Virgo is self-contained; Aquarius is emotionally restrained |
| ♎-♓ | Artistic | *Beauty*
 Libra loves the beauty of symmetry; Pisces loves the beauty of chaos |

Aries on the 6th House Cusp

Independence and freedom are important considerations in the routine conditions of your employment. You need to be unconstrained in your work environment because you work effectively when there is an atmosphere of spontaneity and you are given permission to be adventuresome and risk-taking. You work best when invested with responsibility and free from reporting to superiors; therefore, you may be better suited to self-employment or at least employment that allows you to be in charge. Movement is an important consideration in your job portfolio; therefore, you may be well suited to travelling for work or changing environments regularly. Once the goalposts are in place, it is important that your work environs encourage you to be self-motivated. If your entrepreneurial and visionary character does not find an outlet in the everyday world of work, you are at risk of becoming bored and restless.

Restlessness, boredom, lack of direction or an inability to commit yourself to the job at hand may result in a sudden urge to leave your employment or, if you stay, you become frustrated and short-tempered with those in the environment. A lack of spirit and enthusiasm in your working environment can create tension and stress. Your nature is more akin to taking the risk to leave, rather than trying to steer a sinking ship.

As Aries rules the head, stress may be expressed through headaches, migraines, hearing loss or eyestrain. If you are not mobile enough in your occupation you could feel fatigued and exhausted. However, it is your lack of focus, restlessness and even reckless manner in your work that reveals you are not well suited to your job. It is important to remember that there are ways of minimizing stress at work: movement, a change of pace, a challenge, going to the gym during your lunch break or playing a competitive sport with one of your work colleagues are all healthy outlets. When you feel bottlenecked and the vital signs of life are not responding, you need to expend physical energy to get back on track. Being physical, motivated and challenged are the necessary components of your daily life.

Taurus on the 6th House Cusp

Stability and security need to be primary considerations in your daily life; therefore, working for a corporation or in an atmosphere that is dependable, reliable and well established is beneficial. It is necessary to see your daily tasks through to the end; as a result, you do best in positions that are slower paced and focused on tasks. You work well on long-term projects which develop over time because satisfaction comes from tangible results. It is more difficult to work in situations where results are elusive, changeable or imperceptible. Having a detailed job description and being aware of your responsibilities are also important. While opportunities for growth are always attractive, you are probably more interested in steady growth and practical outcomes. It is essential that you feel adequately valued and rewarded for your work, otherwise you may feel taken for granted. Stability, physical comfort and tangible results are the ingredients of a satisfactory working environment. Without the appropriate mix, stress can accumulate.

Taurus rules the throat and thyroid. Stress may first appear as a sore neck, nagging cough or sluggishness. Over time, accumulated stress may develop into more chronic throat problems. Ways to improve your working environment include surrounding yourself with warm colours, pot plants and pleasing aromas. You seek a solid relationship with your co-workers and it is important not to invest too much in colleagues who do not respond to your warmth or welcome. On a practical level, employment is a satisfying place where your vibrant personality can find solace and reward through hard work and patient building.

Work and values are intimately linked; psychologically, your work reflects your self-worth. Without a sense of your own worth or value you may be trapped in a job that depletes your self-esteem. When your work lacks value, you may transfer these needs onto the material world of finances, attempting to feel rewarded through your possessions. Yet without a connection to the worthiness of work, the money and assets you accrue will never be able to replace what is missing. Therefore, it is important to recognize the need to be valued and appreciated in the work you do, and perhaps the best way to begin is to ensure you find work that you value and welcome.

Gemini on the 6th House Cusp

Being active and mentally stimulated in your daily routines helps you to feel centred. At work you want to be mentally agile, interactive, intellectually challenged and physically mobile. Flexibility is the key, as without this you become bored and restless, which taxes the nervous system. Therefore it is important that your job offers you the scope to work on different programmes and diverse projects.

Mobility, communication and the processing of information are important aspects of your job description. You need a work environment that is not fixed, allowing you the freedom to come and go as you please. It is also important that you are able to unreservedly converse and interact with workmates, as communication helps to alleviate the stress of everyday routines. Your work might be communication-based: writing, exchange of information and ideas, teaching and instruction are all natural activities for you. You fit easily into the new world of information technology and exchange, and are adept at delivering the right message to the right person.

If communication outlets are lacking or there is not enough space to freely move about, you feel agitated, unable to concentrate or sit still. Having physical as well as emotional space at work is important to maintain a sense of well-being. Without flexibility, variety and change you may feel trapped, unable to breathe, even panicky. Your nervous system and lungs are sensitive to stress. Nervousness, anxiety and feeling smothered are the symptoms of stress, reminding you to create more space around you. An important daily ritual is focusing on your breath, bringing awareness to your breathing. Fresh air, space and distance are essential everyday components. Allowing yourself the space to daydream, toss around some ideas with co-workers or tell a funny joke helps to dissipate your nervous energy. Whether you take a walk at lunchtime or picnic in the nearby park, it is important to change the pace and get some fresh air to reinvigorate you.

Cancer on the 6th House Cusp

Creating a nurturing workplace environment and supporting and mentoring others are key aspects to a fulfilling job. Psychologically, you need to feel attached to your work and derive emotional and personal security from your job. Support, closeness, caring and empathy are attributes that you need in your working routine. Therefore, it is not surprising that you may be drawn to social work, family therapy, child care, nursing, health-related professions or childhood education, as all these occupations provide an environment where the focus is on nurturing and caring for others. This may not be your career; however, what is necessary is that your working environment nurtures and supports you.

One of life's most valuable, yet understated, vocations is motherhood. Work and family are connected and an emotional connection with those who share our daily space is important. At work, your family might be your co-workers. Another possibility is that work and family are entwined, such as working in a family business, with a family member or employed in a similar profession to one of your parents. Belonging is intimately bound up with work and it is through your everyday routines that you find your sense of emotional security and a place to belong.

If you lack a sense of safety or emotional connection to your work or the people you work with, you become moody, sensitive or overly dependent, reacting negatively to the environment and those in it. Stress is expressed through your moods. Or you may withdraw into feeling unwell and unappreciated. The solar plexus carries your discomfort; a stomach ache, nausea or having an upset tummy are symptomatic of discomfort in the workplace. Make sure you take care of yourself by providing a safe and nurturing environment for yourself.

Leo on the 6th House Cusp

A playful atmosphere in the work environment promotes being comfortable, focused and connected. You need to identify with your job to make it your own, and you also need be recognized in your workplace and to enjoy the company of your workmates. Work is a place you need to be proud of, feel that it is alive and creative; if not, you feel deflated. When you identify negatively with your work or working environment, you may withdraw or become petulant and condescending.

Feedback and approval are important components of your daily routine. You work best when you are aware that you have your superior's approval or your workmates' endorsement. Ultimately, you need to build your own confidence in your work, but the support of others is necessary at the beginning. Without an adequate sense of approval you may unconsciously expect to fail, and will not apply yourself or strive for achievement. It is important for you to know that there is scope for advancement and that opportunities exist for promotion. With these assurances and the right environment you are a loyal employee and a terrific spokesperson for the company.

You may promote your own products, creative works or talents. Self-promotion and having big ideas come naturally to you. You possess a natural appeal which attracts the right situation when you are optimistic and open. When you lack confidence or doubt your abilities you may compensate by being overconfident or inflated, which tarnishes your natural charm. When you are stressed your cardiovascular system becomes overworked and overwrought. Work stress affects your heart, reminding you that you need to return to being creative and expressive. Your chart indicates that there may be a correlation between work pressure and tension focused on your heart. Leo is connected to the lower back, and pain here is a sign of being out of sync.

Virgo on the 6th House Cusp

Consistency and orderliness are important; therefore, it is difficult for you to work in a chaotic environment. You need to know what is expected of you, responding best when there is a routine. If this is not possible, it is important to create rituals to unify the disparities at work. When boundaries are in place and you are familiar with the working procedures and others' expectations, you are able to relax and benefit from your work.

It is necessary to feel that you are constantly developing in your job and consistently improving in your job performance. You work best when there are specific goals, deadlines or tasks to be completed. The urge to improve is a large part of your nature, but with this disposition there may also be a perfectionist streak. Temperamentally, this urge for perfection might be a defence against feeling inadequate. When you begin to feel stressed or overwhelmed you might become more critical or obsessive, unable to finish the job until it is 'perfect'. Since your work ethic is high, you may be the last one to leave the office because you are finishing off a project or taking on responsibilities that others have relinquished; therefore, discriminating and setting boundaries between your responsibilities and those of others is essential.

It is vital that your working environment is healthy. You may find it necessary to brighten up the atmosphere so it feels hygienic. You need privacy at work; therefore, it is essential that you define your working space and what you can expect from your co-workers. When you are focused and using your analytical and discriminatory skills, the time passes quickly because you are totally involved in what you do. When stress builds up on the job, digestive difficulties may arise. Work pressure increases your anxiety and somatically the pressure is carried by the intestines; therefore, it is necessary for you to analyse and digest what has occurred during each working day.

Libra on the 6th House Cusp

When your working environment is aesthetic, and the atmosphere is peaceful and harmonious, you relax. But when you are enveloped by noise, the surroundings are unattractive or the climate of the workplace is tense and discordant, then you are stressed and at odds with your environment. Space and the feeling of the place you occupy is very important; therefore, it might be helpful to redecorate your work station or your office in colours that are right for you, or to collect works of art or pictures that beautify your work setting.

Your innate social skills give you the capacity to be successful in dealing and interacting with others. You have a natural aptitude for negotiation, counselling, writing, communication, diplomacy, hospitality, interviewing and recruiting, and all these skills are suitable for jobs in human resources or any other occupation involving people skills. Your sociable nature means you can work well with the right colleague or co-worker. Because you are competent when judgement and strategic thinking are necessary, this suggests that jobs requiring reflection, consideration, refinement and perception will suit you. Work is part of your lifestyle and you may forge your career alongside people you like and value. Often you find yourself working side-by-side with your partner or close friend. You might even meet your partner or your close friends through work.

Harmony and cooperation with your co-workers are important, and involvement with those you are working with both during and after hours improves your job satisfaction. Your co-workers are partners and you expect equality and fairness in all your interactions. However, one of your difficulties may be expressing any negative feelings to your co-workers or articulating your disappointment when they have acted selfishly or not taken your feelings into consideration. Unexpressed anger or frustration may lead to an underlying tension in relationships with clients or co-workers. If the working relationship declines, there may be a tendency to blame fellow workers or the conditions of the job, rather than your own dissatisfaction and disapproval. When stress at work is high, you feel out of balance, disconnected and unable to think clearly, and you lose your motivation. When this occurs, claim some space away from work and relationships so you can work out what is happening. Given some space and time off, you will be more willing and ready to launch yourself back into work.

Scorpio on the 6th House Cusp

When the deepest aspects of your nature are called into duty, you feel absorbed, engrossed and are satisfied with what you are doing. Without this, you may feel bored and unchallenged. You may be instinctively drawn to work that involves crisis, elimination and restoration. Scorpio qualities can be used in a variety of work routines: crisis management, medical emergency, psychotherapy, oncology, bereavement work, renovations, garden design, archaeology and research. As long as you feel you are working intensely, getting to the heart of the matter and being deeply engaged in what you are doing, you feel satisfied.

Integrity and honesty are important virtues for your workplace. You also need to respect the work you do, as well as to respect those who work in your industry. Trust is an important component of your working life, and while it may not be prudent to trust those you work with or for, you must trust that you are in the right position, with the right team and working for the right reasons. If you question your motives you may feel fraudulent or dissatisfied with your work. You can work well with others on projects and are open to combining your talents, yet you also work well by yourself. You have a strong work ethic and are highly motivated and focused. However, if you are disempowered in your workplace, power struggles with superiors or co-workers could develop.

The Scorpio spirit is incisive and insightful, energies you bring to your workplace. With your powerful presence you are not afraid of challenges or the truth. Others may react to your intensity with feelings of envy or intimidation, isolating you in the workplace. Integrity and honesty are important to you and many co-workers will not share the same intensity. When stress and pressure build up at work, so do the feelings that you have bottled up. Physically, you feel this in the gut and bowels, reflecting your need to let go. You need time and space to yourself so you can recharge. Even though you are a highly committed individual, the most important commitment is to your health and well-being. At the end of each day it is important to create a ritual that helps you let go of the stress built up during the day. To be able to cross over into your private life you need to create a firm boundary line between your engagement at work and your personal life.

Sagittarius on the 6th House Cusp

Sagittarius is a far-sighted sign, so occupations that permit a sense of adventure, learning, travel, cross-cultural experiences and stimulation are ideal. While this may seem too good to be true, it is important to note that you create your own fortune through positive attitudes and optimism. Your luck in securing the right job is proportionate to the attitude you bring to the situation.

The nature of Sagittarius is to explore further afield, beyond known boundaries; therefore, your work may take you beyond what's familiar, a long way from where you began. Literally, this could mean that you may work elsewhere in the country or overseas, work for an international organization or take up a post in a newly developing field. Education and dissemination of information underpin your work. Human values, ideals, principles and ethics are all part of your orbit, whether you work as an instructor, tutor, liaison office or translator, in education, publishing or teaching, or interact in the global community. It is important that your work supports your philosophy of life and that you are free enough to be able to discuss your beliefs with your co-workers. It may be through working overseas or with foreigners that you are introduced to new beliefs which reshape your philosophy of life.

Inspiration, expansiveness, optimism, travel, freedom, learning and advancement are all important facets of your working life. You need to feel inspired by what you do, otherwise you become restless and uninterested, unable to settle down to a regular position. If your job does not allow you to move about, feel unconstrained and express your ideas, you are unable to settle down to work. You need to feel that your ideals and ethics are respected in the workplace; if these vocational needs are unrecognized or ignored, you might be gripped by inflated and unrealistic expectations. Without focusing on the right career for you, there is a tendency to drift and 'dream' in an unproductive state. Or, if you become stuck in a rigid job with few possibilities for change, you are at risk of becoming depressed. You need to find enthusiasm and the spirit of life in the everyday; therefore, your work challenges you to go further afield than you might ever have imagined possible.

Capricorn on the 6th House Cusp

To support your strong personality you need the assurance that your daily life is structured and regulated. Your work ethic is strong; hence, vocational roles that draw out your leadership qualities, management abilities, proficiency and clarity will help you to find your place in the world. You might find that you are more competent and effective in positions where your responsibilities are well defined and the hierarchical chain of command is unmistakable.

If you are not identified with convention or establishment, it is important to introduce these qualities into your lifestyle. When you do this, you might find you are comfortable in the business world, whether you are self-employed, in partnership or working for a large company; therefore, it is always wise to be open to learning about the world of commerce and industry. It is important for you to respect tradition and customs because they define the atmosphere of your working world.

Being receptive to parental and societal expectations, you respect authority. This is partly because you have a strong sense of maturity and responsibility yourself. While you may not always accept this, it is part of your natural temperament. Therefore, it is sensible that you direct your dependability and conscientiousness towards your lifestyle, forging an authoritative and autonomous career. However, one pattern may resurface with authority figures: your level of competence and commitment may not be shared by those you work with or for. While you feel obliged to respect your bosses and superiors, you may feel their that leadership skills and competence are lacking. Rather than feeling deflated by this, become more resolved to develop your own authority, ambition and principles.

Recognition and approval for your work are important. If your need for recognition is unsatisfied you may be overly ambitious or controlling. It is also important to recognize that your compulsion to achieve may be fuelled by feelings of inadequacy. These might manifest as either a fear of success or an inappropriate command of authority. When the perfectionist streak appears, it is time to schedule a holiday or you may become overwhelmed with work. When you become sick and tired of work, you feel it in your aching joints and your sore back. Stress stiffens your body and you feel cold and distant. It is imperative for you to be aware that the rituals of your daily life need structure. Because work is a large part of daily life you will need to schedule periods when you take time off, even though that may be difficult for you.

Aquarius on the 6th House Cusp

Freedom and space are essential in your everyday life. Not just breathing space, but emotional and mental freedom is a prerequisite for you to feel connected. Sometimes this is accomplished by working independently or in an unorthodox or marginal job. With enough independence, leg room and lack of restrictions, you are prepared to be more committed and present with your work. It is important that your routines allow you to be innovative and unique, because working in a similar way to others or on identical projects with your workmates can generate claustrophobic feelings. Without adequate freedom and independence there could be an overt reaction against or disrespect for authority and hierarchy. Fear of entrapment might lead to irregular employment because you choose to remain outside the system. When you are engaged in repetitive and irrelevant tasks you become disenchanted. When stress builds up it is carried by the nervous system. Anxiety, even a panic attack, or feeling spaced out and disconnected are the signals that you are out of sync with your work routines. When this happens, try breaking up your routines by doing something different.

Stimulation and excitement are also necessary for you. Being mentally agile and alert, you need to be intellectually motivated or you become restless and uninterested. You may be drawn to technology as a way to engage your thinking. Tasks that require you to be original, far-sighted, inventive, future-focused and visionary stimulate you and provide an incentive to become involved. Collegial support and participation are important, but not at the expense of your individuality. At work you are aligned with the well-being of the group, rather than individual members' concerns. Although this might be perceived as being disinterested, it is your natural stance. You have an innate capacity to work with groups, whether as their team leader, facilitator or even as a member, as long as you have enough autonomy and feel equal. Part of your working life may involve groups or teams.

Being attracted to human rights and social and collective concerns, you may become caught up in office politics or be the one who speaks for the group. Overall, you are drawn to jobs that are progressive and innovative as well as those dedicated to improving the human predicament such as green politics, environmentalism, sustainability and conservation. These concerns are part of your lifestyle and working life, as you endeavour to make a difference in the world.

Pisces on the 6th House Cusp

A strong imagination could lead you into the arts, music, design, dance or photography; in fact, a host of creative endeavours might be possible. Or you may feel a strong urge to help others and this could lead you into working with the underprivileged, the handicapped or the disenfranchised. Care and compassion are virtues that you would like to express through your work. You are capable of feeling devoted to your work, so if you do not feel as expressive or uplifted as you would like, then your spirituality needs to feature in your lifestyle. If work does not supply the creativity or spirituality you need, it is important that you provide a space outside of work for this.

You are sensitive to the working environment; therefore, it is important to establish appropriate boundaries. One way is to respect your duties and responsibilities, as you have a tendency to take on others' tasks. Being helpful to workmates and colleagues can often backfire. Without adequate boundaries you may feel overwhelmed with responsibility, feeling that you are in 'over your head'. Another boundary is needed emotionally, as you could become enmeshed with your workmates' or clients' problems, leaving you feeling exhausted and depleted. As a sensitive you have a tendency to take on the negative feelings that are in the environment or in those you work with or for. You need to take care of yourself first, both physically and emotionally, by creating a healthy and pleasing workspace.

You do best when the atmosphere is flexible and provides enough room to let things happen in their own time. If there is too much structure or rigidity you may feel anxious or intimidated. It seems contradictory to suggest that your work should go with the flow, yet it is best for you to be relaxed, unforced and creative. Daily practices like meditation or silence help to refocus and realign your sense of well-being. You need time to reflect and contemplate. When you do not get the time to recharge yourself, you may feel listless, lethargic and directionless. When you sense yourself drifting or going around in circles, it is time to pause and take stock.

Planets in the 6th House
Planets in the 6th house represent the archetypal forces that underpin the routines of our everyday life. Because they are so available on a daily basis, it is imperative that we find avenues for their expression otherwise they affect our equilibrium and well-being. These are the forces that are both the root and the response to our illnesses, our crises and our disappointments. It takes a conscious effort to direct them towards personal growth, well-being and fulfilling work. Most importantly, it is work and effort that are required to actualize their potentialities.

Sixth houses planets had set shortly before we were born. While not passive by nature, planets in the 6th are placed in a house underneath the horizon; therefore, they are instinctive, reflective and orientated to the darkness, not the light. They need to be considered, thought through and intentionally directed towards developing and sustaining a balanced lifestyle.

As the house which locates the people in our everyday lives, the 6th house is associated with those we work with. Planets in the 6th show the archetypal patterns which arise at work and may be experienced through co-workers, bosses and those who assist us in our daily lives. Whether it is through projection or identification, the individuals who we work with can often bring issues with our parents, siblings and partners into the work space. Also, our co-workers, immediate bosses, clients and customers may be the catalysts for critical change in our lives.

Because the 6th house is an area of apprenticeship where we perfect our craft, planets here are helpful in developing techniques and practices to support our lifework. These are the energies that can help ensoul our everyday world; therefore, they need to be productive in our work routines and day-to-day tasks. Like the 6th house itself, these energies are eclectic yet they also need to be purposeful; therefore, it is useful to be as aware of them as we can.

The Sun in the 6th House

Your identity is entwined with what you do; therefore, work is where you are likely to come face to face with your character. Work is where you develop confidence and self-respect. Your workplace is your studio or theatre where you are able to build your identity, discover faith in your abilities and find a sense of fulfilment. It is a vital and creative place and the biggest challenge to discovering its liveliness is you. The Sun has just set, which is a reminder that appreciation for what you do may be internal rather than external.

Being productive is vital to your well-being and integral to your sense of growth and self-development; therefore, it is important that you work where you can excel and be recognized for your capabilities. Work is the sphere where you will forge your identity and self-esteem, growing in self-reliance and capability as you mature. If you work for a boss, they need to be a strong and fostering manager who is able to give you direction and acknowledgement. As the Sun personifies the father figure, patterns with a boss or co-worker may mirror issues with your own father, such as favouritism.

Work is a highly creative place because this is the forge where you temper your sense of identity. It is important to be successful in your work and take pride in what you do. If you are not feeling acknowledged or cannot find your reflection in your work, then you may become depleted and burnt out. Ironically, working gives you energy and vitality when you are connected to what you do; without this identification with your work, you feel rudderless and directionless. However, it is also necessary to shine where you are and find the courage and confidence to stand up for yourself in the working environment. Your task is to put your own label on what you do. Make your own mark on the workplace by creating an impressive imprint. Your position may not yet be created, so it is up to you to design the position that you would like to fill.

Because you need to be personally involved with work, you may be drawn to occupations that showcase your creative abilities. You are inherently good at managing creative productions. However, you may become so involved and focused on work that you lose some perspective on other areas of your life. Therefore, it is wise to establish balance in your daily regime. You need to be identified for what you do; therefore, it is very important that you recognize the value and fulfilment of work. The secret of your success is your ability to be identified with your job.

The Moon in the 6th House

Your 6th house Moon plays a major role in the way you cultivate your work. Being the most personal of all the planets, it suggests that you have your own individual needs and private routines to integrate into the work sphere. Feeling safe, belonging to the team and secure in your routines fulfil some of your work needs. Your work needs to feel familiar. You might make your workplace your nest, keeping continuity between work and home with personal pictures, mementos, your children's drawings or a favourite coffee mug on your desk. While it is important to create a safe environment and relate to workmates like family, it is often your instinct to mother that leads to bruised feelings. If you bring your intimate needs into the workplace you may feel hurt when they are not reciprocated.

Another way to focus your urge to nurture is through occupations of service, care or duty. Instinctively knowing about healing, restoration and caring, you may be drawn to health occupations, working with children or the elderly, midwifery, nursing or other professions involving care to some degree. But there are also other ways in which this image may manifest. Drawn to the past, the Moon responds to collecting antiques, restoring furniture, historical research, genealogy and occupations involving food, restaurant work or catering. However this archetype presents itself, the underlying urge is to feel attached to what you do.

It is your work that provides security, not necessarily the pay cheque or the retirement benefits. Fulfilling employment is when you feel you belong and are where you feel needed. You might prefer shift work, work from home, a family business or a home industry; whichever way this might manifest, it is imperative to recognize that you have to meet your own individual work needs.

You are also highly sensitized to the atmosphere of your working environment, the moods of your workmates and the ethos of the industry you work in. When work stress builds up you will feel it in the gut; it is telling you that you have had a gutful, and it is time to become more separate and to take care of yourself. If you hear yourself saying that you are sick of work, take heed as you may well become sick just to get some time off! Therefore, it is imperative that you take good care of your health, diet and daily regime. But first, make sure that work is a safe and restorative experience.

Mercury in the 6th House

Mercury engages with work by being social, communicative and adaptive. In the 6th house it is important that its analytical, communicative and organizational skills are utilized. In an information-orientated culture, Mercury in the 6th can find many outlets, such as working in IT, developing ideas, writing, lecturing, training, sales and promotion. A long list of occupations that suit the quest for analysing information and promoting ideas include: the media, accounting and economic analysis, advertising, computer work, editing, information technology, being an interpreter, journalist, librarian, postal worker, radio announcer, script writer and statistician. The list is endless. Mercury is a multifaceted divinity, the god of the roads, the marketplace and commerce.

What is certain is that you need to be mobile, interactive and not tied down to a desk. The nervous system bears the brunt of the work stress so your nerves have a tendency to become frayed. You may become so involved with the task in hand that you become disembodied, forgetting to eat regularly, take a break or just get out for some fresh air. If this occurs you run the risk of becoming scattered and anxious. Your mind is racing with all the things that need to be done and it feels as if they must all be done now. If you find yourself being bored at work, you are definitely in the wrong occupation. Part of being successful is being in tune with your body and what it needs, being mindful not to overtax the system by doing too much.

No matter what your position is at work, you easily become the central link in the chain of command as well as a clearing house for news and gossip. Your role in the office may be as the one who is in contact with everyone. Whether you are the youngest or last one to join the work team, you bring innovative and fresh ideas and energy to your workplace. You have an ability to get the message through to whoever needs to hear it, so whether you are a personal assistant advising your boss, a newsreader, gossip columnist, teacher, interpreter, writer or graphic artist, your message needs to be delivered.

Venus in the 6th House

Presentation, image, dress and style are important considerations in your workplace; you also need it to be pleasant and welcoming. It is almost impossible for you to work in unattractive surroundings, unless the end product is artistic or beautiful. Similarly, it is difficult to work in a hostile situation unless, of course, it leads to reconciliation. The archetype of beauty seeks its expression in your daily life. Working as a specialist in art, in a museum as a curator, guide or consultant, or as an art or beauty therapist, could be satisfying. The fashion industry, the perfume or cosmetic trade, clothing design, interior decoration and design, gifts and crafts, and floristry, also express this archetype, as would work involving hairdressing, fashion, make-up and beauty products. The bottom line is to be able to feel engaged with the creation of beauty. Seeking balance and reconciliation, you could be proficient at mediation, personnel work, counselling or arbitration. The hospitality industry is also possible, given your innate skills at diplomacy and your natural charm in a work situation.

Another way to engage with this archetype is through your sensuality, whether that is through massage, music, art, design, placement, essential oils or any occupation focused on touch, taste, sound, smell or sight. Since the feminine archetype underpins your working life, another possibility is working with women and women's issues, whether that is in a personal setting as a counsellor or adviser, perhaps a doctor or psychoanalyst, or as a politician or educator dedicated to women's issues; alternatively, you bring life and beauty to your work.

Feeling equal and in relationship are important. Your partner may be involved in some way with your work, you might meet your partner at work or perhaps you experience your co-workers as partners. The pleasure principle and work are entwined so when you are unfulfilled in what you do, you might seek pleasure through other avenues, such as food, alcohol or shopping. Weight and work could be connected. When you are happy at work you feel attractive and valued, but when satisfaction is missing you feel undervalued and unattractive. Finding work that values and appreciates your skills and resources generates a healthier sense of self-esteem.

Mars in the 6th House

Being the god of action, Mars in the 6th recommends daily movement, activity and exertion. Finding ways to channel aggressive instincts into your daily routines is important; perhaps by working out in the gym, running, swimming, walking or other physical activities. This energy is doing, not being; when it comes to your job you need to find an energetic way to approach work. Physical exertion will go a long way towards satisfying this drive, but it is also important that you can tap into the enterprising and vital spirit of Mars in the work sphere.

Your competitive nature needs to be acknowledged in your working life. You may set goals and deadlines for yourself, compete with others in the workplace or find yourself in a highly competitive industry where wits and will must combine to win the game. It is healthy for you to see work as a game that you are striving to win. Mars in the 6th house suggests strong ambitions which are best expressed overtly, because when everything is out in the open you feel free to go for what you want.

Independence, challenges and adventure are part of your working terrain. It might not suit you to be an adventure hunter but the metaphor is still apt. Whether you are hunting for the right product, being headhunted or tracking down a problem, your work needs to be challenging and competitive. Being entrepreneurial, you work well on your own and following your instincts. You also may be suited to following a trade, whether that is an electrician, a plumber or any other occupation that allows you to fix problems. Strategy and precision combine to make you good at decision-making; therefore, you can be called on to make decisions in a hurry. This exacting nature could manifest in a myriad of ways, from surgical skills to clear-cut decision-making.

When your work is unchallenging, boring or too routine, you become restless, irritated and stroppy. When frustrated and quick-tempered you might find yourself becoming argumentative with your workmates just to get a reaction. Being mindful that you need movement, change and stimulus as part of your everyday life helps to keep you vital.

Jupiter in the 6th House

This archetype seeks instructive and adventuresome occupations; in the 6th house you may be drawn to work that supports the quest to interact with the wider world through education, teaching and sharing knowledge with others. Another option is travel, working in a foreign country, in the tour industry, foreign trade or in a job which requires overseas contact . However, you do not need to physically travel to be engaged with cross-cultural and meaningful employment. You may work with others who come from exotic ethnic backgrounds, different educational histories, unfamiliar religious convictions or differing sexual orientations. They introduce you to the unknown and help to introject meaning into your everyday life. You need to feel that your work is always growing, filled with possibilities and that you are engaged in making a difference.

Work inspires you to move away from past constrictive attitudes. As you question communal ethics, political policies, social parameters and cultural mores, you may be drawn to the fields of political science, ancient history or foreign languages. Jupiter is a social planet so its energy is focused on communal and societal concerns; therefore, you may be interested in advancing ecological, moral or religious attitudes and awareness. You want to stretch yourself and lead a life where you are inspired by learning what exists outside the box. Work is the vehicle that helps you to see the world.

Once you believe in something, you have the enthusiasm to be able to engage others with your passionate ideas. This is potentially useful in sales and when interesting others in products or processes that you believe in. You are able to advertise and market what you know makes a difference in the world. You can also focus this trait on instructing and helping others to improve their well-being and their lifestyle. Whether you are able to find your exuberant spirit on the sports field, in an ashram, travelling or studying, you need to access the abundant energy of Jupiter in your everyday working life. Without a spirited dedication to what you do, you may become restless and prone to excesses. A spiritual exercise, an engaging hobby or stimulating studies are routines that can help to access your need for a philosophical and meaningful daily life.

Saturn in the 6th House

Saturn's task in the 6th house is to become masterful and authoritative in the sphere of employment. That is the potential of Saturn in the work sector; but what is the reality? Saturn often manifests as being critical because of its high standards and perfectionism, attitudes which may be projected onto the environment, expecting work to conform to your values and high standards. The reality, of course, is that work will not be perfect and you will make mistakes along the way. When you realize this, the possibilities for success increase.

The first step is to acknowledge your ambition and goals. Innately, you want to play by the rules, work ethically, adhere to a routine and be acknowledged for your accomplishments. Unfortunately, the corporate world does not always have the same work ethic. While you take your duties and responsibilities seriously, others and even your boss may not share this attitude. In fact, you may have already experienced a string of bosses whose competency and dedication were no match for yours. Or found out that all your hard work and dedication was not used in the final process. Feeling defeated, you may complain about your situation and the lack of management or integrity. You work best when given responsibility and control; often you have to make this happen yourself. Part of Saturn's pattern in the 6th house is that the individual needs to be left alone to craft and shape their own job. But once you recognize that your hard work and dedication is intended for your success, not that of others, you can steer your own course.

Your great assets are persistence, commitment and focus. Control is also important; therefore, you might consider self-employment, or certainly employment where the rules are clear and there is the opportunity to advance. You can work well in a hierarchical structure when there are bosses you respect. Unfortunately, this might be rare. When it occurs then you will take advantage of the learning curve. But if you do not respect your superiors you can turn the situation to your advantage. You can grow into any job, so take your time. Becoming an authority or highly skilled in your chosen field is very important, so you may find that study and training are part of your job spec. Advancement is important so it might be necessary to periodically review your goals and your progress. Time management is also important because you need to be sure you can fulfil the commitments you take on. When the pressures of work become greater than you can bear, you feel it in your back. Bodily aches, a sore back, stiff knees and pains in the neck remind you that it is time to have a break from your work routines. Clocking off is as important as clocking in.

Chiron in the 6th House

As Chiron is the archetype of wounding and healing, it is highly likely that these dynamics will play a role in your job. Literally, this may describe one of many healing occupations, especially the complementary healing professions. Chiron, as the mythic originator of the physical, mental and spiritual approaches to the healing arts, aligns with the modern disciplines of naturopathy, homeopathy, herbalism, chiropractic healing, Feldenkrais, osteopathy, acupuncture, Chinese medicine, crisis counselling, shamanism, dream therapy, psychotherapy, Reiki, astrology and other modalities that work with imagery and symbols as a healing tool. This may not be your career, but you may be involved with these ideas daily in some work capacity.

You may have found your work through your own suffering or experience. By understanding something for yourself, you are able to work with others who are in the same predicament. You may not literally bear the wound or scar, but somewhere deep inside you understand the nature of the wound or ailment. This might be working in the health field with those recovering from addictions or trauma, or in social work with refugees or displaced and disenfranchised individuals. Chiron was also a mentor and teacher. Mentoring professions such as life coaches, inspirational teachers or tutors and coaches dedicated to their students resonate with this placement.

It is important to honour the parts of yourself that do not fit into the system. You might be required to work in a structure, a system or an organization and this may be difficult. Chiron in your daily work suggests that you may feel marginal to the system you work in, and you may be on the periphery of your professional associations. Ironically, you are not. You understand something beyond the system and will not compromise your own understanding in order to belong. Although you might feel foreign to the system you work in, or are the foreigner in the work system, it is important to celebrate your differences and use them to your advantage.

Uranus in the 6th House

Psychologically, you need to feel independent enough at work to do your own thing. Imposition of rules, strict procedures and repetitive tasks do not suit you, as the revolutionary aspect of your character needs expression in the work department. When this does not find its voice you might rebel; however, when the archetype is focused on cutting-edge, adventuresome and future-orientated work it is highly conscientious. You might explore helping others with future planning, work with technological and innovative design, experiment with organizational change or any new employment that is dedicated to advancement and human opportunity.

Emotionally, your work needs to provide enough space and freedom for you to explore a range of possibilities. Feeling unattached, able to move on at any time and ready to take the opportunity when it arrives is ideal. You would not feel comfortable with the same working position for the next twenty years. You are more interested in the possibilities and opportunities of work rather than the realities and procedures. While you work well in a team, it goes best when you are not emotionally attached. You need a clear distinction between your emotional life and your work life, as they do not mix well. Although you need your freedom from emotional entanglements in the workplace, you have good friends and colleagues who become witnesses to and co-conspirators in your life work.

Physically, your workspace also needs to be spacious. Without your own space you might confuse your need to be separate with separation, pushing co-workers away just to be able to breathe. Therefore, it is important to honour this need for physical space and separateness. When work becomes oppressive, you may become restless, irritable and reactionary or slip into despondency. Your work and lifestyle need to provide enough space to feel free enough to explore life's opportunities and possibilities.

Neptune in the 6th House

Work may feel mysterious, even unattainable. This might be due to your expectations and idealism; however, the truth is probably that you create your own work and lifestyle as you go. Like a photographic negative, your work picture is slowly developed over time. You are able to sense and imagine what you want to do, but it takes time for that to actualize. Neptune's nature is uncontained, unformed, fluid with no boundaries, yet the 6th is a house where order and ritual are important. Your task is to find a way to integrate the creative spirit that is spiritual and transcendent with the everyday tasks of productivity and work.

You may not be clear about what you would like to do, but there are two roads you might consider. The first is the creative path where the magical aspect of Neptune can be staged or given a canvas or a screen onto which to project its vivid images. With Neptune in this house you can tap into its boundless imagination to produce moving and inspirational works of art. The medium is your choice. Whether it takes the form of film, dance, acting, painting, writing, music or any other, you can be sure the muse will show up. The second way is the helping professions, as you have an innate ability to be compassionate and empathetic. Both paths are fed by the innate urge to be of service. This is your calling and you feel compelled to find the spiritual in the everyday; a difficult task in a corporate world, but not impossible. One of the main focuses of your work is to bridge what is ideal with what is possible. Therefore, you may be in a variety of positions where you must navigate between the world of the imagination and the world of certainty.

The everyday world of work with its guidelines, routines, procedures and protocol may not be an easy fit for your otherworldly nature, making it a necessity to honour this aspect of yourself through hobbies or rituals. In this way you can appease the soulful need to do creative work, even when you may be occupied in a soulless job. Whether you paint, take dance lessons, sing in a choir, write poetry, volunteer, meditate or bush walk, it is necessary that you revere the spiritual and creative aspects of yourself. When your spiritual nature lacks expression, it presents itself as fatigue, lethargy, loss of concentration and forgetfulness. Physically, Neptunian ailments are hard to diagnose because they belong to the soul, not the body. Therefore, spiritual work is the way to remain well, recognizing that when the pressures of work are overwhelming you find a sanctuary in which to be still and centred.

Pluto in the 6th House

Mythologically, Pluto resides below the visible world, surfacing infrequently. However, when he does make his presence known, it is life-altering. This is a metaphor for your work, which is transforming and confronting. Through work you may be drawn into the deeper aspects of yourself. Work is therapeutic by nature, coercing you into unearthing your power. With Pluto in the 6th house, it is in the work sphere where you encounter your hidden strength, uncover your motives and recognize your ability to deal with crisis and endings. Quite literally, work might involve death, what is hidden, secrets or anything buried beneath the literal or psychological ground we stand on.

Professionally, this gives you a depth of character. Occupations where your critical skills are needed to manage or advise may lead you to therapeutic careers that involve loss, transition, concentration and intensity. Like an archaeologist, you like to peel away the layers to find the truth and have a knack for research, crisis work or change management. You may also be involved with finance, especially investments of other people's resources. Due to the high demands of your work, what is important is that you are aware of your need for privacy and respect.

Reflect on the nature of your vocation and its intensity. You may have a propensity to become fixated or obsessed with work detail, so you need to be vigilant that work does not consume you or abduct you from your personal life. Because the work environment constellates your strength and power, you often experience other colleagues or workmates being intimidated by or envious of you. Unfortunately, there is nothing you can do to change this except to recognize that their discomfort lies with your commitment to the truth. Certainly you cannot allow yourself to be disempowered by the weaknesses of others. On the other hand, you will also draw powerful and insightful people into your orbit who will change your attitudes and direction to work. Work offers you the opportunities to encounter your integrity and honesty, confronting you with the need to be true to yourself.

– Chapter 10 –
PROFESSION
The Career Path and the Tenth House

The cusp of the 10th house is the Midheaven,[38] the highest point on the ecliptic at our moment of birth. Its elevation in the horoscope suggests a complex of factors: it is the most public area of the horoscope, representing our relationship to and experience of the world. This symbolizes the goalposts of our lives. These expectations and aspirations are not only set by ourselves but have been put in place by our ancestors, as the MC and 10th house also represent the parental expectations and values that influence our career choices.

From a traditional point of view, the 10th house has always indicated the course of our work or trade; in a contemporary context, the career is one of this house's most significant features. From a modern view, it continues the tradition as a house focusing on profession, conditions of the career, the role and status in the world: in general, the vocational life path. Of the three houses of vocation it is the only one above the horizon; therefore, it is more public and visible. As the only angular house in the trinity, it also symbolizes where we enact our career and where it is known and acknowledged. Therefore, the sign on the MC or 10th house cusp, its ruler and the planets in the house are the symbols through which our vocation naturally attempts to express itself.

The 10th House	• The nature of your relationship with the public and the world • Your place and status in the society • The public sphere where you find your role, either through a career, your reputation or your contributions • The area where you strive for authority over the course of your life • Your parents' influence on your career
Keywords	Achievement; Ambition; Authority; Career; Contribution; Parent (often suggested as the conditional or 'world' parent); Prestige; Profession; Public; Reputation; Social status; Unlived life (of parent); Vocation; World

The Sign on the 10th House Cusp and its Ruler	• A key to your success; which qualities do the sign and its ruler potentially bring to your role in the world • Vocational qualities that seek expression through your career path in the world • What you need to promote and support your reputation • What needs to be conscious and to develop and mature with career activities • Your contribution to the greater world outside the self
Planets in the 10th House	• Need to find a niche in the world; to express their force though career • Need to respond to the 'calling' and desire to contribute meaning and fulfilment to life • Urge to be in control of the vocational destiny, to be authoritative, reliable, autonomous, successful • Urge to be responsible and focused on fulfilling the life tasks and mission

Since career suggests a course of one's life, the 10th house will play a prominent role in helping to navigate the career path. The 10th suggests where we need to find our authority and autonomy in the world and where we strive to be successful. Situated at the peak of the horoscope, the 10th house illustrates what we would like to achieve in our relationship with the world. It also suggests the public sphere and how we are recognized in that sphere, whether through our professional titles, our achievements or contributions. It is in this arena where we strive to contribute to the world in our own unique way. I often visualize the 10th house cusp as being the spire on a cathedral, a temple or stupa which lifts our attention to the heavens and the heights of what we imagine we might be in the world.

Signs on the Cusp of the 10th House

The Midheaven, the 10th house cusp, suggests career paths that open out onto the world, ones that are potentially fulfilling and successful. The sign indicates what we want to achieve, which qualities are available to support the journey and where we need to locate ourselves in the world. The ruling planet both reinforces and challenges the construction of the career. Wherever and however it is positioned in the horoscope, consciousness needs to be applied to access this ruling planet so it may be used as a guide and collaborator on the vocational journey.

In the natural wheel, the MC is square to the Ascendant. When using an unequal house system like Placidus, which is the one used throughout this book, the angular relationship between the MC and Ascendant changes. In any horoscope, when the solstice signs of Cancer or Capricorn are on the MC, the equinox signs of Libra or Aries respectively come to the Ascendant, forming the square which is exact when 0° of these signs culminate on the MC. As we move away from the solstice points the space between the MC and Ascendant can stretch to a trine or contract to a sextile. And in high or low latitudes this can be even greater. But in terms of imagery, what is important to recognize is that the MC is naturally at odds with the Ascendant, as the following combinations show:

MC Sign	♑	♒	♓	♈	♉	♊	♋	♌	♍	♎	♏	♐
ASC Sign	♈	♉	♊	♋	♌	♍	♎	♏	♐	♑	♒	♓

MC-Ascendant combinations in the natural wheel

Note that in the natural wheel, the sign on the MC is always the square behind the sign on the Ascendant, or the waning square. This suggests it is not instinct nor action that is needed to contemplate this tension, but consciousness of the differences between our personal and public characters. For instance, the Ascendant is our personal outreach into life whereas the MC is our public role; therefore, the way we may want to act and present ourselves may not be appropriate in the public sphere. What we choose to do in our own life is not necessarily appropriate in our professional life, nor is what we do in the privacy of our own homes suitable in public. When the personal life becomes public it serves the personality and no longer the career. Therefore it is important to be mindful of the differences and conscious of the suitable activities needed for both. Over time, with applied conscious effort, we strike the balance.

In contemplating the signs on the MC and Ascendant, be aware that underpinning the combination is a tension, not because of the astrological signs but because of the different orientations of the MC and Ascendant.

Aries on the 10th House Cusp

Professionally, the spirit of Aries suggests making its own decisions and creating its own career; therefore, any vocation that encourages self-governing and entrepreneurial qualities is suitable. As your career trajectory may be consistently changing and presenting challenges, you are suited to working freely and instinctively wherever there is some uncertainty and risk. But how this is assimilated with your personality is the key.

The Aries temperament needs activity; it becomes impatient if it has to wait too long. In any vocation you yearn to let your spirit of discovery soar, wanting to trail-blaze, to adventure, to pioneer, to chart virgin territory and explore what has not yet been discovered. You crave to accomplish the impossible. Self-image is important and personal identity needs to be a focus; therefore, vocations that utilize and encourage personality and identity are appropriate. You learn by making mistakes, breaking rules and dealing with the consequences rather than through books. Being self-motivated, you thrive on competition and challenges from others.

The Fire spirit needs to push itself; therefore, physical work or work requiring courage, nerve, adrenalin and stamina is suitable. Occupations with a goal, a deadline or a risk factor encourage this driving spirit. You like to initiate projects, but not necessarily see them through to completion, so planning, brainstorming, vision and entrepreneurial skills suit you best. Without the fulfillment of these vocational urges, frustration and boredom could be prevalent, igniting an aggressive and self-defeating attitude. Therefore, it is important to recognize that your personality needs to harness your competitive and industrious instincts.

Taurus on the 10th House Cusp

Taurus on the Midheaven suggests employing your sensual, tactile and Earthy nature in your career, perhaps through construction, visual arts or crafts, horticulture, massage or a variety of vocations that employ physicality and a hands-on approach. You need to receive tangible results from what you do; therefore, you may do better in vocations that involve physical, rather than intellectual, spiritual or feeling activities. Although these other realms may be vocationally viable, they need to yield practical, tangible results.

Stability and longevity are important, as you need to proceed along your career path step by step and at your own pace. Allowing yourself to settle, finding your rhythm and learning the job thoroughly takes time; if you feel rushed or pushed you may actually slow down. At the end of each working day you need to know that the task has been accomplished and at least one thing has been struck off the must-do list. Security, reliability and a good track record with the company or organization you are considering is important when assessing the right employment. You like to be attached to what you do, feel stable in your place of work and have a sense of mastery over your workshop. But it is imperative that you value what you do and be valued for what you create. Your career needs to be valued; therefore, the monetary reward needs to be commensurate with your own self-worth.

When your vocational needs are not met, you may feel stuck, despondent or lethargic, unable to draw on your instinctively resourceful and creative nature. When meaning and engagement are lacking in your vocation, you will turn to the material world to satisfy your emptiness. Yet without the soulful expression of your creativity in the world, materiality will not be satisfying either. Vocationally, you need to find a secure place to manifest your abundant resources in order to feel fulfilled.

Gemini on the 10th House Cusp

Gemini needs lots of room to breathe and to move about freely in a career, surrounded by a shifting landscape that inspires thoughts, ideas and techniques. Communication underpins your vocation, giving you many ways to creatively exchange with others. Whether it is through design, writing, lecturing, body movements, laughter or such occupations as a reporter, journalist, writer, teacher, translator or announcer, your calling is to circulate information and express your ideas. Flexibility and the freedom to communicate are paramount. Whatever the choice, you will always need space so you feel unencumbered by the system.

Agility, dexterity and versatility are other qualities to consider; therefore, professions involving graphics, drawing, designing and sketching, all of which include the dexterity of both mind and hand, are compatible: perhaps drafting, calligraphy, design and illustration. As long as information flows, you are content. Perpetually youthful, you are also adept at setting your career sails to take advantage of the winds of change. Duality plays a starring role in your vocation; whether this manifests as having two jobs at once or being torn between two professions, it certainly implies change and flexibility in your professional life and the roles this brings.

Ideas are not meant to be ideologies, communication is not communion. It is satisfying enough to move with your ideas, share your thoughts, write down your experiences and communicate your feelings. When your vocation does not offer this wide experimentation ground or room to test all the possibilities your spirit becomes agitated and nervous, scattering its ideas on barren ground, unable to mature in the world. Your love of facts and the discovery of meaning are so important; communication, learning and being mentally stimulated are imperative for you.

Cancer on the 10th House Cusp

Emotional security and feeling that you belong are possible if you feel safe and contained in your career. You may have a preference for a family environment, thereby attempting to transform the work atmosphere into a family one. Familial issues might be involved in your career; for instance, an environment that has an extended family atmosphere, a family business, working from home, following vocational traditions and customs especially on your mother's side or even vocations centred on family dynamics and issues. You might be drawn to vocations involving family services: family care providers, early childhood educators, day care workers or home services.

Providing safety, comfort and care for those in need is your calling. Your nurturing urges need fulfilment in the world; therefore, occupations involving nurturing, caring and providing support to others are appealing. This may lead to considering a profession as a health care professional or an occupation in primary teaching, nursing or counselling. Being a helper of some kind, such as a family therapist, social worker or being involved in public service, is a career consideration. Professions involving literal nurturing with food, cooking, restaurant and hospitality work, home catering and home industries engage your instinct to be caring and creative in the world. Alternatively, you might consider a career involving the home or products for the home, real estate or domestic jobs; a more person-centred architecture or design business where you help others to be settled could also be suitable.

Emotional security in your personal life is a necessity if you are to excel in the world. Therefore it is always wise to seek the shelter and support of those you love and ask for the help and backing of those in charge.

Leo on the 10th House Cusp

In the body, Leo governs the heart, which is an apt metaphor for your need to be at the centre of your profession, heartened by and 'in love' with the career path you take through life. Your calling is to express yourself and be engaged in creative productions. Whether these are artistic or scientific, therapeutic or practical does not matter as long as your vocation fulfils your desire for the self-exploration of personal talents and skills. You are more satisfied when your career is recognized and appreciated. It is important for your identity to be a central focus in what you do, because your creativity needs to be identified and demonstrated. Whether you make your own products, design your own label or manage your own business, what makes a difference is that your name is attached to your creative output and that it is recognized.

Praise goes a long way in encouraging you to perform well. Approval, especially that of your father, is important for you to feel secure in the world. By design you will also encounter the father archetype in the world through replacement figures such as superiors, bosses, bureaucrats, difficult clients or demanding customers. A hallmark of your vocation is your encounter with authority.

Being loyal, trustworthy, dependable, warm and generous are qualities that enhance your career standing. Self-esteem and confidence are linked with your vocation; therefore, it is important that you are appreciated for what you do. You need to be encouraged to stand back and see the creative results of all your efforts. Since Leo needs an audience you may thrive in professions where you are able to interact with others and use your creative skills. Promoters, teachers, entertainers, instructors, motivators, authors and actors are all called to the centre stage of their own creativity. The Leo temperament is also very natural for working with children, children's products or children's entertainment. Therefore, you may do well in recreational and creative businesses, theatre, amusement and leisure occupations as well as a range of lifestyle occupations.

Virgo on the 10th House Cusp

A virtue of your calling is honouring your desire to be of service. This urge, alongside striving for wholeness, are considerations in any vocational pursuit. Although this urge may be projected onto a literal career, your true vocation is serving yourself in your quest for wholeness. It is important that your vocation fulfils the desire for self-improvement and self-understanding. This quest may lead you into a wide spectrum of health care occupations, social services, holistic healing or sacred professions: for instance, dentistry, medicine, nursing, mental health, social work, clinical psychology or pastoral counselling. Holistic healing careers involving herbs, natural remedies and therapies, nutrition, hygiene, physical realignment and so on, are also well suited to Virgo's sympathy with the natural world. A naturopath is both a literal and metaphoric image that encapsulates this urge to find a path towards wholeness.

Virgo's need to serve could also be satisfied through the repair and service industries, and you may have an interest, even an innate technical skill, that could be utilized vocationally in scientific or medical occupations such as a laboratory technician, scientific research, health inspection or medical research and technology. Or you may resonate with the instinctual and natural world of plants and animals; an example could be a nurseryman attending to plants or a veterinarian caring for animals. Analysing facts and figures is another skill that can be used in a variety of ways, such as auditing mathematics, and accounting where your ability for detail and precision can be utilized. Virgo suggests deconstructing the whole into its various parts to improve its functionality. Whether this is done through dissection, editing or criticizing, your goal is to improve whatever you become involved in. Your quest for perfection needs to be recognized and directed in any profession, otherwise you may feel unsatisfied, obsessing on what is not right.

Your job needs to be constantly improving. Routine and ritual are necessary in order to promote a sense of coherence, as chaos in your world is unsettling. The need to constantly improve and the pressure to be perfect may drive you into working too hard and too long; therefore, it is important for you to remember to balance work demands and personal needs.

Libra on the 10th House Cusp

With a strong need for beauty, harmony and relating you might be drawn to the arts, but not necessarily choose to be an artist. Your aesthetic urges could find expression in vocations related to art, music, design or fashion through organizing, promoting, producing or trading. A wide professional spectrum could be considered, such as interior design, Feng Shui, décor, fashion coordination, beauty therapy, cosmetics, stage design and modelling.

The Libran scales remind us of the inclination to judge. Psychologically, this is Libra's way of discovering what they value, appreciate and like. Through judgement, options and possibilities are weighed up. Vocationally, this instinct to judge can be used in professions where arbitration, perception and clarity of thought are essential. You might also discover your skills at conflict resolution, negotiation, relating and communication, leading into professions involving personnel recruitment, arbitration, political negotiation, counselling, consulting and judging. You are fulfilled when you can negotiate a truce, resolve an awkward situation or introduce the right person into the right situation. As social skills are innate to Libra, you may be drawn to the hospitality industry or occupations where tact and diplomacy are necessary. A natural tendency towards relating may lead you towards the counselling professions, because listening and reflecting back another's feelings, moods and even desires is a Libran trait.

A tendency to overlook the possibility of conflict and negativity could lead to unsatisfying working partnerships. As your need for harmony and cooperation in the workplace is high, an unharmonious environment or unsupportive collegial relationships leaves you anxious and disheartened. Without positive interaction and support, Libra will find it hard to concentrate on any task. What is important for you is relationship and engagement, and it is important that you discover this through your work in the world.

Scorpio on the 10th House Cusp

Being intensely involved with what you do and occupied with what is crucial and critical is motivational for you. Therefore, careers that involve crisis management, repair and renovations or are centred on rebuilding and transformation are consistent with this image. However, you may also be drawn to a range of healing and therapeutic professions that enable you to delve deeply into yourself and others to uncover negative patterns from the past. Through your career, you learn to endure what others find difficult. Understanding cycles heightens your ability to work with crisis or near-death experiences as well as frightful and difficult rescue situations or investigations. Forensics, criminal investigation, medical research, trauma counseling and palliative care are all areas that resonate with Scorpio.

In working relationships you are able to accomplish something with a partner that you could not do yourself, something valuable and transformational. While the need to partner is important, you also need your time alone. Your quality of being able to work effectively on your own and be focused on the task allows you to be skilled at research and investigative work. You are most effective when you feel trusted by those you work with and are empowered by management. Completion is also important, so vocations that are highly changeable might not suit you.

Power is an issue that will be part of your vocational life. Professionals who are influential and transformational may play an important role in your career, or you may be attracted to professions which are commanding and powerful. If you feel disempowered in your career this may be transferred into power struggles with superiors, betrayals or power issues in the atmosphere. It is important to know that you are trusted to perform your duties.

Sagittarius on the 10th House Cusp

Freedom of movement, upward mobility and limitless possibilities are part of your wish list for a career. Qualities you can bring to your career are long-range vision, enthusiasm and intuitive capacities. Principles and ideals are important; therefore, it is essential that your vocational path reflects your personal ethics. Your philosophical and humanistic view of the world can be utilized to inspire and motivate others. Motivating and encouraging others to perform beyond their limits can be developed and may lead you into education, training, coaching, publishing or occupations where knowledge is used for the betterment of the self and community.

The need for freedom is high, because you need to pursue your goals openly and honestly. The Sagittarian archetype loves freedom, nature and travel, and these elements are also important for you to consider in a vocation. An occupation that allows you to explore foreign landscapes, be involved with cross-cultural concerns or with nature is beneficial: a travelling veterinarian, a foreign guide or teacher, perhaps an adventure leader, are images that may appeal. However, your need for exploration does not always have to be physical. Often it may be scholastic or intellectual instead.

Your idealism and interest in social education and reform requires that there is a degree of social involvement in your occupation. Your need to expand your world views and be in contact with ideas and individuals who broaden your philosophy and mental concepts is an important consideration. Education and human concerns, which foster social and philosophical expansion, are ideal. If you feel confined or limited in your vocation, or your work is repetitive and predicable, then you may feel imprisoned, depressed or lethargic. You need your career to push past the restrictions and boundaries set down by the systems of the past.

Capricorn on the 10th House Cusp

Honouring tradition and hierarchy, respecting structures and laws, and creating well defined boundaries and responsibilities are imperative on your career path. You need to honour convention in your vocation, yet not to the extent of being controlled or inhibited. A clearly defined job description helps to maximize your performance. Knowing your tasks, so that you do not try to overachieve or take on responsibility for others' work, is also important. You may feel responsible for the whole system, which impedes your own ability to do well.

The opportunity to advance up the corporate ladder one step at a time, along with a hierarchical culture in the workplace, is consistent with this image. Capricorn is ambitious; first and foremost, your ambition is simply to be able to do the best you can. In this sense ambition is healthy; however, when coupled with insecurity, performance anxiety and the lack of a supportive father figure, your ambition can be projected onto status and outer achievements. Having a sense of your place in the work environment, being responsible for your own area of work, having a title, approval and feedback, regular reviews and mentoring are all helpful in finding security in your career.

Qualities of commitment, dedication, application and discipline come naturally to you. Tangible achievements are important, as you may not thrive with conceptual or undefined duties. While your skills can range from business acumen to garden design, from architecture to construction, the common elements are being productive, employed and task-orientated, all of which are essential for you. Like a mountain goat, you need to be sure-footed on your career path. The route you take needs to be steady, controlled and well planned. When too much pressure to succeed is placed on your young shoulders, you may find that your route has been designed by others' needs and expectations, not your own. You need to know you are in control of your destiny, your own boss, authoring your own script and following your own manual.

Aquarius on the 10th House Cusp

Aquarian ideals are usually altruistic and aspire towards equality and freedom; hence, involvement in humanitarian pursuits or with organizations sympathetic to charitable, ecological or animal concerns may be appealing. Vocation is influenced by idealism and philanthropy. Like Uranus, the ruler of your Midheaven, you need to express your progressive, intuitive and future-orientated qualities through your career so you know that you are creatively contributing to designing the future. You have an instinct for technological and original research and are able to thrive in innovative and modern atmospheres that utilize the latest technologies. Consequently, your career path might lead to technology or a career in visionary design or architecture. You might be satisfied by political activism, economic reform or social justice and equality. Since your flair for the unusual must be acknowledged and considered, you may be suited to a wide range of alternative or complementary helping professions like astrology.

Working with associates, friends and colleagues in organizations could be rewarding, but the need for individual expression and equality in the group is the most important consideration. Your need to express your individuality and be independent may suit vocations that are different, even marginal. You need to feel unrestrained in your job duties and you work better in a democratic structure than a hierarchical one. Aquarius is social but does not necessarily feel the need to attach to others. Therefore, in a work environment, you might appreciate the social interaction but not necessarily want this to become a deeper emotional bond. For instance, you may feel more content when spending the main portion of your working day communicating via technology or working alone, rather than being involved with others. The more space there is, the better you perform. The key to your calling is to be able to give yourself enough permission to be free from the crowd and the traditions of the past, forging your own unique pathway in the world.

Pisces on the 10th House Cusp

An archetypal urge underlying Pisces is to dedicate the vocation to something greater, surrendering themselves to a spiritual quest, a calling to heal and help or be soulfully creative. As mentioned previously, these devotional urges lead in one of two directions: surfacing into a path of service in the world or delving into a creative exploration of their spirituality. However, both paths, whether worldly or not, are influenced by the innate mystical and spiritual nature of Pisces.

Your creative, intuitive and artistic temperament seeks to find its voice through vocation. Although a career needs to incorporate these aspects, this is often difficult to achieve in a science-based world. Artists hear the calling of the Piscean muse. Whether or not the creative vocation can find a place in the external world, it certainly needs to be embraced and honoured in the inner one. The sign of Pisces is also associated with institutions and the urge to seek asylum, retreat and healing. Hence you might be called to a hospice vocation, working in a hospital, refuge, asylum or other institution where healing, sanctuary and well-being are encouraged. Working with the underprivileged or helpless is also part of your creativity.

The urge to merge is also important for the Piscean archetype. This can manifest in your lack of boundaries by either absorbing the feeling life in the atmosphere around you or not being aware of your need for separateness. You need an atmosphere in which you can reach out without feeling held back or unencumbered, knowing what is expected of you. As you are so receptive to your atmosphere and are prone to taking on too much, the need for time and space away from the intense demands of others' expectations is important in any career. Scheduled retreats are necessary in order to reconnect with your spiritual energy, as this fuels so much of your creative and caring nature. Without consistently tapping into the internal spiritual springs you may feel exhausted by the demands of life, confused and directionless in your work, disappointed that the world lacks compassion. In your own way you find your path through the world by honouring the creative and sacred qualities deeply embedded in your nature.

Planets in the 10th House
Planets in the 10th house are the archetypal forces that seek to be expressed through vocational pursuits and carry both parental and societal expectations. They seek to be known through the public sphere; therefore, they are more inclined to be projected out onto the world or expressed through activity, achievement and accomplishments.

Tenth house planets are just about to culminate. They have been developing as they rise towards the Midheaven. This is metaphoric of the strong urge to express themselves in the world through appropriate channels, as this house respects traditions and systems. At some point along the vocational path this archetypal force seeks expression on the world stage. But the world in the 10th house is set in the context of the individual and their experience, not necessarily the world at large.

These are the energies that we perfect over time, ones that shape our roles in the world and contribute to our creative outcomes. They are metaphoric of our career, and reflecting on their symbols and images can assist us in considering our career choices and occupational opportunities.

The Sun in the 10th House
Solar occupations have been traditionally linked with speculation and risk-taking in entrepreneurial business ventures. While the Sun is not psychologically associated with risk, except perhaps the risks of self-discovery, the solar sphere of the 5th house (the Sun's natural house) rules speculation and gambling and conjures up images of commodity traders, promoters, stock exchange personnel, investment bankers and high-risk investors who have become associated with solar professions.

The Sun represents vocations that father and foster others, and with the Sun in the 10th house leadership is part of the career trajectory; hence, positions such as foremen, presidents, magistrates, community leaders, business managers, instructors, principals and team directors are reflective of the Sun shining through the 10th house. On a personal level the need for your father's approval may be high and this could be unconsciously transferred onto superiors in the workforce when your father's approval feels lacking or is withheld. Your father may also be influential in the choice of vocation; this is not always conscious, as his unlived professional life may cast a shadow over your own career path.

The Sun personifies entertainment professions, amusements, self-improvement, creative expression and careers involving spectators. Acting, the theatre, the performing arts, motivational training, teaching, sales, advertising and promotions are all consistent with the urge to express the self. This also could manifest in careers involving amusement centres or professions which deal with leisure and recreation. As the Sun is the natural ruler of the 5th house, working with children and children's products, early childhood education, child counsellors, children's recreation or amusement, children and educational toys, children's wear, and so on, are all typical of the Sun.

Of all the planetary types, the solar type is one of the most difficult to characterize. What is necessary is that you enjoy what you do and feel personally identified with your vocation. There is a strong affinity with creativity and a need to be acknowledged and congratulated. Ultimately, what is important is that you are able to identify with your career and able to place your creativity and yourself at the heart of what you do.

The Moon in the 10th House

In classical astrology the Moon is associated with the public. When combined with the lunar need to nurture, vocations like health care, social work, family counselling or therapy, nursing and involvement in the public service are possible. Other lunar professions which deal with the public are chefs, bakers and brewers, waiters and other occupations dealing with food and agriculture such as the food industry, including catering, hotel management and promotion.

Besides the public, the Moon is emblematic of women and women's issues, leading to professions concerning women's rights, health care and social services. Specialized medical areas such as gynaecology and specific issues of infertility, pregnancy, hormonal changes and rites of passage could play a role vocationally. The Moon is also concerned with the home, so a range of professions dealing in home services such as real estate, products for the home, home design, domestic services, furniture, antiques and making the home secure and safe are within the lunar portfolio. The mothering and nurturing side of the Moon involves child care professions such as day care workers, teachers, early childhood educators, counsellors, family care providers, obstetricians, midwifery and paediatricians. Any of these professions might be a fulfilling career.

Astrological statistics have linked the Moon to the profession of writing, perhaps in a broader sense because this profession uses the right side of the brain and works in an imaginative way. Professionals such as writers, songwriters, poets, playwrights, artists, scriptwriters, novelists and creative journalists are under the spell of the Moon and may find creative writing an important part of their vocation. What is of importance is that you feel at home with your career and are able to use your strong perceptive and intuitive nature in your work.

Mercury in the 10th House

As the ruler of Gemini and Virgo, Mercury's occupations suggest both gathering and analysing information. The Mercurial archetype suggests professions that involve data, ideas and information technology, such as the information industry which now involves computers and the Internet. Statistician, scientist, accountant, economic analyst and librarian are Mercurial occupations which involve research and data processing.

Mercury was the messenger of the gods and its astrological function is to deliver messages and communiqués. Therefore, a host of Mercurial professions includes lecturers, teachers, writers, interpreters, journalists, radio announcers, editors, postal workers, the computer and information industry, news reporting and advertising, any of which might be of interest when contemplating your career. Mercury is the patron of travellers, and astrologically rules short trips; therefore, occupations involving the travel industry such as being a driver, courier, tour guide and organizer, interpreter, flight attendant and cab driver are also consistent with this placement. Mythological Mercury was also the god of commerce, and vocations involving trade, negotiation, contracts, verbal skills, argument and persuasion are akin to his nature. You might consider the field of commerce, commodity trading or the stock exchange, as these could be an appropriate sector that helps to focus some of your abundant nervous energy.

The analytical side of Mercury also combines with the urge towards health in professions such as clinical psychology, psychiatry and psychiatric nursing, being a dietician, health care work and medical analysis. The Virgo side of Mercury represents industries that provide services to their clients. With this archetype atop your horoscope it is important that you have flexibility and continuous change in your vocation. The influence of youthful Mercury means that many interesting assignments and positions await you in your chosen career.

Venus in the 10th House

Venusian professions include being an art specialist, art museum worker or curator, art or beauty therapist, model, fashion designer and promoter, working in the perfume or cosmetic industry, the music industry, singing, interior decoration and design, gifts and crafts, floristry, pottery and theatre and set design. An innate style and culture could lead you into a myriad of professions that deal with fashion, whether that is buying clothes or home furnishings or redecorating homes.

Venus is also inclined towards the development of social skills and interaction and is linked to professions which highlight these traits. The hospitality industry, community relations, hosting industries, hotel management, receptionists, wedding planners and caterers come under the domain of Venus. Professions which include diplomacy and protocol, such as being a diplomat, ambassador or lawyer, or working in customer services, social arrangements and personnel management are also ruled by Venus, so these are all careers which might be worth your consideration.

Venus is also connected with partnerships and working in a one-to-one situations. Venus in the 10th house suggests careers that involve partnerships, working as a counterpart to another, working in close affiliation with others or in a profession which complements others. This could include counselling, especially career counselling or relationship therapy, tutoring, business partnerships, personal recruitment, management or being a personal assistant. You may also be inclined to work in industries that promote a sense of worth, whether that is psychological or economical, such as personal coaching or investment strategies. You might find that you have an innate skill in dealing with money, helping others to become more financially aware and/or secure.

As the ruler of Taurus and the 2nd house, Venus is also linked to professions involving finance as well as agriculture. Using the senses and the creative flair could be fulfilled when following a career in massage or aromatherapy, or even as a food and wine merchant or connoisseur. Whatever your passion, you need to incorporate your own sense of style and grace into what you do.

Mars in the 10th House

Mars suggests occupations that promote an independent and entrepreneurial spirit, such as goal-orientated work that involves a competitive drive but allows freedom. Mars is strongly placed in your horoscope, suggesting that you have a strong ambition and natural drive. If your competitive spirit is stifled then you might experience aggression from being displaced in your work environment, whether through your clients, your co-workers or your superiors. Excelling when you are challenged or when you have the opportunity to pioneer a project, you can do well in inventive and explorative careers, especially when you are encouraged to use your entrepreneurial spirit.

Careers involving danger, adventure and adrenalin are governed by Mars. This archetype feels the need to participate and be challenged; therefore, competitive or adventure sports, the fire brigade, the police force, ambulance work or being a paramedic are good outlets for this. Statistically, Mars has played a leading role in the horoscopes of sports champions. Mars is physical, so using your physical energies in competition sports, training or labour may play a vocational role. A physical education trainer, coach, dancer or dance instructor, gymnast, athlete, physical labourer and construction worker are all images that resonate with the physical side of an elevated Mars.

Classically, Mars's professions have been associated with sharp objects or tools, linking them to careers such as a surgeon or dentist, or occupations using mechanical instruments such as a machinist, mechanic and carpenter. As the god of war, Mars is linked with military professions such as the armed services, the National Guard, security services and providers. Rigorous training, discipline, focus and being alert are aspects of a Martian vocation. No matter how you encounter Mars in your profession, it is imperative that you feel independent enough to strike out on your own and are self-regulated and motivated.

Jupiter in the 10th House

Careers involved in expanding people's understanding of themselves and the world around them, or administering to their religious and soul needs, are well suited to this placement. Philosophers, philosophy and literature teachers, the clergy, motivational instructors, educators and coaches come under the influence of Jupiter and any of these roles would provide a focus for this expansive energy. Jupiter is associated with the sporting industry, team sports, horse racing, sporting goods, adventure and adventure guides, so it offers abundant occupational choices. Having the urge to exceed the expectations that were set down earlier in your life, you strive to expand beyond the limits that were set by your family and culture.

Jupiterian vocations educate and inspire others to a greater understanding; therefore, professors, university lecturers and tutors, and teachers of higher wisdom utilize the archetype of Jupiter in their careers. Cross-cultural contacts, travel and dealing with international concerns are also part of the pattern, including vocations in the Foreign Office, import-export trade, protocol, ambassadorship, foreign buying and selling, being an interpreter, missionary or travel consultant, and working in foreign affairs or international contacts. As part of education, Jupiter rules the dissemination of information and ideas through publishing, writing, advertising and the telecommunications industry.

As the chief Olympian, Zeus (Jupiter) was the most influential of the gods and this archetype seeks to influence and impact others with their ideas, generally through all forms of education. Teaching, instructing, publishing, coaching, guiding and mentoring are the common denominator of all Jupiterian professions. Your urge will be to disseminate knowledge that enhances and improves the quality of life for everyone. Perhaps you are a student or traveller, but whatever your vocation, it is imperative to infuse your visionary and optimistic spirit into any role you play in the world.

Saturn in the 10th House

As Saturn tends towards perfection, you may be motivated to try even harder when it is culminating. Professions that encourage a need for excellence and precision can direct some of this energy; however, you need to be aware of a perfectionist tendency that may inhibit your freedom to be creative and tolerant. If the need for perfection becomes compulsive, a workaholic temperament may be triggered. With Saturn in the 10th house you were probably aware from a young age of the expectations placed upon you and of the role being forged for you in the world. This feels stifling and oppressive; however, to rebel might be an act against yourself, because when your defensiveness is stripped away you still have ambition and an authentic urge to succeed. Moreover, you also have the self-sufficiency and incentive to do well. The labour of Saturn in the 10th house is to shape your own autonomy and become your own authority. While your professional path will include working for others, you will probably feel more satisfied when you are self-directed. Respecting your boss might be difficult when you find that you are more competent.

Occupations allowing a sense of authority are important. Your need for responsibility and autonomy is high, so positions such as executive, technician, scientist, corporate manager, school principal, teacher, law maker, politician and councillor could fulfil this need.

Saturn is also associated with many trades, especially the building trades, but also may be connected to agriculture and real estate. Contractors, bricklayers, builders, gardeners and landscape designers, architects and building designers, people who work in the construction industry, labourers, real estate dealers, land developers and engineers all come under the jurisdiction of Saturn. The need for hierarchy is important to Saturn, as is respecting one's superiors. With your need for autonomy and authority, a common pattern might be having clashes with management when trying to attain a position of influence and control. Your bosses and superiors will be both challenging and supportive, assisting you to find your authority and confidence in the world.

Chiron in the 10th House

In classical myth, Chiron is the ancient link to the archetype of the healer–hero and reminds us of the archetypal urge to heal the self. In contemporary times, Chiron symbolizes the quest for wholeness, individuation and the attempts to integrate body and soul. In vocational pursuits Chiron tends towards the complementary healing professions that address the need to reconcile the body–mind split. Having this archetype strongly placed in your vocational sector means you may feel drawn to the healing arts, especially complementary and alternative medicine and healing.

With Chiron in the 10th house there are many possible paths leading into the healing professions: naturopathy, homeopathy, herbalism, chiropractic, and Ayurvedic and Chinese medicine. These are all alternative healing practices which attempt to work with the body and mind. Dream therapists, channellers, practioners of Reiki and other New Age healing modalities, astrologers and others working with imagery and symbols as healing tools are all resonant with this image. Chiron was also a mentor and teacher so you may be drawn to mentoring professions such as life coaching, inspirational teaching, meditation instruction or health education.

As a foster figure, Chiron is also associated with the marginalized, and you may feel called to work with refugees, the homeless, the handicapped, the underprivileged and the outcast. You have an innate understanding of what it feels like to be disenfranchised and may be drawn to working with those who are less privileged. Whether this is through social work, a caring or medical profession, trauma counselling or even private practice, you find your capacity to heal is drawn from your understanding and acceptance of your own wounds. Your innate capacity to heal and to understand trauma is forged through your own experience. Ironically, it is your wounds and complexities that call you to be a healer and educator.

Uranus in the 10th House

Being innovative, Uranus rules the technological revolution, new and cutting-edge technology, the electronics industry and the most innovative electronic and engineering fields. Being futuristic, it is drawn to scientific research and innovation. Computer programmers and technicians, Internet-based occupations, radio and television and the broadcast media are akin to its nature. As an altruistic planet, it rules humanitarianism and social reforms, including the areas of politics, compassionate occupations, promotion of causes, professional and humanitarian associations and social services. This archetype leads to vocations which encourage inventiveness, science and technology.

Occupations that deal with the human condition and the advancement of the individual, such as psychology, and especially approaches like group psychology, Adlerian, Gestalt and psychodrama, are of interest. Astrology, community work and reforms, and many of the New Age occupations like crystals, channelling, complementary therapies and medicine, all appeal to the nonconforming aspect of Uranus. It is the extraordinary and non-traditional vocations that call you. Therefore it is not too extreme to consider being a rock musician, a metaphysician or even a science fiction writer. To be true to yourself you need to find a unique and unknown road. Expect the unexpected. When you were born your vocation probably did not exist; if it did, it was probably not one that your parents would have considered.

Neptune in the 10th House

Neptune suggests that you are called to seek a vocation that will satisfy your creative yearnings, soulful urges and the need to be of service to others. However, your career path is not clear, and neither can you expect it to be. What you can expect is that you will be caught up in the chaos of life and will need to learn to feel at peace with letting it take you where you need to go.

Wherever Neptune is in the horoscope is where we find the urge to make contact with the divine. Neptune in the 10th house suggests that you seek the divine in your vocation and you desire to follow its calling into the world. Neptune resonates with the longing to find soul, as it feels suffocated by the mundane, literal and tedious aspects of life. It longs for connection and often languishes in a sense of divine discontent. Its urge to embrace or surrender to the divine can manifest in longing, idealization and fantasy, often experienced as a calling to help others.

Neptune can find fulfilment through the helping professions, including a wide spectrum of occupations such as nursing, social work, hospital work, psychology, working with physically disabled or mentally handicapped individuals, the ministry and other spiritual vocations. Working with the elderly, the poor, the sick or the underprivileged, volunteer work, and all the intuitive vocations such as clairvoyance, psychic healing and spiritual coaching, dream and image therapy all appeal to this archetype. Neptune is also associated with the drug and chemical industries, and careers in pharmacology, psychiatry, chemistry, working with oils and essences, and in drug and alcohol rehabilitation.

Poetry, art, music, photography and camera work, the film and video industries, dance, and the fashion and glamour industries satisfy the creative urges of Neptune. You may have the soul of an artist whose fate is to search for creativity and spirituality in a world that is devoid of soul. You may feel you do not belong in the world, yet your destiny awaits you there. Rather than being caught in the exhaustion of ambivalence, it is helpful to realize that you need to express your creativity, rather than expect the world to be your muse.

Mythological Neptune also ruled the seas and there may be a deep yearning to work with the sea in a variety of ways such as oceanography, in other aquatic occupations, boating or ships. However, this is often metaphoric of the deep urge to express feeling and soulfulness through your career. With Neptune in your 10th house, you may first have to surrender your ideals, images and expectations before you find the right path.

Pluto in the 10th House

Pluto's name means 'riches' and wherever Pluto is located in the horoscope is where you will metaphorically find buried treasure. It is the place where subterranean and unexpressed feelings in your family are buried, which suggests that your vocational path may unearth the shades, ghosts and secrets of your familial past. Yet it also suggests that you are uncovering valuables and riches not yet conscious in your family.

Pluto is associated with loss, unexpressed grief, traumatic and shameful feelings, secrets as well as a host of unacceptable feelings such as anger, rage, resentment, jealousy and envy. In a vocational sense, Pluto deals with vocations which dig deep, into either literal or psychic ground to locate the truth and encourage the release of whatever has been repressed. Hence psychotherapy, oncology and bereavement counselling are all vocations which are worth considering. Pluto rules research and investigative vocations such as depth psychology, medicine, loss, grief and bereavement counselling. Other suggestions for this placement include working underground, plumbing, medical research, investigative reporting, working for the police or governmental undercover agencies, detection and archaeology.

Pluto is the realm of the dead and in a vocational sense you might be involved with this literally or where the cycle of destruction and renewal is prevalent. Burials, the undertaking professions, coroners, mortuary work, wills and legal vocations concerning inheritances, the dead and the rights of the dead, insurance agents, demolition and renovation work are all consistent with this image. The power of Pluto to influence the masses and transform public opinion is reflected in such careers as marketing research, the media and other vocations of influence, and politics.

With this placement, your solitude and need to be alone are confronted on your path. This might suggest that you are ambivalent about being public or known, making your need for privacy and solitude in your working life an important priority. With Pluto on your Midheaven, your destiny involves people in powerful positions, influential organizations and transforming occupations. It is important for you to recognize that you make an impact on your world even if you are unaware of it.

– Chapter 11 –
VOCATIONAL TRANSITIONS
Planetary Cycles and Transits

Career Transitions
Two of vocation's major transitions are the entry into the work force and the exit from professional or working life. In between there are many job changes, promotions, opportunities and even career adjustments. It is common to change jobs during our working careers, especially in late adolescence and our early twenties while we are finding our way into the work force. American statistics suggest that people will average about a dozen jobs by their mid thirties. Job changes can occur within the same career trajectory yet often the career itself changes. By our mid thirties we may have made a handful of career moves along our vocational route.

Each generation has new attitudes and experiences. As times change, so do the vocational goalposts that are beyond our control, such as retirement age, employment opportunities, social security benefits and economic stability. Social, political, technological and economic developments alter the landscape of work as we have known it. What we encounter as we enter the work force will be very different from when we leave. One of the certainties on our career path is change and it is wise to take full advantage of transitions involving your career.

Career changes can be either proactive or unplanned. Proactive career changes are often made due to a variety of factors, such as dissatisfaction with the current position, feeling unchallenged at work, an inability to use our best skills and talents, economic reasons or disliking the culture of the workplace. As our personal and spiritual values mature, we may no longer feel aligned with what we do and may seek a change in career. This is common during midlife as well as other major life phases. But wanting to change one's career does not guarantee that it will happen; a proactive change requires strategy and planning, backed up by courage and passion.

Unplanned changes are due to circumstances beyond our control, such as retrenchments, business closures or moves, hierarchical and organizational changes, new management or personal difficulties such as mental or physical health, injury, divorce or financial complications. In these cases we still have a choice in how we respond and participate with the change. Although an unplanned career change is distressing, it is part of an ongoing larger career picture that is still developing.

Astrology can be insightful in both instances, using personal transits and generic planetary cycles. Let's begin with an overview of astrological transitions in order to understand how they might parallel vocational transitions.

Astrological Transitions

Planetary movements have always revealed and interpreted the changing dimension of time. Attempts to measure time using planets have existed since antiquity; for instance, the changing face of the Moon helped ancient man to measure and record the passing of time. Each planetary cycle has its own unique timing, whether that is the fast-moving Moon which takes 27.3 days to orbit the Earth or slow-moving Uranus which takes a lifetime of 84 years to encircle the Sun. Each cycle records one revolution through the zodiac. In the time Uranus takes to complete one cycle through the zodiac, the Moon has recorded over 1100 cycles. Every day is marked out by the faster moving planets, while the slower ones differentiate the major phases of the life cycle.

Transits are the most popular method of advancing the horoscope or viewing it in the context of times past, present or future. A personal transit compares a particular planetary position at any given date with the natal planets and angles of an individual's horoscope, also noting the movement of that planet through the signs and houses. As part of this process, the astrologer outlines a time frame for the planet's movement across this part of the chart.

The social (Jupiter, Saturn) and outer planets (Chiron, Uranus, Neptune and Pluto) are catalysts of change that challenge our habitual patterns. An outer planet's transit to a significant aspect of the personal horoscope is the mechanism that augurs consciousness, separation and change. These planets also signify vocational changes; therefore, it is wise to welcome their presence and participate with their energies as they come into focus.

Transits are collective images, as everyone experiences the same planetary movements simultaneously. However, each individual has their own unique orientation to the planetary passages. When a planet interfaces or aspects a personal horoscope, the planetary effect is experienced individually and responded to in a unique way. Transits may first manifest externally through an event or an individual. Although the transit may be experienced as an external event, it unearths innate psychic structures that confront us with an authentic way of being. This may be accompanied by feelings of disconnection, confusion or trauma as we awaken to unknown aspects of ourselves. When an innate psychic complex begins to unravel the psyche may respond defensively, yet paradoxically it may be excited by the possibility of change. Astrologically, the symbolism of the transiting planet identifies the nature of the experiences and the process that is unfolding.

But transits are not only external events: they have an inner emotional and psychological factor. Unlike secondary progressions, which are embedded in the natal chart, transits are not inborn. Therefore, a transit often feels as if it originates from outside, imposing itself on us rather than emerging organically. Hence transits are sometimes described as 'fated' or unexpected. Progressions are reminiscent of DNA, because they are an individual's personal genetic code, whereas transits symbolize what happens to an individual during the course of their lives, both on an outer and inner level. Transits are compelling forces and harbingers of great change and growth.

Transits are snapshots of points in time, phases that characterize the shifting tides of life. The term 'transit' also refers to the passage of a planet in relationship to its own natal placement, for instance transiting Saturn in aspect to natal Saturn. These transits record the process of ageing and correspond to initiatory periods in the life cycle. Aspects within the larger planetary cycles occur for everyone at similar ages. These are known as generic cycles, specific to a generation, marking out the rites of passage and the natural developmental chapters of life.

Vocational Times

When an individual is ready to make changes in their life, signposts appear. These might be a dream, an opportunity that presents itself in the outer world, a change of circumstance or simply an inner knowing. Generally, these signposts come into view when we participate with the transition, having let go of outdated ways of being and entered into uncertainty. This ambiguous period is often referred to as 'liminal', an in-between phase amid what has past and what has not yet arrived. In the fluid space between the securities of everyday routines we become receptive to the signposts. When we involve ourselves in the transition, and are mindful of the unconscious aspects of the process, it becomes more apparent how to take the next step in our life. A complex of events and feelings often take place around times of change and initiation. With each step we take towards our vocation, we step away from the herd, and this is a challenging and exciting stage in our vocational quest.

Vocational times or major shifts in life direction and purpose are reflected in planetary cycles, transits and progressions. When major transits or progressions pass through the vocational houses or aspect vocational signatures in the horoscope, directional changes become focused on the career. Transits and progressions reflect vocational times in a myriad of ways. Through experience the astrologer becomes more confident in recognizing the important vocational times. The following summarizes some of the significant vocational transitions:

- A significant career transition is signalled when a slow-moving planet, including Saturn and Chiron, transits an angle. Neptune and Pluto will cross the angles probably only twice in a lifetime, which gives these transits a high priority. When one of these planets transits the MC, the individual is challenged to be authentic about their life direction and purpose, because their relationship with the world is altering.

- Transits to the Midheaven are especially pertinent, as this is the angle directly concerned with life purpose. Since all four angles are strongly focused on the life direction they must be considered separately. For instance, let's imagine each of the outer planets transiting the MC:

Pluto suggests a confrontation with power and influences that are often beyond our control. Psychologically, there is a death of the ideals and fantasies about who we are or could be in the world. Surrounding us are the power games of the corporate world; the misuse of power is exposed in some way and we are forced to be as true as we can be to our own course of life. The system we are working in is being transformed.

Neptune crossing the MC dissolves the illusions about who we are in the world, yet restores our dreams and visions about what we may be. It reconnects us to our creativity and helps to dispel the illusionary veils around who we have become.

Uranus crossing the MC illuminates the path for us and offers a myriad of opportunities to inspire us to become one of a kind.

Chiron transiting the MC suggests that we face our sense of marginalization and wounding in the world so we can take an authentic place, not the path that others have expected of us.

Saturn culminating gives us feedback on our progress to date. It will culminate twice, perhaps three times, in a lifetime. During the second or adult cycle, it helps to consolidate who we are in the world, as well as give us a sense of our authenticity and autonomy.

All these planets crossing the angles will reshape and change the life direction. This is a top priority in assessing vocational times.

- Saturn, Chiron, Uranus, Neptune or Pluto transiting one of the four angles suggests an encounter with one's life course. Each angle corresponds to a particular life direction: for instance, transits across the Ascendant-Descendant axis augur change in the personality, the self, relationships and partnerships. Transits across the MC-IC axis are directed towards personal security, familial life and goals and direction in the world. Therefore, it is important to note the slower-moving transits to all the angles, but the MC is the angle focused on career direction.

- Transits of the nodal axis through the houses illuminate our life path and inspire us towards the direction we need to take.

The North Node will point towards what needs to be developed while the South Node might suggest what needs to be emptied out. When the nodes move through the houses of substance or conjoin the angles of the horoscope, it is important to be aware of vocational issues. Transits of the outer planets to the natal nodes need to be considered too, as these transits awaken the calling and reconnect us to our purpose and direction in life.

- Saturn in transit helps to define and shape our relationship with the outer world. Its transits often correspond with challenges and responsibilities, which forge a path through life. It is especially significant when it transits the 2nd, 6th and 10th houses, as these transits identify our place in the world. As it culminates on the MC, the efforts made in establishing ourselves in the world become evident. Saturn's transits consolidate and define the individual's role in the world. Note its transits through the 2nd, 6th and 10th houses as being important times of structuring and focusing on vocation.

- The progressed Moon indicates our feeling responses, sense of security and comfort. From a vocational perspective, as it progresses through the horoscope but especially through the 2nd, 6th or 10th houses, our career hopes become more mature and deeply felt because the progressed Moon is a symbol of how comfortable we are feeling with our job and career.

- The transits of the outer planets to significant constellations in the horoscope suggest that the individual can experience a greater facet of themselves. These are often significant vocational times, synchronizing with changes of direction in the life course. Transits forming important aspects to the horoscope are always worth exploring in terms of career, as the individuation process is deeply aligned with vocation. Outer planet transits are synchronous with the emergence of deeper aspects of the self; therefore, at these times there is often self-revelation and insight into one's direction and purpose.

- Consider the natural planetary cycles and the life cycle generally. Reflect on the critical times in planetary cycles that synchronize with important life cycle passages; for instance, the oppositions and returns of the Jupiter cycle often correspond with developmental stages in education, outreach into life and vocational possibilities. In the Saturn cycle the squares, oppositions and returns are times of consolidation and foundational change. Critical times in the Jupiter and Saturn cycles play an important role in our vocational search; the Pluto waxing square, the Neptune waxing square, the Uranus opposition and the Chiron return are also important times to consider.

The movement of the social and outer planets, the lunar nodes and the secondary progressed Moon give shape to patterns embedded in the life cycle, stressing particular phases of life which can be significant in vocational transitions. We will now study each major planetary cycle and how this might be utilized when considering vocational changes and developments.

Jupiter and Saturn

These are the 'social' planets. As they transit the horoscope they reflect the experience and influence of the socialization process, such as social development, skills and training, educational opportunities and changes, responsibility, authority, ambition and what it means to be a member of the community. Transits of these planets are important to note in terms of their generic cycles, as well as the personal transits through the houses and significant aspects to natal planets.

Jupiter

Jupiter reflects the personal quest for understanding and the way in which human beings instinctively expand the conscious horizons of their lives. It is the archetype of the religious quest, the urge for meaning and insight. Its restless search for truth, wisdom and understanding develops the capacity to become skilled and successful in the world. Jupiter describes the social, educational and cultural experiences that enhance and expand understanding.

By nature, Jupiter wants to develop and broaden what it transits. It may point to where new insights are revealed, where opportunities become possible or growth is imminent. But the expansive quality of Jupiter operates within limits: it is not unbounded, nor limitless in its possibilities. Its potential is best realized with purpose and intent. When uncontained, the temperament of Jupiter can be inflationary, ungrounded, prejudiced and can have a sense of entitlement.

Every Twelve Years

Jupiter's cycle is just under 12 years – 11.88 years, to be exact. It spends an average of one year in each sign of the zodiac, retrograding every year for four months. In that time it retrogrades for about 10°; when direct, it will go forwards by about 40°. Important ages in the Jupiter cycle are its oppositions at *approximately* the ages of 6, 18, 30, 42, 53, 65 and 77, as well as its returns at the *approximate* ages of 12, 24, 35, 47, 59, 71 and 83. Remember, these are transitions; therefore the year before and the one after these ages will also be noteworthy.

Jupiter can transit a zodiacal point once or three times. When it passes once, the timing of the transit can be quite fast; however, when it transits a zodiacal degree three times, the timing takes at least nine months.[39] Even though a transit may pass quickly without any noticeable advantages, the nature of Jupiter brings subtle opportunities for expanding and understanding our vocational quest. The transits of Jupiter inject insight and purpose into our life direction, encouraging growth and development in our careers.

Seven Jupiter cycles mark out an average lifespan and each twelve-year period is significant for the planning and development of our career. Every return marks a new phase of discovery and growth. Each twelve-year phase could be likened to a developmental assignment in our vocation. Alchemists considered seven stages in their alchemical opus; likewise, we might consider the seven Jupiter cycles as being transformative passages in our life work, because from a vocational viewpoint each twelve-year period calls for a particular task.

The launch of each cycle is important, as the individual enters a liminal period where the past cycle is waning and the new one is emerging, yet nothing has yet been fully established. The essence of the old cycle is the foundation stone for the new one. At these turning points there are new visions emerging, new sets of beliefs and principles. This is accompanied by an urge for a broader, more encompassing career experience as well as a desire to move further afield. There may be an impulse to explore further education, to travel or seek new communal experiences as a means of working with the emergent cycle. Therefore, I take note of the year in an individual's life when they are experiencing a Jupiter return as this will be significant in envisioning the path ahead. I encourage the individual to reflect on this transition: are any new opportunities available? What are their dreams and images about possibilities? Where do they imagine these may lead them? Astrologically, the time frame will be twelve years so it is important to promote farsightedness and encourage imagination at this time. It is a time of review and reorientation: looking back on the past twelve years of achievement, and then looking forward to next twelve years of possibilities.

The other crucial point during the cycle will be the opposition phase, approximately six years after the return. This is a phase when there is more perspective and objectivity about the current cycle. It is a time when there are more job prospects, with opportunities to consider further training, to plan or to set goals for future career movements. In terms of this time in the cycle, reflect back six years to the return: what were the new ideas and visions that were emerging and how have these progressed? What is becoming apparent in the career aspirations that have been developing over the past six years? Other Jupiter cycles can be considered in respect of the current one to ascertain a pattern of what might emerge at the opposition. Consideration of timing in other Jupiter cycles may reveal a motif or pattern based on the past experience of previous cycles. Reflect on this cycle vocationally. The following table takes into account the *approximate* ages of the Jupiter cycle, its returns and oppositions.[40]

Jupiter Cycle	Age Span	Age at Return	Age at Opposition
1st cycle	Birth to age 12		6
2nd cycle	12-24	12	17-18
3rd cycle	24-36	23-24	29-30
4th cycle	36-48	35-36	41-42
5th cycle	48-60	47-48	53-54
6th cycle	60-72	59-60	65-66
7th cycle	72-84	71-72	77-78
8th cycle	84-96	83-84	89-90

When contemplating Jupiter's role in vocation it is apparent that at the first return at age 12, the transition to secondary education is highlighted, while at the opposition at 18 the transition to tertiary education is emphasized. This second cycle involves the discovery of our vocation and what we want to do in the world. The second return ushers in the third cycle and corresponds to our apprenticeship in the world, while the return at 35-36 signals the midlife development of our vocation. Each of the transitions will be unique, but underlying each one is the same archetypal resonance which is vocationally significant.

Through the Houses
The personal cycle of Jupiter through the houses begins as it passes from the 12th house across the Ascendant. It will spend an average of one year in each house; therefore, *approximately* nine years after it crosses the Ascendant it will culminate on the MC, bringing the fullness of its cycle into the vocational sector. Jupiter's transits through the vocational houses demarcate the growth of our personal values, resources, skills, job experience and confidence in the world.

Jupiter's transit into the 2nd house comes after its year in the 1st, where a personal cycle has begun with new dreams, expectations and goals. As it enters the 2nd house these goals can be more realistically assessed and foundations set down to achieve the objectives of the new cycle. Jupiter's nature is expansive and so 2nd house themes are broadened, such as the growth of one's skills and talents, the development of self-esteem, an increase in personal and material worth and the liberty to be able to spend resources to support and develop vocational pursuits.

When Jupiter enters the 6th house it has spent the previous year in the 5th, where the confidence to be more expressive, creative and imaginative has improved. The courage to be more explorative and to take risks may have developed to the extent that by the time Jupiter enters the 6th, the individual is ready to change their job or lifestyle. Jupiter extends our world so work may widen, becoming busier or more dynamic. This year broadens employment opportunities; therefore, there may be opportunities for travel or study through work.

As Jupiter crosses the MC into the 10th house, the cycle culminates. During the past year as Jupiter has transited the 9th, the individual is preparing, knowingly or not, for an expansion in their career. Groundwork is being done through study, education, travel, personal growth, beliefs and values to provide greater meaning and opportunity in the career. As Jupiter transits the 10th house, an individual finds that their work in the world may become aligned with their talents, beliefs and ethics. In Chapter 1 we looked at the two brief cases of Dane Rudhyar and Susan Boyle, who each experienced their world widening when Jupiter transited their 10th house.

If natal planets are in these houses then Jupiter's conjunction to them promotes their role in the vocational quest. Their archetypal essence is energized and given meaning to assist their expression in the career during that year. Jupiter can help to support the mastery of this energy; therefore, there may be inspiring courses or motivational teachers who are able to encourage the planetary archetype to be more functionally operational in the career.

Saturn

Saturn embodies the process of maturation. It represents the quest for autonomy and personal responsibility through discipline, focus, commitment and work. Its impetus is to strive to be the best one can be; yet, the shadow cast in this pursuit is perfectionism and criticism. Saturn also symbolizes the suitable structures, rules, authority and foundations which enable individuals to mature socially and take appropriate roles in society. These structures can be fostering, mentoring and supportive; yet on the other hand they could be rigid, limiting and controlling. Saturn is the experience of hierarchy, especially of parental discipline and law. This is enacted through society's rules and regulations, which are often projected onto bosses and other authority and worldly figures. Saturn also describes how we define ourselves in the world through our career, work, hobbies, affiliations and organizations. By transit it brings these archetypal themes to the fore.

Saturn, like Jupiter, governs the socialization process. It is more concerned with containment and boundaries, unlike Jupiter which aspires to go beyond social conventions. Saturn concentrates on the preservation of tradition, respecting customs and abiding by the rules. It is also focused on contributing to and maintaining a coherent society; hence the archetype is vocationally important, as

Saturn moderates and judges personal contributions with a system. It symbolizes ambition, authority, autonomy, status, quality and merit. Our familial, social and cultural experiences of rules and regulations contribute to how we, as children, adolescents and adults, participate within the system. Even in our rebellion against policies and systems, the archetype of Saturn is operational. Therefore, each one of us needs to find our own way to integrate and accommodate Saturn's principles and laws into our life. This is a major part of our vocational learning.

Cycles of Saturn
The 29.5 year Saturn cycles can be divided into secondary sub-cycles of 7-7.5 years. Approximately 7-8 years after birth, Saturn makes its first waxing square to its natal position; 14-15 years after birth, it is in its oppositional phase and at age 22 it reaches its waning square in the cycle. When it returns at age 29-30, the first cycle is complete and the next begins. All these periods in the cycle can be drawn together in a developmental cycle. We could view the whole life cycle in this way:

Saturn Cycle	Age Span	Age at Return	Age at Waxing Square	Age at Opposition	Age at Waning Square
1st cycle	Birth to 29.5		7-8	14-15	22
2nd cycle	29.5-59	28-30	36-37	44	51-52
3rd cycle	59-88	58-60	66	73-74	81
4th cycle	88+	88-89			

Saturn's aspects identify critical times in each cycle. As the task of Saturn is to mature, become self-governing and take one's role in society, the returns mark an important initiation. The first return at the end of the decade of our twenties initiates us into adulthood when we become personally responsible for our careers, while the end of this cycle signals the review of what we have done to achieve our potential. Saturn can be a difficult taskmaster, preferring to be directed, focused and employed in constructive projects.

Each of the three cycles of Saturn mark out our career path: the first cycle is our training ground; the second is applying our vocation in the world while the third becomes how we continue to contribute to both the inner and outer world, no longer being identified with our career as we once were. In all three phases the vocation demands a different expression. We might consider the waxing squares of the cycle as being the impulse to begin to consciously construct the new cycle; the opposition as a time of great input, understanding and feedback on what we are doing; while the waning square is reflective and considered. It is a time when we become more aware of what we have done in the cycle and how we might re-evaluate and reorientate our purpose and goals. The return marks a potent initiation into the new phase of life and participation with our vocation.

Transiting Saturn brings establishment and structure into focus. By transit it may point to areas of the life where more discipline, responsibility and hard work need to occur. As Saturn is the planet of consequence, it might synchronize with feedback and reality checks from authority figures. The personal cycle can be plotted from the time Saturn crosses the Ascendant, then approximately 21-22 years later it will be near the MC. The personal cycle maps Saturn's development through the personal spheres and interpersonal spheres of the horoscope to its culmination in the 10th house, then through its dissemination and eventual withdrawal in the 12th house to prepare for the next cycle that commences again at the Ascendant.

The Personal Cycle

When Saturn transits the houses of substance, we become more consciously aware of our own worth, value, abilities, responsibilities, ambitions and the urge to take a position in the world. On average, Saturn will transit each house for nearly 2-3 years. When it enters the 2nd house the new cycle is still in its infancy. Saturn through this sector helps to build the structures and foundations that will contain the new cycle's growth. Saturn carries its ambition and urge for professionalism throughout the cycle, and this is the time to lay the groundwork for future success. As the 2nd house also addresses financial resources this will be a time to budget, forward plan and save, endeavouring to invest in long-term assets that will mature when you really need them. This transit is often cited as a time when difficulties with money arise; however, the problem may not be money, but the consequence of not being responsible, not making appropriate investments or a lack of discernment in business. It is a time of valuing and safekeeping one's resources. Negative patterns of self-worth and self-esteem that are consciously reworked during this phase can be sustained throughout the cycle.

When Saturn reaches the 6th house it is time to assess the daily rituals, including work. This transit may highlight what is disappointing, as well as long-term patterns and attitudes to work; yet, in essence, it is an effective time of integration and dedication. Changing work may not be appropriate until the details of why the job has become unfulfilling are identified. It is a time when unsupportive habits can be changed and when new routines and rituals can be initiated to support the well-being of daily life. Without reflection or contemplation on what is not working, the stress of discontent may become somatized, lodged in the body as pain, discomfort or illness. The 6th house draws together work and health in a subtle way. The body will remind us of our frustrations and distresses at work. As the transit through the 6th takes hold we can become more responsible and engaged with our true occupation, exploring alternatives through courses or projects. It is the time to restructure the work resumé, change unsupportive habits, specify what is missing in our work and endeavour to find a balance between the pressure of work and the need for self-care and self-management.

Saturn's ascent to its natural habitat of the 10th house and crossing the MC is a priority in a vocational analysis. In terms of the personal cycle there is a culmination of 20+ years of work. According to our age, this experience will be received differently; nonetheless, it is a time of realization about the importance of career and the recognition of one's skills and aptitudes. Saturn crossing the MC suggests attainment; however, this is dependent on the work done during the cycle. During the adult cycle, if the work is rewarded we could imagine a promotion, more responsibility, a new title, a managerial position, etc. If there has been no engagement with the work then this transit may be an anticlimax and nothing may come to pass. As Saturn enters the 10th house the focus is on career and its alignment with our personal life and our roles in the world. It is a time of recognition and respect, although this does not always take the form of outward acknowledgement. As Saturn transits the 10th it is important be identified with our work and vocation. It is a time of being comfortable and centred in the world.

Another major vocational aspect is when transiting Saturn aspects an inner planet, especially the Sun. Each planet has its creative focus and Saturn's transit will encourage this to be structured, disciplined and applied constructively. In this way, Saturn's transits to the inner planets can organize their role more effectively in the career. Saturn's strong aspects to the Sun forge a sense of identity, authority and assurance, which can then be applied to the career.

Chiron

Chiron does not move steadily through the zodiac, spending the most time in Aries and the least in Libra. The following table summarizes the time per sign from Chiron's last zodiacal cycle.

Sign	Approx. Transit Time	Sign	Approx. Transit Time	Sign	Approx. Transit Time	Total Time Spent in Element
♈	8.33 yrs	♌	2.23 yrs	♐	2.60 yrs	Fire = 13.2 years
♉	6.93 yrs	♍	1.83 yrs	♑	3.56 yrs	Earth = 12.3 years
♊	4.46 yrs	♎	1.66 yrs	♒	5.48 yrs	Air = 11.6 years
♋	3.09 yrs	♏	1.96 yrs	♓	7.83 yrs	Water = 12.9 years

We have our Chiron return at the age of 50. Other crucial times during the cycle are the waning and waxing squares and the opposition, which are unique for each Chiron sign. The following table shows the *approximate* age period, according to the natal sign of Chiron, when an individual will experience the crisis points. For instance, someone born with Chiron in Aries will receive the waxing square of Chiron to its natal position between the ages of 16 years 6 months and 19 years 9 months. Please note that this table shows only the approximate age spans for Chiron's transits to its natal position. These ages may vary because of Chiron's irregularity of orbit and retrogradation.

Natal Chiron in the Sign of	First Waxing Square between	Opposition between	Last Waning Square between
Aries ♈	16 yrs 6 mths & 19 yrs 9 mths	20 yrs 2 mths & 26 yrs 11 mths	28 yrs 4 mths & 33 yrs 1 mths
Taurus ♉	9 yrs 10 mths & 14 yrs 20 mths	15 yrs 3 mths & 20 yrs 2 mths	26 yrs 10 mths & 28 yrs 4 mths
Gemini ♊	7 yrs 2 mths & 9 yrs 10 mths	13 yrs 4 mths & 15 yrs 3 mths	26 yrs 10 mths & 30 yrs 3 mths
Cancer ♋	5 yrs 9 mths & 7 yrs 2 mths	12 yrs 8 mths & 13 yrs 10 mths	30 yrs 3 mths & 35 yrs 6 mths
Leo ♌	5 yrs 1 mths & 5 yrs 9 mths	13 yrs 10 mths & 17 yrs 1 mths	35 yrs 6 mths & 40 yrs 2 mths
Virgo ♍	5 yrs 5 mths & 6 yrs 3 mths	17 yrs 1 mths & 23 yrs 1 mths	40 yrs 2 mths & 42 yrs 10 mths
Libra ♎	6 yrs 3 mths & 8 yrs 1 mths	23 yrs 1 mths & 29 yrs 9 mths	42 yrs 10 mths & 44 yrs 3 mths
Scorpio ♏	8 yrs 1 mths & 11 yrs 8 mths	29 yrs 9 mths & 34 yrs 9 mths	44 yrs 0 mths & 44 yrs 6 mths
Sagittarius ♐	11 yrs 8 mths & 16 yrs 10 mths	34 yrs 9 mths & 36 yrs 7 mths	43 yrs 9 mths & 44 yrs 6 mths
Capricorn ♑	16 yrs 10 mths & 21 yrs 8 mths	36 yrs 1 mths & 37 yrs 0 mths	41 yrs 10 mths & 43 yrs 9 mths
Aquarius ♒	21 yrs 8 mths & 23 yrs 1 mths	32 yrs 10 mths & 36 yrs 1 mths	38 yrs 4 mths & 41 yrs 10 mths
Pisces ♓	19 yrs 9 mths & 23 yrs 1 mths	26 yrs 11 mths & 32 yrs 10 mths	33 yrs 1 mths & 38 yrs 4 mths

Chiron transits awaken the potential for healing by accepting our mortal limitations. As the mediator between Saturn and Uranus, Chiron initiates us into the greater realms of the self, personified by the outer planets, through the encounter with our mortality and limitations, symbolized by Saturn. A Chiron transit can reveal an important spiritual path, reconnect us to our spiritual heritage and stimulate a more meaningful and authentic way of being. Chiron's transit discloses parts of the self that have always felt alien, isolated or disabled. Through consciousness and acceptance these marginal aspects can be reintegrated.

From the vocational viewpoint, Chiron's transiting influence will be felt most dramatically as it crosses the MC or another angle, or aspects the Sun or Moon or an inner planet. Since its cycle is irregular, the house(s) containing Aries will have the longest Chiron transit, while the house(s) containing Libra will have the shortest. Vocational wounds and disillusionments may be revealed when Chiron transits the 2nd, 6th and 10th houses.

For instance, during the 2nd house transit these wounds may be connected to feeling that our skills and talents are undervalued psychologically and financially. Complexes around money, personal values or self-esteem might arise so they can be recognized and better integrated into our life. In the 6th, the acceptance of our feelings of marginality in the workplace or disenfranchisement and conflict with our co-workers might arise to reveal deeper wounds around belonging and the existential pain of incarnation. As Chiron culminates in the 10th house our feelings of being a foreigner in the system are reconciled so that we can take our rightful place in the world. Chiron's transit to the MC helps to heal the feelings of being the 'foreigner' in the system and invites us to accept the creativity in being marginal and an outsider.

As Chiron transits an inner planet, the archetypal nature of this planet is invited to be more integrated into the whole system. One of the ways that its nature can become more assimilated is through its amplification and imagination. For instance, when Chiron transits the Sun it identifies wounds not only in the individual's spirit and confidence, but also their inheritance through the male lineage of the family. This awareness allows their sense of self-assurance and faith to be reconciled and applied more directly on their vocational path.

During a Chiron transit the archetype may be personified as a life guide, mentor, career adviser or personal or spiritual counsellor, especially when it transits a personal planet or the Descendant; however, since this is inherently part of Chiron's archetypal nature it may manifest during any major transit. Chiron's movement encourages the quest for an imaginative and restorative place where the physical and the spiritual world coincide; therefore, its transits might parallel numinous visions, spiritual awakening or mystical experiences which can be applied to our creativity and vocational pursuits. Chiron symbolizes the place between the world of form and spirit and during its transit we often find ourselves in-between the 'real' world and the 'other' world. Through Chiron we learn to accept other realities and the wound of feeling marginal and not belonging.

The Outer Planets

The outer planet transits differ from Jupiter and Saturn, because their influence is beyond the realm of familial, social and cultural expectations, inviting the individual into a deeper experience and understanding of themselves. The transits of the outer planets lead into the exploration and experience of the unknown. One way of thinking about this in terms of vocation follows:

- An outer planet transit can correspond to events in the outer world, which mirror and awaken the psychic life; therefore, new opportunities, openings, difficulties or impasses at work arise to confront us with change.

- Outer planet transits awaken the experience of 'fate', something which feels beyond our control. These transits summon us to address larger patterns and the complex issues of life; therefore, in the context of the vocation, issues may arise in our personal life, our work environment, the organization we work for, or even globally that are not of our making. In these cases our control lies in our response to the situation, as we are able to control our responses but not the event itself. Our free will is the choice to respond appropriately.

- Outer planetary transits usually involve disorder, with a breaking down of defences and barriers. During this state creativity can be discovered and awakened. Vocationally, these transits may expose an unlived creative force which is awakened, transforming our attitude and approach to our vocation.

- Outer planet transits encourage authenticity and reconnection with our vocational intentions.

- These transits offer the opportunity to consciously participate in what is happening. It is our choice whether or not we collaborate with these changes to ensure optimum career outcomes.

• Physical symptoms, emotional reactions, psychological shifts and spiritual awakening accompany these transits. Our understanding of our vocational needs and desires at this time is heightened by the consideration of the metaphors, images and symbols arising during this period.

The cycles of the outer planets affect an individual's experience of the life cycle and ageing. Their full cycles are much longer than those of the other planets: Uranus's full cycle encompasses 84 years, Neptune's is 165 and Pluto's is 248 years; therefore, the critical moments in the cycle, such as the waxing and waning squares and the opposition, only occur once.

However, their transits are also experienced in a personal way when impacting natal configurations in the horoscope. In a vocational analysis we will be particularly alert for transits to the MC, its ruler, as well as the other angles and major aspects to the inner planets, especially the Sun. Each transit is unique for each individual; however, there are archetypal themes and symbols that are important to consider for each planet.

Uranus

Uranus jolts us into awareness and its process is both invigorating and destabilizing. Its intention is change, mostly long-term. By transit its temperament is to break down outworn structures and conventions that are past their use-by-date. From a vocational viewpoint this might be experienced as dramatic or innovative changes in the career sector, revolutionary workplace agreements or regulations, management restructuring or a sudden change that affects the working life. An initial reaction might be anxiety, panic, a sense of abandonment or an experience of disconnection and disengagement from one's work. It may feel as if we have been ejected from what seemed stable and certain; however, Uranus's nature reforms and modernizes the career trajectory.

During a Uranus transit it is quite common for many opportunities to arise. It is always important not to rush or jump ahead when opportunities come up, but to respond when the time seems right for change. Many of these opportunities may not be appropriate; however, they do acknowledge possibilities and potentials. Later in life we look back and appreciate these as alternative unlived lives.

As its archetypal nature is highly intuitive and future-focused, insights and experiences during the Uranus transit are often omens well ahead of 'real time'.

To take the road less travelled is the course that Uranus encourages; therefore, in a vocational sense there is often an adventure into the unknown. But, to explore these possibilities, one needs to risk and be open to the options that are being presented. This is why the Uranus transit often feels like a wild ride that could end up anywhere.

Its cycle of 84 years means that it spends an *average of 7 years* in each house;[41] therefore its movement through the houses of vocation is most notable when it first crosses into them. In terms of the life cycle, its opposition between the ages of 38 and 42 is generally highly significant from a vocational perspective, as it is during this midlife period that the monotony and boredom with work may be acute and the impulse to change the career course is heightened. For innovative individuals this is often critical, as many of their biographies attest. For those established in their vocations this is a time when there can be an acceleration of work, growth and creative output.

Neptune

The conspiracy during a Neptune transit is to transport us closer to our imaginative and creative possibilities. During this process it is difficult to imagine where the transition will lead us and where it will end. The feeling is often of being adrift, without an anchor, buoyed up and down on the seas of life. Liminality, the experience of drifting between two fixed points, is heightened during the transit. The transit often accompanies confusion, not knowing and uncertainty; however, this is the nature of Neptune – to dissolve the boundaries between what is known and what is not, so that we may be more sensitive and vulnerable to our inner creative and spiritual being.

Under a Neptune transit the veil between the 'real' and the 'imagined' worlds is thinner than at any other time. Sensitivity to the invisible, the unconscious and the unknown is heightened. In terms of vocation this is often a period of soul-searching, disillusionment or disenchantment which brings to the fore the sense that something is missing. However, it is also a time when our search for the creative and more meaningful aspects of our nature is able to find a direction in the world.

To participate with the transit suggests taking one step at a time. The process is not complete; therefore, there is no clear conception of what needs to be amended or be done. During this time there is an energetic susceptibility; physiologically, one's sense of vitality is lowered, so feeling alert, focused and able to be active is often impaired during this transition, leaving an individual feeling fatigued, tired and directionless. It is a time when the inner life is active with dreams and images of possibilities which later can help to reshape the career direction.

Since Neptune spends *an average of 14 years* in a house, its influence on the houses of vocation has its main impact as it leaves a house of life and enters the first 5° of the 2nd, 6th or 10th houses. In terms of the life cycle its square at the age of 41 occurs during the midlife transition when the disenchantment with one's life's work may be acute. A bittersweet longing for something more soulful and meaningful builds up as the urge to change the career course intensifies. However, at this juncture of the life cycle there is still ample time to engage with the creative and spiritual opportunities that are arising. Those who are on their creative path may experience the early forties as a time when their creativity and spirituality are peaking.

Pluto

Metaphorically, the transits of Pluto turn off the lights in our life so we can get accustomed to seeing in the dark. Under this passage we become aware of what is hidden, buried and ignored in the basement of our selves. Pluto encourages us to look deep into the self and celebrate the depth and integrity of the soul.

From a vocational perspective a transformation is occurring. This might suggest a company takeover, a retrenchment, a promotion to a position of influence and power, a loss or a dramatic shift in status. Whatever the change may be, the focus is on power and integrity within your profession and yourself. The awareness of power and the urge to be more potent and influential is brought into your workplace. This may be confronting and intimidating to others but is necessary to encourage honesty in your working environment.

Trust is an issue during a Pluto transit. In terms of vocation this may be with a boss, a co-worker, a client or even with you yourself. There is a learning curve about discrimination and who is trustworthy; but first there is often betrayal before the awareness comes of who is trustworthy. The transit teaches us to be more authentic with our feelings, honest about our intentions and to let go of outworn connections when they are no longer emotionally sincere. During the transit the person may feel that their best skills and talents are not functioning. Often lethargy, depression and forgetfulness can accompany these dark images of the self. This is the process of Pluto: to dig down into the underbelly of the self and restore to consciousness the strengths and resources that have been left in the dark.

Pluto can spend from 12-32 years in a sign. Like the other outer planets its main impact on the 2nd, 6th or 10th houses will occur when it enters the first 5° of the house. Its orbit is very erratic and therefore its waxing square can happen at any point between the ages of 35 and 91.

Pluto's orbit of 248 years means that every generation will receive their waxing square at different times and a few generations may also experience the opposition. Below is a 'rough guide' to the timing of these aspects but, for the exact timing of your personal Pluto square or opposition, please consult your ephemeris. These ages are *approximations*.

Sign	Age	Sign	Age	Sign	Age	Sign	Age
♈	86-91	♋	46-58	♎	36-42	♑	60-73
♉	74-86	♌	39-46	♏	42-50	♒	73-85
♊	58-74	♍	35-39	♐	50-60	♓	85-91

The Pluto in Virgo and Libra generations receive the waxing square during their midlife transition. This is often a very personal encounter with the darker contents of the unconscious. After such an experience one is generally no longer as fearful of letting go into the unknown. When the individual brings this awareness back into their career they are usually more grounded and stronger in their convictions and ambitions. After such an encounter the ability to transform the course of the vocation is stronger.

The Lunar Nodes

As the lunar nodes are intimately connected to our vocation, their cycle and transits through the horoscope are significant. The nodal cycle is 18.6 years; returns occur between the ages of 18-19, 37-38, 55-56 and 74-75, marking important initiations on the vocational pathway. At each of these times, the memory of what we are meant to do or what we are called to do is stirred. We arrive at a crossroads where the mundane aspects of our lives are infused with more spiritual and imaginative content.

The first nodal return, between 18 and 19, often synchronizes with the original call or the first conscious experience of having a greater purpose in life. The second return between 37 and 38, at the beginning of the midlife transition, suggests revisiting our original career intentions, as our life experiences may have taken us away from our vocational path. There is a renewed dedication to fulfilling our calling. A period of reflection on and contemplation of the career begins, along with a more embodied sense of being purposeful. In our mid fifties the nodes return to their natal place for the third time. In the midst of this decade the progressed Moon also returns, and Uranus and Neptune trine their natal position, highlighting the mid fifties as a time of perception, insight and imagination. At this stage the third nodal return suggests a deepening of connection to vocation. Spiritual aspects not previously considered in terms of the vocation become important. The meaning and significance of what we do prevails as an inner question. It is often during the midpoint of this cycle that retirement becomes a reality. Finally, the fourth return at 74-75 is a phase when vocation is no longer in the world but a more personal, inner experience supported by our activities, interests, hobbies and volunteer work.

When working with the transits of the lunar nodes through the houses it is important to also consider the eclipses that accompany the transiting nodes. On average, the nodes will transit one house of the horoscope in 18-19 months, bringing more consciousness to this polarity in the chart. Accompanying this transit will be 3-4 eclipses that fall across this house polarity, occurring near the North and South Nodes. Therefore, each house polarity is highlighted by the transit of the lunar nodes every 18 months. Their environment and atmosphere will emphasized during this period, especially in the week preceding and following each eclipse.

The North Node transit points to the environment where more conscious developments are taking place. This is an area of intake and assimilation, of beginning to develop the role that this environment plays in the life schema. The South Node highlights past issues and concerns that need resolution. This is a place of release, where past experiences and instinctive responses can activate the new growth indicated at the North Node.

Here are some keys to understanding the transit of the nodes through the houses. The transit of the nodes through the horoscope is important vocationally as they draw attention to areas that need development in the contemporary career. Imagine that the cycle begins when the North Node transits the Ascendant. Since the North Node retrogrades through the zodiac, the first house it transits will be the 12th. At the same time the South Node will transit the 6th house. One way to imagine this is to consider the South Node as the task of release and dissemination, whereas the North Node has a mission to develop and grow in the area that is represented by the house.

☊☋ Transit	☊ The North Node: Mission	☋ The South Node: Resource
☊ in 12th ☋ in 6th	**Understanding** To delve deeply into understanding hidden motives and compulsions. To make peace with the past	**Routine** To utilize life rituals and routines to develop understanding. Work and health play important roles in the broad schema of life
☊ in 11th ☋ in 5th	**Communal participation** To find a place in our circle of friends and colleagues so we know we belong to a wider community	**Creative self-expression** To unleash our innate creativity and self-expression so that we are able to fully participate in the process of life
☊ in 10th ☋ in 4th	**Career-focused** To continue to forge our role in the world and strive to heed the call to vocation	**Belonging/settling** To be secure and settled enough to focus on our career and being in the world

☊ in 9th ☋ in 3rd	**Searching for the truth** To quest for meaning, search for understanding, explore beyond familial boundaries	**Becoming mindful** To let go of detailed and rational considerations so we can freely move forwards and explore wider horizons
☊ in 8th ☋ in 2nd	**Honouring the depth of self** To become involved in truth, being honest about feelings and vigilant about integrity	**Reaping past rewards** To free up our resources and talents so we are able to become more deeply connected and intimate with others
☊ in 7th ☋ in 1st	**Respecting relationships** To feel an equal and active part of all our relationships. To allow ourselves to partner	**Relinquishing the focus on self** To let go of the spotlight on the self and move in the direction of cooperating and relating with others
☊ in 6th ☋ in 12th	**A health regimen** To concentrate on daily routines, work habits and health to sustain physical and mental well-being	**Secure in the divine** To have confidence in letting life flow, secure in the faith that divine guidance is at hand if needed
☊ in 5th ☋ in 11th	**Aspiration and applause** To audition, perform and express the self. To be creative and expressive	**The support of friends and loved ones** Letting ourselves receive love and attention from others
☊ in 4th ☋ in 10th	**Building a nest** To give attention to securing ourselves emotionally through focusing on the inner world, home and family	**Acknowledgement** To acknowledge the work that we have done well and develop maturity, autonomy and authority in the world
☊ in 3rd ☋ in 9th	**Communication and ideas** To learn and develop our ideas, to communicate our feelings and present our beliefs in a logical way	**Educating others** To share our innate wisdom with others, disseminate our beliefs and support the integrity of human values

♌ in 2nd ☋ in 8th	**Banking our resources** To value and appreciate who we are, building a healthy sense of self-esteem and a bank account	**Intimacy and involvement** To celebrate the emotional resources of our life; honour the emotional attachments
♌ in 1st ☋ in 7th	**Self-focus** Shining the light on the self, projecting the self, encouraging space, independence, self-expression and freedom	**Social and relating skills** Being conscious of social and relational skills in order to be independent and free from others' expectations

Secondary Progressions

When working with individual charts there are often crucial secondary progressions that parallel career transitions. As progressions are unique images in each individual's chart, I do not make general statements about the nature of progressions specifically related to career change. Instead, I assess each chart separately in terms of the secondary progressions and relate the contemporary progressions to the individual's inner experience, listening to how that may be reflected in the outer world. However, in working with clients in terms of vocational change, I have observed some repetitive themes.

One of these themes is the progressed Sun in major aspect to a superior planet, i.e. the planets exterior to the Earth's orbit, or Mars–Pluto. Another theme has been a planet changing direction; this implies that the archetypal energy is seeking a new mode of representation. If Mercury is retrograde at birth it will go direct in the progressed horoscope by the age of 21. Its change of direction impacts learning, communication, ideas and intellectual interests. If Venus is retrograde natally, she will go direct by the age of 42. Innate values and tastes may shift, which may impact upon the vocation. Each planet's station and change of direction will have its own unique effect. I also monitor the progressions of the inner planets. I specify progressed Mercury as the vocational development of learning and communicative skills; progressed Venus as the maturing of relational skills and self-esteem; and progressed Mars as the growing will to promote the self and the courage to be proactive. While there are many progressions that might correspond with career changes, it is important to consider each chart separately.

The Progressed Moon

The progressed Moon is unique. Unlike any other secondary progressed planet, it completes a cycle of the horoscope every 27.3 years. Like Saturn, it will complete three full cycles in an average lifespan. In the first cycle the progressed Moon returns two years before the Saturn return. In a way it heralds the Saturn return and the end of the decade of the twenties. Saturn is the structure and backbone of our developmental process but the progressed Moon is its feeling life. It is a constant barometer of our moods, sensations and reactions. It symbolizes emotional maturing and in its progression through the horoscope registers and remembers emotional reactions and feeling responses. It is a metaphor for our feeling and instinctual memory. As the Moon progresses in subsequent cycles through the same house, sign polarity or it aspects the same planet, feeling memories from the previous cycle(s) are potentially brought to consciousness. In terms of vocational development the progressed Moon reminds us of our needs and authentic feelings. As an agent of the unconscious it also brings suppressed feelings to the surface through our reactions and moods, reflecting the way we feel about our work or those we work with.

When the progressed Moon moves into one of the vocational houses, it emphasizes the need to be more comfortable with work and more mindful of caring for the self at work. During this time we are more responsive to our habitual behaviours and emotional patterns at work. This allows us to become more conscious of our attitudes, instincts, feelings, motives and responses to vocational needs and ambitions. Work demands more focus and attention when the progressed Moon passes through the 2nd, 6th or 10th house. During its first cycle to age 27, the focus is on the development of career through learning, training and experience; the second cycle between 27 and 55 is on building and sustaining the career; while the third cycle between 55 and 82 focuses on the acknowledgement of our lifework and vocation.

As the Moon progresses through the 2nd house, we instinctively set foundations for our career and begin to establish ourselves with an increasing sense of self-esteem and worth. We are becoming more aware of our attitudes towards personal resources, skills and talents and how we are reimbursed for them through our work. During this period we become receptive to nurturing our sense of worth and protecting our resources and assets. Throughout this period we can be more perceptive about our financial patterns through our emotional reactions to income, money and self-worth.

With the Moon's progression though the 6th, we become aware of the tasks and rituals that provide security and comfort through our work. The need for a healthy and fulfilling lifestyle is becoming more apparent, as is the need to care for the self physically and emotionally. The Moon is absorbent and, when in the 6th, the individual is highly sensitive to the moods and feelings in the work environment. The focus is on work: are you becoming too involved with work and entangled with those you work with? If so, there will be emotional reactions and strong feelings will arise in the context of the working situation, or stress may become somatized in the body as aches, pains and discomfort. As the Moon progresses through the 6th, the focus is on a balanced lifestyle, making every effort to create a supportive and nurturing work environment.

As the Moon progresses through the 10th, the need to care for the self in the world becomes a priority. We are challenged with balancing the needs of the private self with our career needs: how to be in the world, yet remain personally contained and safe. During this time one's direction and life path is in high focus; therefore, our emotional resources become stretched. However, it is also a time when we are beginning to feel at home in our career and also in the world. The Moon is in the public sector; it is time to feel comfortable with our status, our professional standing and our sense of achievement in our career to date. As the Moon crosses the MC, the past two years of conceptualizing and preparing to be more secure in our work begins to take hold.

Planets in the vocational houses are potential allies in the vocational quest. When the Moon enters the house they occupy, the archetype becomes more sensitized and focused in the direction of career. Take note of any planets in these houses, and as the Moon progresses into that house, be aware of how these archetypes can be best directed and supported in service to the vocation.

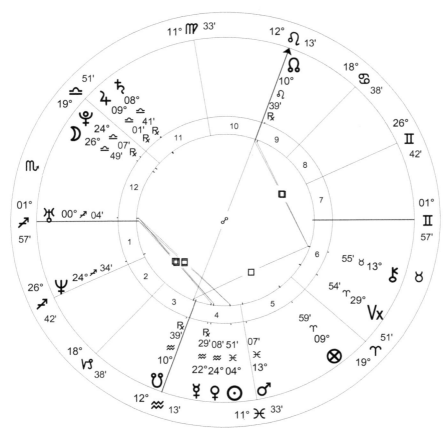

Lleyton Hewitt, 24 February 1981, 00:01 a.m.; Adelaide, Australia

An Early Retirement

Career changes occur in every profession. In professional sports it is common for these to happen early and sometimes dramatically. While I was finishing this chapter in June 2015, the Wimbledon Championships, which are the oldest and probably the most prestigious tennis tournament in the world, were taking place. When Lleyton Hewitt, an Australian tennis professional, had finished his match the crowd gave him a standing ovation, not because he had won (he had lost) but because he was retiring from competition. He was 34 years old.

At age 15, Lleyton was the youngest player to ever qualify for the Australian Open. The next year, still relatively unknown, he won the 1998 Adelaide International, defeating Andre Agassi in the semi-finals. That year he turned professional at 17 years old. In 2001 he defeated Pete Sampras to win the men's singles at the US

Open, becoming the youngest male to be ranked World No. 1. The following year, he won Wimbledon in the men's singles, thereby keeping his No. 1 ranking for 75 straight weeks. Transiting Jupiter, in its second cycle through his horoscope, conjoined his North Node and MC three times during the final six months of his reign as world champion. During Jupiter's third cycle across the MC and into the 10th house, Lleyton announced his exit from the professional tennis circuit.

After his Wimbledon exit, Hewitt said: 'Pretty much sums up my career, I guess. My mentality – going out there and you know, "never say die" attitude. I've lived for that the 18, 19 years I've been on tour'.[42] What is most noticeable about Hewitt's horoscope is the North Node on his Leo MC and Uranus rising with the Ascendant.

All three vocational house cusps are ruled by Fire. The rulers of the MC and the 6th house are widely conjunct in Pisces. The Sun-Mars conjunction and Uranus conjunct Hewitt's Sagittarian Ascendant testify to his passion and 'never say die' attitude. The 18-19 years 'on tour' coincide with the nodal cycle from the age of 15 to 34, his professional life in tennis. At 34 the nodal cycle once again transited his Saturn and Jupiter conjunction, which is where it was at 15. Both Saturn and Jupiter rule angles and the natal nodes are angular; this combination involves destiny and direction. At the time of writing, Lleyton does not officially retire until after the Australian Open in January 2016, but the transition has already begun.

During this transitional time there are major movements in his horoscope reflecting these changes:

- Jupiter will move through the 10th house opposing his Mercury, Venus, Sun and Mars, and apply to natal Jupiter. He is in the final phase of the cycle that began 12 years ago.

- Saturn, having retrograded back across his Ascendant and natal Uranus, will go direct and transit his Ascendant-Uranus conjunction for the third time. This is a fitting image of an ending, yet also the signal of the birth of a new cycle.

- Neptune is transiting the midpoint of his Sun-Mars conjunction in Pisces, separating from the Sun and applying to Mars. The Sun rules the MC and the Neptune transit reflects that his identity with his profession is shifting, perhaps dissolving. Mars, being the ruler of the 6th house, is now in focus: the imagination shifts towards the concerns of lifestyle, health and new routines to find a new work-life balance.

- Uranus is hovering on the cusp of his 6th house, signalling a new approach to and experience of work.

- A notable progression is the Sun at the 10th degree of Aries opposing his Saturn-Jupiter conjunction, symbolizing the emergence of a more authoritative, mature and social identity emerging. The Sun is also conjunct his 5th house Part of Fortune.

When Lleyton retires at the end of the 2016 Australian Open, transiting Jupiter will be conjunct the transiting North Node. Jupiter is in the final phase of its third cycle and a new round will begin at the end of 2016. At this time the transiting North Node will enter the 10th house and begin to return to its natal position on the MC where it begins its third cycle. A new career awaits.

A Later Call
Mary is a regular client whom I have seen twice a year for many years. She is beginning to think about retiring so she can have more time for herself. Having found her vocation later in life, she has been able to spend the last 15 years feeling satisfied and engaged with her work.

Mary is a striking example that vocation can call us at any time. Over the years that I have been seeing Mary, she has had several jobs, including managing a bed-and-breakfast, gardening and various secretarial positions. However, it was her job as an assistant at a primary school that inspired her, at age 47, to apply to university for a degree in early childhood education.

Natal Neptune is in her 6th house. At 47, transiting Neptune had just crossed Mary's MC for the first time and Uranus, ruler of the MC, was approaching her 10th house Moon. This was a breakthrough for Mary because she had always perceived herself as not only uneducated but also unintelligent. At age 48 she started the university course and from the very first assignment she was consistently awarded distinctions and high marks. The school where she conducted her first teaching trial offered her a job when she graduated and a professor helped her to publish one of her projects. Mary was the eldest in her class; I always imagined that her fellow students were heartened by her soulful presence.

With Aries rising and ruling Mars conjunct the Ascendant, Mary found her innate stamina to complete the university degree and follow her vocation. Mercury is also rising. University helped her to temper and direct her rapid thinking in a more dynamic direction. With Mars and Mercury rising, the ability to speak, teach and direct is out front. With the Moon in the 10th she found teaching children to be her passion, and as Uranus conjoined the Moon the vocation was awakened. This inspirational story is an aspect of Mary's Neptune in the 6th which helped her to visualize a new path for work much later in life, much later than she could have ever imagined.

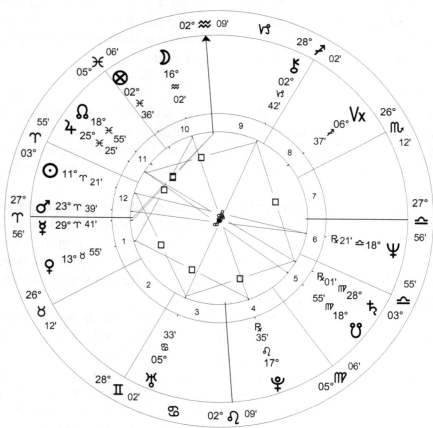

Mary, 2 April 1951, 8.00 a.m.; Melbourne, Australia

Transitions In and Out of Work

Although transitioning in and out of work is highly stressful, career change is an essential element of vocation. As mentioned at the beginning of this chapter, the two major transitions that contain all the others are the transitions from student to working life and from the working life to a private life. I have often observed that themes and experiences as we enter our working life are similar to those as we exit it.

Recently, a 64-year old client, who had been retrenched, came to the consultation with questions about his future life direction. Yet his feelings of anger, rejection and abandonment were so strong that we could not look forwards until we had looked back. George was adopted, a wound that he had carried all his life. His retrenchment had opened the wound again and the pain of rejection was once again acute.

The system that rejected him this time was not the family system but the corporate one. Using his horoscope's images of Saturn square Chiron and Pluto conjunct the Sun (and possibly the Moon – because he was adopted, the time was not available), we explored his lifelong theme of feeling rejected in conjunction with his potent ability to deal with crisis and pain. George recognized the rejecting female boss and the board of directors as embodying his abandoning parents. So the issue was more innate, and in working with his horoscope we could speak of these patterns and separate the primal issue of relinquishment from the current issue of retrenchment.

George was a psychiatric nurse. When he was in his late teens his best friend became schizophrenic. On visiting his friend in hospital, George 'accidentally' met the director of the hospital, who encouraged him to apply for a job in the administration division. He became so interested in the work he saw on the wards with difficult patients that he started training to become a nurse, supported by the director and his co-workers. This became his career.

I felt that George had come to the consultation because he knew that he could not exit his career with such bitterness, having entered it with such support and acknowledgement. He needed to honour his vocation, even though the system had let him down in the end. Through our discussion he recognized some vocational patterns. Ironically, after the retrenchment George was in a good position financially. As he was about to retire in the coming year anyway, it *was* time to leave this work. We affirmed that his vocation would find another way to express itself in the world.

When we enter the work force our career is ahead of us. While we might have strong opinions, ambitions and goals, we really do not know where our career will take us. When we exit the work force, we look back and recognize the threads that have been woven together to create our career. And many of these threads are woven by chance, many by our will and intention, and many by others who come and go in and out of our lives.

I consider the astrological images around the times we enter and exit our working life in order to find common themes that help to reflect the vocational pattern. This is an insightful exercise in deepening our understanding of our calling. Also of interest are the generic planetary cycles that are operational at the time. The following table summarizes the times. I have specified the time of entry as being anywhere from adolescence to our early twenties and the time of exit as being in the period following the second Saturn return. Of course, this period is unique for each individual; however, many governments do specify 'school leaving' or 'retirement' ages.

Transition into Work		Transition from Work	
Approx Age	**Significant Generic Planetary Cycle**	**Approx Age**	**Significant Generic Planetary Cycle**
15	First Saturn Opposition	58-59	Second Saturn Return
18	Second Jupiter Opposition	59-60	Fifth Jupiter Return
19	First Nodal Return	61-63	Waning Uranus Square
21	Uranus Square Uranus	66	Third Waxing Saturn Square
22	Waning Saturn Square	66	Sixth Jupiter Opposition
24	Second Jupiter Return		

Other Generic Cycles During these Transitions

20-21	Waning Progressed Moon Square	65	The North Node conjuncts the South Node
20-21	Neptune Semi-square		

We may retire from our work, our careers and our professions; however, we never retire from our vocation, as this is part of who we are. In later life we find a new way to be with work, no longer intently centred on the outer world of work, but focused on an inner and more private relationship with our creative self.

Let's turn to some examples of vocation and how this becomes our life work.

Chapter 12

LIFE WORK
Patterns in the Opus

When we start our vocational journey we never know where it will lead. We may imagine it, have hope for it, even work hard for it, but we do not know its outcome. It is a mystery and, like all good mysteries, it takes time to discover the plot, understand the characters and separate fiction from fact. Although we seek some certainty, it is not always there. But when we look back on our vocation it is easier to see the turning points, the crossroads, the steps, the blocks, the dead ends and the detours. The further away we are from the starting point, the more we recognize the early signs, the accidental fortunes, the coaches and the challenges that weave our vocational tapestry.

Astrology is a marvellous guide to vocation as it has many images and indicators that help us to imagine career possibilities. Yet how the symbols literalize is often more evident in hindsight; so in looking back we learn how to see ahead. Let's look at two well known individuals who have followed their vocational path. Having both felt an inner urge from a young age, each set out on a path that led to where they could never have imagined; such is the gift of following the call to vocation. Although case studies are often directed towards demonstrating a point, the only point I would like to demonstrate here is that we all have the spirit of vocation inside us and in following, rather than controlling, its curved pathways we find what we may never have imagined possible.

The first study is Thomas Moore, an American writer, known for his bestseller *Care of the Soul*, although he has written more than a dozen other insightful books, one being *The Planets Within*, a contemporary re-visioning of the Renaissance scholar Marsilio Ficino's soulful astrology. Tom Moore has also written a perceptive book on vocation called *A Life at Work*.[43] The second study is Leonard Cohen, the Canadian singer-songwriter, whose encounter with the poetry of Federico García Lorca at 15 illuminated an inner landscape where he encountered his *daimon* and poetic voice. By following the chords of only one aspect in Cohen's horoscope we can see its living image throughout his vocational journey.

Thomas Moore: A Religion of One's Own

Thomas Moore has had many careers, all reflective of his vocation, one that we might call a 'religious' vocation; not organized or formal, but a religion that reveres the gods and the sacredness of life. Or, as Tom writes, a personal religion that 'is both an awareness of the sacred and concrete action arising out of that awareness'.[44] This understanding of the sacred has infused his careers as a monk, a musician, a university professor, a psychotherapist and a writer, with his teaching about being mindful of the soul. Today his vocational path leads him throughout the world to teach about archetypal psychology, imagination and spirituality, but the heart of his instruction is concerned with tending to the soul. Even though the first course of his life was spent in a formal religious location, destiny has directed him towards a more worldly setting.

Tom was born on 8 October 1940 at 9.33 a.m. in Detroit into an Irish-Catholic family. We will travel down some of the roads in his horoscope to reflect on how the vocational images we have discussed are alive in Tom and his chart.

The Daimon of Vocation

At a young age Tom encountered his *daimon*, that inner urge or autonomous spirit that pushes us to act, often in a direction that changes our life course. In his book, *Dark Nights of the Soul*, Tom describes two 'life-defining moments' from his childhood. These early experiences constellate inborn images that have remained thematic throughout his life. He writes:

> One was the day when – I must have been twelve years old – I saw a brochure telling me that I could be a monk and live in the simple, sparse room they showed in a photograph. That little booklet spun me around, and I haven't exited that spin since. The other, more mysterious, was the day I clung to an overturned rowboat in a large Michigan lake, as my grandfather desperately struggled to save me. I don't know exactly how this near-death moment affected me. I think it was preparation, too; a meeting with death and an early invitation to take life seriously.[45]

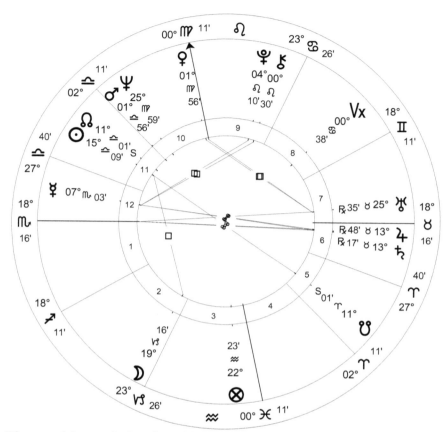

Thomas Moore, 8 October 1940, 9.33 a.m.; Detroit, Michigan, USA

The discovery of the brochure at the age of 12 was an eternal moment that told Tom about his deeply genuine 'religious' values and ultimately his vocational path. In the life cycle, age 12 marks our first Jupiter return, a transitional period filled with questions about life, ideas that seek meaning and often a sense of being called or awoken to something new. We are on the cusp of adolescence, the beginning of major hormonal and bodily changes, as well as transitioning between primary and secondary schooling, which is an apt metaphor for Jupiter's first initiation. I have also heard many clients' stories of being ill at this age, and who during the critical phase of their illness became conscious of something larger in life than they had known before. Jupiter stretches the boundaries of the familiar and for a moment we glimpse a possibility, albeit an image of a possibility. At 12 we cannot yet discern the difference. When he was 12, Jesus sat among the teachers of the temple, listening and asking questions. Those who heard him were amazed at his depth of understanding. A return is a crossroads between the old and new cycle. In the Jupiter cycle this crossroads is about meaning and vision for our life. And whether we are aware of this or not, at the intersection there is a sign. For Tom, it was the brochure.

Besides the Jupiter return, there were major transitions taking place in Tom's natal horoscope; the subjectivity of the personal horoscope was now entwined with the life initiation symbolized by Jupiter's return. Tom was born shortly after the first quarter Moon; therefore the Sun is square the Moon, an aspect that suggests tension between what one identifies as essential and what one needs. Both luminaries are highlighted by the transits of outer planets, an astrological flag that tells us the archetypal world is permeating the personal. During this time transiting Neptune had been squaring his Moon; Uranus was approaching the square to the Sun and during the next 18 months would also oppose the Moon. During this same period transiting Saturn was conjunct his Sun and square his Moon. These transits are of high priority in a lifetime, as the transcendent archetypes of Uranus and Neptune separate the core identity from the secure base it has always known. The self is provoked to find new experiences and different styles of belonging. Simultaneously, Saturn potentially forged a new base for Tom.

A year later, Tom did join the seminary where he 'could be a monk and live in the simple, sparse room'. Being a monk and living in a room of his own would have some appeal: his Moon in Capricorn is reserved, needing containment and structure, behaving autonomously and self-reliantly. At age 13, when the Moon was opposed by transiting Uranus, there was something bigger, what he calls his *daimon*,[46] compelling him to take the risk to leave the sanctity of his personal home and family to seek another way to be nurtured and educated. Philosophy and music, poetry and prayer, words and worship, all of which are so deeply resonant with Tom's horoscope, could be nurtured here. Carl Jung suggested it was the irrational factor of *vocation* that induced an individual to follow his own soul and become conscious.[47] Yet this requires courage and tenacity, perhaps the gift of the Saturn transit to the Sun and Moon.

Venus, ruler of his Sun and North Node, is in Virgo conjunct the Virgo Midheaven, which is a strong vocational symbol. Venus in

Virgo values the sacred, the rituals of an everyday life and the sensual. Over time, Virgo has become trivialized as we lost our connection to the cyclical nature of the goddess and failed to remember to honour her mysteries and rituals. To Virgo, both mystery and ritual are vital.[48] Therefore, this image also supports the monastic life; however, there are many more expressions of this goddess whom the Greeks knew as Aphrodite. But in 1952-3 in America, the image of Venus in Virgo for a young Catholic adolescent could be well contained by the rituals of the seminary. There is no doubt that the calling to the mysteries, rituals, sacred values and honouring of the feminine way will be a lasting aspect of Tom's vocation. But Venus will find other ways to express her aesthetic and erotic sides. At 12-13 he cannot yet know how these threads will be woven into the tapestry of his life.

Tom wonders about how his second 'life-defining moment' affected him; as he said, perhaps it was 'a meeting with death' or 'to take life seriously'. This profound experience is reminiscent of images that arise from deep inside us, as they are original metaphors of the self. Like Odysseus grasping what is left of his raft, Tom clings to the overturned rowboat. But, unlike Odysseus's story, it is not a feminine character who rescues him but his grandfather, a masculine guide. In later life, Tom writes about Odysseus as 'a sacred story', 'the mystery drama of Everyman, the deep story of us all, men and women, as we try to make our way through life'.[49] Perhaps as Tom makes his way through Poseidon's stormy waters of the unconscious he can hold onto the image of the strong masculine.

Tom's Ascendant is Scorpio and Mars is the traditional ruler. Mars is conjunct Neptune, an archetypal amalgam of the personal masculine and Poseidon's stormy seas upon which Odysseus struggled to remain alive. Traditionally, Mars in Libra is complex, as the assertive and self-serving nature is responsive to others' desires before their own. Being conjunct, Neptune dissolves the Martian will so it can be directed towards others. From a personal perspective this is difficult, as the desire nature may be sublimated or repressed. But Tom was rescued from going under by a strong masculine presence. The personal masculine planets are both in Libra; therefore the masculine is other-orientated, responsive, at times reactionary, but engaged in relationship. His feminine personal planets are in Earth, self-contained and introspective. The strong masculine figure of his grandfather is symbolic of mentor figures who have helped him to steer the stormy seas of the unconscious. His most significant mentor was James Hillman, who for 38 years helped him to navigate Neptune's domain. When his mentor died, Neptune, along with Chiron, was transiting the IC. The profound synchronicity of Neptune's transit across the deepest part of the horoscope, the part that Neptune itself rules in Tom's chart, is the reminder that when we are tossed around by unconscious life, the soul keeps us afloat. Soulful images are encapsulated by his Neptune-Mars conjunction in the 10th house; Mars as the helmsman of his chart will steer its course through the stormy waters of the unconscious.

Pluto is the modern ruler of the Ascendant. It is conjunct Chiron in the 9th house. Chiron is sextile Mars and at their midpoint is Venus on the MC: a planetary pattern focusing on the vocation. Pluto is the archetype of death; Chiron is symbolic of accepting suffering and pain as the human legacy. Together, both archetypes demonstrate that death and suffering are soulful conditions. So at an early age Tom met death, or did it rise to meet him? The amalgam of these archetypes resonates with his becoming a psychotherapist and then a teacher, speaker and writer on soul wisdom: a doctor of the soul. It is almost a textbook image for his Chiron-Pluto conjunction in the 9th and Tom has written extensively on the wisdom and soul experience of suffering. When the depth of this conjunction is harnessed with his ability to navigate the seas of the unconscious and the imagination (Neptune-Mars), he brings its worth, valuing the beauty of the soul, to the world (MC-Venus).

Tom writes that besides leaving home and entering the monastery at thirteen, it was 'leaving the religious life at twenty-six'[50] that was also a major turning point. It was the period when a sweeping new cycle of Uranus and Pluto began and also a major turning point in the social fabric of America. This was taking place in Tom's 10th house. Both planets had conjoined the MC while he was in the seminary, indelibly altering his vocational path. Pluto transited his MC- Venus conjunction between the ages of 16 and 18; Uranus transited the MC when he was 21-22. Both were slowly excavating this vocational house during his later adolescence; perhaps a need to be part of the world, a world in great turmoil and change, was stirring.

Tom has degrees in musicology, theology and his Doctor of Philosophy in religion which he received in 1975. When he was denied tenure at the university where he taught, he launched his next career. Vocational pathways zigzag and are never certain. So often when discussing vocation I hear this theme that retrenchment, loss of the job or denial of a promotion or permanency opens up a new course of life. At this point Tom is now in his mid thirties, on the cusp of his third Jupiter return that would initiate him into the next phase of his vocation, as well as bring him to the cusp of midlife.

His next career as a psychotherapist literally represents his vocation as a healer of the soul. In this capacity he was able to witness the soul, not from a 'fix-it' way of thinking but from a model of accepting the soul's suffering and pain. This approach to psychotherapy is underscored by his 9th house Chiron-Pluto conjunction while his Neptune-Mars conjunction was well versed at plunging into the unconscious. Being influenced by poets, mystics, writers, romantics and imaginative thinkers like Ficino, Jung and Hillman, Tom began articulating his own ideas through writing.

But then, as Tom explains, things changed when he was about fifty:

> Then, at a rather late age, around fifty, things began to happen. I was married for the second time and became a stepfather, and in that same year I had a daughter. A book sold well and for the first time in my life I had some money to buy a house and raise a family.[51]

This book was *Care of the Soul*, which became a bestseller and led Tom into a more public arena. Hugh Van Dusen, from HarperCollins Publishers, said: 'We bought it for a lot of money from an unknown author.'[52] He was no longer an unknown author, nor without money. It is not surprising that this success was simultaneous with his marriage, as his public vow to Venus reflects his own developing worth and accessibility. Venus on the MC disposits the Sun and rules the 7th house of relationship; therefore, it will be love and relating that unfasten his deeper values. In becoming a father, he actualized his North Node-Sun, ready now to become a communal father (11th house), which ironically is what it seems he set out to do at the age of 13.

It is not surprising either that powerful astrological transitions were occurring. Turning fifty marks the return of Chiron. When Carl Jung wrote about this period near fifty, he suggested that 'too many

358 Vocation: The Astrology of Career, Creativity and Calling

aspects of life, which should also have been experienced, lie in the lumber-room among dusty memories; but sometimes, too, they are glowing coals under grey ashes.'[53] At the Chiron return, the 'glowing coals' of the imprisoned spirit are rediscovered, and the subsequent period is spent reintroducing them into life. Mercury, the god of letters, ideas, alphabets and language, is in Tom's 12th house in Scorpio. It rules the MC and is square to Pluto and Chiron. All these factors suggest a depth of imagery, the power of communication, transformational words and influential ideas. Mercury is also opposite Jupiter and Saturn; Jupiter encourages philosophy and ways of thinking about the depths while Saturn confronts Mercury with being disciplined and contained. Mercury also rises after the Sun: it is the evening star. Together, these astrological images point to an introspective Mercury or Hermes in his role as psychopomp.[54] Ruling the MC, it is the archetype that leads the vocational quest and it lies in wait like 'glowing coals'. From this moment on, Tom has been a prolific and enormously successful writer on the soul.

In generational terms, Chiron was in high focus due to its return. But Pluto was highly significant in a more personal way. In these years, Pluto was back and forth across Tom's Ascendant, a potent astrological image of emergence, bringing the natal possibilities of transformational ideas and beliefs out into the everyday world. The character is empowered or at least the image of power is aligned with character. It was highly significant that Jupiter, Saturn, Chiron, Uranus and Neptune were all in the Cancer-Capricorn polarity, aspecting his Sun and Moon. In February and October 1990, Saturn was exactly conjunct his Moon in Capricorn while in September of that year it turned direct within 1° of his Moon. Tom's Moon is in the 2nd house of values and money; as previously mentioned transiting Saturn conjunct the Moon suggests a stable time to lay down new foundations, so well epitomized in the outer world as Tom's house and family. In 1991 Neptune squared the Sun three times, while the following year Uranus also squared it. Saturn, Uranus and Neptune were all in Capricorn, unearthing and transforming Tom's relationship to his talents, values and relationship with money. In 1990 Chiron opposed the Moon while Jupiter squared the Sun and opposed the Moon. These are once-in-a-lifetime transits, high-priority astrological images, just like when Tom was 12 and 13.

Thomas Moore continues to write and in 2014 he published *A Religion of One's Own*, a fitting tribute to a theme he intimately knows. Notably, Saturn moved back and forth across his Ascendant while Uranus began its opposition to the Sun. Jupiter again squared the Sun and opposed the Moon, as it had done in 1990, two cycles ago. Vocation will always be a burning ember, but the new Saturn cycle and the Uranus transit to the Sun suggests that Tom might identify himself with it in another way; it will be another chapter in his vocational journey.

Other Vocational Images
As we have explored throughout this book, the Ascendant, its ruler(s), the Sun and the Moon are potent vocational images. Tom's case displays this, with major transits to these positions synchronizing with critical vocational passages in his life. The MC, its ruler Mercury, and Venus conjunct the MC have also played an important role in Tom's vocational path. The Neptune-Mars conjunction in the 10th house, and the Chiron-Pluto conjunction in the 9th, are also highly significant. Other themes that I would take into account, but have not woven into his story, are:

Sun in Libra Conjunct the North Node. The North Node being close to the Sun suggests that Tom was born in the eclipse season; therefore, a solar eclipse occurred near his birth. This eclipse occurred a week before Tom was born at 8°♎. This suggests a potential sensitivity to these cycles, which occur every 18-19 years; hence the ages of 18-19; 36-38; 54-57 and 72-76 are vocationally significant. The nodal returns at 18, 37, 55 and 74 are also times when we are divinely reminded of our calling. Each one marks an initiatory stage in the development of our vocation.

The Sun, the archetypal father, being on the North Node also suggests the influential impact of fathers, grandfathers, mentors and authorities on Tom's life direction. However, it also places him in a fatherly role in the community.

The North Node in Libra in the 11th brings to mind the necessity of consciously working towards participating with a community. Tom's creative potential can be utilized by groups, organizations, friends and colleagues. As part of a vocational picture it suggests that Tom needs to disseminate his creativity and spirituality to the community. However, it also intimates that he will find confidence, distinctiveness and be able to develop character by working with groups and being in groups. While his instinct might be to remain a lone creative wolf, destiny calls him out into the world to share with others what he has fathomed in himself.

The Houses of Vocation

The element of Fire is on the 2nd and 6th house cusps, while Earth is on the 10th cusp, signalling tension in the vocational sphere between the incompatible elements of intuition and sensation. But Tom has six planets in Earth and five of them are in these houses: the Moon is in Capricorn in the 2nd, Jupiter and Saturn in Taurus in the 6th, with Venus and Neptune in Virgo in the 10th. These archetypes help to ground his idealism and visionary spirit. What becomes substantial is that discipline, traditional values, social practicalities and boundaries can structure his creative potential. Jupiter rules the 2nd and is in the 6th, and Mars rules the 6th and is in the 10th, so a circuit improves the connection between these houses.

Sagittarius is on the 2nd house cusp, ruled by Jupiter in Taurus. This suggests that Tom may value philosophies, visions, ethics and possibilities before the mundane realities of life. Money is not of interest in itself, unless it is a philosophical concept or can be traded for education, travel or learning: products that promote meaningfulness. As mentioned previously, income might be derived from education or publishing. It is interesting that when Tom did well from publishing, Pluto had just opposed Jupiter, ruler of the 2nd. Pluto is the mythological god of 'wealth', while Jupiter promotes abundance. Saturn, Uranus and Neptune were all transiting the 2nd, with Saturn on the Moon. The focus was on stabilizing the vocation in a meaningful way.

Aries is on the 6th house cusp, with the ruler Mars in the 10th in Libra. Although Tom's chart is low in Fire, it appears on the cusp of the everyday house; therefore, while it may not be his natural temperament, his work could be mobile, entrepreneurial and independent, working best on his own at his own pace. Important daily rituals that support his sense of well-being need to focus on physical activity, mobility, changes of pace and activity.

As previously discussed, Virgo is on the MC with Venus conjunct, and this plays a prominent role in the chart. Beauty, symmetry, the erotic, love and personal values (Venus) seen through the lens of a sacred everyday life (Virgo) is an endearing and enduring theme on Tom's vocational path.

Leonard Cohen: An Aspect of Vocation

Leonard was born on 21 September 1934 in Montreal, Canada. His time of birth is quoted as 6.45 a.m. 'according to the records'[55] or 'from memory'.[56] However, I have often wondered if the records and the memory have, like Leonard, become romanticized because this moment happens to be the same as that of the rising Sun.[57]

Looking back, this image is reminiscent of the many rebirths in Leonard's life and in a way is symbolic of his first birth into a prominent and distinguished Jewish family, with a proud paternal

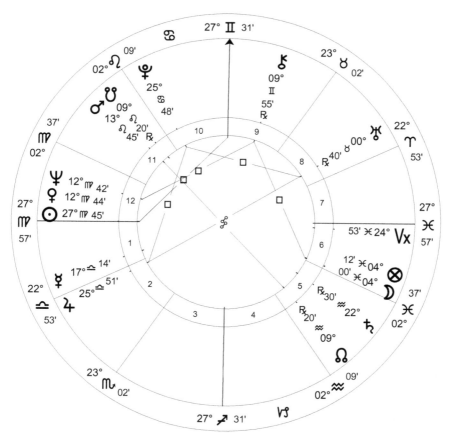

Leonard Cohen, 21 September 1934, 6.45 a.m.; Montreal, Canada

lineage. Like the dawn, Leonard inherited a rich tradition. But what would he make of this new day for the rest of his life?

Leonard came from a strong religious tradition. His mother was the daughter of a rabbi and his paternal grandfather had taught in a rabbinical school in Lithuania. Sagittarius on the IC ruled by Jupiter in the 2nd house is fitting for a family who 'built synagogues and founded newspapers'.[58] This inheritance would find its own expression through Leonard's personal religious quest and his diverse publications of poetry, fiction and songs. Religious iconography would be transferred into his words and lyrics in a subtlety unique way. Turning to his horoscope, let's first analyse the major vocational statements before focusing on one aspect in the horoscope: his Neptune-Venus conjunction in the 12th house.

Vocational Factors

As already mentioned, the Sun is conjunct the Ascendant, symbolizing a vital and charismatic personality. When cold, one is attracted to the warmth of the Sun, and this is an image of Leonard's innate ability to 'heat up' his surroundings. It also suggests the foundation for an appealing personality and a creative and life-affirming outlook.

The North Node is in Aquarius in the 5th house, the natural house of the Sun, where the potential and development of personal creativity, self-expression and performance are located. In Aquarius, the North Node suggests Leonard's path leads him in many alternative directions, some of which are rebellious, anti-establishment, but highly unique. It is an unconventional path and sometimes one in which he stands alone, yet which beats with the heart of the collective. The North Node's traditional ruler Saturn also occupies the 5th house in Aquarius, its own sign, contributing to a disciplined and self-assured approach to his creative projects. At its highest peak is mastery of the creative form; at its base is the path which takes a slow and challenging climb.

The South Node is in Leo, the sign of the Sun, so in various ways the solar energies are intricately woven into the fabric of Leonard's vocation. Mars is also in Leo on the South Node, an image of the warrior-soldier which he strongly identified with in his life and his songs; he entitled one album *Field Commander Cohen*. Whether he was with soldiers in Israel or Cuba, he was fascinated with war and violence. 'War is wonderful' he told a *ZigZag* journalist[59] and told another of having a 'deep interest in violence'.[60]

A childhood story encapsulates this archaic image of his soul: his father was a commissioned officer in the First World War who still kept his wartime gun in the cabinet beside his bed. As a young boy Leonard stole into his bedroom, took the gun out of the cabinet and, cradling it in his small hand, he 'shivered, awed by its heft and the feel of the cold metal on the skin'.[61] Such is the nature of psyche's powerful images that move us to explore life's taboos and boundaries. Mars on his South Node stirs deeply embedded images that will seek expression through his vocation; when consciously honoured and directed, they are not violent nor warring forces, but challenging and compelling drives. In the tail of the dragon he finds an abundance of masculine erotic power, evidenced in his writing, his songs and his life.

Mercury is the ruler of his Ascendant and MC. It is widely conjunct Jupiter, the ruler of the other two angles: the IC and Descendant. Both archetypes are interested in learning, thinking and conceptualizing; but together they are concerned with meaningful ideas, cross-cultural concepts, visionary ideals and hermetic notions. Both rule all the angles, directors on the course of life. As ruler of the MC and Ascendant, Mercury is expressed through the public and personal roles. Jupiter is in the 2nd, squaring Pluto in the 10th. Mercury is drawn into this aspect as well, endowing its expression of ideas and language with breadth and depth, a feature of Leonard's writing.

In company with Jupiter and Pluto in vocational houses is the Moon in Pisces in the 6th, reflecting light on his everyday life, which had been strongly secured by his relationships with his mother and elder sister. As a symbol for everyday life the Moon in Pisces seeks its daily dose of inspiration, creativity and formlessness. In a way it suits the demands of a creative life because security can be held by the instinctual knowledge of life's rhythmic yet uncertain tides. Women have played a major role in Leonard's life as nurturers, lovers, muses and 'robbers', and became the creative inspiration for much of his life work. At the beginning of 1978 his beloved mother died; by the end of the year his partner and mother of his children had left him. That year, his poetry book *Death of a Lady's Man* was released. Saturn had entered his 12th house and was opposing the

Moon; in many ways being a Lady's Man brought an emotive and powerful sensitivity and feeling to his writing.

The 2nd and 10th house cusps are in Air but Water is on the cusp of the 6th and, as mentioned previously, this combination is difficult because Air looks for separateness whereas Water seeks engagement. Intellect and feeling will be strongly featured in the vocational landscape. The 6th house Piscean Moon supports imaginative work while the 2nd house Libran Jupiter finds value and worth in philosophical ideals. Pluto is in Cancer, which is intercepted in the 10th house and ruled by the Moon in the 6th. When the planets in the vocational houses can find a united voice, their alchemy produces haunting and inspired images and words.

Mercury as ruler of the MC and the Ascendant is a powerful indicator of Leonard's call to be a writer, an in-depth and evocative storyteller. But it is the bittersweet lyrics, aching melodies and passionate poetry that infuse his writing. A strong aspect in his horoscope speaks to this and shows how a powerful alignment of planetary archetypes needs to be considered when thinking about vocation.

An Aspect of Vocation: Leonard's Neptune-Venus Conjunction

Lyrical poetry, artistic expression, beauty and musical love affairs are the legacy of Neptune conjunct Venus in the 12th house, a bittersweet blend of passion and sorrow, devotion and escape, sacrifice and longing, and Love Itself,[62] all reproduced in his lyrics and his lovers. This conjunction echoes throughout his artistry, his spirituality and his prosperity. The oceanic 12th house tides sweep this conjunction up in fantasy, deceit, romance, bleakness and the yearning for what is unattainable. Poetry and music would become the instruments to express these formless, haunting soul sounds.

Leonard Cohen was 15 when Chance revealed her hand in a used book store in his hometown of Montreal. Amid countless volumes he found a book of poems by the Spanish bard Federico García Lorca. Between the pages he was introduced to the *duende*, an earthy spirit who seizes artists, confronts their mortality and inspires them to create passionate 'black sounds',[63] possessing not only the artist but its audience as well. The soulfulness and depth of imagination represented by Leonard's Neptune-Venus conjunction in the 12th house resonated with Lorca's poetry. Three times in that year Saturn traversed this creative 12th house combination, giving the image a form and legitimacy in Leonard's life. Saturn would transit this house twice more in his life, and at each of these times his connection to the *duende* would be strengthened.

Along with his Moon in Pisces, the Neptune-Venus conjunction characterizes a strong feminine spirit, a creative and spiritual essence, a muse and inner guide. For a man in the first stage of life, the muse is generally projected onto women, who are ethereal and enchanting. In Jungian terminology this is his *anima*, the feminine soul, so aptly imaged in the horoscope as Neptune conjunct Venus. The feminine muse is a central character in his career and has inspired, frustrated and assisted his expression of the divine through poetry and song, a living testament to the 12th house conjunction ignited by Lorca's poetry.

Some of Cohen's mortal muses are named in song, some are not. Suzanne is perhaps best known. She was a bohemian dancer who, as in the eponymous song, designed her gypsy clothes from second-hand fabrics bought at the Salvation Army Store on Rue Notre Dame. Suzanne lived in Old Montreal near the St Lawrence River. When Leonard visited she would invoke the Spirit of Poetry before tea and mandarins from Chinatown were served.[64] Suzanne embodied Leonard's inner feminine, ultimately the reflection of his own half-crazy gypsy dancer. Intimate in song, yet never in reality, Suzanne was an early personification of the enmeshment of love with fantasy, thematic in his lyrics and poetry. 'Suzanne' would also mark a turning point in shifting the ballast of writing from poetry to song. With his strong Neptune it would be done in ways Leonard could not imagine and through the agency of women.

'Suzanne' was published as a poem in 1966 but recorded the same year by Judy Collins. The opening verse was a poetic account of the time he spent with Suzanne in the summer of 1965, just before the first of three Uranus-Pluto conjunctions in Virgo. Pluto had gone direct, having excavated his Neptune-Venus conjunction during the previous two years; Uranus was also going direct and transiting the conjunction for the last time while Saturn was retrograding in opposition. Starting in 1966, Saturn would oppose the Sun as it began its ascent over the Descendant; Leonard was being identified.

Ironically, Leonard's partner and mother of his children was named Suzanne. This was not the muse who inspired the song, perhaps not even a premonition, but the personal motif that would be enmeshed with the archetypal one. When they separated after Leonard's mother's death, Saturn was again in his 12th house, traversing the Neptune-Venus conjunction, just as it had done when he first encountered Lorca and the *duende* of the poet. Personal feelings of love and grief, emptiness and sorrow, loss and creativity, became entangled with mourning for his inner muse.

It was 1967 and the 'Summer of Love'. Judy Collins was organizing a workshop at the Newport Folk Festival where Leonard would participate and perform. Author, poet and songwriter, he was now emerging as a singer. Another workshop member was Joni Mitchell. Like Leonard, Joni was on the cusp of becoming famous. On 16 July 1967 their paths crossed at the festival and they became lovers. He took her to Montreal and his room at the Chelsea Hotel. Joni also has a Venus-Neptune conjunction. Her Venus at 28°♍29' wraps around Leonard's Sun-Ascendant and her Piscean Moon sits exactly on his Vertex, near his Descendant, which highlights the poetry of this destined connection. Both Canadian, they share a Moon in Pisces and the *duende*. For the first time he became the lyrical inspiration for another's music in Mitchell's songs like 'That Song about the Midway', 'A Case of You' and 'Rainy Night House'.[65] Neptune is a shape-shifter; now Leonard becomes the muse, a recollection that the muse is part of himself.

Thematic in many of Leonard's poems and lyrics is the split, sometimes the amalgam, between the saintly and the sexual feminine, which is another symptom of his Neptune-Venus. But in the song 'Chelsea Hotel', his sexual partner had no angelic aura. He once named Janis Joplin as this woman in the song with whom he shared a one-night stand. Being attainable and carnal, she did not reflect the sacred side of his Neptune-Venus. In 1994, Leonard apologized for the indiscretion of naming Janis publicly, but it was an apology to a ghost. Janis had died on 4 October 1970 as Pluto lay exactly on Leonard's Sun-Ascendant.

In that same year, 1994, Chiron transited his Neptune-Venus. His religious search led him to Buddhism and by 1994 he had taken up residence in a Zen monastery on Mount Baldy. Dwelling in his 12th house, he reflected on his obsession with unrequited love and his helplessness in responding to love that was offered. He self-analysed that it was due to 'some fictional sense of separation'.[66] He was masterful at weaving fiction into his personal life and his songs. Leonard's muse was holy when unattainable but unsustainable in the flesh. It was the dilemma he expressed in many songs; for instance, 'I long for love and light, but must it come so cruel and oh so bright'.[67] Venus-Neptune may fear being annihilated by the loss of love or drowned in its oceanic feelings. This imagined or fictional loss is repeated in each encounter, making it feel real. In the transition from Leonard's love life to his monastic life he began to become aware of the truth his music had always known.

His five-year relationship with actress Rebecca de Mornay had faded before entering the monastery. Rebecca has four planets in Virgo, spanning his 12th house. They share Venus in Virgo and her Mars is conjunct his Sun-Ascendant; hence another suitable muse for his soul. Ironically, he remembers meeting her when she was very young at a boarding school in England. Rebecca was about six, but he was in his early thirties and performing a concert at the school she attended. Years later, when Rebecca asked Leonard how he could remember her from twenty-something years before, he said: 'It was something about your light'.[68] The light is not light seen with the eyes or rationally recollected; the memory belongs to the soul.

The monastic life gave Leonard the opportunity to express his Neptune-Venus conjunction in another way. Yet, while he was becoming spiritually affluent, his financial resources were being siphoned away. As his value for the spirit was enriched, his finances began disappearing. When Leonard left the monastery to rejoin the world, it eventually became apparent that his manager Kelley Lynch, a former lover, friend and helpmate, had depleted his bank accounts. Love and larceny could also be attributed to his Neptune-Venus conjunction, as the financial affairs of this aspect are difficult to value in a material way. Yes, there is the possibility of deceit and deficit; yet, equally, there may be magic and salvation.

As a way to regain his financial footing, the theft propelled Leonard back into the public spotlight. Being in his seventies, robbed of his life savings, he still had his vocation and the call to perform. On 11 May 2008, at 8.05 p.m., after a 14-year break, he took centre stage in Fredericton, Canada, to commence his world tour that would last nearly three years. This tour would be drug-free: no escape into alcohol or cigarettes. He would rely on the truth that he now knew: he could not command the music; rather, he was its instrument. The 15-year-old boy who discovered the *duende* was still alive in Leonard.

When he stepped on stage the applause was thunderous. At that moment in the sky, Venus was setting; Neptune had reached the lower meridian. And transiting Saturn sat again on the cusp of his 12th house. During the tour it would transit his 12th house for the third time, evoking the first cycle when he encountered the *duende*, the second cycle when he began to know that the anima-muse was his own soul, not the outer woman, and now. Impoverished, yet enriched, he nervously began to sing his ode to Neptune-Venus, 'Dance me to your beauty with a burning violin ...'.[69] Reviews of the tour likened his concerts to a love-in, a religious ceremony, a papal visit. The *duende* was moving through Leonard and casting its spell on his audiences. He was its channel, not its casualty.

Leonard not only recouped his losses but he became applauded and appreciated in new places and new ways. The chords of his Neptune-Venus had found another octave and the muses once again danced around the Sun.

– APPENDIX 1 –
Planet and Sign Vocational Correspondences

Consider the connections given below, between the planets and signs and lists of occupations and careers. Expand this list by adding your own associations. Study the charts of people who may lead these occupations and reflect on which planetary archetypes have influenced their choice of career. Please note that these are generalized associations.

Mars/Aries	Venus/Taurus	Mercury/Gemini
Airline industry	Accountant	Advertising
Ambulance work	Architect	Antiquarian bookseller
Armed services	Aromatherapist	Audio-visuals
Army	Boat building	Courier
Athletics	Brewer	Disc jockey
Butcher	Builder	Driver
Coaching	Confectioner	Graphologist
Construction industry	Decorator	Illustrator
Dancer	Design	Interviewer
Electrician	Farming	Journalist
Electronics	Finance	Lecturer
Engineer	Financial advisor	Literary agent
Explorer	Florist	Media
Fireman	Gardener	Newsagent
Gym instructor	Grocery trades	Post office worker
Marines	Horticulture	Publicity
Metallurgist	Insurance	Reporter
Motor mechanic	Market manager	Retailer
National Guard	Masseur	Sales
Paramedic	Musician	Teacher
Police	Nursing	Telecommunications
Professional sport	Organic farming	Telephone operator
Security services and	Painter	Translator
providers	Potter	Travel writer
Self-employed	Restaurant owner	Writer
Trade unions	Singer	Youth worker
Trader	Soft furnishing	
	industry	

The Moon/Cancer	The Sun/Leo	Mercury/Virgo
Antiques	Actor	Accountants
Catering	Advertising	Acupuncturist
Chef	Arts teacher	Arts and crafts teacher
Child care	Business management	Clinical psychologist
Childhood educator	Celebrity	Copywriter
Conservationist	Child counsellor	Craftsman
Counsellor	Children's recreation	Critic
Doll maker	or amusement	Dietician
Domestic services	Children and	Economist
Family care provider	educational toys	Editor
Family planning	Children's wear	Film editor
Furniture restoration	Cosmetics	Health
Genealogist	Creative work	Homeopath
Gynaecologist	Design	Horticulture
Historian	Exhibition consulting	Industrial analysis
Home decor	Fashion industry	Landscape gardener
Home design	Foreman	Librarian
Home economics	Hotel administration	Literary critic
Kindergarten teacher	Jeweller	Mathematician
Midwife	Manager	Microbiologist
Nanny	Model	Naturopath
Nursing	Property development	Organic foods
Obstetrician	Retailing	Personal assistant
Paediatrician	Supervisor	Physiotherapist
Real estate	Theatre work	Psychiatric nursing
Restaurant business	Theatrical agent	Social work
Silversmith		Veterinary science

Venus/Libra	Pluto/Scorpio	Jupiter/Sagittarius
Ambassador	Anthropology	Adventure guide
Art curator	Archaeology	Attorney
Art therapist	Banking	Barrister
Beautician	Big business	Bookseller
Community relations	Cosmetic surgery	Coaching
Cosmetics	Criminal investigation	Educator
Customer services	Deep sea diving	Foreign correspondent
Designer	Detective	Foreign services/trade
Diplomacy	Forensics	Guide
Fashion buyer	Funeral services	Interpreter/translator
Fine china	Geologist	Journalist
Florist	Gynaecologist	Judge
Gifts	Investigative journalist	Language teacher
Hairdresser	Mining	Lawyer
Hospitality	Pathologist	Printer
Hotel business	Plumbing	Protocol
Interior decorator	Police	Publisher
Landscape design	Prison officer	Riding instructor
Lawyer	Property development	Sales
Millinery	Psychoanalyst	Solicitor
Modelling	Psychologist	Space industry
Perfume industry	Research	Sporting goods
Personnel	Researcher	Sports
management	Scientific researcher	The law
Personnel work	and analyst	Travel industry
Potter	Surgeon	University lecturer
Receptionist	Tax specialist	
Wedding planner		

Saturn/Capricorn	Uranus/Aquarius	Neptune/Pisces
Accountancy	Alternative therapies	Caring professions
Architecture	Astrology	Clairvoyant
Archivist	Astronomy	Counsellor
Armed Forces	Biologist	Dancer
Building industry	Broadcast media	Diver
Civil servant	Community work	Drug rehabilitation
Conveyancing	Computer technology	and counselling
Dentistry	Electrician	Fashion industry
Engineering	Engineer	Film
Gardening	Humanitarian work	Furniture design
Geologist	Information	Geriatric nursing
Governmental work	technology	Hospital work
Medical profession	Internet-based	Magician
Mineralogist	occupations	Make-up artist
Mining industry	Inventor	Musician
Mountaineer	Medical research	Navy
Orthopaedic medicine	Metaphysics	Nursing
Politics	Meteorologist	Painter
Scientist	New Age occupations	Photography
Stock exchange	Political science	Priest
Stockbroker	Psychology	Set designer
Stone mason	Radiographer	Social work
Teacher	Recording industry	Welfare
Town planner	Rock musician	Wine merchant
Trade unionist	Science fiction writer	Working with the
	Scientist	homeless
	TV engineer	

Armstrong, Lance	18 September 1971, no time Dallas, Texas, USA	No recorded time Chapter 5
Boyle, Susan	1 April 1961, 9.50 a.m. Blackburn, Scotland, UK	Birth certificate Chapter 1
Client	22 August 1965, 5.14 p.m. Geelong, Australia	Birth certificate Chapter 1
Client	18 August 1970, 6.05 p.m. Beijing, China	From client Chapter 2
Client	2 April 1951, 8.00 a.m. Melbourne, Australia	Hospital records Chapter 11
Cohen, Leonard	21 September 1934, 6.45 a.m. Montreal, Canada	From biography; S Simmons, *I'm Your Man* Harper Collins (2013) Chapter 12
Diana, Princess of Wales	1 July 1961, 7.45 p.m. Sandringham, England, UK	From Diana and her mother Chapter 5
Greer, Germaine	29 January 1939, 6.00 a.m. Melbourne, Australia	From Germaine Greer Chapter 5
Hewitt, Lleyton	24 February 1981, 0:01 a.m. Adelaide, Australia	From mother and hospital records Chapter 11
Jolie, Angelina	4 June 1975, 9.09 a.m. Los Angeles, California, USA	Birth certificate Chapter 6 and 7
Martin, Ricky	24 December 1971, 5.00 p.m. Hato Rey, Puerto Rico	Birth certificate Chapter 5
Moore, Thomas	8 October 1940, 9.33 a.m. Detroit, Michigan, USA	From Thomas Moore Chapter 12

Rockefeller, John Jr.	29 January 1874, 10.00 a.m. LMT Cleveland, Ohio, USA	From biography *John D Rockefeller, Jr., A Portrait* (Harper, 1956) Chapter 2
Rudhyar , Dane	23 March 1895, 1.00 a.m. Paris, France	Birth certificate; Rudhyar later rectified the time to 0.42 a.m. Chapter 1
Spitz, Mark	10 February 1950, 5.45 p.m. Modesto, California, USA	Birth certificate Chapter 5
Trump, Donald	14 June 1946, 10.54 a.m. Jamaica, New York, USA	Birth certificate Chapter 5
Winfrey, Oprah	29 January 1954, 4.30 a.m. Kosciusko, Mississippi, USA	From memory Chapter 5

ENDNOTES

[1] 'The Road Not Taken' by Robert Frost from *The Poetry of Robert Frost*, Holt, Rinehart and Winston (New York: 1969), 105.

[2] Thomas Moore, *Care of the Soul*, Harper Collins (New York: 1994), 181.

[3] AA Milne, *Now We Are Six*, Puffin Books (New York: 1992).

[4] Kahlil Gibran, *The Prophet*, Alfred A Knopf (New York: 1982), 25.

[5] James Hillman, *The Essential James Hillman: A Blue Fire*, edited by Thomas Moore, Routledge (London: 1990), 172.

[6] Quotes are from CG Jung, *Volume 17, The Collected Works: The Development of the Personality*, trans. RFC Hull, Routledge & Kegan Paul (London: 1954), para. 299-305.

[7] Solar Writer Vocation is one of many Solar Writer reports designed and published by Esoteric Technologies. Available from: http://www.esotech.com.au/products/solarwriter/ [Accessed 9 January 2016].

[8] See Ptolemy, *Tetrabiblos*, translated by JM Ashmand, Symbols & Signs (North Hollywood, CA: 1976), Book IV, Chapter IV; and William Lilly, *Christian Astrology*, The Astrology Center of America (Bel Air: 2004), Book 2, Chapter LXXXIV.

[9] For a classic reference on the houses of the horoscope, see Howard Sasportas, *The Twelve Houses*, Flare Publications (London: 2010).

[10] The two case studies in Chapter 12 are examples of this calling.

[11] *Dane Rudhyar, A Brief Factual Biography*, © James Shore (USA: 1972), 3.

[12] Dane Rudhyar's birth certificate listed 1 a.m. as his time of birth; Rudhyar rectified this to 0.42 a.m., resulting in the 14th degree of Sagittarius rising. Astro-Databank reports: 'Leyla Rael quotes him, rectified by him to 0:42 a.m. from a given time of midnight to 1:00 a.m. Same in Sabian Symbols No.810. Didier Geslain archive holds the birth certificate, which gives a time of 1:00 a.m.' Available from: http://www.astro.com/astro-databank/Rudhyar,_Dane [Accessed 9 January 2016].

[13] Hillman, *The Essential James Hillman: A Blue Fire*, 24.

[14] The planets have been consistently linked to deities, from the Babylonian through to the Egyptian and Greek ages, finally being classified as their Latin counterparts. For instance, the planet Mercury was known as Nebo, Thoth and Hermes through these periods. Although the planet Pluto was not discovered until 1930, he was a major deity in the ancient pantheons, known as Hades in Greek mythology and Dis in Roman.

[15] For a discussion on the *daimon* see Chapter 12.

[16] For a discussion of root metaphors in vocation, see James Hillman, *Suicide and the Soul*, Spring Publications (Irving: 1978), 24.

[17] Brian Clark, *Considering the Horoscope*, Astro*Synthesis (Melbourne: 2010).

[18] This is one of many translations of Heraclitus's phrase which links character to fate. See James Hillman, *The Soul's Code*, Random House (New York: 1996), 256-7.

[19] Demetra George, *Astrology and the Authentic Self*, Ibis Press (Lake Worth: 2008), 84.

[20] Howard Sasportas, The Stages of Childhood in *The Development of the Personality*, Samuel Weiser, Inc. (York Beach: 1987), 32-6.

[21] As an example, Pluto may be the life and death feeling surrounding labour or a perinatal loss in the family synchronous with birth; Neptune might symbolize the uncertainty and complications surrounding the

delivery, the bleary and bewildered sense of feeling lost in approaching a new destination; Uranus reveals the unexpected disconnection or severance that took place near birth, an abrupt sense of entry and/or disassociated feelings; Saturn rising might suggest a long and difficult labour; and Chiron on the horizon signals foreign feelings, a birth scar or a separation from the mother.

[22] See Robert Hand, *Night & Day: Planetary Sect in Astrology*, Arhat Media (Las Vegas: 1995).

[23] See Melanie Reinhart, *Incarnation,* The Centre for Psychological Astrology (London: 1997), 116. A new edition *Incarnation: The Four Angles and the Moon's Nodes* is published by Starwalker Press – see http://www.melaniereinhart.com/melanie/chironastrologybooks.php [Accessed 9 January 2016].

[24] These ages are also repeated by the Metonic and Saros cycles. The Metonic cycle is the 19-year cycle in which New Moons recur. The Saros cycle is 18 years, 10-11 days. This cycle was used to predict eclipses that occurred in sequence every 18 years 10-11 days. There are 19 Saros Series of Eclipses; 19 are north and 19 are south. Each of these cycles that involves the Sun, Moon and Earth is closely aligned with the nodal axis and has a mathematical harmonic.

[25] See Brian Clark, The Fool with a Thousand Faces, http://www. astrosynthesis.com.au/category/tarot-articles/ [Accessed 10 January 2016].

[26] The True Node moves through the zodiac in a meandering way – it will slither backwards through the zodiac for about 4 months then reaches a plateau near the same degree for 2-3 months, then slips back again to repeat the same movement, similar to the movement of a snake. The True Node highlights certain degrees of the zodiac more than the Mean Node. CJ Jung, in the *Red Book: A Reader's Edition*, WW Norton (New York: 2009), 414, states 'the becoming of the soul follows a serpentine path'.

[27] Rudhyar introduces his ideas in *The Astrology of Personality*, Servire/Wassenaar (Netherlands: 1936), 316-23 and continues in *Person-Centered Astrology*, ASI Publishers (New York: 1980), 266-300.

[28] Demetra George records the first use of these terms in the Persian literature of the 4th century; see George, *Astrology and the Authentic Self*, 164.

[29] P Thomas, *Epics, Myths and Legends of India*, DB Taraporevala (Bombay: 1961), 91.

[30] Mythic imagery suggests the cycle of the eclipses as the Sun and Moon are near the nodal axis.

[31] Rainer Maria Rilke, *Letters to a Young Poet*, trans. Reginald Snell, Sidgwick and Jackson (London: 1945), 39.

[32] CG Jung, *Volume 8, The Collected Works: The Structure and Dynamics of the Psyche*, trans. RFC Hull, Routledge & Kegan Paul (London: 1960), 246.

[33] For an insightful commentary on creativity, see Rosemary Gordon, *Dying and Creating: A Search for Meaning*, Karnac Books (London: 2000), Part III.

[34] Gordon, *Dying and Creating: A Search for Meaning*, 147.

[35] James Hillman, A Contribution to Soul and Money in *Soul and Money*, Spring Publications (Dallas: 1982), 35.

[36] In English, the word 'appreciate' is significant in understanding the 2nd house: it means 1) to recognize the value in something and 2) to increase in value. When we value our resources they appreciate in worth. By the law of correspondences this suggests that we not only feel more valued, but also are richer.

[37] One of the more diverse associations with the 6th house is small animals and pets, a tradition left over from medieval times when animals, such as sheep, hogs and goats, were seen as service providers for milk and food. In more contemporary times, pets are part of our daily life and need attention and day-to-day care. They focus our attention on the here and now. Animals personify the instinctual life and caring for pets is akin to caring for our soul.

[38] For systems like Whole Sign Houses and Equal Houses where all houses are 30°, the Midheaven is not the 10th house cusp and is shown in the chart as a separate point.

[39] Timing depends upon the orb used for the transiting planet applying and separating to the natal planet. In this case I am using a 1° orb.

[40] The retrograde cycle each year affects the timing of the cycle.

[41] The timing of a transit through a house is not uniform. It depends on the size of the house, which is dependent on the house system used, season and latitude of birth. In using an average, we would say Uranus transits a house in 7 years because its cycle is 84 years. However, when we look at Susan Boyle's horoscope, her 11th house spans 50° while her 12th house measures 55°. This suggests that Uranus will transit her 11th house in about 11.5 years and her 12th house in about 13 years.

[42] This was reported by ABC News through their website: http://abcnews.go.com/Sports.

[43] Thomas Moore, *A Life at Work*, Broadway Books (New York: 2008). The book is subtitled *The Joy of Discovering What You Were Born To Do*.

[44] Thomas Moore, *A Religion of One's Own*, Gotham Books (New York: 2014), 4.

[45] Thomas Moore, *Dark Nights of the Soul*, Piatkus Books (London: 2006), 24-32.

[46] Moore describes the *daimon* in terms of vocation as 'a passion, an urge you can't ignore, and a direction that you yourself may never have chosen. The appearance of the *daimon* is like an eruption or even an intrusion into your life.' Moore, *A Life at Work*, 121-2. He also amplifies this spirit in many other writings, for instance in *Dark Nights of the Soul*, 16-17.

[47] See Introduction.

[48] See Brian Clark, *Mythic Signs: The Zodiacal Imagination*, Astro*Synthesis (Melbourne: 2002).

[49] Thomas Moore, *Original Self,* HarperCollins (New York: 2000), 3.

[50] Moore, *A Life at Work*, 74.

[51] Ibid, 76.

[52] From an article by Emily Yoffe, *How the Soul is Sold*, 23 April 1995, *New York Times*. Available from: www.nytimes.com/1995/04/23/magazine/how-the-soul-is-sold.html?pagewanted=4 [Accessed 9 July 2015].

[53] Jung, *Volume 8, The Collected Works: The Structure and Dynamics of the Psyche*, para. 772.

[54] Psychopomp is a leader or sender of souls generally into the underworld.

[55] Sylvie Simmons, *I'm Your Man: The Life of Leonard Cohen*, HarperCollins (New York: 2013), 4.

[56] Lois Rodden's Astro-Databank is now maintained by *astro.com* and the chart is listed as 'A' data. Available from: www.astro.com/astro-databank/Cohen,_Leonard [Accessed 9 January 2016].

[57] John Etherington, Leonard Cohen's 'Secret Chart', *Apollon*, Issue 1, CPA (London: 1998). Available from: www.cpalondon.com/Issue%20One.pdf [Accessed 9 January 2016].

[58] Simmons, *I'm Your Man: The Life of Leonard Cohen*, 6.

[59] Robin Pike, *ZigZag*, October 1974, as referenced in Simmons, *I'm Your Man: The Life of Leonard Cohen*.

[60] Donald Brittain and Don Owen, *Ladies and Gentlemen... Mr Leonard Cohen*, documentary film, 1965, as referenced in Simmons, *I'm Your Man: The Life of Leonard Cohen*.

[61] Simmons, *I'm Your Man: The Life of Leonard Cohen*, 9.

[62] This is the title of one of Cohen's musical poems that captures the archetypal essence of this 12th house union. See Leonard Cohen's 'Love Itself', from *Book of Longing*, Penguin (London: 2007), 54.

[63] This is Lorca's own expression – see Federico García Lorca, *In Search of Duende*, New Directions (New York: 2010). See Liel Leibovitz's description of the *duende* in *A Broken Hallelujah*, WW Norton (New York: 2014), 54.

[64] Simmons, *I'm Your Man: The Life of Leonard Cohen*, 124-7.

[65] All songs written and copyrighted by Joni Mitchell. See www.jonimitchell.com [Accessed 9 January 2016].

[66] Simmons, *I'm Your Man: The Life of Leonard Cohen*, 413.

[67] Lyrics from 'Joan of Arc' by Leonard Cohen, © Leonard Cohen Stranger Music Inc, Sony Music Inc.

[68] Simmons, *I'm Your Man: The Life of Leonard Cohen*, 375.

[69] Lyrics from 'Dance Me to the End of Love' by Leonard Cohen, © Sony/ATV Music Publishing LLC, Stranger Music Inc.

Astro*Synthesis

Astro*Synthesis was founded in Melbourne in 1986 as an astrological education programme. Since that time Astro*Synthesis has consistently offered an in-depth training programme into the application of astrology from a psychological perspective. The foundation of the course has been constructed to utilize astrology as a tool for greater awareness of the self, others and the world at large.

From 1986 to 2010, Astro*Synthesis offered its dynamic four-year teaching program in the classroom. Astro*Synthesis now offers the complete program of 12 modules through distance learning.

For a detailed syllabus or more information on Astro*Synthesis E-Workbooks, E- Booklets or reports please visit our website:

www.astrosynthesis.com.au

CPSIA information can be obtained
at www.ICGtesting.com
Printed in the USA
BVHW092015150223
658579BV00004B/255